A HUNDRED
OR MORE
HIDDEN THINGS

A HUNDRED
OR MORE
HIDDEN THINGS

The Life and Films of
Vincente Minnelli

Mark Griffin

Da Capo Press
A Member of the Perseus Books Group

Designed by Pauline Brown

Set in 11 point Fairfield Light by the Perseus Books Group

Library of Congress Cataloging-in-Publication Data

Griffin, Mark.
  A hundred or more hidden things : the life and films of Vincente Minnelli / by Mark Griffin. — 1st Da Capo Press ed.
      p.   cm.
  Includes index.
  ISBN 978-0-7867-2099-6 (alk. paper)
  1. Minnelli, Vincente. 2. Motion picture producers and directors—United States—Biography. I. Title.
  PN1998.3.M56G75 2010
  791.4302'33092—dc22
  [B]
                                                              2009042445

First Da Capo Press edition 2010

Published by Da Capo Press
A Member of the Perseus Books Group
www.dacapopress.com

Da Capo Press books are available at special discounts for bulk purchases in the U.S. by corporations, institutions, and other organizations. For more information, please contact the Special Markets Department at the Perseus Books Group, 2300 Chestnut Street, Suite 200, Philadelphia, PA 19103, or call (800) 810-4145, ext. 5000, or e-mail special.markets@perseusbooks.com.

10 9 8 7 6 5 4 3 2 1

For Lester

CONTENTS

A HUNDRED
OR MORE
HIDDEN THINGS

INTRODUCTION

I WAS SIXTEEN YEARS OLD when I saw the movie that changed my life. During a summer vacation in which I was expected to evolve from sophomore to junior, I actually went a step further and found myself. My life-altering cinematic experience came courtesy of *On a Clear Day You Can See Forever*, the second-to-last directorial effort of the great Vincente Minnelli. This decidedly offbeat musical not only featured a time-traveling protagonist with paranormal powers but came complete with a poignant theme about the liberating effects of self-acceptance—a message all too eagerly received by St. Dominic Regional High School's resident misfit.

I watched *On a Clear Day* over and over in the summer of 1984 I found it healing and empowering. My friends thought I had lost it. They began to look at me funny. In an era dominated by *Return of the Jedi* and *Ferris Bueller's Day Off*, was I actually claiming to have achieved some sort of cosmic consciousness through repeated viewings of . . . a *Barbra Streisand movie*? It was suggested that I should try getting out more often or maybe join a rugby team . . . before it was too late. But after discovering that *Village Voice* critic Andrew Sarris had once referred to the object of my obsession as "an underrated masterpiece," there was no stopping me. This high-level endorsement was the only excuse I needed to study said masterpiece with an even more attentive eye.

I was mesmerized by what Sarris had referred to as "Minnelli's morbidly beautiful mise en scène," and there was an unusual quality about the film that I was eager to reconnect with. Although *On a Clear Day* was a large and lavish major studio production, there was also something endearingly personal about it. Minnelli seemed to exhibit a genuine empathy for his heroine, who throughout the film grapples with the effects of a split self.

As I would soon discover, Daisy Gamble—the psychically gifted, identity-challenged chain-smoker at the center of *On a Clear Day*—was the kind of conflicted character that Vincente Minnelli had practically patented. Here was another engaging oddball to add to the director's already impressive collection of visionaries, dreamers, artists, and outcasts. An awkward, unassuming "go-alonger," Daisy is so ashamed of her extrasensory abilities that she attempts to suppress this part of herself, terrified that someone will discover that she is (in her own words) "un-normal." Besides her supernatural skills, Daisy harbors another secret—there is a more alluring, alternate identity buried within her. Several lifetimes ago, this neurotic wallflower from Mahwah, New Jersey, was Lady Melinda Tentrees, a clairvoyant noblewoman and 1814's "It" Girl. Melinda's captivating personality, regal bearing, and eye-popping ensembles effortlessly upstage Daisy's modern-day existence.

After coming to terms with her previous incarnations, Daisy experiences an exhilarating moment of self-discovery: The most important person you will ever be is the one that you are right now. As she begins to blossom as vibrantly as the azaleas, peonies, and posies that have surrounded her in virtually every frame, Daisy embraces her authentic self: "*On a clear day . . . rise and look around you and you'll see who you are. . . . On a clear day, how it will astound you that the glow of your being outshines every star.*" I took the message to heart. And apparently so had Minnelli. *On a Clear Day* had inspired me to look at myself in a very different way. The gift of self-empowerment had been bequeathed to an insecure adolescent in need of reassurance. I was beyond grateful and very curious to know more about the man behind the movie.

I had been a card-carrying Judy Garland fanatic since childhood, and because I had seen all the films in which "the world's greatest entertainer" had been directed by her second husband, I thought I was rather well acquainted with Vincente Minnelli. Largely because of *Meet Me in St. Louis*, I equated his name with an unmistakable style and the kind of exquisitely crafted extravaganzas that had long ago vacated the neighborhood movie house and taken up residence on the late show. Though, as I soon learned, there was more to Minnelli than what initially dazzled the eye.

During the remainder of my summer vacation, I ravenously consumed some of the other important titles in the director's oeuvre: *The Pirate, An American in Paris, The Band Wagon, Tea and Sympathy, Gigi,* and Minnelli's tragically mutilated final film, *A Matter of Time*. While these movies were often boldly innovative, even ahead of their time, somehow they also felt strangely familiar. Despite the fact that almost all of these pictures had been produced long before I was born, it was as though Vincente Minnelli had somehow been eavesdropping on my dreams. No, better than that . . . he was telling the story of my life on film, and by this point, my friends were *begging* me to get out more often. Though I really didn't care. Minnelli's movies were taking me to important places within myself and that was all that mattered.

Eventually, I was able to see beyond my sixteen-year-old's self-absorption and recognize that Minnelli wasn't telling the story of my life on screen but his own. Or at least it seemed so. "My romanticism has never precluded me from my work which, in the final analysis, is the story of my life," Minnelli observed in his 1974 memoir.[1] A lifelong workaholic, the director was probably referring to the countless hours he put in on Hollywood soundstages over the years. Though I hoped that what he also meant by this was that his work actually contained the story of his life. For I purely loved the notion of Minnelli as a mild-mannered subversive who labored under the constraints of the studio system yet somehow managed to sneak autobiographical elements into his films . . . buried-treasure style.

If Minnelli's movies are indeed autobiographies in code (and many can certainly be "read" that way), his achievement is all the more extraordinary when one considers the fact that all but three of his pictures were made during his twenty-six-year association with Metro-Goldwyn-Mayer, Hollywood's preeminent "Dream Factory"—but a factory nonetheless. I was intrigued. Just how had Vincente managed to produce such self-reflexive and personal work while toiling away at the most conservative and lockstep of the major studios? And what exactly was the work telling us about his life?

After scrutinizing the films, I started reading everything I could about Minnelli. I was interested in what made Vincente tick, not only as an artist but as an individual, though most of the information I could find about him focused almost exclusively on his directorial achievements. Before too long, references to auteur theories, surrealism, and *Cahiers du cinéma* began creeping into my conversation. I learned that although Minnelli had won an Oscar in 1959 (for his direction of *Gigi*) and several of his titles invariably turned up on lists of the Best Films Ever Made, he was more acclaimed in Europe than he was in his own country.

I now felt very protective, almost proprietary about my favorite director, and it irked me that he was sometimes treated like a second-class citizen. Although most critics and film scholars would readily acknowledge that Vincente Minnelli was "the master of the decorative image," they seemed reluctant (until recently) to discuss his work in the same way one would approach Orson Welles, John Ford, or Jean-Luc Godard. Why? Did Judy Garland, Technicolor, and a score by Lerner and Loewe automatically disqualify Minnelli from being taken seriously as a director?

"The curse of Vincente Minnelli is really the curse of eighty-five percent of Hollywood's great artists," says film scholar Jeanine Basinger:

> Jerry Lewis is a great filmmaker but, you know, he just acts funny. Raoul Walsh is a great director but he just makes action and gangster films. It's really the curse of people not taking Hollywood seriously. A lot of artists get dismissed on the basis of something like, "If it isn't Ingmar Bergman, it can't be good." In some ways, people fear fantasy. They fear escapism. They're afraid it's trivial. And people don't want to take film on it's most artistic terms. They don't want it to fly and soar and be visual and stunning. Because none of that is "serious." All of this is reflected in the way people approach Minnelli, apologizing for him or downgrading him. . . . Say that someone is watching the dream sequence in *Yolanda and the Thief* and they're easily dismissing it. Then suppose I told them that it had been directed by Fellini, would they still be so quick to dismiss it? Of course they wouldn't.[2]

Whenever some shortsighted film authority attempted to write Vincente off as a glorified window dresser, I wanted to lead them (by the hand) to the nearest copy of *Lust for Life*. In Minnelli's critically hailed 1956 biopic, Anthony Quinn's Paul Gauguin lashes out at Kirk Douglas's Vincent van Gogh. "You paint too fast!" Quinn's fiery postimpressionist tells the mad genius. "You look too fast!" is van Gogh's unforgettable reply. As the director's most fervent followers have always maintained, it would appear that we've been looking too fast at the work of Vincente Minnelli.

For many Minnelliphiles, part of the mystique and fascination with his work is that it is so richly layered that a single film can be appreciated on many different levels. "I feel that a picture that stays with you is made up of a hundred or more hidden things," the director once said.[3] A well-dressed, thoroughly entertaining movie such as *Gigi* can be enjoyed as the tune-filled, sensory-rich experience that it is. Or, if one chooses to lift the ornate lid and peer inside, there are countless "hidden" elements to be discovered, including sharp-eyed social critiques, a feminist manifesto, and erudite references to great artists and their works. Oftentimes, the sumptuousness and sheer artiness of Minnelli's presentation has tended to distract viewers from the fact that there was plenty going on beneath the elegantly appointed surface.

Though as Minnelli pointed out to interviewer Henry Sheehan, he always intended that the decorative trappings should be in service to the story: "Most people don't realize that the décor, what [the characters] hold and the surroundings tell an awful lot about the character. And that's what I'm concerned with—the character."[4]

From Madame Bovary to Eddie's father, the characters in Vincente Minnelli's films are some of the most beloved in all of cinema, which is a bit surprising when one considers the fact that they are anything but your typical Hollywood heroes. Virtually all of Minnelli's movies are stories about unconventional individuals who find themselves at odds with the world around them simply by being who they are. Their very identity is the source of their dilemma, and these nonconformists must seek refuge in fantasy, art, or an alternate reality in order to heal themselves. From Little Joe Jackson, whose soul is caught in a tug-of-war between heaven and hell in Minnelli's first feature, *Cabin in the Sky*, to Nina, an impressionable chambermaid who lives vicariously through the memories of a faded courtesan in *A Matter of Time*, a Minnelli character is almost always a dweller on two planets. These are people who are not only displaced but split right down the middle. Without question, this was a recurring theme that Vincente had more than a passing interest in exploring. Why? Was the duality that turned up time and again in the films reflecting some part of his own experience?

After Minnelli's death in 1986, suggestions that the director may have had a divided life of his own began to appear in print. Along with such iconic figures as James Dean, Cary Grant, and Rudolph Valentino, Vincente Minnelli has always been a sexually suspect character. Just consider the "evidence": Minnelli was a former window dresser and costume designer. He had an unerring eye for décor. An alleged affinity for eye liner. A romantic association with Judy Garland. In the eyes of some, Minnelli was seriously overdue for his own float in a gay pride parade.

In our postmodern, politically correct world, everything—and everybody— must be clearly marked with a very precise label. "Bisexual" is the one usually hung on Minnelli, though it was generally assumed that despite his marriages to four women (some of whom were also rumored to have been bisexual), Minnelli was a "closet case"—an essentially gay man who, due to societal conditioning and career pressures, felt compelled to marry and procreate. Denying who he really was would at least satisfy society, a politically conservative studio, and *Modern Screen* subscribers.

In Jon Marans's recent play *The Temperamentals*, "Vincente Minnelli" appears as the physical embodiment of the closet. Marans concocted an episode in which Minnelli is approached by gay activist Harry Hay and asked to lend his support to the Mattachine Society. "I have Minnelli using this metaphor about homosexuality," says Marans. "He talks about a woman's perfume and how it will lose all of its heavenly aroma once you open up the bottle. In the same way, he thinks you shouldn't open up the bottle of homosexuality. Minnelli has this theory that 'You should never discuss it for fear of making it mundane and letting it all out into the open.'"[5]

In this out and proud post-Stonewall age, it probably wouldn't take most observers long to do the math and consign Minnelli to the closet. But then again, hadn't some of Minnelli's own movies, most notably *Tea and Sympathy* and *Designing Woman*, pointed out that just because something looks one way doesn't necessarily mean that it is that way? Was it possible that, just as people had looked "too fast" at Minnelli's work, snap judgments had been made about him as a person? Had Vincente been stereotyped into a corner? Minnelli may have been effeminate, androgynous even, but did this automatically add up to gay? Even in our more socially conscious times, there are some observers (including an exceedingly sequined relative) who seem convinced that everyone is barking up the wrong tree.

"My sister, Liza, passionately resents the suggestion that her father had a secret gay life," Judy Garland's daughter, Lorna Luft, wrote in her 1998 family memoir. "The Vincente I remember had a roving eye and a weakness for beautiful women, some of whom he married. Granted, one marriage might be a cover, but three?"* Those closest to Minnelli seemed to be contradicting the frequently repeated rumors about him. Or was this denial in the first degree?

When my longtime dream of writing a Minnelli biography became a reality, I knew that my subject—while colorful and endlessly fascinating— was also a complete enigma. "Vincente Minnelli was Hollywood's great mystery man," Garland confidant Tucker Fleming told me. "I think he's quite a complex figure and there have always been so many question marks about him. . . . You really have your work cut out for you."[6] Though who was I to go rummaging around in somebody else's life? Especially when that someone had been so guarded and self-protective? Then I reread Minnelli's 1974 autobiography, *I Remember It Well*, and came to regard the title as something of a challenge. In *Gigi*, Maurice Chevalier croons a wistful tune by the same name, in which he misremembers some of his romantic interludes. By borrowing the title of the song, Minnelli seemed to be winking at the reader— these are the memoirs of a notoriously forgetful man. In other words, this autobiography is my version of events. What I choose to remember. The truth may be a very different story.

---

* An Emmy-winning 2001 television movie adapted from Luft's memoir, *Life with Judy Garland: Me and My Shadows*, seemed to diverge from its source material where Vincente Minnelli was concerned. In one scene, Garland (Judy Davis) confides to MGM arranger Roger Edens (John Benjamin Hickey) that she expects Minnelli (Hugh Laurie) to propose to her. Edens is visibly surprised and attempts to warn his protégé about the director: "I don't think he's marrying material." (Quotation from Lorna Luft's book *Me and My Shadows: A Family Memoir* [New York: Pocket Books, 1998].)

So I began searching for the real Vincente Minnelli. Before too long, I found myself playing a variation on "Limehouse Blues," the celebrated sequence in Minnelli's 1946 revue musical *Ziegfeld Follies*. In this indelible production number, Fred Astaire is in pursuit of Lucille Bremer—first while fully conscious and then when he's in the midst of a delirious dream. Astaire is lured into the darkened depths of his own subconscious by the most Minnellian object imaginable—an Oriental fan. As Bremer disappears into the shadows, the fan she clutches seems self-propelled, flitting about like an unusually beautiful butterfly. Although Astaire makes several attempts to capture the fan, it's always just out of reach. I knew exactly how Fred felt, for trying to find Minnelli was like chasing after that fan.

My subject practically defined "elusive." Minnelli may have been a public figure, but the most important parts of his life had been locked away deep inside of himself. How do you go about finding someone who really knew a thing or two about staying hidden? Early on, I realized I wouldn't be able to find Vincente on my own. So I organized a search party. I knew that it would be necessary to conduct as many interviews as possible and get people talking. As Vincente had been the subject of so much speculation and rumor, hearing directly from those who actually worked with or knew him would be absolutely essential. Only this posed another set of challenges that I had been warned about.

When I profiled the late screenwriter Gavin Lambert for a magazine, I mentioned that I was interested in writing about Minnelli and talking to as many of the director's surviving colleagues as possible. Although Lambert was encouraging, he had two very succinct words of advice: "Hurry up." How right he was. Considering that Minnelli's first feature was released in 1943 and that his Broadway career stretched back to the early 1930s, finding people to talk to postmillennium was not going to be easy. And even if I managed to track people down, how forthcoming would some of these press-savvy Hollywood veterans be if I broached the very personal subject of Vincente's sexuality? Even though we were living in supposedly less repressive times than Minnelli had, most of his colleagues had graduated from the MGM School of Public Relations and they were masters at deflecting uncomfortable questions.

Apprehensive yet insatiably curious, I began to move forward. During a three-year odyssey, I contacted as many Minnelli coworkers, friends, former neighbors, and true believers as I could find. Armed with an antique tape recorder and aided by an enterprising though overworked research assistant, I ended up talking to hundreds of people who were exceptionally generous in terms of sharing their memories, insights, private correspondence, and photographs with me. Amazingly, many of the people I spoke with had never gone on record before.

There were also plenty of surprises along the way. An elderly interview subject in Delaware, Ohio (where Vincente had spent his formative years), casually mentioned Minnelli's brother to me. *Vincente Minnelli had a brother?* The detail-obsessed director had overlooked his sibling in his autobiography. Why? Another person I talked to was curious to know what I had discovered about that terrible tragedy involving Vincente's adored Uncle Frank. The terrible tragedy. Yes, of course. *What terrible tragedy?* Early on, a fellow biographer had advised me to play dumb when talking to people, but it quickly became clear that no playing would be necessary. Just because I had seen *The Sandpiper* more times than was psychologically advisable didn't mean that I really knew anything about the man who had created it.

Some people were dying to tell me Minnelli stories, having saved up revealing anecdotes for nearly seventy years. Others played it close to the vest, choosing their words with almost excruciating caution. And more than a few people attempted to steer the conversation away from Minnelli, preferring to discuss Judy Garland, the weather, or their own careers (one veteran actress took the opportunity to pitch me the story of what she hoped would be her comeback vehicle—the saga of a centerfold-turned-mafia-wife).

In conducting research, I asked a thousand different questions, though virtually everyone I spoke to had the same one for me: "So, have you talked to Liza?" The answer, unfortunately, was no—though an attempt was made. After all, many of my interview subjects had stressed how unique and endearing the bond had been between father and daughter. If anyone really knew Vincente Minnelli, they knew his bond was his pride and joy. And over the years, the high-octane headliner has done an admirable job in terms of celebrating her father's cinematic legacy (including two helpings of *Minnelli on Minnelli*, a televised tribute in 1987 and a Palace Theater stage show in 1999). Nevertheless, I wasn't at all surprised that she did not consent to be interviewed. Although Liza obviously adored her father—and she remains one of his most devoted champions—she has been unwilling to either acknowledge or explore some of the complexities of his life. Despite several efforts, I was unable to contact Vincente's other daughter, Tina Nina Minnelli. This was another disappointment as I'm sure she has a compelling story to tell, and one very different from her famous sister. Thankfully, many people were willing to talk.

I found that often the most challenging interviews proved to be the most rewarding. Nina Foch, who appeared in Minnelli's classic *An American in Paris*, bristled at some of my questions about the film, but she turned quietly reflective and almost melancholy when I asked what her director was like as a human being:

> I don't really know where his private life was but I think it was very complicated. He was not at all the kind of person to be very forthcoming about his private life but I remember I was in his study one day and I spotted this set of drawings that Vincente had done. One of them really caught my eye. I said, "I love that. Give that to me." It was just something that came off his sketch pad but it was really beautiful. But also, if you looked at it long enough, you could see that he was a very complicated soul. I remember thinking, we may be friends but I really don't know Vincente at all. . . . I wonder if anybody really did.[7]

Taking everything into account—the enigma of Vincente Minnelli as both an individual and an artist, his unconventional upbringing, an ambiguous sexuality, a show-business career that afforded him the opportunity to work with everyone from Josephine Baker to Jack Nicholson, long-concealed family secrets, and no less than Judy Garland and Liza Minnelli as supporting players—it's truly astounding that Minnelli's story has received so little attention.

Film historian and Minnelli disciple George Feltenstein has made some attempts to rectify this. Feltenstein has long wanted to produce a documentary that would explore the director's life and career. But when he presented his ideas to some documentarians, he found that his enthusiasm was met with an inexplicable indifference: "I remember that the filmmakers' objection was, 'Well, there's no story there.' I said, 'What do you mean there's no story there? There's an amazing story there. . . . *The story of his life is in his films.'* You know, Judy Garland had that lyric that Roger Edens wrote for her, 'The history of my life is in my songs. . . .' Well, the history of Minnelli's life is in his films. And when you look at all those films, you see the pained artist, the passionate romantic. All of those things. How is it people cannot see this?"[8] Looking too fast, yet again.

In some ways, this project is a thank-you note that's been twenty-five years in the making. So many summers ago, Vincente Minnelli's message of hope and encouragement managed to find a restless teenager stashed away in Lewiston, Maine. And the inspirational effects of Minnelli's movies helped an unconfident young man return to St. Dominic Regional High School with head held high. I'd like to believe that in seeking the truth about my subject and attempting to present him as a complete person, that I'm belatedly returning the favor. For as I had been told many years ago, to see yourself is to see forever.

Lester Minnelli's yearbook photo, Willis High School, 1921.
PHOTO COURTESY OF BRENT CARSON (PHOTOGRAPHER UNKNOWN)

Delaware Days

THERE WAS SOMETHING ABOUT THAT YEAR . . . 1903. It seemed too turn-of-the-century and antiquated, so later on, he would tell people that he was born in 1907, which sounded more modern and Jazz Age. In the best show-business tradition, shaving a few years off his age would make his talents seem all the more remarkable, coming from one "so young."

The name on the Chicago birth certificate read "Lester Anthony Minnelli," though that would change, too. Just as 1903 would be abandoned in favor of 1907, the name Lester would eventually give way to "Vincente," which had a more artistic ring to it. Right from the start, reality needed to be improved upon. Painted over. "The biographer of his early years is hard put to sift fact from legend," S. J. Perelman would write of Minnelli in 1937. Though who needed facts when you could slap a couple of coats of illusion over the unvarnished truth and create a little magic? Doing so seemed perfectly natural, as everybody in Lester Minnelli's life was in the business of make-believe. "Vincente grew up in an atmosphere of grease paint and footlights," his father once told a reporter. At least this much was true.[1]

In either 1900 or 1902—depending on who was doing the remembering—Lester's father, Vincent Charles (better known as V.C.), and Uncle Frank (better known as F.P.) formed what was originally called the Minnelli Brothers Mighty Dramatic Company Under Canvas. Despite the epically proportioned name, it was a modestly budgeted traveling theater company with ten actors and about twenty crew members. "We demand ability, wardrobe, appearance and sobriety," the Minnelli Brothers announced to prospective performers.

Lester's father,
Vincent Charles
(V.C.) Minnelli in 1938.
Along with his brother Frank,
V.C. managed the Minnelli
Brothers. Mighty Dramatic
Company Under Canvas,
which brought musicals and
melodramas to
Midwestern towns.
PHOTO COURTESY OF
LYNN RAMEY
(PHOTOGRAPHER UNKNOWN)

In return, actors were guaranteed respectable treatment, a long season, and "tickets from Hong Kong, if you are what we want."[2] While it wasn't the Ziegfeld Follies, it wasn't peddling snake oil either.

Barnstorming across central and northern Ohio, Indiana, and Illinois, the Minnelli Brothers brought musicals, melodramas, and the occasional minstrel show to towns with names like Sandusky, Chillicothe, and Zanesville. They performed under canvas, usually in vacant lots, promising patrons that "the big tent will positively not leak, so a performance will be given, rain or shine."[3]

A Minnelli Brothers production was billed as "a good, clean attraction with so small an admission that it will never be missed."[4] In fact, for as little as a dime, one could see the Minnellis' "suburbanized versions" of such venerable stage melodramas as *Saintly Hypocrites and Honest Sinners* or *Mrs. Wiggs of the Cabbage Patch* (though all of the characters were renamed and some of the plot elements camouflaged so that the Minnelli Brothers could avoid paying hefty royalties to the playwrights).

The stately V.C. would serve as the company's musical director, accompanist, and composer of original songs.* Though it was Lester's beloved Uncle

---

* One of V. C. Minnelli's tunes, "The White Tops," a Sousa-like "march and two-step," was a popular selection in the repertoires of circus bands across the country. Lester Minnelli's mother, Mina Gennell, penned the rarely heard lyrics.

Lester's mother, Mina Le Beau, in 1938. In her touring days, she performed under the stage name Mina Gennell and the press dubbed her "The Dresden China Doll."
PHOTO COURTESY OF BRENT CARSON (PHOTOGRAPHER UNKNOWN)

Frank who handled the logistics and hit upon the idea of creating what was essentially a "portable theatre." With their equipment in tow, the Minnelli Brothers could pitch their tent in any town, even if it didn't offer a venue spacious enough to accommodate the large audience needed to turn a profit. Ever the industrious impresarios, the Minnelli boys came equipped with their own electric-light plant, folding chairs (for reserved seats), and bleachers (for general admission). If all that wasn't enough, the Mighty Dramatic Company could even deliver a vivacious star who had once graced the Broadway stage.

Lester's mother, Mina Le Beau, had adopted the stage name Mina Gennell and had won acclaim as an actress in productions in Chicago (where her family had settled).* While appearing on the bill of a Charles A. Loder revue, Mina met V. C. Minnelli. It was anything but love at first sight, as almost immediately, the star and her musical director clashed over her accompaniment. Eventually the smoke cleared and the leading lady found herself attracted to this ambitious, obstinate Italian American, who knew his way around a tune and how to charm everyone into doing things his way.

---

* In Vincente Minnelli's 1974 autobiography, he refers to his mother's family "emigrating from France." (Vincente Minnelli, with Hector Arce, *I Remember It Well* [Garden City, NY: Doubleday, 1974].) Mina Le Beau (born Marie Emelie Odile LeBeau) was actually of French-Canadian descent. Her father, Flavian Le Beau, was born near Montreal. There is a strong probability that Mina's maternal lineage includes Native American ancestors.

In November 1894, V.C. and Mina were married in Chicago. To those who followed her career as a high-spirited soubrette, Mina seemed to be sacrificing a bright future on the Broadway stage in favor of marriage. Though she didn't seem to mind. "Mother definitely lacked an emotional affinity for the theatre," Vincente Minnelli would observe. "Though she was well on her way to becoming a star—acting was just a living to her."[5]

Despite her ambivalence to the theatrical profession, "The Dresden China Doll" (as Mina had been dubbed by the press) would appear in countless Minnelli Brothers specialties, including *A Tom Boy Girl*, *Tess of the Storm Country*, and *The Girl of the Golden West*.[6] Though legitimately talented, Mina harbored few illusions about the theater, having survived the inhumane demands of performing fifteen shows a day at one point in her career. By the time she became the leading light of her husband's company, "The Dainty Star" had seen it all.

A publicity photograph of Mina as Lady Babbie in *The Little Minister* speaks volumes.[7] The image reveals a diminutive woman with unusually large, haunting eyes. There is no attempt to "turn on" for the camera. The absence of personality is all the more surprising when one remembers that this is the grandmother of the most animated performer of all time, Liza Minnelli. In later years, Lester would remember his mother as a "simple" woman who "blossomed" on stage. Though, as Lady Babbie, Mina is decidedly unglamorous, and her slight look of peeve suggests that she might find greater fulfillment scrubbing the pantry than stealing an extra bow. *I'd rather be anywhere but here*, her expression seems to be saying.

A year after their marriage, the Minnellis prepared to welcome their first child, but what should have been a joyous occasion would have a tragic outcome. "Before I was born, twin brothers had been carried off by mysterious childhood diseases endemic to the times," Vincente Minnelli would write in his ironically titled memoir, *I Remember It Well*. "Another brother named Willie . . . died when I was an infant. Little wonder that mother was overprotective of me, her last surviving son."[8] While it makes for a poignant story (in the best melodramatic tradition), Vincente's version of events is incorrect.

Between 1895 and mid-1900, Mina reportedly gave birth to five children, but only one survived to greet the new era. In August 1895, a set of twins was delivered: William Francis Minnelli and an unnamed sibling (referred to only as "Baby Minnelli" in interment records) who either arrived stillborn or succumbed shortly after birth. At the age of two years and five months, William would die of diphtheria in January 1898, some five years *before* Lester was born. In April 1897, one-month-old Vincent C. Minnelli died of

Lester Minnelli's brother, Paul (right), with his Delaware neighbors Lynn (left) and Marcia Ramey. In later years, whenever interviewers broached the subject of siblings with Hollywood's Vincente Minnelli, elder brother Paul would vanish from the family tree.
PHOTO COURTESY OF
LYNN RAMEY
(PHOTOGRAPHER UNKNOWN)

"cholera infantum." Other than a scrawled number on the 1900 Federal Census report, no information has emerged about another Minnelli infant, more than likely stillborn or surviving only a few hours.

In later years, Vincente Minnelli would freely admit that he was "notoriously poor" at recalling names, dates, and details. Though in the case of his own siblings, the forgetfulness seems rather deliberate. For Lester was not, in fact, his mother's "last surviving son." There was an older brother, born in September 1899 in Chicago, who not only survived infancy but lived to the age of sixty, and his name was Paul.

After contracting meningitis as an infant, Paul Felix Minnelli would struggle with what would now be termed developmental disabilities. "Mrs. Minnelli told my mother that Paul was seven years old before he could say, 'Mama.' That was the first word," recalled the Reverend Lynn Ramey, who grew up next door to the Minnellis.[9] Paul was living with his disability in an era that was less than enlightened about his condition. When he was twenty, the Minnellis' eldest son would be certified as "feeble-minded" by state authorities.*

---

* A medical certificate entitled "Inquest of Lunacy, Epilepsy or Feeble-Mindedness" from July 22, 1920, describes Paul Minnelli's behavior as "childlike" and determined that as a feeble-minded person, Paul was "incapable of receiving instruction in the common schools." Even so, surviving classmates in Delaware, Ohio, recall Paul Minnelli attending school—though he was usually in a lower grade.

In later years, whenever interviewers broached the subject of siblings with Hollywood's Vincente Minnelli, elder brother Paul would vanish from the family tree.* With rare exceptions: In 1937, Alice Hughes wrote a *New York American* profile of Vincente and observed, "He makes no attempt to entice his younger brother to the big city, away from his home town, which is Delaware, Ohio."[10] While Hughes misidentified Paul as a younger brother, it is one of the few instances where an article about Vincente Minnelli makes some reference to his otherwise unacknowledged sibling.

As Paul turned three and a half and his disabilities were becoming more apparent, Mina discovered that she was expecting again. The baby would arrive in February. In the theater, the winter months were known as the "lean season," as engagements were harder to come by, especially for traveling players. Sure enough, as they awaited the arrival of their fifth child, Mina and V.C. found themselves engaged by different theater companies. Mina continued performing—as a visibly pregnant ingénue—until the latest possible moment. When she could hold out no longer, she retreated to her mother's house. On February 28, 1903, Lester Minnelli made his debut in Chicago. Years later, there would be an enormously successful return engagement.

***

AS SOON AS LESTER WAS OLD ENOUGH, his parents worked him into the act. "I played the children's parts whenever there were any to play," he recalled. It was Lester's unforgettable performance in the Minnelli Brothers' production of the creaky melodrama *East Lynne* that sealed his fate as an actor. Five-year-old Lester was playing "Little Willie," who dies in his mother's arms during the play's overwrought climax. Mina, in character as the distraught mother, clutched her son's "lifeless" body and exclaimed, "Gone! And never called me mother!" Mistaking his mother's dramatically charged portrayal for real life anguish, Lester suddenly sprang back to life and did his best to reassure a thoroughly embarrassed Mina that he was still among the living. "No Mama. I'm not dead. I was *acting*," Lester announced as the audience roared.[11]

"Acting never appealed to him," V. C. Minnelli would later say of his son's early retirement from the spotlight. "He was a quiet boy and [he] would

---

* In 1978, while Vincente Minnelli was being honored at the Athens International Film Festival, journalist Peter Lehman asked the Oscar-winning director, "Do you have any brothers or sisters?" Between puffs on his ever-present cigarette, the seventy-five-year-old auteur responded, "No. We had twins who died when they were infants." No mention was made of Paul Minnelli. (Peter Lehman, Marilyn Campbell, and Grant Munro, "Two Weeks in Another Town: An Interview with Vincente Minnelli," *Wide Angle* 3, no. 1 [1979]: 65.) In 1994, Delaware historian Brent Carson met Liza Minnelli after she performed at the Polaris Amphitheater: "I mentioned Paul Minnelli to her and she said, 'I never knew that he had a brother.'" (Brent Carson, interview with author, 2007.)

sit in the dressing tent and watch the men make up. Before the season was over, the cast would not go on without Vincente's o.k. of their make-up. If he said, 'Eyebrows too black' or 'Not enough red,' the change was made to suit him."[12]

At a very young age, Lester began displaying some legitimate artistic talent. It wasn't long before his doodles morphed into designs. As Minnelli would recall years later, "The fact that my father and uncle owned the show made it possible for me, at an early age, to make suggestions for settings and costumes. . . . My proudest moment was when my mother wore a costume that was made up of about 75 percent from my rough design and suggestions. It was this early triumph which probably influenced my entire career."[13]

***

WHEN THE MINNELLIS WEREN'T OUT bringing culture to the provinces or getting on or off a Pullman car, their home base (and winter headquarters) was Delaware, Ohio. Smack dab in the center of the state, Delaware was the birthplace of the nineteenth president of the United States, Rutherford B. Hayes, and the home of Ohio Wesleyan University.

"When the Minnellis came to Delaware, they didn't have very much money and of course, they were trying to find a place to stay," recalls family friend Anne Dinovo.[14] "So, my father offered that they could stay in a house he had on Park Avenue until they found their own place. Well, they never found a place. They lived in the house my father owned—free of charge— for many, many years. . . . They had a lot of courage but very little money. But the whole world was a stage to that family. . . . The father was always dressed like the jack of diamonds and I don't think he had a dime in his pocket, poor guy."*

When Lester was five, the *Journal-Herald of Delaware* announced the Minnelli Brothers Farewell Tour: "Regardless of the so-called hard times . . . Minnelli Bros. are making great preparations for the coming season." V.C. did his best to put a positive spin on what appeared to be his swan song as an impresario, telling a local reporter, "If hard work, excellence and 'the goods' count, that should make 1908 our banner year."[15] The reports of the company's imminent demise proved to be premature. Although the Minnelli Brothers managed to press on for a number of years, there were indeed hard times ahead.

---

* At one point, V.C. and family moved in with Lester's grandparents. Their home at the corner of N. Washington Street and Fountain Avenue in Delaware came complete with a rolling front yard and a spacious front porch. The house is a dead ringer for the Smith residence in *Meet Me in St. Louis*.

A fire destroyed their entire operation at one point, necessitating a $10,000 reconstruction effort. Neighbors in Delaware also remembered that the Mighty Dramatic Company was sidelined by the Great Flood of 1913. Although the Minnellis survived these setbacks, even they were no match for a new-fangled invention that was proving to be more of a legitimate threat than a passing fancy. As Vincente remembered it, "Motion pictures had finally done the theatre in. The movies started to be good and more or less killed the tent show business."[16] Decades later, when he received his Best Director Oscar for *Gigi*, Vincente Minnelli was all too aware of the supreme irony: The same film industry that had awarded him its highest honor had put his father out of business.

For V.C., folding up the tent in many ways represented the collapse of the dream. "Father wasn't happy about the development,"[17] Lester would say of the derailment of the elder Minnelli's career on the road, though Mina seemed to relish the fact that her touring days were finally over. She would embrace her latest role as full-time mother and housewife with the kind of wholehearted enthusiasm that had been missing from some of her tent theater appearances. Besides, the Minnellis weren't out of the business altogether. They would eventually open their own studio in Delaware and teach young ladies, such as Dorothy Florance, how to dance: "Mrs. Minnelli had a cane that she walked with and boy, she'd crack your legs with that cane if your pointe work wasn't proper," Florance recalled. "A nice little lady but a very strict teacher."[18]

***

AS LESTER GREW UP, there was agreement from all corners that he was anything but your typical son of Delaware. From an early age, the budding artist found it necessary to piece together an impenetrable private universe from whatever bits of the fantastic he managed to find in the everyday. "I had learned to recycle my experiences in real life and apply them to my creative endeavors," Minnelli said.[19]

If his days in Delaware happened to be uneventful or unkind, Lester's glittering inner world was always waiting. Real life—with its Catholic guilt, strict discipline, and feelings that never seemed to fit—could always give way to an alternate universe, one that was fantastic, exotic, and drenched in color. A daydreamer without equal, he'd imagine himself carousing in Rudyard Kipling's barracks or sailing aboard a pirate ship bound for the Spanish Main. Or he might spend an afternoon sketching in his father's chicken coop. Despite the cackling and rustling of feathers, the relative solitude and sanctuary he found there formed what Minnelli would later refer to as "my first studio." Or, when he felt more sociable, he might gather a few friends together and stage a not-so-amateur theatrical in a neighbor's barn, which he had decorated with a skull and crossbones.

For the most part, V.C. seemed to encourage his son's creativity, though Lester's artistic flair may have also churned up some unsettled feelings in the elder Minnelli. "My father treated me with a grave courtesy, perhaps regretful that his son was so socially timid," Vincente would recall decades later.[20] Lester's timidity was one thing, though far more disconcerting to V.C. was his son's undeniable effeminacy. In a pre–politically correct era, having fathered one child who had been branded "feeble-minded" and another who seemed unusually sensitive must have been discouraging to a man as proud as V. C. Minnelli.

Having survived tough crowds and unforgiving critics, V.C. was somewhat unyielding where Lester's creative endeavors were concerned. "It's good . . . but it isn't up to your usual standard," V.C. would remark when presented with his son's latest chicken-coop masterpiece. The seeds of Vincente Minnelli's legendary perfectionism were sown in Delaware. Taking his cue from V.C., Lester would confront his own reflection in the mirror: "Here you are, nine years old, and what have you done? You're nothing . . . nothing but a failure."[21]

As there would always be an emotional distance between father and son, and Paul was unable to keep up with his younger brother's spectacular flights of fancy, Lester bonded with his Uncle Frank. "He was flashier than Dad, and more current," Lester would say of the flamboyant uncle who introduced him to the bright lights beyond Delaware through loaned copies of *Life* magazine or *Snappy Stories*.[22] Frank regaled his nephew with backstage anecdotes, and Lester would inundate his uncle with questions about everything pertaining to show business.

Lester's strict Catholic upbringing and the years he'd spent touring in the company of adults had matured him beyond his years, making him seem unusually serious for a youngster. "He was very nice, very quiet and very reserved for a child," recalls Margaret Brawley, who attended St. Mary's Parochial School with Lester. Brawley remembers that during the holidays, the nuns would encourage Lester to put his unique talents to good use. "Vincente used to come around—he was probably in the sixth or seventh grade—and he'd go up to the blackboard and draw pictures. . . . We weren't allowed to touch them or erase them because they were just perfect." Lester's artistic abilities won him the kind of positive attention that he was not otherwise awarded from his peers. "The sisters and students just clamored around him," says Brawley, describing a scene that could have been lifted directly

Some early evidence
of Lester's artistic flair.
ILLUSTRATION
COURTESY OF
BRENT CARSON

from Minnelli's cult musical *Yolanda and the Thief*, in which a convent's star pupil is singled out for special attention.[23]

John Hanrahan was one of Lester's boyhood friends. "He just knew that Minnelli was going to be somebody great and important," Bill Hanrahan says of his father's friendship with the future director. "He said there was just something about Vincente Minnelli—even as a child—where you just knew he was going to be big time."[24]

Others remember that Lester was regularly teased and bullied in school. Some of this may have been attributable to "The Minnelli Gallery" of twitches, facial tics, and lip pursings—nervous habits that would become more pronounced over time—though the taunting young Lester received in school probably had more to do with his effeminacy than anything else. "He was quite flamboyant," says Delaware historian Brent Carson. "He was very theatrical acting at times—even when he wasn't acting. I think that during his early years, he was probably made fun of."[25] Lester's preference for play-acting and drawing over fishing and football also led neighbors to make certain assumptions.

The Minnellis: V.C.,
Paul, and Mina at home on
London Road in Delaware,
Ohio. Lester had already
moved on to the bright lights
of Broadway.
PHOTO COURTESY OF
BARBARA BUTLER
(PHOTOGRAPHER UNKNOWN)

"I think he was gay," says Delaware native Virginia Barber, whose father, Robert Stimmel, was a childhood friend of Lester Minnelli's. "Of course, in those days, people never mentioned anything about that. You just didn't back then. There were two words I never heard growing up here. One of them was 'gay' and the other one was 'Jew.'"[26]

The Minnellis' Catholicism, Paul's disabilities, Uncle Frank's flamboyance, Lester's effeminacy, and the fact that the Minnellis were "theater people"—all of this resulted in an alienating effect in the small-town confines of Delaware, Ohio. True, the Minnellis were well liked within the community, even admired, but just the same they would forever be viewed as somehow apart. Lester especially would feel the full impact of being branded "different."

As the adolescent Lester was considered reserved and sensitive, it is curious that the editors of his high school yearbook would honor him with an epithet like "From the crown of his head to the soul of his foot, he is all mirth."[27] Though, as Minnelli noted years later, "My timidity began to leave me during that last year at Willis High School." Surrounded by students from

Lester Minnelli steals the
show as the malevolent
"Deadeye Dick" in the
Glee Club's production of
Gilbert and Sullivan's
H.M.S. Pinafore.
PHOTO COURTESY OF
BRENT CARSON
(PHOTOGRAPHER UNKNOWN)

what he would later describe as "Delaware's middle class," Lester finally loosened up.[28] Minnelli's thoughts on the latest Adolphe Menjou picture or his references to Modigliani were no longer met with blank stares. His jokes—no matter how Noel Coward-ish in tone—landed. The year at Willis seemed to fly by, with Lester stopping the show as the malevolent "Dick Deadeye" in the Boys' and Girls' Glee Club production of Gilbert and Sullivan's *H.M.S. Pinafore.*

Just as Lester was beginning to blossom, graduation day arrived. As Minnelli received his diploma, it was with the knowledge that many of his friends would be heading off to Ohio Wesleyan in the fall. Lester would not be among the incoming freshmen. "I don't know what I would have studied in college but the idea of going was ingrained in me," Minnelli remembered. "I saw all the kids in high school were going and I was very disappointed that I didn't have the money to go to college."[29] The modest income that V.C. and Mina earned from teaching dance to Delaware's aspiring Isadoras was enough to keep the family afloat but not to send Lester off to campus.

In August 1921, only months after Lester received his high school diploma, a family tragedy would further taint what should have been a carefree period for the recent graduate. As the *Delaware Daily Journal Herald* reported: "Mr. Frank P. Minnelli, aged 51 years, one of the best known theatrical men in Ohio, took his own life by firing two 32 caliber revolver bullets through his body as he stood in the Pennsylvania Railroad yards." Frank left behind a letter addressed to his wife and brother that read: "Untold suffering has justified my act, good-bye."[30]

It was a heartbreaking end for Lester's adored Uncle Frank, whom the *Delaware Journal* reported had been "mentally unbalanced by illness." The papers attributed Frank Minnelli's severe depression to a year-long battle with "dropsy and heart trouble." Though at least one friend of the family was more matter of fact: "As for Frank, he hit the skids," recalled Dorothy Eveland. "He became a drunkard and a penniless bum. His body was found one morning in a Delaware railroad yard. A very sad end."[31] Though it was devastating to Lester, Uncle Frank's suicide may have also provided his nephew with the motivation he needed to launch himself.

After Minnelli became famous, newspaper profiles would suggest that it was around this time that Lester "secretly planned a campaign" to leave Delaware and pursue his artistic ambitions in the big city. New York was his first choice, but he'd settle for Chicago if necessary. Of course, the big move required money. "I think the first job he ever had in Delaware, my father gave him," says Barbara Butler. "My father owned a confectionary and Lester was hired to work there. As the story goes, Lester was carrying this tray up the stairs one day and he dropped it and everything spilled all over. My father was unhappy with him and fired him. Mrs. Minnelli asked if my father would take him back as they were in very poor circumstances at that time. So, Lester came back for awhile."[32] One job lead to another. He worked in an angler's shop, painting artificial fishing flies. He created the advertising curtain for the local movie house. Finally, he had saved up enough to put his "secret campaign" into action.

{2}

Window Dressing
the World

MINNELLI SAID GOODBYE to Delaware and, true to his word, never looked back.* It was on to Chicago—and in the midst of the Roaring '20s, no less. That "toddling town" was teeming with activity, anarchists, and bathtub gin. Al Capone was at large. The *Daily Tribune* headlines blared all the latest: "$22,000 to Fight Booze," "To Uphold Law in Scopes Trial, Prayers Go On," "Bandits Bind Miss Bingham, Steal $1,500." Amid Chicago's speakeasies, nightclubs, bookie joints, and brothels, Minnelli absorbed what he described as the city's "raucous vitality."[1] It was certainly a far cry from the well-mannered tranquility of Delaware, Ohio.

Fortunately, Lester wasn't alone in the big city. Upon his arrival, he moved in with his Grandmother Le Beau (Mina's mother) and his Aunt Amy,† a former trapeze artist who had toured on the vaudeville circuit. Their modest house at 1220 West Polk Street was near Notre Dame de Chicago, where Grandmother Le Beau and Aunt Amy would faithfully attend early Mass and listen to the sermons offered by the Fathers of the Blessed Sacrament. But not Lester, who by this time admitted "falling out" as a practicing Catholic. His mind was on more worldly matters—namely finding a job.

With his artist's portfolio tucked under his arm, Lester embarked on a job search, which abruptly ended when he was "seduced" by a spectacular

---

* According to city directories, Lester Minnelli was still residing with his parents in Ohio as of 1922. He most likely moved to Chicago the following year.

† Aunt Amy's baptismal name was Marie Levina Le Beau.

Florentine-style window display at Marshall Field. After inquiring about employment opportunities at the store, Lester was led to the top floor office and introduced to one Arthur Valair Fraser,* Marshall Field's display director. An innovative force in the world of window display, Fraser had combined papier-mâché and wax figures to create what would ultimately evolve into the department-store mannequin. After examining Lester's watercolors, "The King of Display" (as Fraser was known) hired him on the spot. With one fortuitous visit, Minnelli had gone from the ranks of the unemployed to Mr. Fraser's fourth apprentice. It was the best kind of window shopping.

Lester and his fellow trimmers had their work cut out for them. As the Midwest's largest department store, Marshall Field featured sixty-seven windows in need of dressing. The store's meticulously designed window displays were unequaled and the envy of other retailers. Although Lester was disappointed that his new position didn't allow him to be as creative as he'd hoped, it was at Marshall Field that "the Minnelli Touch" was born. The future director would discover which combination of colors pleased the eye, how the trappings surrounding a subject were just as important as the subject itself, and that even the smallest details enhanced the big picture. As Minnelli would later strive "to bring the sleek lines of modernism into the theater," he hoped to take Marshall Field's "excellent windows into the twentieth century."[2] But for the moment, Lester's greatest challenge involved deciding which tie went best with which display model suit.

Fifty years after working at Marshall Field, Minnelli would write about the experience in the telegraphic notes for his autobiography. "Don't think anyone gay in the window dressing department," he mused. In the published version of his memoir, he assured readers that his fellow display men "were all married and raising families."[3] While this may be true, Minnelli seemed eager to distance himself from anything that smacked of the homoerotic, including the traditionally gay milieu of window dressing. Perhaps the need to publicly distance himself had something to do with the fact that during his years in Chicago, Minnelli almost certainly embarked on a relationship with another man—one named Lester Gaba.

"Lester always maintained that he had some kind of dalliance or liaison with Minnelli," says designer Morton Myles, who knew Lester Gaba when both resided on Fire Island. "I can't say yes or no for certain, but he always alluded to the fact that they had an affair. . . . It may have started as a trick

---

* Misidentified in Minnelli's memoir and other sources as "Mr. Frazier."

Lester Gaba's Hannibal
High School yearbook
photo from 1924 (when
he was still known as
"Abe"). "Lester always
maintained that he
had some kind of
dalliance or liaison
with Minnelli," says
designer Morton
Myles, who
befriended Gaba
in his later years.
PHOTO COURTESY
OF STEVE CHOU

and then turned into a friendship. Anything is possible. But on the other
hand, Lester was known to embroider quite a bit. I mean, there wasn't a
New York City taxi driver that he didn't have when he was short on change
for the fare."[4]

While it's been said that opposites attract, Minnelli and Gaba could not
have been more similar. There was the uncanny coincidence of their first
names (though Gaba's real first name was "Abe," and it's unclear when he
started calling himself "Lester"). In terms of their physical appearance, there
was more than a passing resemblance between the two. Like Minnelli, Gaba
was from middle America (Hannibal, Missouri), and he, too, had left his
hometown while still a teenager. Landing in Chicago, Gaba worked at Marshall Field as an errand boy, though the two Lesters most likely met when
both were working for Balaban and Katz, where Minnelli designed costumes
and Gaba designed promotional posters.

Gaba had the same need to express himself visually that Minnelli did.
Both were constantly window dressing the world and transforming the everyday into something far more enchanting. As Gaba recalled, "As soon as I
was old enough to make a crepe paper rose, I began to help my father trim
the windows of his clothing store in Hannibal. And it's probably the best
experience I ever had."[5] Gaba could sketch almost as well as Minnelli, but
it was his whimsical soap sculptures—southern belles and white knights
carved out of ordinary bars of Ivory that won him the most attention. A decade after their friendship—or affair, as the case may be—blossomed in
Chicago, Minnelli and Gaba would resume their relationship in New York.
Through it all, Minnelli remained devoted to his one true love—his career.

Lester Gaba told *Esquire's* Hugh Troy that he had "never met a creative person whose mind is so inseparable from his work, and who is so willing to sacrifice everything—amusement, friends, and self—to achieve his ambitions as is Minnelli."[6]

* * *

DESPITE MINNELLI'S GRUELING WORK SCHEDULE at Marshall Field, he somehow managed to find time to attend recreational education classes at the School of the Art Institute of Chicago.* "I went to the life classes a couple of times but couldn't keep it up because I was working," Minnelli recalled years later.[7] Encouraged by the positive response he had received for his acting forays back in Delaware, Lester gave performing another try, appearing in an amateur production of Eugene O'Neill's *Where the Cross is Made* at the Radical Playhouse.

He also regularly attended the theater, but never as just another passive spectator. Throughout a performance, Lester was continuously busy, creating what he would later refer to as "memory sketches" of the incandescent stars on stage, including showstoppers such as Ina Claire and Mary Nash. Encouraged by friends, Minnelli began selling his memory sketches backstage for $10 ($15 if the purchaser was especially well dressed). Oftentimes he was able to make direct sales to the actors whose likenesses he had captured, including some of his future collaborators, such as Fanny Brice and Ethel Barrymore. One evening, after the curtain fell, Lester met professional photographer Paul Stone backstage. Stone took notice of Minnelli's work and was immediately impressed. "If you can do that, you can learn to photograph," Stone told Lester. When the photographer offered Minnelli more money than he was earning at Marshall Field, he had no choice but to agree. It was time to get behind the camera.

Paul Stone snapped theatrical luminaries, society matrons, wedding parties—and, when nobody was looking, male nudes.† Lester Minnelli proved to be a characteristically quick study, though he lacked Stone's finesse in dealing with the celebrities and high-society types who streamed into the photographer's Raymor Studio, which happened to be across the street from Marshall Field.

---

* Although Minnelli's enrollment at the Art Institute was short lived, his attendance would contradict later newspaper reports that insisted that "he never had an art lesson in his life."

† One of Stone's subjects in later years was future Hollywood adonis Steve Reeves, whose god-like physique would earn him the title "Mr. Universe" and starring roles as Hercules in several sword-and-sandal epics.

Minnelli would remember Stone as a "high strung, nervous type" who suffered a breakdown only a few months after Lester began working for him.[8] During Stone's extended absence, it fell to Minnelli to photograph the likes of actress Ina Claire.* Lester was so bashful shooting a star that he worshipped that he hid behind the camera, quaking. Social unease aside, Paul Stone's studio was beneficial for Minnelli, as it furthered the education that had begun in Mr. Fraser's window-display department at Marshall Field. Lester learned how important lighting was in terms of creating the proper mood; he discovered that he had a knack for presenting subjects so that they appeared utterly glamorous yet perfectly natural. After agreeing to photograph a determined leading lady from her "best side," Lester would sweet-talk her into trying a different angle. Almost always, Minnelli's way proved to be the more visually arresting.

There may have been a different kind of education taking place at Stone's studio as well. With a parade of handsome, well-built young men stopping in to be photographed with their clothes off, it's possible that Raymor Studio was something of gay sanctuary. In fact, in a deleted passage from his autobiography, Minnelli noted, "Paul Stone's assistant gay—didn't have much to do with him."[9] Was it Minnelli's strict Catholic upbringing that wouldn't allow him to have "much to do" with Stone's unnamed gay assistant? Or was it the fact that by the early '70s, when Minnelli was preparing his memoir, he had a vested interest in presenting himself as the exclusively heterosexual father of superstar Liza Minnelli?

Minnelli's remark is curious—and all the more so as it was while he was working in Stone's studio that he began to pattern himself after the most colorful fop of them all—James McNeill Whistler. In later years, Lester would tell the story of discovering his idol in one of two ways: A Raymor Studio sitter left behind a copy of E. R. and J. Pennell's biography of the flamboyant painter and Minnelli was instantly smitten, or he happened into an art gallery one Sunday afternoon and was taken with the Whistlers up on the wall. Whichever way it went, Minnelli latched on to Whistler's story as though it were the modern-day dandy's guide to life. Lester no doubt recognized something of himself in descriptions of Whistler being "absorbed in his work when that work was in any way related to art." Whistler's life story so completely captured Lester's imagination that he began to emulate the artist's dandified ways—from his ostentatious style of dress to his reverence for color, which Whistler once described as "the most magnificent mistress possible."[10]

---

* Ina Claire, who would go on to star in such Hollywood classics as *The Awful Truth* and *Ninotchka*, was Minnelli's first choice for the role of Aunt Alicia in his Oscar-winning musical *Gigi*. The actress turned down the role.

A master of self-invention, Whistler's story pointed the way to Minnelli's own personal transformation. For it was in Chicago that Lester Minnelli became Vincente Minnelli. At first, he used his father's name, "Vincent C.," before deciding to add the final "e" to his first name for a touch of sophistication and old world elegance. "Vincente Minnelli" said man of the world. Artist. Aesthete. The name change signaled a whole new beginning. Lester from Delaware simply ceased to exist.

It was yet another example of how Minnelli and his companion Lester Gaba were on the same wavelength. "Lester Gaba wanted you to believe that he was a genie born out of a bottle in midtown Manhattan," says Morton Myles. "He didn't like any allusions to Hannibal, Missouri. If someone appeared who knew him from his early days in Chicago, they got very short shrift. If someone brought up Chicago, you never saw that person again in his presence. . . . He invented himself as a New York character. It probably was the same with Minnelli."[11]

In the midst of transforming himself, Vincente suddenly found his surroundings uninspiring. "I yearned to be a participant like Whistler instead of a spectator, and I was itching to move on," Minnelli recalled of his later years in Chicago.[12] The same kind of driving ambition that had propelled a teenager out of Delaware, Ohio, now brought him through the doors of the opulent Chicago Theatre. Once again, Minnelli would exhibit his portfolio (which now included photos of glamorous stars he had snapped at Stone's studio) and find that it met with immediate approval.

Frank Cambria was director of productions for Balaban and Katz, the Chicago-based theater chain that presented live stage shows between screenings of feature films. Cambria introduced Minnelli to A. J. Balaban, who was impressed not only with Vincente's portfolio but with the young man's gumption. Although Vincente couldn't sew a stitch, that didn't stop him from pitching himself as the head costumer for Balaban and Katz's nonexistent wardrobe department, promising to enhance their live shows with "a custom touch." He was hired. Although initially billed as "Creator of Costumes," Minnelli would eventually design sets for a number of Balaban and Katz extravaganzas as well.

"The Balabans didn't have access to the best movies because they were latecomers to the scene in Chicago," says David Balaban, whose great uncle, A. J. Balaban, ran the family business with an awe-inspiring military precision:

> There were already other chains that operated many more theaters than the Balabans. So, Balaban and Katz had to come up with another way to attract people to their theaters. The way they did that was through opulent architecture,

air-conditioned theaters, and through the design of these stage shows which
were a combination of vaudeville, musical revues, and very highbrow classical
music. . . . They were marketing themselves as the premier quality place to
see a show. . . . That was the atmosphere that Vincente Minnelli was thrown
into.[13]

The live portion of the Balaban and Katz weekly spectacular rotated
among several theaters in the Chicago area, and Minnelli made the rounds
along with the sets and costumes. "The time that Minnelli was with Balaban
and Katz was a very formative period," says David Balaban. "It formed the
foundation for a lot of his aesthetic beliefs because he had a lot of freedom
to basically create these shows from scratch. . . . It would have been the best
kind of training for being a director."[14]

In 1928, Balaban and Katz merged with the motion-picture chain
Paramount-Publix. This corporate marriage would have a life-altering impact
on Minnelli. At first, his employers would only occasionally dispatch an
all-too-happy-to-oblige Vincente to their flagship theater, the New York Paramount. Once there, he would lend his talents to stage productions that would
play before Broadway audiences prior to heading out on the road.

Since his Delaware days, Minnelli's "secret campaign" had involved
bundling up his art books and making his way to New York. And now, not
only had that long-cherished dream materialized, but, as Vincente recalled,
"It was everything I expected it to be."[15] Not only was New York a neon-
drenched utopia, but the city seemed to operate on the same kind of nervous
energy that Vincente did. Only one thing was lacking to make the scenario
perfect: permanent residency. After his initial visits, Minnelli had made up
his mind that at the earliest opportunity, he would move to Manhattan. And
as fate would have it, Balaban and Katz had the very same notion. If Vincente
wanted to remain in their employ, he would have to relocate to New York.
So, Minnelli packed his bags.

A Glorious
Garden of Wonders

IT WAS THE STUFF of countless Mickey Rooney–Judy Garland musicals: A wide-eyed kid with loads of talent and insane ambition making the leap from his family's small-time theatricals to The Great White Way. *Milking applause instead of milking a cow*.[1] Though at the moment Minnelli arrived in New York in the early '30s, the great metropolis seemed like a movie set that was still under construction. They had just taken the wraps off of the Empire State Building. Three square blocks were being leveled to make way for John D. Rockefeller Jr.'s Radio City center, and Mrs. Harry Payne Whitney was announcing plans for a new museum devoted exclusively to American art.

And at the outset of the Great Depression, Broadway was offering, for those who could afford a ticket, escapist fantasy in the form of extravagant musical revues. The more lavish the production, the better. There was the Ziegfeld Follies, Earl Carroll's *Vanities*, and George White's *Scandals*. These eye-popping extravaganzas offered over-the-top opulence, "lewder than nude" showgirls, and grand spectacle—everything audiences needed to forget about the harsh realities of the world *out there*, where over 4 million people were unemployed.

There was theater. And then there was street theater. Like countless artists both before and after him, Vincente had naturally gravitated to Greenwich Village. Even in those days, the parade of eccentrics and oddballs wandering around were often more entertaining than any of the legitimate attractions offered in Times Square. The Village was not only a haven for artists, radicals, and self-styled bohemians but had long ago established itself as America's preeminent gay mecca. In the Village, the unorthodox was the norm and flamboyance flourished. Here, even more so than Chicago, was a dramatically heightened environment that nearly mirrored Vincente's colorful inner world.

Minnelli's first residence in the city was, as he described it, "a tiny Greenwich Village nest, sublet from vagabond-dancer Jacques Cartier."[2] The address was 89 Bedford Street, two blocks off of the better-known Christopher Street. According to census records from 1930, Vincente lived alone in the one-room apartment and was paying the landlord $65 a month for rent, more than any other occupant in the building. Apparently it was around this time that Minnelli began playing with the facts about his age: He informed an unsuspecting census taker that he was twenty-four years old when he was actually twenty-seven.[3]

The personal transformation that had begun in Chicago continued in New York. Inspired by his surroundings, Minnelli went full tilt Village artiste. He began sporting a long coat and a flat black hat with a wide brim. The look was memorably described by one observer as "a triumphant marriage of Harlem and the Left Bank." It may have been around this time that Vincente began wearing make-up as well. A touch of eyeliner. A trace of lipstick. As he had grown up advising the actors in his father's troupe on how to paint their faces, this probably seemed perfectly natural to him. Besides, why should cosmetic enhancement be reserved for center stage? Although the youthful Minnelli had once been described as "quite handsome in an almost Mongoloid way," Vincente was all too aware of the fact that he had not been blessed with matinee-idol good looks. So why not indulge in a bit of exterior decorating? After all, he had told the census taker that he was "actively employed as an independent artist." So why not look the part?[4]

As for the "actively employed," he was constantly in demand, creating exquisite costumes for the Paramount-Publix circuit and "designing the equivalent of a Broadway show every week."[5] And of course, there was no end of fascinating people to meet both in and out of the theater.

One of Vincente's earliest champions was an indefatigable young woman named Eleanor Lambert. Although not yet the extraordinarily influential force in the fashion world that she would later become, Lambert had already developed an unerring eye for spotting legitimate talent. She immediately recognized something unique and unusually beautiful about Minnelli's ever-expanding portfolio.

"She was kind of a talent spotter," says Lambert's son William Berkson:

I witnessed this probably all of my life with her. . . . People would come to her office or they would come at tea time. Somebody's always got . . . *some-*

thing. In the later days it would be a guy with a new line of bridal outfits. In the old days, it was the latest designer. The enthusiasm and the energy she had went beyond business. In other words, a lot of what she was offering was just free advice. She really just seemed to delight in finding the next big thing. . . . So, a lot of what she did was basically say, "Sit right here. You better get to know me because I can see that you're a comer and I can clue you in."[6]

Lambert saw to it that Minnelli met all the right people.

Another who was taken with Vincente's artistic abilities was Joseph Monet, editor of the notorious Van Rees Press. Monet hired Minnelli to illustrate a new edition of the quasi-erotic *Casanova's Memoirs* in a manner reminiscent of English surrealist Aubrey Beardsley. Vincente's art nouveau–style drawings of androgynous figures engaged in boudoir shenanigans of every description made clear what the Venetian adventurer's recollections only hinted at.

***

JUST AS HE HAD FOR DELAWARE'S movie house years earlier, Vincente would design the curtain for the ninth edition of Earl Carroll's *Vanities*. Unlike the modest drape at The Strand, Carroll's curtain, at 300 feet wide, was on the grandest of grand scales, and it would be on full view before a seen-it-all Broadway audience. The curtain would also serve as the centerpiece of Carroll's gleaming new art deco theater. Inspired by the exquisite (and exquisitely expensive) curtains Erté had designed for the Folies-Bergère, Vincente was determined to achieve a similarly stunning effect—though at a fraction of the cost. Rising to the challenge, Minnelli devised a visual stunner: a "living" curtain in absinthe green chiffon with silver embroidery that featured "strategically placed openings" in the fabric through which Carroll's comely showgirls could insert arms, legs, or other parts of their anatomies: Peek-a-boo. The effect was dazzling.

Although critic Robert Benchley would dismiss "the definitely Negroid sense of color," the theatrical community was abuzz over Minnelli's audacious opulence. Vincente's ability to produce sumptuous, eye-catching effects on a very thin dime had not been lost on budget-conscious Earl Carroll. The impresario promoted Minnelli to scenic and costumer designer for the 1932 installment of the *Vanities*.

Carroll would also be responsible for Minnelli's first appearance on film. In a 1933 promotional short entitled *Costuming the Vanities*, Carroll and his bashful costume designer are seen reviewing wardrobe sketches for star Beryl

Wallace (who would later become the showman's wife). While Carroll looks directly at the camera, Minnelli does everything to avoid it. His shyness is palpable. It appeared that there was more than a little bit of Lester left in suave sophisticate Vincente Minnelli after all.

While the *Vanities* was still on the boards, Vincente was summoned to assist glamorous Grace Moore, the first in a glittering line of great lady stars in his life. "The Tennessee Nightingale" (as Moore was nicknamed) had triumphed in the Metropolitan Opera's production of *La Bohème* four years earlier. Now Karl Millocker's comic operetta, *The DuBarry*, was being prepared for Moore and she had personally requested twenty-nine-year-old Minnelli as the art director, hopeful that he could do for her what he had done for Earl Carroll and his curtain. Similar to the type of exacting star Vincente would encounter some forty years later when he worked with Barbra Streisand, Moore was legitimately talented, equipped with a mercurial temperament, and had very "definite ideas about what was seemly for her," Minnelli recalled decades after their uneasy collaboration.[7]

Moore's ideas about the way she should be presented on stage clashed with many of Minnelli's most inventive concepts. When Vincente proposed that Moore wear a brief kimono-style drape in a brothel sequence, the star huffed and stormed out. Moore's coach ride to the palace of Louis XV had been imaginatively conceived by Minnelli so that that the audience could glimpse the rear of the coach and its rotating wheel through the carriage's back window, but when Minnelli suggested that stagehands rock the coach back and forth to complete the illusion, Moore complained that she was queasy and nixed the idea. To make matters worse, the notoriously absent-minded Minnelli sent the leading lady a congratulatory telegram on opening night—only it was addressed to popular singer *Florence* Moore. The star was not amused, and she was probably even less so when she read Brooks Atkinson's review of *The DuBarry*, which began by praising Minnelli's "richness of color and sweep of line" before getting around to her performance.

Having established himself as one of the most visually inventive talents on Broadway, Minnelli was made a set designer by his bosses at Paramount. Not long after the promotion, Paramount shifted its stage-show operations to Astoria, Long Island, where the East Coast division of Paramount Pictures was headquartered. No sooner had Minnelli been promoted than Paramount decided to drop its costly stage shows in favor of big band appearances.

The career-driven workhorse was suddenly out of a job. Though, as it turned out, not for very long. After spending only a couple of months among the ranks of the unemployed, Vincente received a call from the newly opened

Radio City Music Hall. Was he interested in a position as the Music Hall's chief costume designer? The offer couldn't have come at a better time for Minnelli. And without question, "The Showplace of the Nation" needed all the help it could get.

On December 27, 1932, when Radio City had opened its doors, the response from the press and public alike had been positively underwhelming. Rather than presenting a bold, modern attraction to complement the Music Hall's gleaming art deco design, the inaugural production staged by Robert Edmond Jones proved to be a fustily old-fashioned affair—a virtual funeral rite for vaudeville, complete with Fraulein Vera Schwarz and the Flying Wallendas. A catastrophe in nineteen acts, the entire performance had been conceived and supervised by Samuel "Roxy" Rothafel, Radio City's director general. The day after the disastrous opening, Brooks Atkinson took Rothafel to task in the *New York Times*: "The truth seems to be that maestro Roxy, the celebrated entrepreneur of Radio City, has opened his caravansary with an entertainment, which on the whole, does not provoke much enthusiasm."[8]

It was resoundingly clear to the management that something drastic had to be done before Radio City went under quicker than the *Lusitania*. While the Music Hall's theaters were temporarily closed, no end of changes took place. Robert Edmond Jones resigned, as did costume designer James Reynolds. Emergency meetings were called. Roxy and company would need to chart an entirely new course.

A mix of movies and live stage spectacles had proven to be a winning combination for Minnelli's former employer, Balaban and Katz. Other theater chains had found success with this varied approach as well. So it came as no surprise when Radio City announced that it was adopting the stage and screen format. When it reopened on January 11, 1933, Radio City's revamped program included a feature film (Frank Capra's *The Bitter Tea of General Yen*) and a considerably shortened stage show. This would prove to be a winning formula. "From January 1933 until it closed as a movie house, Radio City Music Hall invariably, inflexibly, and with no exception, always changed its show on Thursday," says historian Miles Krueger. "Every single week there were new sets, new costumes, new ballets, new choral numbers. They had a men's chorus and visiting comedians and acrobats and God knows what. Everything for about 35 cents. That's how they could fill 7,000 seats."[9]

While the Music Hall's format was being overhauled, Radio City's management decided that an entirely new production staff was needed to breathe some life into what was supposed to be the "live" portion of the bill. Someone remembered Minnelli's striking contributions to the Earl Carroll extravaganzas, and by February 1933 Vincente was in place as Radio City's chief costume designer.

Minnelli would be working closely with Roxy Rothafel, a former marine drill sergeant. As Vincente would soon discover, dealing with Roxy was a major occupational hazard. Like virtually everyone under Rothafel's command, Minnelli found the irascible impresario "obstreperous and fault-finding."[10] This was certainly the case with art director Clark Robinson, who threw in the towel after yet another heated exchange with the impossible-to-please Rothafel. In terms of finding an immediate replacement for Robinson, Roxy didn't have to look too far.

Although he was still as wet as the Music Hall's walls, Minnelli was now Radio City's new art director—this in addition to his already overwhelming costuming duties. It was a head-swelling double dose of responsibility—though almost immediately, Vincente would find himself cut down to size. Roxy, an equal opportunity put-down artist, would make the mild-mannered, soft-spoken Minnelli his whipping boy of choice. As Vincente recalled, "Instead of doing the job of three men, I would now be doing the job of six . . . and getting a proportionally larger share of Roxy's sarcasms."[11]

In July 1933, Minnelli was handed his first assignment as art director, and it would call upon every ounce of his artistic ingenuity to fill the role. Vincente's training under Balaban and Katz would prove invaluable as he conjured up such sumptuous set pieces as a "Water Lily" ballet, a Cuban-themed sketch (complete with a pair of mammoth fighting cocks), and a Parisian dress boutique in which the shapely "Roxyettes" would strut their stuff—all of it crammed into fifty minutes. Within a matter of days, Minnelli would be expected to whip up another batch of equally imaginative settings and a dazzling array of costumes. It was Vincente's designs for December's "Scheherzade Suite" (complete with Persian rugs and elephants) that made both the New York Times and Roxy take notice. "You know, I've been picking on this fellow," Rothafel admitted to his beleaguered staff. "All that picking brought fine results. . . . He's an artist."[12]

No sooner had his commanding officer tossed Minnelli a bit of long-overdue praise than Rothafel was sent packing. The management had more than likely received one too many complaints regarding Roxy's take-no-prisoners tactics. Although the ulcer-inducing confrontations with Roxy were over, the nonstop work and continual sleep deprivation were still very much a part of Vincente's exhaustively paced existence. He fought off fatigue with gallons of black coffee. Racing to keep up with the grueling production schedule,

Vincente and composer E. Y. "Yip" Harburg in the '30s. Minnelli said of his equally talented friend: "I was drawn to his rare good nature, and he must have seen in me a kid who needed more polish and dash."
PHOTO COURTESY OF LILY MELTZER AND THE HARBURG FOUNDATION

the hourly backstage dramas, and the constant demands of everyone around him, Minnelli had precious little time to claim as his own: "I'd stay up all night and light the new show, then we'd start planning the next one at lunch the following day."[13]

If he had been a self-declared "failure" at nine, Minnelli was single-mindedly determined to make up for his "misspent" youth. Virtually every minute of the day was consumed with getting a new show ready. When he wasn't placating neurotic stars or fixated on some bit of visual minutia, Minnelli somehow found time to acquire a remarkable collection of friends—a veritable Who's Who of the entertainment world.

E. Y. Harburg (whom everyone called "Yip") was outgoing, a deep-dyed socialist and an inveterate ladies' man. Though he was a dreamer like Vincente, Harburg was in many ways Minnelli's polar opposite. Despite their distinctly different personalities, Yipper and Vincente became fast friends. In October 1934, when Minnelli was given an opportunity to direct his first show at Radio City, he invited Harburg to contribute an original song, "Jimmy Was a Gent," to *Coast to Coast*. Billed as a sophisticated revue in four scenes, the production transported audiences to several exotic locales. It would serve as something of a blueprint for Minnelli's first Broadway spectacular, *At Home Abroad*.

It was Harburg who introduced Vincente to two people who would become his closest friends: Ira and Leonore Gershwin. With a gentle, self-effacing demeanor similar to Vincente's, Ira Gershwin was accustomed to letting others hold court. He never seemed put out by the fact that both professionally and socially, he was overshadowed by his younger brother George. When Minnelli stepped out with the Ira Gershwins, Lee inevitably took charge—which wasn't too difficult, as both her husband and Vincente were certified introverts. Through the years, Lee would become something of a surrogate mother to Minnelli—fussing over him, introducing him to all the right people, and ribbing him about his confirmed bachelor status.

Vincente found another lifelong friend in the form of eccentric pianist and professional hypochondriac Oscar Levant (whom Bosley Crowther dubbed "the gifted vulgarian"). Levant was a fixture at Gershwin parties, always at the ready with a blistering wisecrack or a self-deprecating one-liner. Oscar was every bit as rabbity and nervous as Minnelli. But unlike the eternally tight-lipped Vincente, Levant tended to narrate the finer points of his neurosis, constantly complaining about ailments, both imaginary and all too real.

It was at the Gershwin's apartment on 72nd Street that Vincente would meet and mingle with some of the brightest talents on the New York scene. Minnelli and composer Harold Arlen would reminisce about their days with Earl Carroll. Vincente would bring dramatist Lillian Hellman up to speed on all the latest backstage gossip. The delightfully witty "Prince of Broadway," Moss Hart would keep Minnelli entertained with some side-splitting theatrical anecdote that would turn up in one form or another in one of the devastating comedies Hart wrote with collaborator George S. Kaufman. As with Minnelli, there had been "a lot of speculation about Hart's sexuality."[14] And just like Vincente, Hart would end up tying the knot at the age of forty-two. Marriage—even so late in the game—would put an end to all of the whispers.

***

IN 1932, LESTER GABA packed a clean shirt and his lucky penknife and headed off to New York. Considering everything that Gaba and Minnelli already had in common—Marshall Field, the Chicago Art Institute, Balaban and Katz—was it yet another uncanny coincidence that they both moved to Manhattan around the same time? Or had Minnelli gone on ahead and smoothed the path for his uniquely talented friend? Whatever the case, once they were reunited, Minnelli and Gaba were closer than ever. Or at least as close as two fiercely ambitious, career-driven artistic types could be.

Although Gaba's career would never ascend to the same heights at Minnelli's, throughout the latter half of the '30s, he seemed to be everywhere at once. His clever soap sculptures turned up in ads for Ivory Snow detergent;

he staged fashion shows, wrote magazine articles, and designed a successful line of costume jewelry; and his one-of-a-kind Gramercy Park apartment was featured in *House Beautiful*. The dining room, with its "mad" Venetian mural and "an honest-to-goodness canopy," looked like a set piece straight out of a Minnelli-designed Music Hall number. If the name of the game was publicity, then Lester Gaba was one skilled competitor.[15]

Lester Gaba: soap sculptor, mannequin designer, and "the Andy Warhol of his day." *Esquire* referred to Gaba as "one of Minnelli's closest friends."
WESTERN HISTORICAL MANUSCRIPT COLLECTION, UNIVERSITY OF MISSOURI–COLUMBIA

"He preceded Andy Warhol in knowing how to bring attention to himself," says designer Morton Myles. "Just being a painter or just writing about fashion, he realized would not do it. And so, he had to do all of these unusual things to create attention."[16]

If Gaba was looking for attention, he found plenty of it, courtesy of one of his most bizarre creations. "The Gaba Girls" were a series of mannequins that were so incredibly lifelike that shoppers who breezed by the fashionable figures in the windows of Best and Company or Saks Fifth Avenue invariably did double takes. The most famous of the Gaba Girls was a tall, statuesque blonde named Cynthia who possessed an "eerie, almost human quality" that was both fascinating and unnerving.[17]

Cynthia quickly became a society column staple. Harry Winston loaned her diamonds for an evening out. The press had a field day spotting Cynthia at El Morocco, in the balcony of the Broadhurst, or having her hair done at Saks Fifth Avenue's Antoine salon. Lester Gaba relished the attention but resented the fact that he was being upstaged by his own creation. When Cynthia fell out of a beauty parlor chair and shattered, Gaba wasn't exactly prostate with grief. He told a reporter: "Cynthia had become a Frankenstein to me, and I was rather relieved that she decided to—retire."[18] After her untimely "passing," Cynthia was replaced by a real-life surrogate—Gaba's own mother. As Morton Myles recalls, "People used to say, 'He gave up "The Girls" and now he's got his mother.' . . . I remember attending a party when I first moved to Fire Island and when Lester arrived, he was pulling his mother Mamie in the type of little express wagon that we used for hauling groceries on the island. That's an image you don't forget. She immediately

The beautiful Marion Herwood Keyes. Minnelli's devoted secretary was also known as his "unkissed fiancée."
PHOTO COURTESY OF PETER KEYES (PHOTOGRAPHER UNKNOWN)

became the center of interest arriving that way. I remember she once said, 'I'm really like the Queen of Sheba, I suppose.'"[19]

Between toting around Cynthia and Mamie, Gaba somehow managed to work in a relationship with Minnelli. If Vincente was knee-deep in preparations for the latest Radio City extravaganza, Gaba would patiently wait for him to finish his backstage duties. In 1934, the two went on a cruise to Bermuda together. When *Esquire* profiled Minnelli in 1937, Gaba (whom the magazine described as "one of Minnelli's closest friends") recalled that everything they did and saw throughout the trip was "so much fodder for Minnelli's brain, [as he was] constantly attempting to twist everything into an idea for a stage show."[20]

Just as Vincente's relationship with Lester Gaba had everybody guessing, so did his association with a striking, modishly attired young woman named Marion Herwood. As Minnelli recalled, "The work at the Music Hall was getting so involved that it was decided that I should have a secretary. I hired Marion."[21]

They were always together, often working late into the evening. Always at her right elbow was Marion's Titan-sized notebook, in which she jotted down Minnelli's latest inspirations. But was their relationship all just strictly business? After a Walter Winchell item appeared suggesting that Vincente and Marion were "that way about each other," Minnelli's mother phoned from St. Petersburg, Florida (where the Minnelli family had relocated in the late '30s), and inquired about his intentions. Vincente assured her that he and his dutiful secretary were just good friends—though it seems that even Herwood thought otherwise.

"I've come to assume that they practically got married," says Marion Herwood's son, Peter Keyes. Each time Minnelli made the move from Broadway to Hollywood (first for a brief stint at Paramount in the late '30s, then with MGM for keeps), Herwood went with him. It was during Vincente's second attempt at breaking into the movies that his faithful assistant was dealt a devastating blow. Without explanation, Vincente suddenly shifted his attention from Herwood to MGM's resident showstopper. "I think [Minnelli] may have broken things off around the time he went after Judy Garland," says Peter Keyes. "At that point, my mother indicated that she had a nervous breakdown out in California and that one of her brothers was terribly important in supporting her through a very difficult period and helping her out of the depression."[22]

Friends of the costume designer Irene, whom Herwood assisted on Minnelli's 1945 movie *The Clock*, remembered that Marion considered herself a Minnelli fiancée despite the fact that Vincente's embraces were at best polite and that he had never so much as kissed his intended. After Herwood recovered from her broken engagement and the breakdown that followed, she would resume her work as a costumer on such MGM classics as *The Picture of Dorian Gray* and *The Postman Always Rings Twice*. And she would eventually marry an investment banker.*

---

* In later years, Minnelli and Marion Herwood Keyes occasionally corresponded. "I have thought about you many times and it is a joy to hear from you," Vincente wrote to his former assistant in the early 1970s. Herwood Keyes was also one of dozens of Minnelli colleagues whom writer Joel Siegel interviewed for his exhaustively researched though ultimately aborted biography of the director.

"A New Genius
Rises in the Theater"

Oh, what wouldn't I give for
Someone who'd take my life
And make it seem gay as they say it ought to be,
Why can't I have love like that brought to me?
My eye is watching the noon crowds,
Searching the promenades, seeking a clue . . . [1]

ALTHOUGH BILLY STRAYHORN had written the lyrics to "Something to Live For" in Pittsburgh in 1939, they may well have applied to Minnelli during his New York years. Vincente had achieved so much professionally by the time he was in his early thirties that, Lester Gaba and Marion Herwood aside, there hadn't been much time to cultivate significant relationships. For the man who had once said, "Creating magic for my audience is all that I live for," romance was really an afterthought—though for Vincente, "searching the promenades" wasn't always about looking for love.

"When I was very young and exploring New York City, Minnelli was working at Radio City Music Hall," recalls designer Jack Hurd, who in later years served as a set decorator on such MGM productions as *It's Always Fair Weather* and *Butterfield* 8:

Next door to Radio City, at Rockefeller Center, there's a skating rink. That's what they call a cruising spot for gay pick-ups. Well, he picked me up there one evening and brought me back to his apartment. He showed me models of sets and things, which he had around the apartment. Then he wanted to have sex but I didn't find him attractive. He had make-up on. He was too feminine. So, I left. . . . Years later, after the war, I ran into him between the sound stages at MGM, where I was then working on sets. I reminded him of what took place years ago and oh, god, . . . he went to L. B. Mayer and he wanted to get me fired. He didn't want me around. And he was still freakish, wearing make-up—lipstick and eye stuff. He was married to Judy Garland by then and everybody would say, "What the hell does she see in him?"[2]

Though he was shy and self-protective, Vincente somehow managed to cultivate an impressive collection of friends. They would congregate in the West 53rd Street studio that Minnelli acquired in 1935 and in his "modernistic" apartment, which came complete with a Japanese valet named Hara.* Regular visitors included Yip Harburg, choreographer George Balanchine, writer Paul Bowles, and composer Kay Swift, who christened Minnelli's salon "The Minnellium." There were other visitors as well.

If Paul Stone's Raymor Studio had been something of a gay refuge back in Chicago, The Minnellium may have offered the same kind of sanctuary in Manhattan. "Clearly Minnelli's aesthetic interests and the world in which he lived was very queer," says historian David Gerstner:

> His New York circles were very gay and he cultivated a coterie of people that was interested in the queer arts. There was [Pavel] Tchelitchev, the out homosexual painter. Minnelli was friends with [Ballets Russes director Serge] Diaghilev. He said that he had been photographed by George Platt Lynes. And his New York theatrical productions were very much indebted to a lot of gay artists. . . . He was in that milieu that was so central to his whole aesthetic. And this set the stage for everything that followed.[3]

***

ALTHOUGH VINCENTE'S RESPONSIBILITIES at the Music Hall were multifaceted and ever expanding, they were also limiting. What Minnelli really wanted

---

* When the *Dunkirk Evening Observer* profiled Minnelli in December 1936, it described Hara as "a soft-slippered, slant-eyed servitor" as well as Vincente's "best friend and severest critic." In *The Sewing Circle*, author Axel Madsen makes reference to "the rumors about [Minnelli] and his Japanese valet," but little is known about Hara, and the suggestions that he was more than just a personal assistant to Minnelli aren't accompanied by any substantial evidence. ("Valet Critical," *Dunkirk Evening Observer*, December 31, 1936; Axel Madsen, *The Sewing Circle: Hollywood's Greatest Secret. Female Stars Who Loved Other Women* [New York: Birch Lane Press, 1995].)

to do was direct. His first offer came from "the theater's bargain basement"—the Shuberts. Like everyone else, Vincente knew that the Shubert organization was a "shlock operation," though now brothers Lee and Jake (also known as "J.J.") were attempting to produce shows of higher quality. They hoped that by signing Minnelli, this would be a signal to theatergoers that the Shuberts were going legit.

The first of the three Shubert revues Minnelli agreed to oversee was originally called *Not in the Guidebook*. Vincente and collaborators Howard Dietz and Arthur Schwartz (whose songbook would later comprise the score for Minnelli's *The Band Wagon*) envisioned their *Guidebook* as a colorful "musical holiday" in which stars Beatrice Lillie, Eleanor Powell, Ethel Waters, and Reginald Gardiner would romp through such exotic locales as Japan, Austria, and Africa. All of the globe-trotting prompts one of the weary adventurers to ask, "Why don't we just take a trip around Paul Whiteman?"[4]

"I had total autonomy and no expenses were spared in mounting the production," Minnelli recalled. While this arrangement freed him up creatively, he was also operating under the onus that if the show didn't come off, there would be nobody to blame but Vincente Minnelli. He seemed to prefer it that way, telling *Newsweek*: "One person should do everything in musicals, then original ideas remain un-tampered." Credited with staging, settings, and costumes for what was ultimately retitled *At Home Abroad*, Minnelli knew that his professional reputation and future career were riding on the whole extravagant enterprise. In a sense, Minnelli was the whole show. And already there were some who wanted to give him the hook.

In a letter to business partner William Klein, J. J. Shubert let it rip: "I wish you would ask for a manuscript of *At Home Abroad* and read it yourself. I read it and believe me when I tell you that there wasn't one outstanding thing in the play. . . . If you asked me to invest a five cent piece in the proposition, I would absolutely refuse to do so on its cold-blooded book and lyrics. My only hope is that it succeeds and gets over." Of course, J. J. Shubert's damning assessment of the material was obviously colored by what Vincente described as the intense "love-hate relationship" that existed between the Shubert brothers. "[They] had no personal dealings with each other," Minnelli recalled. "Each headed his division of the company in separate but equal fashion. . . . Lee was marvelous, it was Jake who was the monster."[5]

Minnelli had no time to get caught up in the in-fighting. Digging his heels in, he prepared to work like never before. With this production, Vincente was determined to bring a modernistic sensibility to the Broadway musical as well as a thematic continuity that had been conspicuously absent from most theatrical revues. He was also intent on creating a show that would have a fresh, bold look. He devised ways to effectively spotlight each member of the company, fully aware that this was the kind of production the trades termed "a personality show." And what personalities. First and foremost, there was the inimitable Beatrice Lillie. In a priceless sketch entitled "Dinner Napkins," Lillie appeared as the delightfully discombobulated Mrs. Blogden-Blagg. The snooty matron attempts to order "one dozen Double Damask Dimity Napkins," which, after many mangled attempts, comes out as "two dizzen dozen doozan dankin nippers, only dibble drimmisk."

Though she was clearly *At Home*'s headliner, Queen Bea (as the press affectionately dubbed Lady Peel) was the first to admit that the show's success was dependent on the extraordinary ensemble that Vincente had carefully assembled: "We had the latest thing in tap dancers in Eleanor Powell, a long-legged, statuesque girl, who as Ashton Stevens used to say, 'looked as if she had a mother.' Ethel Waters invariably stopped the show with a Jamaican plantation number, which in these much altered times would probably bring out a picket line. . . . And I brought over from London a new leading man, Reginald Gardiner, who began by doing brilliantly original imitations of wallpaper."[6]

Although virtually every sequence in *At Home Abroad* was a knockout, Minnelli and librettist Howard Dietz locked horns over two elaborate production numbers: the scintillating Eleanor Powell showcase "The Lady with the Tap," and "Death in the Afternoon," a surrealistic ballet featuring the young Danish dancer Paul Haakon. The acerbic Dietz (whose Playbill bio included the memorable admission, "I am thirty-nine years old and drink like a fish") wanted to eliminate these sequences. Dietz may have registered concern because both numbers were dance-centric affairs that weren't dependent on his clever lyrics to succeed. Believing that both numbers were integral to the show, Vincente fought to retain them and ultimately prevailed. Minnelli was vindicated when these sequences were singled out for praise by the critics.

Minnelli was partial to "Death in the Afternoon" because of its "overtones of apprehension."[7] The sequence concerned a young Spanish matador (Haakon) marching off to the bullring to meet his fate. The ballet employed innovative lighting techniques, and it was awash in a violent shade of scarlet that, years later, MGM designers would come to refer to as "Minnelli red." Apart from the stylistic flourishes, the ballet also featured a fairly blatant helping of homoeroticism, as the handsome torero is dressed by two male attendants who seem unusually attentive.

If naysayer J. J. Shubert had been unwilling to invest a nickel in the "cold-blooded" *At Home Abroad*, he probably found himself warming up to the show as 2,000 people jammed Boston's Shubert Theatre on September 3,

Reginald Gardiner surrounded by adoring fans in a promotional photo for *At Home Abroad*, which took Broadway by storm in 1935. The *New York Times* declared: "What gives *At Home Abroad* its freshest beauty…is the scene and costume designing of Vincente Minnelli."
PHOTO COURTESY OF PHOTOFEST

1935, for the world premiere. Despite the impressive turnout, the production's creative team second-guessed themselves right up until the eight o'clock curtain. But as the evening got underway, the perspiration and panic attacks gave way to hopefulness. "Beatrice Lillie was given a near ovation at her first appearance," the local press noted. By evening's end, it was clear that Minnelli and company had a Broadway-bound hit on their hands.

While acknowledging that a bit of "skillful surgery" was in order, the *Boston Post*'s Elliot Norton (who would emerge as one of Minnelli's most vocal early champions) concluded, *"At Home Abroad* is that loveliest of things to see in the theatre—a hit."[8]

Once the company returned to New York and prepared for the Broadway unveiling, *At Home Abroad* was retooled and scaled back. On opening night at the Winter Garden (September 19, 1935), lighting effects failed to come off and cues were missed. To an exhausted Minnelli, these relatively minor blunders seemed like signs of an unmitigated disaster. Fearing the worst, the director left the theater immediately after the curtain came down and went straight to bed, fully intending to skip the opening-night party. But the unqualified raves drew Vincente out from under the covers.

"What gives *At Home Abroad* its freshest beauty . . . is the scene and costume designing of Vincente Minnelli," the venerable Brooks Atkinson declared in the *New York Times*. "Without resorting to opulence, he has filled the stage with rich, glowing colors that give the whole work an extraordinary loveliness. Nothing quite so exhilarating as this has borne the Shubert seal before." *The New Yorker* concurred: "The settings, done by a young man called Vincente Minnelli, seem to me the best I've seen in a long time, being uniformly stylish, cheerful and intelligently in key with what's going on."[9]

Prior to *At Home Abroad*, no one had ever simultaneously designed and directed a Broadway musical before. As critics used words like "innovative" and "original" to describe Minnelli's work, he was both flattered and surprised that his efforts had made such an impression.

Vincente Minnelli was the toast of Broadway, a critic's darling—the subject of adoring magazine profiles and the nucleus of an incredibly eclectic coterie of friends. Yet this wasn't enough. Even now, when Vincente studied his reflection in the antique mirror in his Chinese red bathroom, it was still Lester staring back. "Here you are. . . . And what have you done?" always seemed to be the question behind that wanting look. For Vincente, the answer was always "not enough." Even now, his father's admonition, "Not up to your usual standard," was always nagging at him.[10] In a very real way, "the usual standard" for Minnelli was one of almost superhuman achievement. No matter how hard he worked, nothing on stage could ever quite measure up to the magnificent images swirling around in his brain.

While audiences were still flocking to see Bea Lillie deliciously poke fun at all sham and pomp in *At Home Abroad*, Lee Shubert approached Vincente with an irresistible idea: resurrecting the Ziegfeld Follies. Although Ziegfeld had died in 1932, his widow, Billie Burke (still several years shy of achieving immortality via her role as Glinda in *The Wizard of Oz*), had given her blessing to a Shubert-produced *Follies* in 1934. The production was well received and even turned a modest profit in the midst of the Depression. Even though "The Great Glorifier" was gone, the opulent spectacle that was the *Follies* could still cast its spell. Encouraged by the reception for the 1934 edition, the Shuberts were ready to give the *Follies* another go, and Minnelli agreed to join them. Though they were never known for their extravagance, the Shuberts spared no expense in mounting the 1936 installment. They assembled a dream team that included Ira Gershwin (lyrics and sketches), Vernon Duke (music), and, direct from Diaghilev's Ballets Russes, George Balanchine (choreography).

The Shuberts had already tapped revue veteran John Murray Anderson to direct, while both sets and costumes were being entrusted to Vincente, who would be paid $1,500 for his services. At least that's how it read on paper. As those close to the production recalled, Minnelli provided "major uncredited assistance" to Anderson in a variety of ways. This included everything from establishing the visual concept of the show (which would be in "the spirit of a fashion photograph by Cecil Beaton") to directing at least two of the sequences. One of these was "Night Flight," an impressionistic ballet featuring the eternally unsmiling Harriet Hoctor and choreographed by Balanchine, who would become a Minnellium regular.

Working on the *Follies* would allow Vincente an opportunity to work with collaborators as diverse as Fanny Brice, Bob Hope, the Nicholas Brothers, and future MGM choreographer Robert Alton. One participant especially excited Minnelli's imagination: an exotic, utterly scandalous import from the Folies-Bergère named Josephine Baker.

Nearly forty years after designing Baker's jaw-dropping ensembles for the *Follies*, Vincente could still vividly recall encasing "her svelte figure in a shimmering sari" for "Maharanee," a musical number in which one of Baker's admirers pays tribute to her by singing, "Who brings glamour to cafes, to the Ritz and Zelli's, in her Schiaparellis? . . . It's the maharanee." For "Island in the West Indies," Minnelli outfitted "the Black Venus" in a scandalously brief thong "ornamented by white tusks." Though it was Act II's "Five A.M." that inspired Minnelli's pièce de résistance: Baker as a weary trollop, returning to her flat at an ungodly hour wearing an extravagant, nearly one hundred pound gold mesh gown offset by a plum-colored ostrich cape. Only the finest would do for Vincente's glorious bird of paradise.

Although Minnelli fixated on what F. Scott Fitzgerald referred to as Baker's "chocolate arabesques," he was equally exacting with every other aspect of the production. "I don't think there has ever been a greater disciplinarian or a more exacting perfectionist in the musical theatre than Vincente Minnelli," composer Vernon Duke observed. "Where other directors wasted a lot of valuable time wrangling with costume designers, arguing with overpaid stars or kidding around with chorus girls, with Vincente—once the rehearsals started—it was all work and no play. We all felt like cogs in Minnelli's magical wheel and kept ourselves well oiled."[11]

It was Ziegfeld's greatest star, Fanny Brice, who stole the show both on stage and off during the run of the *Follies*. Whether spoofing Busby Berkeley's over-the-top extravaganzas in "The Gazooka" (a "Super-Special Musical Photoplay in Techniquecolor on the Widescope Screen"), lampooning the modern-dance movement in "Modernistic Moe," or romping as the beloved Baby Snooks, Brice was the comedic centerpiece of the whole shebang,

Fanny Brice
(as Baby Snooks) getting
the best of Bob Hope in
Ziegfeld Follies of 1936.
"Vincente Minnelli, who
doesn't appear on the
stage at all, is the
star of the new
Ziegfeld Follies . . ."
wrote Elliot Norton in his
Boston Post review.
PHOTO COURTESY OF THE
SHUBERT ARCHIVE

though after the curtain came down, the star was continuously plagued by ill health and bouts of insomnia.

During the show's two-week tryout in Boston, the creative team realized that *Ziegfeld Follies of 1936* was shaping up as too much of a good thing. As Ira Gershwin noted, "This *Follies* was rare in that although the customary out-of-town phrase 'It needs work . . .' applied, the problem here was one of wealth of material rather than lack. . . . We had too much show with too many elaborate production numbers."[12] After a major overhaul, a significantly scaled back *Follies* was finally judged ready to meet an audience, which it did in December 1935.

While Fanny Brice almost always ran away with the reviews, she was for once eclipsed by another in the notices that appeared the day after the opening: "Vincente Minnelli, who doesn't appear on the stage at all, is the star of the new *Ziegfeld Follies*, which had its world premiere last night at the Boston Opera House," wrote Elliot Norton in the *Boston Post*.[13]

This was followed a week later with another, even more glowing tribute: "It is the well-pondered opinion of this column that Vincente Minnelli . . . has a greater theatrical genius than the late Florenz Ziegfeld. . . . With all his vast capacity, [Ziegfeld] never had any such amazing ability to create and project theatrical beauty as has this Italian-American." It was high praise and well deserved, though Minnelli would later quip, "I got out of Boston not a moment too soon before I was either canonized or burned at the stake."[14]

The *Follies* would be further fine-tuned in Philadelphia, but while it was there, an exhausted Fanny Brice collapsed on stage. As the star carried much of the show, the producers prayed that Brice would be well enough to bring the production into New York. Miraculously, the comedienne rallied, and *Ziegfeld Follies of 1936* made its Broadway debut on January 30. By early May, however, Brice was out of the spotlight altogether after her doctor diagnosed neuritis of the spine. Rather than attempting to replace their one-of-a-kind headliner, the producers decided to temporarily close the show with plans to bring it back after a summer hiatus. Vincente would describe the laying off of both cast and crew as "another example of the Shubert's up-yours philosophy."[15]

Before it reopened in September, *The New Ziegfeld Follies of 1936–1937* (as it had been retitled) required some revamping, as much of the show's topical humor had become dated during the months the production was on hiatus. Minnelli wasn't called back to assist with the retooling, as his services were already required on the next Shubert-produced opus.

Billed as "Vincente Minnelli's Gay Musical," *The Show Is On** would be the first production to feature the director's name above the title. And just in case any theatergoers missed it, the playbill would include another reminder: "The Entire Production [was] Conceived, Staged and Designed by Vincente Minnelli."† John Murray Anderson, goodbye. As Vincente later noted, "Given carte blanche, I filled it in as if it were a Southern belle's dance program."[16] Among those invited to contribute original songs were friends Vernon Duke, Richard Rodgers and Lorenz Hart, Hoagy Carmichael, Harold Arlen, and Yip Harburg (who would be called in to doctor the show as well).

In preparing musical material, Minnelli remembered a sort of parody of a Viennese waltz that George and Ira Gershwin had begun but dropped before they went to Hollywood to work on the Fred Astaire–Ginger Rogers vehicle *Shall We Dance.*‡ Vincente sent a telegram to the Gershwins asking them to revisit their "Straussian take-off" so that he could work it into the

---

* The original title was *Tickets for Two*.
† It's worth noting that despite Minnelli's all-encompassing credit, Eddie Dowling was responsible for "stage direction," Edward Clark Lilley is credited with directing the sketches, and Robert Alton handled the choreography.
‡ It was Minnelli who suggested this title for the classic musical, which had originally been saddled with the name *Stepping Toes*.

"It is practically my life ambition to see them both on the same stage," Minnelli said of Bea Lillie and Bert Lahr, the stars of *The Show Is On*. Reporter William A. H. Birnie observed of the revue's director: "His remarks are low-keyed and polite, as if he were coaching a church benefit . . . but even such veterans as Lillie and Lahr pay strict attention to what he says." PHOTO COURTESY OF THE SHUBERT ARCHIVE

show. The Gershwins came through, and "By Strauss," with its lilting melody and inventive rhymes ("Ya ya ya—Give me Oom-pah-pah!") became one of the highlights of *The Show Is On*.

If *At Home Abroad* had offered audiences a picture-postcard tour of the globe, *The Show Is On* would make the theater itself the evening's primary destination. "The thought just came to him when he was walking in Central Park one afternoon," Marion Herwood said of her employer's inspiration for his latest revue. "He wanted to do a bigger, newer, more unusual musical than had ever been done before. The subject he liked was the show game. . . . He thought of contrasting the old and new, of revealing scenes with the color and glamour of the '90s and then following this with ultra-modern jazz song numbers."[17]

As for featured performers, Minnelli had very definite ideas: "I can think of only one leading comedienne, and that would be Beatrice Lillie. The comedian, of course, must be Bert Lahr. It is practically my life ambition to see them both on the same stage." Lillie needed little convincing: "It may be safely concluded that when an invitation came along to play in a new musical under the direction of Vincente Minnelli, who handled *At Home Abroad*, I set off at a fast trot for cocktails at his studio. Vincente's gentle salesmanship may have done it—perhaps he picked up the technique when he worked for Marshall Field's Chicago department store."[18]

Even the inimitable Lillie would have to be on her toes to keep up with her seasoned costar—one of the most original and outrageous talents in the business. Whether he was refining his trademark "gnong, gnong, gnong" in a burlesque house or delighting millions of moviegoers as the Cowardly Lion in *The Wizard of Oz*, Bert Lahr was a certified showstopper. The master buffoon was also "the worryingest rehearser in the business," according to sketch director Edward C. Lilley.[19] A fidgety, neurotic button-twister, Lahr seemed light years away from the elegant, eternally composed Lady Peel. Yet they clicked, both on stage and off. And *The Show Is On* gave these two ingenious comedians ample opportunity to display their sublime chemistry and individual versatility.

Lillie was a caution as a nineteenth-century crooner perched high on a "perilously migratory moon," warbling "Buy Yourself a Balloon" while flinging garters into the audience. Bert Lahr had them rolling in the aisles with "The Song of the Woodman," Arlen and Harburg's send-up of Nelson Eddy–style anthems such as "Stout-Hearted Men." Appearing in lumberjack regalia and wielding a papier-mâché ax, Lahr offered an ode to deforestation: *What do we chop, when we chop a tree? A thousand things that you daily see. A baby's crib, the poet's chair, the soap box down at Union Square.* "That song was written specifically for Mr. Lahr's talents—to point up his immense mimicry and range," says Arlen scholar R. Bobby. "Minnelli said, 'There's a spot in the show where I need a great number for Lahr.' Arlen and Harburg were in Hollywood and they came up with this hilarious song which shows how brilliant they were at writing material for a specific performer."[20]

David Freedman, whom Vincente dubbed "The master of all sketch writers," had been responsible for some of the wittiest material in *Ziegfeld Follies of 1936*. For *The Show Is On*, he managed to top himself, though it certainly didn't hurt that his writing partner for "Mr. Gielgud Passes By" was none other than Moss Hart. In the sketch, Bea Lillie embodied the actor's nightmare—a chatty latecomer who yaks her way through a performance of John Gielgud's *Hamlet*. Reginald Gardiner's frustrated Gielgud finds himself competing with her as he attempts to portray Shakespeare's Melancholy Dane. Lillie's thoughtless chatterbox explains that an opening night is the one place she's certain to meet up with her friends and have a nice, long chat.

During rehearsals for *The Show Is On*, Minnelli was profiled by the *World-Telegram*'s William A. H. Birnie, who noted that Vincente looked "as if he had wandered out of an art gallery and wished he could remember his way back." The reporter also observed Minnelli directing: "His remarks are

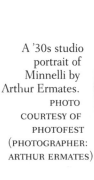

A '30s studio portrait of Minnelli by Arthur Ermates.
PHOTO COURTESY OF PHOTOFEST
(PHOTOGRAPHER: ARTHUR ERMATES)

low-keyed and polite, as if he were coaching a church benefit. But an attentive visitor notices that even such veterans as Bea Lillie and Bert Lahr pay strict attention to what he says." Birnie's portrait of Minnelli included a certified eyebrow raiser: "He shies away from any activity that might be considered effeminate."[21] This after Vincente had confessed an affinity for Tchaikovsky symphonies and Whistler etchings and owned up to taking dancing lessons at Arthur Murray's.

The Show Is On opened at the Winter Garden on Christmas Day 1936, and Santa delivered a hit. The production continued Minnelli's extraordinary winning streak. The misfit from Delaware, Ohio, was now the most sought after talent on Broadway: "It happened to me. I was a winner. The offers started pouring in. The re-creation of the War of the Roses using real roses? In time. A musical version of Medusa, starring Merman and the inmates of the New York Herpetological Gardens? Maybe next year. A Hollywood contract? Come now."[22]

For some time, the same critics who had been heaping hosannas on Vincente for his work in the theater had wondered how long it would be before Hollywood's "bogeymen of Technicolor" would scoop Minnelli up and carry him away. Already there had been one close call. Playwright Lillian Hellman was determined to bring her buddy Vincente and movie producer Samuel Goldwyn together. Hellman found that as moguls go, Goldwyn was straightforward and possessed of genuine integrity, and she believed Vincente could be a tremendous asset to the producer. But Minnelli wasn't as taken with Goldwyn as Hellman was. "I have an offer from Sam Goldwyn, but he doesn't seem to understand what my work is about," Minnelli wrote to Yip Harburg in April 1936. "He seems to want me very much as a designer, and seems shocked and grieved to learn that this is only a part of what I am doing in the theatre and would want to do in pictures. . . . There must be some way for the movies to use my small but exquisite talent without labeling me as a designer or as a director."[23]

It was clear that if Vincente did surrender to the silver screen, it would have to be on his own terms. And his employer would have to fully understand how truly unique that "small but exquisite" talent of his was. After instructing his agents to look into the offers from various movie studios, the highest bidder turned out to be not Goldwyn or MGM but Paramount Pictures. Terms were met. A contract was signed. Minnelli was going Hollywood at $2,500 a week.

"Just as he was conceded to be the one person who could return the musical stage to the glories of the Ziegfeld reign, Minnelli is snapped up by Paramount," the *Boston Traveler*'s Helen Eager noted in an article headlined "A New Genius Rises in the Theater." The newly anointed genius was surprisingly candid about his reasons for heading west: "He told us, quite frankly, that the money offered him by the film company was too attractive to turn down."[24]

Paramount's publicity machine kicked in before Minnelli had a chance to pack his bags. The October 30, 1936, edition of the *Los Angeles Times* carried a tiny, telegraphic item buried between stories about Binnie Barnes and Gloria Swanson that read, "Importance of musicals in present studio activities is stressed with the signing of Vincente Minnelli by the Paramount organization. This producer and director of footlight attractions will act as general advisor on the melodic features that are made hence forward at the establishment."

5

A Small
but Exquisite Talent

IN JANUARY 1937, Minnelli drove through the Paramount gates for the first time. Never one to start small, he proposed that his first production should be an innovative musical mystery entitled *Times Square*. Minnelli envisioned the film as an all-star extravaganza that would incorporate scenes from actual Broadway shows currently on the boards. In his pitch to studio chief Adolph Zukor, Vincente maintained that the expense of importing Great White Way headliners to Hollywood or dispatching a film crew to New York would be justified as moviegoers would be all too eager to spend their Depression-era dimes to see theatrical luminaries most of them had only heard about. Zukor listened, as did head of production William LeBaron. Still reeling from the losses on *Alice in Wonderland*, the lavishly mounted all-star epic gone wrong, Paramount executives were understandably leery about committing to anything as grandiose as *Times Square*. Nevertheless, Vincente continued to develop the screenplay with Russian writer Leo Birinski, who had scripted the Greta Garbo vehicle *Mata Hari*.

After studio executives expressed their doubts about *Times Square*, Minnelli shelved the project, and despite his great enthusiasm, it remained unproduced. Paramount then asked Vincente to turn his attention to *Artists and Models*, a picture he was assigned to serve in an "advisory capacity." This breezy musical comedy was being readied for Jack Benny and Ida Lupino. The very definition of madcap, the movie represented a change of pace for irascible, one-eyed director Raoul Walsh, who later excelled at helming such gangster flicks as *The Roaring Twenties* and *White Heat*. "Public Melody

Number One," a witty spoof of the G-Man genre, would be the sole sequence that Minnelli conceived that would be retained in the final cut of *Artists and Models.**

Collaborating with fellow New York transplant Harold Arlen, Vincente whipped up a frenzied pastiche featuring a characteristically manic Martha Raye and Louis Armstrong. Looked at today, "Public Melody Number One" might be considered a sort of rough sketch for the Jim Henry's night club sequence in Minnelli's first feature, *Cabin in the Sky*. But when Minnelli viewed the much-altered version of "Public Melody" that ended up on the screen, he dubbed it "a full scale mess, missing all the nuances we'd supplied."[1] Vincente had also prepared an elaborate surrealistic ballet for *Artists and Models*, but it was deemed "too artistic" for a Paramount programmer and dropped.

Understandably, Minnelli was frustrated. After being hailed as Broadway's new genius, he found that Hollywood was oddly indifferent to him. Imaginative concepts that had been eagerly embraced by Minnelli's New York colleagues didn't inspire anywhere near the same enthusiasm in Tinseltown. With his cryptic communication style and sketches for dream ballets tucked under his arm, Minnelli was considered too avant-garde, too cosmopolitan, and, well . . . just *too much* for Hollywood. Busby Berkeley's kaleidoscopic choreography for *Footlight Parade* was one thing, but a Jack Benny vehicle taking time out for a surrealistic ballet was simply going too far. *It will never go over in Duluth, kid*, one can almost hear the cigar-chomping producer say.

When Lee Shubert offered Vincente a return to Broadway in the form of a new musical entitled *Hooray for What!* the unhappy transplant didn't hesitate. After he wrangled himself out of his lucrative Paramount contract, his eight-month adventure in Hollywood was over. Although he would be missed by a small circle of West Coast intimates, the rest of the industry barely took notice of his departure. Little did they know that he would be back, and next time out, it would be to stay.

With the joyous sound of New York traffic once again ringing in his ears, Minnelli told columnist James Aswell: "I have just returned from Hollywood where all the world's a succession of stages. After years spent working in the theater on one stage at a time, I found it just a bit terrifying to create a scene that covered almost a quarter of a mile. . . . In my opinion, the screen as a musical comedy medium has not as yet been fully and completely developed."

---

* *Artists and Models* was a hit at the box office and even inspired a sequel, 1938's *Artists and Models Abroad*, which featured Lester Gaba's high-profile blonde mannequin "Cynthia."

Roy Roberts, Ed Wynn, and Vivian Vance in Minnelli's *Hooray for What!*
Vance replaced future MGM arranger Kay Thompson, who was originally cast as the
show's singing spy. "Kay Thompson was fired from that show," remembers songwriter
Hugh Martin, who was in the chorus. "She was fired not by Vincente but by the
stupid Shuberts. Vincente was as horrified as we all were."
PHOTO COURTESY OF THE SHUBERT ARCHIVE

Even though he had just skulked away from Hollywood's sound stages in de-
feat, Minnelli expressed very definite ideas about how screen musicals could
be improved upon. He called for songs that actually advanced the plot and
looked forward to "the perfection of color film."[2]

Less than a year after abandoning Broadway to teach Hollywood a thing
or two, "the new genius of the theatre" was back with little to show for his
trouble. While Minnelli was away, the Great White Way had matured. Star-
driven, plotless revues like *The Show Is On* suddenly seemed extravagantly
wasteful in F.D.R.'s New Deal America. Even musicals were expected to
sober up and have something important to say.

As conceived by Yip Harburg, the antiwar extravaganza *Hooray for What!*
would deliver first-rate songs (such as "Down with Love") as well as political
substance. Harburg had channeled his very real revulsion regarding the rise
of fascism into a riotous farce. The musical's plot concerned Chuckles, an
amateur inventor who stumbles upon a formula for an all-powerful gas. ("This
gas will revive the dead. I've got a big offer from the Republican party.") After
making his discovery, Chuckles is suddenly sought after by world leaders,
munitions makers, and the glamorous international spy Stephanie Stephano-
vich. After secret agents get hold of the formula for the gas and sell it, each

of the world's great dictators all believe that they alone are in possession of the ultimate secret weapon. But one of the spies has scrambled the formula so that what is ultimately unleashed on the world is laughing gas.

Howard Lindsay and Russel Crouse, the talented team that would later give Broadway a record-breaking triumph in the form of *Life with Father*, were brought on board to assist Harburg with his scenario. Harold Arlen would write the music. Vaudeville veteran Ed Wynn was cast as Chuckles. Agnes de Mille would choreograph the show's "Hero Ballet." While Howard Lindsay was credited as the show's book director, the entire production would be staged by Minnelli, who admitted, "I approached my first book show as if it were a revue. . . . The only difference to me was that one set of characters carried through from beginning to end."[3] Given the content of *Hooray for What!* and its very topical satire, Minnelli would not be able to rely solely on his designs to win the audience over. The scenic effects would be in service to the story this time, not the other way around.

Nevertheless, during the show's pre-Broadway tryout in October 1937, critics couldn't help but notice how pretty political satire could be. "An air of luxury predominates, for Vincente Minnelli has outdone himself in providing beautiful costumes and backgrounds," Elinor Hughes noted in her *Boston Herald* review. Also singled out for praise was "a striking blonde girl with a husky voice and an original style."[4] Her name was Kay Thompson. Although Thompson was clearly a rising star and had walked away with some of the best notices in Boston, it was not long after her out-of-town triumph that she was informed that her services were no longer required.

"Kay Thompson was fired from that show," says composer Hugh Martin, who was also in the cast. "I was outside her dressing room when it happened and I never heard such sobbing in my life. . . . She was fired not by Vincente but by the stupid Shuberts. Vincente was as horrified as we all were. . . . But Kay lost her job in *Hooray for What!* and it was given to Vivian Vance, who later played 'Ethel' in the *I Love Lucy* series."[5] Despite the raves Thompson had received, the Shuberts suddenly decided that their leading lady was too angular and bony. Vivian Vance (Thompson's understudy) was the kind of voluptuous Joan Blondell type that the Shuberts found sexy. Vance, who idolized Thompson, suddenly found herself in a very awkward position, but at Kay's urging, she went on.

Along with Thompson, Agnes de Mille was ousted. She was replaced with future MGM choreographer Robert Alton. During its out-of-town overhaul, *Hooray for What!* suddenly became less about Harburg's antifascist themes and more about Ed Wynn's off-the-wall buffoonery. There were reports of friction between Wynn and Minnelli. Other roles were recast. But despite all of the backstage bedlam, *Hooray for What!* was pronounced a hit when it opened on December 1, 1937.

* * *

IT WAS COMPOSER VERNON DUKE who suggested that Minnelli next direct a musical version of the S. N. Behrman play *Serena Blandish*. Minnelli liked the idea but took it a step further –a musical version of *Serena Blandish*— but with an all-black cast. He envisioned Cotton Club headliner Lena Horne in the title role of a young woman being groomed to meet high society. And if Minnelli had his way, Ethel Waters would strut her stuff as the irrepressible Countess Flor Di Folio.

In April 1938, it was announced that S. J. Perelman would be tackling the adaptation, and the incomparable Cole Porter was set to compose the score. It seemed that *Serena* had all the makings of another Minnelli-designed block-buster. But then, as quickly as the project came together, it began to unravel. In September, the *New York Times* broke the news: "Not that anyone ever took it too seriously, but Vincente Minnelli has dropped his plan to present a Negro version of *Serena Blandish*, leaving Mr. M. to consider other ventures."[6]

Mr. M. had also been toying with the idea of mounting "a surrealistic fantasy set to jig time." Tentatively entitled *The Light Fantastic*, the new show was being planned as a third collaboration for Minnelli and Bea Lillie. Vincente also hoped that for this outing, his friend Dorothy Parker would contribute a sketch or two. All of this was put aside, however, when legendary impresario Max Gordon offered Minnelli an opportunity to design a new musical. With a score supplied by Jerome Kern and book and lyrics by Oscar Hammerstein II (the same team that had revolutionized Broadway a dozen years earlier with *Show Boat*), there were great expectations for the new production, *Very Warm for May*.*

Advance publicity promised that the musical would be "reminiscent of the song and dance fun-fests that used to tenant The Princess Theatre." The story, which concerned young performers in a summer stock theater getting mixed up with gangsters, was infused with the kind of "let's put on a show!" exuberance that would soon become a trademark of the Mickey Rooney–Judy Garland musicals of the '40s. Needless to say, this was material that a fugitive from the Minnelli Brothers Mighty Dramatic Company Under Canvas could relate to completely.

Hammerstein would direct the book, and Minnelli would stage the musical numbers. The cast included future stars Eve Arden, June Allyson, and

---

* The musical was originally entitled *In Other Words*, after one of the songs in the show.

Hiram Sherman,
Grace MacDonald, and
Eve Arden in *Very Warm for
May*. Minnelli would write off
the 1939 Broadway musical as
"my first disaster." In later
years, Arden would refer to
the show as "Very Cold
for October."
PHOTO COURTESY
OF PHOTOFEST

Vera-Ellen. In the role of "Smoothy Watson," a handsome young dancer named Don Loper was cast. He would become one of Vincente's closest friends and a fixture in the Freed Unit at MGM. "Don Loper's big claim to fame was that he danced with Ginger Rogers in *Lady in the Dark*," remembers Tucker Fleming. "In later years, he became quite a designer and he had a big house in Bel Air and he used to entertain a lot—straight parties and gay parties. Even at the gay parties everybody had to wear black tie. He was very pretentious. Wore patent leather shoes. . . . He was very social and the type of guy that would have appealed to Vincente."

Very Warm for May premiered at The Playhouse in Wilmington, Delaware, in October 1939. The local press was encouraging, and the audience response was equally enthusiastic. The gorgeous ballad "All the Things You Are" seemed destined for the Hit Parade. It looked as though Minnelli had another hit on his hands. Then, producer Max Gordon arrived on the scene and decided it was time to *produce*.

Minnelli and choreographer Harry Losee were informed that their services were no longer required. Hassard Short (who had worked on some of Cole Porter's musicals) and Albertina Rasch were called in to restage scenes and revise the choreography. Gordon began pressuring Hammerstein to drop the show's gangster subplot. Although he initially resisted Gordon's "suggestion," Hammerstein eventually gave in. When *Very Warm for May* opened at the Alvin Theatre on November 17, 1939, it was a very different musical from the one audiences in Wilmington had enjoyed. Remarkably, even with a sizable chunk of its story missing, the show was well received. "Strangely enough, on opening night we were greeted with laughter, applause, and even bravos," remembered Eve Arden, queen of the wisecrackers. "Max Gordon, our producer, was ecstatic. I had a chilling feeling that he was being premature, knowing the unpredictability of critics, and I was right."[7]

Out of respect for Kern and Hammerstein's previous achievements, the critics stopped short of savaging the show—though just barely. Although Max Gordon had expected an extended run to rival the 289 performances that Rodgers and Hart's *Babes in Arms* had racked up a year earlier, the Alvin's box office remained unnervingly quiet. After a dismal 59 performances, the curtain came down on what Minnelli would dismiss as "my first disaster" and Arden would come to refer to as "Very Cold for October." Only one element of *Very Warm for May* had a life beyond its final curtain call. The winsome "All the Things You Are" would be recorded by a host of popular singers, from Sinatra to Streisand.

Just up the street from the funeral atmosphere at the Alvin, the Booth Theatre was staging an original play entitled *The Time of Your Life*, which had opened to rapturous reviews. Heralded as "a prose poem in ragtime," the drama had been written by William Saroyan— a bearish, hugely talented, and more than slightly eccentric true original. Unlikely as it seems, after Saroyan and Minnelli were introduced, they became buddies, though Saroyan biographer John Leggett believes that the playwright may have harbored some ulterior motives in befriending Vincente. "Saroyan was always imagining that by getting to know some influential person, that he would advance his career," Leggett says. "Minnelli would have appealed to him simply because of his Broadway stature."[8]

To Minnelli, Saroyan seemed a good choice as the book writer for a proposed all-black revue with no less than Rodgers and Hart furnishing the score. Minnelli and producer Bela Blau commissioned Saroyan to write the script, paying him $200 to begin the project, which was in some ways *Serena Blandish* revisited. "[Saroyan and Minnelli] took the subway to Harlem," says Leggett. "They went to the Apollo Theatre and they were impressed by seeing the black male dancers there and out on the street. It pleased Saroyan's imagination but I don't think they every really got anywhere with that project."*

---

* Years later, Minnelli became interested in mounting a revue entitled *The Black Follies*, a project that Alan Jay Lerner's assistant, Stone Widney, proposed to him. The show was envisioned as an all-black Ziegfeld Follies. "We went out and talked to him about that," remembers Widney. "He said, 'This is a wonderful idea. . . . You have to go to Chicago and see all the people who are in the jazz scene. It should be big. Extravagant.' When we came away from the meeting, I said, 'I think this is going to be a little over budget.'" *The Black Follies* was never produced. (Stone Widney, interview with author.)

At one point, Yip Harburg replaced Rodgers and Hart as the revue's composer. Saroyan continued to churn out sketches at an incredible rate, amazing Minnelli with his swiftness. Despite the remarkable talents involved, the all-black revue never materialized. Even so, memories of his visit to the Apollo and the lindy-hoppers dancing in the streets would remain in Minnelli's mind when it came time to direct his first film.

***

IT WAS ONE OF THE MOST IMPORTANT introductions in the history of Hollywood: Arthur Freed meets Vincente Minnelli. In terms of movie musicals, it was almost as noteworthy as the day Fred met Ginger, though, in later years, nobody could recall the details of the meeting. Did Yip Harburg make the introductions, or was it Roger Edens? Minnelli remembered it happening in the spring of 1939, while others believed that the two first met during the run of *Very Warm for May*. Whatever the circumstances, the point was that Arthur Freed had come calling and Vincente knew that this could be opportunity knocking.

A native-born South Carolinian, Freed had tirelessly scaled the show-business heights, first as a Tin Pan Alley tunesmith. In collaboration with composer Nacio Herb Brown, Freed would make his mark supplying lyrics for such sublime standards as "You Were Meant for Me," "Good Morning," "The Wedding of the Painted Doll," and one of the most enduring and instantly recognizable tunes in the history of popular music, the unforgettable "Singin' in the Rain."

Just as the movies were beginning to talk, Freed found himself at MGM, and his songs graced the soundtrack of 1929's Best Picture Academy Award winner, *The Broadway Melody*. A decade later, Freed served as the uncredited associate producer on *The Wizard of Oz*, one of the finest films (musical or otherwise) to come out of Hollywood and the movie that made Judy Garland, "the little girl with the great big voice," a major star.

"Yep," "Nope," and "Terrific" were considered unusually long-winded responses for Arthur Freed, so he got right to the point: "How would you like to work at Metro, Vincente?" Minnelli was ordinarily as tongue-tied as Freed but his answer came quickly: "I've been there." Vincente explained that his experience at Paramount had soured him on the movies. Freed persisted. "They simply didn't understand you. Come on out for five or six months, take enough money for your expenses. . . . If you don't like it at any time you can leave." Minnelli would be working for Freed but without a title. He'd be devising musical numbers, maybe even directing some. What's more, he'd be doing it at the biggest studio in Hollywood. Said Minnelli: "Before I knew it had happened, I had already started."[9]

Suddenly, Minnelli found himself going Hollywood all over again, but this time there was a significant difference: The movies were ready for Vincente Minnelli. "I was getting a fraction of my salary at Paramount," he noted with obvious disappointment. But otherwise, Metro-Goldwyn-Mayer would prove to be a gold mine for Arthur Freed's colorful new protégé.

As Minnelli was packing his bags, he received word that his mother had died at the age of sixty-eight in St. Petersburg, Florida. After Mina's death, Vincente's elderly father and his brother, Paul, would be cared for by his Aunt Amy. While Vincente would keep up a correspondence with his relatives and he provided for them financially, his new employer would keep him so busy that extended visits were out of the question. Besides, Minnelli had a new family now. It was called the Freed Unit.

MGM's Dream Team:
Minnelli and producer Arthur Freed on the set of *The Clock*, 1945.
Director Stanley Donen said of his Metro colleagues, "Arthur Freed thought
Vincente Minnelli was remarkable. He gave him anything he asked for. . . .
He fought for it and got it."
PHOTO COURTESY OF PHOTOFEST

6

"A Piece
of Good Luck"

MINNELLI ARRIVED IN CULVER CITY on April 22, 1940. According to the terms of his contract with the studio, he'd be serving in a "general advisory capacity in connection with the preparation for and production of photoplays which contain musical numbers" as well as "the creation, preparation and direction of musical numbers."

As he didn't have a title and wasn't assigned to a specific picture, Minnelli was encouraged to roam around and observe the inner workings of the massive studio, which churned out fifty-two pictures a year. MGM may have been an assembly line like every other studio in town, and perhaps the most conservative of the majors, but it prided itself on producing gleaming Rolls-Royces, not Fords. If 20th Century Fox featured Alice Faye as *Lillian Russell*, MGM could claim Greta Garbo as *Queen Christina*. Sure, Paramount may have had Gary Cooper, but Metro had "The King," Clark Gable. Even when an MGM film (say, one produced by Joe Pasternak) wasn't legitimately top of the line (say, *Song of Russia*), it was always slicked up so that it appeared so. With what seemed to be infinite resources at its disposal, Metro had the ability to conjure up Paris in 1883, Oscar Wilde's London, the San Francisco earthquake of 1903, or Munchkinland.

"MGM was self-sufficient in that it had the best of everything," says actress Marsha Hunt, who made several pictures for the studio. "You had the feeling that [studio chief] Louis B. Mayer, who surely had his faults, was not a man to sneer at because he really understood motion pictures. He loved them passionately and he had an ability to find and bring onto the lot the very finest talents from anywhere."[1]

If MGM was able to boast that it had the most impressive collection of artists (both in front of and behind the camera) in all of Hollywood, Arthur Freed would eventually siphon off the cream of the crop. As Metro scholar Hugh Fordin points out, the producer knew exactly where to go to import such top-of-the-line talent: "Freed didn't want anybody from Hollywood. Freed wanted everybody from Broadway . . . Minnelli, Gene Kelly, Stanley Donen, Chuck Walters, Robert Alton, Connie Salinger, Betty and Adolph . . . all of these people came from New York."[2]

When Broadway's dynamic duo, Betty Comden and Adolph Green, first landed at MGM, they were informed that they had been assigned to the Freed Unit. "We didn't really know what 'the Freed Unit' was," Comden admitted.[3] What it was has been described as "Broadway-on-Hollywood." Part artist's colony, part repertory company, it was a collection of diverse, remarkably talented artists who all had one thing in common: Arthur Freed. The producer, who was known for cultivating prize-winning orchids and amassing works by French Fauvist Georges Rouault, also had a knack for collecting the best in the business.

"It was called 'the Freed Unit' but there never was a unit," says film historian Richard Schickel. "It was just a bunch of artists clustered around Arthur. They were just over in a corner by themselves making movies and I don't think there was as much oversight on that group of actors and directors and writers as there was in other areas of MGM's production. . . . That was almost like a piece of good luck." Typically, an MGM movie was created by a committee or micromanaged by an omnipresent producer, but, true to form, Arthur Freed would buck the trend. He allowed his writers, directors, and choreographers almost complete autonomy. And the results spoke for themselves. "You can immediately see the difference between a musical from MGM and those done at Paramount and Fox," says actress Betty Garrett. "There's just something different about an MGM musical. Somehow they're more professional, more sophisticated. There was just a touch that Arthur had that nobody else in the business really had." Some believed that Freed's greatest gift was simply knowing who to hire.[4]

"The thing that has been said most often about my father was that he was a great finder of talent and an appreciator of talent and he gave all of these artists a chance to do their thing," says Arthur Freed's daughter, Barbara Freed Saltzman. "He talked MGM into hiring a lot of these people, and once he had them, he let them do whatever they did best. So, that was really one of his greatest talents—finding talent, encouraging it and not just doing it all by himself, but letting other people come up with their own ideas and then he'd go to bat for them."[5] Even by MGM's standards, the team that Freed assembled was truly extraordinary.

First and foremost, there was composer-arranger Roger Edens. Ethel Merman's one-time rehearsal pianist, Edens was brought to Metro by Freed, who put the tall, well-mannered Texan to work as a musical adaptor. Before Judy Garland ever attempted "The Boy Next Door" or "On the Atchison, Topeka, and the Santa Fe," Edens would have tried those tunes on for size first, determining how Garland's powerhouse pipes could be shown off to best advantage on each note. Almost immediately, Edens became indispensable to Arthur Freed. In fact, many believed that Roger Edens *was* the Freed Unit.

"I can tell you that one of the greatest advantages my father had in life and throughout his movie career was Roger Edens. He was a lovely man and a great assistant to my father in everything," says Barbara Freed Saltzman.[6] Just how essential Edens was to the Freed Unit was spelled out later in his career, when he produced two musicals— *Funny Face* and *Hello, Dolly!*—at studios other than Metro. Although they were made elsewhere, both films exhibit an unmistakable Freed Unit sparkle from start to finish.

After her abrupt dismissal from Minnelli's *Hooray for What!* Kay Thompson reinvented herself as a vocal coach and arranger, landing at MGM in the early '40s. Thompson could always be counted on to fire up a number with her own distinctive brand of "bazazz." For Garland's "A Great Lady Has an Interview" sequence in *Ziegfeld Follies*, Thompson would not only provide the number with a scintillating, ahead-of-its-time be-bop sound but also help Judy find the comedic nuances of the piece. "Kay would write twenty ideas while I threw out nineteen," says composer Ralph Blane, who collaborated with Thompson on *The Harvey Girls*. "They would just come to her like that, she was so fast! As a matter of fact, Kay could have been a great composer had she settled on one theme or idea."[7]

Orchestrator Conrad Salinger was, in the opinion of André Previn, "the greatest arranger of American musical-comedy that ever lived."[8] Salinger could take a well-worn tune, such as "Limehouse Blues," and turn it into a masterpiece that not only shimmered and soared musically but also brilliantly underscored the emotional content of the sequence it was accompanying. "He knew orchestration absolutely," says Freed Unit musician-librarian Frank Lysinger. "He could take something like a very simple kind of English folk song and arrange it in a quiet way, and then, when the same tune is reintroduced later in the film, he could build it up practically into a symphony. He was just brilliant in so many ways."[9]

Choreographer Robert Alton would showcase Ann Miller's trademark hundred-taps-per-minute in the memorable "Shakin' the Blues Away" in *Easter Parade* and even made Peter Lawford look relatively graceful doing "The Varsity Drag" in *Good News*. "Everybody deferred to Robert Alton," says writer Jess Gregg. "He was the master but he was also a very droll man. He was married and had a son but he confessed to us that sometimes when he was sitting in the park, the other men who used the park would call him *Evelyn*."[10]

Combining their talents and expertise, the members of the Freed Unit would create some of the finest musical films Hollywood ever produced. "These people were all geniuses," says Michael Feinstein. "They all created a unique voice and they were a unique part of an era of American music that is largely gone, largely lost and so special in the end result. When I listen to the achievements of Conrad Salinger or of Roger Edens or the dance arrangements of Saul Chaplin—like his arrangement of 'Get Happy'—or the exquisite music for *Summer Holiday* that Salinger orchestrated, I hear something that is never going to happen again. . . . The team that was assembled at MGM was just a stellar array of talent."[11]

While Edens, Thompson, Salinger, and Alton would form the nucleus of the Freed Unit, the circle would eventually widen to admit the likes of writer-lyricist Alan Jay Lerner, choreographer-director Charles Walters, orchestrators Lennie Hayton and Johnny Green, and designer Irene Sharaff. Soon to be included in this incredible mix of artists was Vincente Minnelli, whose work would call upon all of these remarkable talents at one time or another. "Arthur Freed thought Vincente Minnelli was remarkable," says director Stanley Donen. "He gave him anything that he asked for. . . . He fought for it and got it."[12]

While Arthur would always have his back, Minnelli may have also felt at home in the Freed Unit for personal as well as professional reasons. As writer Matthew Tinkcom says, "I think there was a kind of community there that was receptive both to his aesthetic and to whatever kind of ambiguous sexuality we're talking about. . . . At least on the Metro lot and especially in the Freed Unit, there was a kind of laissez-faire attitude toward there being queer employees. The Freed Unit was, in fact, a kind of place where queer talent could flourish."[13]

The unusually high concentration of gay artists in one department led to disparaging remarks about "Freed's fairies," homophobic jokes, and no end of salacious stories about many of the principal players. As the rumor mill had it, Conrad Salinger was a giant talent—and in more ways than one. "The reputation about him was that he had a basket to gasp at," says Jess Gregg.

"And of course, he was into fellas. I mean, that whole MGM crowd was—people like Connie Salinger and Bob Alton—everybody was gay and everybody took it for granted. There was no need to advertise the fact. People suspected that you were—whether you were or not."[14]

**

AT VIRTUALLY THE SAME TIME Minnelli landed at the studio, so did a fellow New York transplant—the luminous Lena Horne. Among Vincente's initial, usually uncredited assignments at MGM were shooting Horne's "specialty numbers" in musicals helmed by other directors and otherwise exclusively populated by white performers.* "I never felt like I belonged in Hollywood," Horne remembered. "At that time, they didn't quite know what to do with me—a black performer. So, I usually came on, sang a song and made a quick exit." Despite the fleeting nature of her appearances, Horne was well teamed with Minnelli, who made no secret of his fixation on the star. "He was obsessed with Lena in that period, and I would have thought doing everything he could to help her," says illustrator Hilary Knight, an ardent Horne devotee in his own right. "What's so interesting to me is why there's this heavy concentration on blacks as exotics that runs through his involvement with [Horne] and in other movies like *I Dood It* and *The Pirate*. There's that whole exotic black thing that he was completely obsessed with."[15]

Vincente's obsession is readily apparent in *Panama Hattie*, which was released in 1942. Adapted from the Broadway hit that had starred Ethel Merman, this gobs-gone-wild extravaganza directed by Norman Z. McLeod would be utterly forgettable if it were not laced with Cole Porter tunes and graced with Horne's two Minnelli-mounted production numbers. Lena's all too brief rendition of "Just One of Those Things" is charged with more vitality and style than anything contained in McLeod's uninspired footage, which was deemed so wanting that it was overhauled by Roy Del Ruth after an unsuccessful preview. Horne's number, which is framed in adoring close-up, sets the standard for the way the star would typically be presented during her tenure at Metro—as a glamorous, almost ethereal songbird segregated from the movie's main storyline. For "The Sping," Horne is decked out in cockleshell accessories, costumed in a Carmen Miranda cast-off, and accompanied by the dancing Berry Brothers. Horne's numbers here and her later appearances in *I Dood It* and *Ziegfeld Follies* are sort of cinematic second

---

* It's been suggested that Minnelli may have been responsible for Horne's "You're So Indiff'rent" sequence in 1944's *Swing Fever*, a wartime musical directed by Tim Whelan.

cousins to the stylish showstoppers that Minnelli had mounted on stage featuring Ethel Waters and Josephine Baker.

Vincente's work on *Panama Hattie* would provide him with a crash course in movie making. "He didn't know anything about the technique of motion pictures, and we couldn't expect him to," cinematographer George Folsey would later say of Minnelli's first attempts behind the camera, not so fondly recalling Vincente's "twenty-seven moves of the boom . . . up, down, in, out, dollying all around, panning and crossing over, and all of this on musical cues."[16] While his dazed colleagues attempted to keep pace with his hyperactive shooting style, Minnelli viewed this all as on-the-job training. "I was learning how to move the camera," he would later remark.[17] He was also learning that certain effects that had played well at the Winter Garden appeared one dimensional and stagy on film. Nevertheless, Metro's newcomer had a few new tricks to teach those Technicolor bogeymen. Color and lighting—two areas in which Vincente excelled—would evolve under his unerring eye. But for the moment, it was small steps forward.

As was the case during his aborted Paramount tenure, Minnelli was called upon to conceptualize musical numbers that would enhance films by some of Metro's veteran directors, such as Busby Berkeley. Vincente's concepts, which had been considered too outlandish or artsy at Paramount in the '30s, were eagerly incorporated at MGM in the '40s. *Strike Up the Band*, the fifth screen-teaming of Mickey Rooney and Judy Garland, provided Minnelli with an opportunity to concoct a visually inventive sequence that would win him the right kind of attention. After giving him a tour of the set, Arthur Freed ordered Minnelli to hurry up and get inspired: "We need a big production number here. Mickey and Judy are in the house, and he's telling her he wants to be a famous band leader like Paul Whiteman. Something big has to happen."[18]

Minnelli sprang into action. Spotting a fruit bowl on the set, he was reminded of a recent *Life* magazine layout. Using these images as his inspiration, he devised a spectacular sequence built around the ballad "Our Love Affair." Mickey and Judy would assemble an edible orchestra featuring a pear-headed violinist, a tangerine-topped percussionist (playing grapefruit drums), and a passionate, grape-headed conductor à la Leopold Stokowski. "All I did was supply the idea," Minnelli would later say. "The studio did the rest."[19] The critics took notice: "The episode is an outstanding example of imaginative entertainment," *Variety* raved.

Minnelli's sequence was memorable, but even more important to the studio, it was economical. "This is the genius who took a bowl of fruit and made a big production number out of it," Louis B. Mayer would proudly say whenever introducing Vincente to studio visitors. It was Arthur Freed, however, who orchestrated Minnelli's most important on-set introduction—to Judy Garland, then eighteen years old and already a Top Ten box-office star. "I was attracted to her open manner, as only a man who has been reserved all his life can be," Minnelli said.[20]

Vincente would work with Garland more closely on her next screen teaming with Rooney, *Babes on Broadway*. In a haunted-theater sequence, Garland and Rooney would pay tribute to "ghosts with greasepaint." It was Vincente's idea to have the film's talented young stars impersonate theatrical luminaries of the past. Mickey would salute Richard Mansfield in his signature role as Cyrano De Bergerac, and Judy would offer an homage to Sarah Bernhardt as Joan of Arc in "L'Aiglon." In musical moments, Rooney would portray George M. Cohan in *Little Johnnie Jones*; Garland would perform a sprightly "I've Got Rings on My Fingers" as Blanche Ring. Minnelli's impersonation idea was ultimately overruled by director Busby Berkeley, who underestimated his stars. Berkeley insisted that neither juvenile should attempt impersonations. Instead, they should simply play themselves, trying each role on for size. Although Garland and Rooney gamely gave it their all, the compromised approach threw the sequence off kilter. "It wasn't very successful," was Minnelli's assessment of the finished version.[21]

It was while making uncredited contributions to *Kathleen*, Shirley Temple's sole effort for MGM, that Vincente reportedly stopped the show with something other than his conceptual ideas for the film's big production number "Around the Corner." Several of the contract dancers who worked on the film claimed that Minnelli appeared on the set wearing cosmetics—lipstick, mascara, eye shadow—enough chemical enhancement that Max Factor should have been beaming with pride. As dancer Dorothy Raye recalled, "There was an absolute silence on the set. I mean silence! Nobody had ever appeared looking like that. None of us could think of what to say."[22]

While the stories about Minnelli's fondness for make-up would proliferate in the years after his death, Jess Gregg doesn't buy it: "You hear people today say things about him wearing eye shadow and magenta lipstick and I think that's a damn lie. Particularly in Hollywood, it would have been fatal. Not only fatal but worse than that—it was unfashionable. Drag was so out then. . . . I think people have made up a story to be shocking and to get people to listen. I really don't think it's true."[23]

Though others insist it is. "He was very effeminate in many ways and he did show up wearing very pale lipstick," says Judi Blacque, a contract dancer who appeared in multiple Minnelli productions, including *Meet Me in St. Louis*. "Of course, we never inquired. We just took it for granted. There were so many unusual people in Hollywood that it got so that you didn't pay attention to those oddities."[24]

While it was satisfying to see even some of his most offbeat ideas reach the screen, Minnelli was accustomed to directing full-scale Broadway productions with major stars. So far, his screen assignments at two studios had consisted of stylish segments inserted into movies directed by others who walked away with all of the credit.

Vincente's year-long period of exploration and experimentation was coming to a close, and there were important decisions to be made. If he remained at Metro, would Minnelli find himself in the same predicament that Lena Horne was in, allowed to dazzle but only in small doses? What's more, in New York, Vincente had been the ringleader of The Minnellium, his very own coterie of outrageously talented and erudite friends. In Hollywood, he was very much alone. Still something of a nonentity at the studio, Vincente was not yet being invited to the posh parties hosted by the wives of the studio moguls. And although a few of his New York friends also found themselves in California, they were either fully engaged with projects of their own or busy figuring out how to get back to Broadway.

"Honey in
the Honeycomb"

HOW DID MINNELLI, an artist both unconventional and avante garde (even for Hollywood), ever hope to get anywhere at the most lockstep studio in town? He would adapt. He would dazzle them. It had worked in Chicago. They couldn't get enough on Broadway. But if his ideas had been too extravagant and offbeat for Paramount, how would they ever find a home at MGM, the studio that touted all-American values in the form of *Boys Town*, *Young Dr. Kildare*, and the Andy Hardy series?

Fortunately for Vincente, he had managed to ingratiate himself with Metro's top echelon—Arthur Freed, Roger Edens, and even Mayer, who hadn't forgotten Minnelli's salvage efforts on *Panama Hattie* or his small but striking contributions to the Mickey-Judy musicals. The fact that Vincente had devised sequences that were inspired yet economical immediately endeared him to the front office. Such a talent could only be viewed as an invaluable asset to the studio, as MGM was preparing a seemingly endless roster of ambitious productions, most of them grand-scale musicals.

Always a Metro specialty, musical films dominated the production schedule, and many were being specifically designed to boost wartime morale, such as the patriotic Judy Garland–Gene Kelly vehicle *For Me and My Gal*, for which Minnelli would conceive some of the vaudeville montages. Other musicals were of an even more escapist nature, and falling into this category was a promising though undeniably risky property: a film version of Vernon Duke and John LaTouche's all-black musical *Cabin in the Sky*, which had a modestly successful run on Broadway, racking up 156 performances in 1940.

A whimsical morality tale, *Cabin* concerned the forces of heaven and hell vying for the attention of shiftless gambler Little Joe Jackson. On the side of the angels is Little Joe's devout wife, Petunia, who finds herself in direct competition with the vixenish Georgia Brown, a temptress sent direct from Hotel Hades.

For all his monosyllabic responses, Arthur Freed was a shrewd character who recognized that Vincente was perfectly suited to the story not only because of *Cabin's* theatrical origins, or the fact that it contained elements of surrealistic fantasy, but because Minnelli, as the perpetual outsider, would readily identify with a cast composed of African Americans. Realizing how blissfully wed Minnelli and the material would be, Freed fought tooth and nail for Vincente to be named *Cabin's* director. The producer even endured what was later described as a "fur-flying donnybrook" with Metro's powers that be, all in the name of Minnelli. And it certainly wouldn't be the last time Freed would have to go to bat on Vincente's behalf. Though it was decided that Freed's flamboyant protégé could be entrusted with the job, Minnelli knew that during the next three months the real trial would begin: "I'd have to prove my worth all over again in films."[1]

The studio wasn't only taking a chance on a first-time director, for, despite its Broadway pedigree, *Cabin in the Sky* was actually pushing the envelope. Metro executives knew that this type of "experiment" had worked before. King Vidor's all-black musical *Hallelujah* had performed surprisingly well for the studio back in 1929. And Eddie "Rochester" Anderson, Rex Ingram, and Oscar Polk—all set to star in *Cabin*—had previously appeared in the 1936 Warner Brothers fable *The Green Pastures*, which had also featured an exclusively African American cast. Even so, Freed had been forewarned that *Cabin* would do no business south of the Mason-Dixon line, which may account for the fact that the movie was one of the most conservatively budgeted of the producer's career. The studio shelled out $40,000 to transport *Cabin* to the screen, though executives remained dubious about the film's prospects, especially with no bankable stars above the title.

True, Ethel Waters brought her Great White Way cachet to the role of the eternally self-sacrificing Petunia Jackson, but prior to *Cabin* her most recent screen appearance had been in *Cairo*, in which she appeared as Jeanette MacDonald's maid. That particular role had been refused by newcomer Lena Horne, who would land the role of the alluring Georgia Brown—though Horne's name really didn't mean anything at the box office either. Dooley Wilson had starred as Little Joe Jackson in the stage version of *Cabin*, and he had recently appeared in the Oscar-winning *Casablanca*, in which he crooned "As Time Goes By" for Humphrey Bogart. While Wilson was red hot, Freed was determined to secure more of a box-office draw for *Cabin's* male lead. He decided on the gravelly-voiced Eddie Anderson, well known to radio fans as Jack Benny's faithful sidekick, "Rochester." A trio of black icons—Louis Armstrong, Duke Ellington, and John W. "Bubbles" Sublett— would appear in supporting roles.

Only weeks after production launched in August 1942, Minnelli discovered that his first full-length feature was already generating considerable controversy. Almena Davis, a reporter for the *Los Angeles Tribune*, visited the set during the shooting of the dance-hall sequence and told her readers:

> Everywhere you have been impressed with the complete absence of race prejudice as such, on the set. No one here, you are convinced, would refuse to eat with anyone else on account of color, or work, or even sleep with dark skinned folk. The much vaunted liberalism of the artist is present, you realize, but all the while the consciousness that there IS something wrong with Hollywood faintly disturbs you. . . . You try and match the continual parade of stereotypes; the crap shooting scenes in *Cabin In The Sky*; the dialect, the traditional ignorant, supertsicious [sic] celluloid darky, with the camaraderie which the director displays with the colored actors. You try to match the so-called "progressiveness" of Borros Morros, Donald Ogden Stewart, Vincent Manilli [sic] with their reactionary, often vicious treatment of the Negro character. And it doesn't match.[*]

Despite the dissenting voices—both in the press and at the studio— Minnelli found a source of unwavering support in Lena Horne. "Vincente and Lena were inseparable," Horne's daughter, Gail Buckley, recalled. "The coincidence of their simultaneous Hollywood careers strengthened their natural bond of sensitivity. . . . They dined together every night while *Cabin* was in preparation. Lena carried her lonely childhood everywhere and Vincente gave her the kind of brother-sister relationship she needed so badly. She was thrilled with Vincente's *Cabin* concept. She thought he was a genius."[2]

While it's been suggested that Vincente and Lena may have been romantically involved, it's more likely that Horne's friendship with Minnelli was similar to the kind of closeness she shared with her gay friends: composer Billy Strayhorn and playwright Arthur Laurents. "Vincente Minnelli and I stayed friends," Horne said of her fellow Manhattan transplant. "He and

---

[*] Russian-born Borros Morros served as the musical director on dozens of Hollywood films, including John Ford's *Stagecoach* and the same version of *Artists and Models* that Minnelli had contributed to. (Almena Davis, "How 'Bout This?" *Los Angeles Tribune*, October 19, 1942, 9–10.)

I were New Yorkers and we had that kind of empathy to draw upon."[3] While studio hairdressers—save for the legendary Sydney Guilaroff—refused to touch Horne's hair and she was hardly welcome in the MGM commissary, Vincente treated Lena as an equal. Minnelli sought his star's input on developing the *Cabin* screenplay, which differed from Lynn Root's libretto. He even turned to Horne for assistance in downplaying any elements of the characterizations that might be perceived as racially insensitive.

As Minnelli later observed, "Once we decided to go ahead with the film, we gave no thought to public reaction. We would never knowingly affront blacks . . . or anyone else for that matter." One larger-than-life force of nature would remain perpetually offended, however. "When we made *Cabin in the Sky*, there was conflict between me and the studio from the beginning," Ethel Waters admitted. "For one thing, I objected violently to the way religion was being treated in the screenplay."[4] Others felt that Waters wasn't so much rankled by the script as by how much attention Vincente was lavishing on his third-billed star.

Early on it became more than clear that there was only room for one star in an Ethel Waters production—and her name was not Lena Horne. "Miss Waters considered herself quite rightly, to be an enormous star and [she] regarded Lena as an upstart and her enemy on every front," Gail Buckley noted.[5] If Waters had once enjoyed Vincente's undivided attention during the staging of *At Home Abroad*, Minnelli now only seemed to have eyes for Horne, and he took great pains to make sure that her striking looks were photographed to best advantage. Needless to say, this did not sit well with Waters, who had convinced herself that Minnelli was developing a star at her expense. "I guess she's just jealous 'cause she ain't got what I got," Lena's Georgia Brown says of Ethel's Petunia Jackson, and many close to the production were convinced that the sentiment didn't only apply to the characters.

Even musically, *Cabin*'s leading ladies were at odds. Waters had introduced Harold Arlen's "Stormy Weather" at the Cotton Club in 1933, though Horne offered the definitive rendition of the song in a 1943 film of the same name and claimed the tune as her own anthem. Waters fumed when she heard Horne croon "Honey in the Honeycomb" in a sassy style that to Ethel's ears sounded like an imitation of her own distinctive delivery. "All through that picture there was so much snarling and scrapping that I don't know how in the world *Cabin in the Sky* ever stayed up there," Waters recalled, conveniently forgetting that she had instigated most of the snarling and scrapping.[6]

All of the pent-up rage and resentment that had been smoldering within Ethel for years—dating back to her unhappy upbringing in a Chester, Pennsylvania, ghetto—detonated on Minnelli's set, with a petrified Horne the

Ethel Waters, Eddie "Rochester" Anderson, "Bubbles" (John W. Sublett),
and Lena Horne in Minnelli's first full-length feature *Cabin in the Sky*.
Waters and Horne were at war on screen and off as Minnelli played referee.
PHOTO COURTESY OF PHOTOFEST

object of Ethel's unrestrained fury. As Gail Buckley described it, "[Waters] flew into a semi-coherent diatribe that began with attacks on Lena and wound up with a vilification of 'Hollywood Jews.' You could hear a pin drop. Everyone stood rooted in silence while Ethel's eruption shook the sound stage. . . . She was still more or less raving when Vincente dismissed the company and suspended shooting for the day."[7]

Despite all the behind-the-scenes bedlam and a mercurial leading lady with a hair-trigger temper, Vincente's first full-fledged directorial effort bears no evidence of all the discord. What emerges is an enchanting musical fable—a kind of African American answer to *The Wizard of Oz*, complete with recycled tornado footage from that 1939 classic.[*] The tight budget ($662,141, compared to the over $2 million lavished on *Oz*) resulted in what seemed like cramped quarters in many scenes, but this actually worked in Minnelli's favor, as a genuine sense of warmth and intimacy was created.

For his first time out, Minnelli hits far more than he misses. Ethel's poignant performance of "Happiness Is a Thing Called Joe" begins with Petunia crooning

---

[*] Like the Kansas sequences in *Oz*, the original theatrical prints of *Cabin in the Sky* were enhanced by a warm sepia tone, though Minnelli's musical is rarely, if ever, shown that way. Vincente told interviewer Henry Sheehan that the sepia enhancement was Arthur Freed's idea.

at the bedside of her wounded husband. Midway through the tune, there is a deft transition to the Jacksons' backyard, where an exuberant Petunia is at her clothesline, still singing the same tune but presumably weeks later and in the company of an almost fully recovered Little Joe. Miraculously, her prayers have been answered.

Minnelli's female leads may have clashed bitterly off screen but they are both sublime in the film. Hearing Waters croon the title tune in her trademark raspy delivery, or witnessing her strutting and high-kicking her way through a spirited reprise of "Honey in the Honeycomb," gives one a pretty good idea of what a showstopper Waters must have been on Broadway. After a saucy bubble-bath number, "Ain't It the Truth," was axed, Horne's performance became a largely nonmusical one, but she makes every appearance count nonetheless. Each time Georgia Brown moseys into a scene, Minnelli indulgently allows Horne a *Modern Screen* "moment" while the camera simply bears witness to her incandescent beauty.

"Vincente Minnelli has done a really inspired job in the direction of the picture, without which it would not be the good entertainment that it is," enthused the *Hollywood Reporter*. "He handles his characters and story pace with a knowledge of the mannerisms and the superstitions of the Negro, leveling on the important sequences and doing a quick shift with the unimportant bits that were required to hold the story together. It is his first picture effort and the job stands out." The *New York Times* said *Cabin* was "as sparkling and completely satisfying as the original stage production," and *Daily Variety* dubbed it "a fantastic piece of American folklore."[8] MGM's risky venture also paid off at the box office. In its initial release, *Cabin* earned a respectable $1,606,624.

But did Minnelli's first film, which was written, produced, and directed by white artists, have anything meaningful to say to African American audiences? "The fact that *Cabin in the Sky* is an all-black film, that was made during a period when blacks didn't have a wide range of representation on screen, makes it incredibly important," says film scholar Charlene Regester. "Because black audiences were craving these images and you've got a 'Who's Who in Black Hollywood' in that film, people flocked to see it, although they were very much aware that some of the representations were stereotypical. . . . I think if black audiences went to see *Cabin in the Sky*—and I'm just speculating on this—they went sort of ambivalently positioned."[9]

Eva Anderson, the wife of Eddie "Rochester" Anderson, remembers that years after the film's release, her children were teased in school because of their father's participation in the film:

They were very ashamed because the kids at school were calling their father "Uncle Tom" and stuff like that. A lot of younger people resented the film, but look at it this way, if we didn't have *Cabin in the Sky*, we wouldn't know Eddie Anderson. We wouldn't see Ethel Waters perform. . . . I think that it was a very important film in those days and I think it's still important today. It shows people what we were all about then and how we came to be what we are today. And by looking at the film, you can see we definitely came a long way.[10]

When *Cabin* is screened for contemporary audiences, it is usually accompanied by warnings that the picture is "a product of its time" and that it may reflect some of the racial prejudices that existed when it was produced. Others believe that *Cabin* still offers compelling evidence of how boldly cutting-edge and ahead of the curve Minnelli could be.

"I would say that the film comes directly out of his New York experience where Minnelli developed what I see as his queer aesthetic," says film scholar David Gerstner:

Part of the queer thing is that Minnelli shows his nonracist cards for the period, which is to say, he wants to work with the broadest section of people possible and there's this belief that all people are talented. If there was this prevailing idea that black people weren't allowed on a Hollywood set or that blacks were inferior, Minnelli didn't buy into any of that. To me, that's part of a really interesting queer dynamic. It's as though he's asking, "What kind of aesthetics can we produce as an intermingled group of people?" So, I think *Cabin* is really significant in that way because it not only shows his queer aesthetic that he took from New York and brought to Hollywood but also a queer sensibility in terms of the way he sees relationships between people.[11]

Vincente didn't have time to bask in the glow of the warm reviews heaped upon him when *Cabin in the Sky* was released in the spring of 1943. To the ever ambitious Minnelli, being next assigned to salvage efforts on somebody else's picture had to have been a deflating letdown. Though he was understandably disappointed, Minnelli was also "flattered" that his superiors at Metro turned to him in an attempt to rescue an incurably muddled mess preciously entitled *I Dood It*. Originally intended for Roy Del Ruth, who had cranked out scenarios for Mack Sennett's Keystone Kops, *I Dood It* was concocted as a showcase for two hopelessly mismatched MGM contract players: Red Skelton and Eleanor Powell. Why a brash, raucous comedian and the screen's most stylish stepper were considered perfect chemistry has been lost to some best forgotten casting session.

An uninspired Minnelli signed on but, like his colleagues, approached *I Dood It* strictly as a job, painfully aware that any attempts at meaningful artistic expression were futile. Screenwriters Sid Herzog and Fred Saidy were called in to revamp Buster Keaton's final silent film, *Spite Marriage* (1929). While they may have updated the story of an imbecilic pants presser besotted by the star of a creaky Civil War saga, their *I Dood It* certainly didn't improve upon the quirky charm of the original.

In the end, *I Dood It* would emerge as a confused mélange of contrived comedy, big band interludes, and cardboard espionage. Primarily a vehicle for Skelton's overcooked buffoonery, the finished film bears little evidence of Minnelli's trademark directorial flourishes. For those who had been waiting for the kind of movie in which Eleanor Powell attempts to slip Red Skelton a Mickey Finn but ends up ingesting it herself, the wait was over. Ordinarily, when handed a less-than-inspired property, Vincente could at least be counted on to smarten up the mise-en-scène and distract the viewer with some eye-popping decor, but instead, Skelton and Powell romp through stagnant settings or against backdrops that are either bland or insanely cluttered.

Minnelli is on assured footing with a musical audition sequence, though even that seems suggestive of a hasty assembly. Lena Horne sings a sprawling Kay Thompson arrangement of "Jericho," and Hazel Scott lets it rip on an instrumental "Takin' a Chance on Love." Performing against a spangled diaphanous backdrop, Horne and Scott add a touch of class to the proceedings, but still, *I Dood It* is such a confused hodge-podge that nothing can truly save it.

Adding to the everything-but-the-kitchen-sink ambiance, even Minnelli's French poodle, Baba, is trotted out by Butterfly McQueen at one point.[*] The presence of Vincente's canine companion is telling, as *I Dood It*, though profitable, was a real bowser. Still, the critics weren't unkind.

As the *Hollywood Reporter* noted, "Minnelli's direction is astonishingly expert when it is considered that he has merely one previous picture to his

---

[*] McQueen's sequence was no laughing matter to two lieutenants stationed at the Santa Ana Army Air Base. In September 1943, they wrote to Minnelli and expressed their outrage: "We were shocked by the scene in *I Dood It* in which Red Skelton mistakes the idiotic black dog for the negro girl. The slur on the colored people was one of the most vicious we have seen emanate from Hollywood for some time." Decades later, Minnelli insisted that no racial insensitivity was intended: "I was surprised by such an interpretation. Like my general attitude to the picture, this was the farthest thing from my mind." The letter to Minnelli, which was dated September 12, 1943, was from Lieutenants "Twinelmann" and "Darby," stationed at the Santa Ana Army Air Base, and concludes with: "You directors have a personal responsibility to see that not even one scene, even in jest, encourages anti-democratic attitudes." The letter is contained in the Margaret Herrick Library at the Academy of Motion Picture Arts and Sciences in Beverly Hills, California.

credit. Such a wacky affair could have gotten out of hand in many places but never does." *Time* didn't mention Minnelli but noted, "Most of Skelton's comedy is Bob Hope laid on with a ball bat. Red goofed up over a kiss, Red getting off lines like 'I press men's pants but this is the slack season,' appeals chiefly to the primordial. . . . But now and then Skelton's broad and cheerful silliness comes so thick and fast that the effect is like being held down and tickled."[12]

8

5135 Kensington Avenue

WHILE VINCENTE WAS SHOOTING *I Dood It* and enduring Red Skelton's pratfalls, a number of MGM's most capable screenwriters (Victor Heerman, Sarah Y. Mason, and William Ludwig among them) had each taken a crack at transforming a wispy, character-driven slice of Americana into a tightly plotted, action-oriented screenplay. Sally Benson's *The Kensington Stories*, serialized in *The New Yorker* as *5135 Kensington*, recounted a bygone era of Friday night Whist clubs and suitors making their intentions known with ten-pound boxes of Page and Shaw candy.

It was the story of the Smiths, the quintessential American family, living in St. Louis at the turn of the century. Papa is a lawyer. Mama is a dutiful housewife. Their only son, Lon, is preparing to head off to Princeton. Eldest daughter Rose is beginning to receive long-distance telephone calls from Yale boys, while Esther is infatuated with the boy next door. Tootie and Agnes, the two youngest, occupy themselves by burying dolls that have succumbed to at least four fatal diseases.

Two events upset the natural order of things in the Smith household: the arrival of the Louisiana Purchase Exposition, better known as the St. Louis World's Fair, and the father's shocking announcement that, because of a job promotion, the entire family will leave St. Louis and move to New York.

Arthur Freed believed that Benson's charming stories, though slight and essentially plotless, had the makings of a heartwarming musical that would incorporate popular songs of the period, such as "Skip to My Lou" and the 1904 Sterling and Mills standard, "Meet Me in St. Louis, Louis," which would inspire the film's title. With a musical in mind, Freed naturally hoped that the material could be shaped into a vehicle for his brightest star, Judy Garland.

In adapting the stories and attempting to inject some conventional plotting into Benson's wistful nostalgia trip, some of the original scenarists went too far. In one misguided treatment, the teenaged Esther Smith is embroiled in a kidnap and blackmail plot more appropriate to *I Wake Up Screaming* than *Meet Me in St. Louis.*

"Freed had a number of screenplays that we were forced to read that were dreadful," remembered the next writer in line, Irving Brecher. "Not one of them left me with any impression. Those scripts were rejected in toto. We didn't get anything from them, so we went back to the short stories."[1]

Brecher and collaborator Fred Finklehoffe* started from scratch, restoring the whimsical, homespun qualities of Benson's original narrative. This version of the *St. Louis* screenplay fleshed out episodes that Benson had only alluded to—a sisterly cakewalk, a ride on the trolley, and a Christmas Eve cotillion. By July 1943, Brecher had turned in a completed script, and although it looked promising, there was unified resistance to *Meet Me in St. Louis* by MGM's upper echelon.

"The studio did not want to make *Meet Me in St. Louis*," Brecher recalled:

> The reason it was made and we were rushed into doing a script was because at that time in Hollywood, there were only two existing Technicolor cameras and they were always in demand because color meant a lot at the box office. All of a sudden, one of the cameras became available and MGM had a contract, which it had to exercise within a brief period of time, to use it. In desperation, Freed and his bosses got the idea with this story, "If it has Judy Garland and color, maybe we'll make a few bucks." When it got close to where they were going with casting and all of that, I talked to Freed and we were discussing directors and I said I didn't think anybody could do it better than Minnelli.[2]

Brecher had never worked with Minnelli, but he certainly knew of his reputation—and not only as a director:

> I met Minnelli when he was shooting *Cabin in the Sky*. I sensed even in those days that he was maybe a queer. I wasn't sure. But he didn't come on to me

---

* Although he ultimately shared screen credit with Fred Finklehoffe, Brecher would contend that he was solely responsible for the entire screenplay of *Meet Me in St. Louis*. Brecher's assertion seems to be borne out by studio records, which reveal that after contributing to a rough continuity outline, Finklehoffe moved on to other assignments while Brecher carried on alone.

and he didn't swish. But there was something about the way Minnelli would open a cigarette box and take one out and light it . . . very effete. It was almost like a caricature of a gay guy. And there was something about the way he used his hands and twisted his lips and wore green eye shade and hung with all the gays, like Don Loper, the dance director, who was out and I mean *out*. Vincente was part of the Freed Unit, which was the gay community there. Freed wasn't gay but the rest of them were. . . . At any rate, Freed liked the idea of reaching for Vincente as the director of *St. Louis*. And without question, Minnelli was perfect for that picture.[3]

Even before shooting a single frame, Vincente was under pressure. If all went according to plan, he'd be entrusted with MGM's most valuable asset, a twenty-one-year-old supernova named Judy Garland. If the picture was a hit, it could make his career. There was just one problem. Garland didn't want to make *Meet Me in St. Louis*. The star had finally graduated to more mature roles in *For Me and My Gal* and *Presenting Lily Mars*. The idea that she should regress and play yet another wholesome teenager—and opposite a couple of scene-stealing child stars to boot—didn't exactly thrill her.

Several key players associated with production #1317 would take credit for cajoling Garland into boarding that St. Louis trolley, including Irving Brecher, who recalled reading the entire script to Judy at the urging of studio chief Louis B. Mayer. "I had a hell of a time with her," Brecher recalled:

I had to make her believe that her scenes were the most important in the picture. So, when I was reading to her, I threw away the kid sister's stuff because Judy was afraid Tootie would steal the picture. . . . Like anyone could steal a picture from Garland. Judy had been to my home a number of times at parties and she liked me and kind of trusted me but she was very ambivalent and troubled about *St. Louis*. I finally broke her down and she weakly said, "Do you really think I'll be alright?" I said, "It's your picture, Judy. It'll be the best thing you ever did." And I hoped I was telling the truth.[4]

In Minnelli's 1974 memoir, it is Garland's director who attempts to convince her of the project's special merits. "I wasn't aware of her feelings when I first discussed the role with her," Vincente remembered. "She looked at me as if we were planning an armed robbery against the American public."

"It's not very good, is it?" Judy challenged Vincente, expecting that Minnelli, the urbane New York sophisticate, would dismiss *St. Louis* as nothing more than sentimental, candy-colored tripe.

"I think it's fine," Vincente answered. "I see a lot of great things in it. In fact, it's magical."[5]

With Garland more or less persuaded, the other essential bit of casting concerned Tootie, the mischievous five-year-old member of the Smith household, partially patterned on Sally Benson herself. The role required an unusually adept child performer who could convincingly play precocious, execute a sprightly cakewalk, and become tearfully inconsolable on cue. From the moment casting ideas were floated, Margaret O'Brien was the only serious contender. Minnelli would claim credit for "discovering" O'Brien after witnessing her audition for *Babes on Broadway*, the musical in which she would make her debut. O'Brien's dynamic audition included her impassioned plea, "Don't send my brother to the chair! Please don't let him fry!"

Production began on December 7, 1943. "It's strange but I can remember everything that happened on that set," Margaret O'Brien says. "It was a very quiet set because Vincente Minnelli kept everything quiet and lovely for the actors."[6] Through the eyes of a talented six-year-old everything may have seemed quiet and lovely, but the studio's production reports tell a different story. Injuries and illnesses were almost a daily occurrence. Joan Carroll required an emergency appendectomy. Mary Astor suffered from an acute sinus condition. Margaret O'Brien battled hay fever, influenza, and nervous spells. A month into production, Margaret's mother, Gladys, wrote to Freed and explained that she was pulling her daughter out of the picture for a few weeks. As she put it, "I was beginning to be greatly criticized for allowing my child to work so hard."[7]

And then there was Judy.

Minnelli's skittish leading lady was still unable to completely relate to the story. Once before the cameras, Garland mocked what she perceived to be the trite, juvenile aspects of the script. On the first day of principal photography, newcomer Lucille Bremer (cast as the oldest Smith sister, Rose) was imbuing her performance with the kind of wholehearted sincerity that Garland ordinarily invested in her roles, no matter how banal. "I want you to read your lines as if you mean every word," Minnelli told Garland. Known as the quickest quick study in the business, Judy complied, but she seemed thrown by Minnelli's unconventional approach. Discouraged, Judy confided in Arthur Freed that Vincente's cryptic direction wasn't providing her with the guidance she needed. "She says she doesn't know what you want," Freed repeated back to Minnelli. "She doesn't feel she can act anymore."[8]

When Garland griped to veteran actress Mary Astor about Vincente's mystifying direction, the colleague Judy referred to as "Mom" offered a sharp dose of motherly advice. "Judy, I've been watching that man and he really knows what he's doing," Astor responded. "Just go along with it, because it means something."[9]

Although Garland attempted to go along with Minnelli, she didn't surrender completely. When Vincente summoned the cast for yet another rehearsal, Judy defiantly sped off in her roadster. Minnelli had his star intercepted at the studio gate and brought back to work. Getting Judy to the set and keeping her there would become a regular concern for a number of production assistants on the MGM payroll.

"Well, of course, Judy was always late," recalls June Lockhart, who costarred in the film as Eastern debutante Lucille Ballard:

> It was rather interesting because we would come into make-up at six-thirty and then get *under*-dressed because in that film, we even wore the underwear of the period. Then they'd give us a robe and we'd wait because Judy hadn't arrived yet and then we'd wait some more and finally, at about twelve-thirty, they'd say, "Well, Judy's come through the gate. You can all go to lunch. Come back around two." So, we'd come back at two and then they would say, "Well, she doesn't want to work today. So, you can all go home." And this happened a lot. But let me tell you, when she came on the set all dressed and ready, she knew her lines and where her marks were and she was funny and entertaining to be with and I think by then, was thoroughly enjoying playing the part.[10]

It also didn't hurt that for *Meet Me in St. Louis*, Garland would have the privilege of introducing three original songs: "The Boy Next Door," "The Trolley Song," and "Have Yourself a Merry Little Christmas"—each one a masterpiece. The trio of songs would advance the plot as effectively as the dialogue or action. "I had read the script and I knew there was a Christmas scene," recalls composer Hugh Martin, who wrote the songs with partner Ralph Blane. "I was doodling on the piano while Ralph was working on lyrics. I worked on this tune for a couple of days and couldn't make it go anywhere. It just sort of lay there after the sixteenth bar. About the third day, Ralph said, 'I know I'm not supposed to be listening, but you were playing a very pretty little madrigal type tune for a couple of days and then I didn't hear it anymore. It really bothered me because I think you had something good there.'"[11]

Something good indeed. Although "Have Yourself a Merry Little Christmas" would become a holiday institution as indispensable as eggnog, the original lyrics posed a problem, as they included such downbeat lines as "Have yourself a merry little Christmas. . . . It may be your last." As Martin remembers, Garland liked the song but not the suicidal lyrics: "Judy quite

Margaret O'Brien and Judy Garland in *Meet Me in St. Louis.* "Vincente Minnelli kept everything quiet and lovely for the actors," O'Brien says. "He was certainly in charge but in a very charming, gentle, and understanding way."
PHOTO COURTESY OF PHOTOFEST

wisely said, 'If I sing that song to little Margaret O'Brien, the audience will hate me. They'll think I'm a monster.' So, they came to me and said, 'Judy loves the melody and she wants you to write a new lyric, please.' Being stupid, I said I wouldn't and I stuck to my guns." It was the boy next door to the rescue. "Tom Drake came to me and said, 'You're being an absolute horse's ass and I'm not proud of you and if you miss this opportunity to have a great, classic Christmas song, I will never speak to you again.' And I thought, well, he's a sensible man and he's not too dumb and I went home that night and I wrote the lyric that was in the movie."[12]

Lovingly photographed by George Folsey,* Garland would never look better on film than she did in *St. Louis.* Apart from a standout vignette in *Thousands Cheer,* released the year before, *St. Louis* would be the first feature since *The Wizard of Oz* that allowed Judy's legions of followers to view their Metro goddess all aglow in vibrant Technicolor. Despite the fact that Garland had been reluctant to take on another dewy ingenue, there is an appealing

---

* "George Folsey told me that he did not shoot 'The Trolley Song,'" says film historian David Chierichetti. "Folsey was busy setting things up for the 'Boys and Girls Like You and Me' number that was cut, so Harold Rosson [who was the cinematographer on *The Wizard of Oz*] shot 'The Trolley Song.'" (David Chierichetti, interview with author.)

freshness and genuine warmth to her Esther Smith. Freed from Andy Hardy, Busby Berkeley, and her outmoded ugly duckling image, a new Judy Garland emerges in *Meet Me in St. Louis*, and she's a real beauty.

Make-up artist Dorothy "Dottie" Ponedel refined Judy's look for the film, giving her a fuller lower lip and introducing what was to become Garland's trademark arched eyebrow. More important than any cosmetic enhancements was that Garland also found a close friend and trusted confidante in Ponedel. "It was amazing to watch the two of them together," Meredith Ponedel says of her Aunt Dottie's legendary rapport with Judy. "Vincente respected the fact that Judy would respond to Dot when she wouldn't respond to anybody else."[13] However, midway through production on *St. Louis*, Garland suddenly became very responsive to Minnelli. And was it possible that Vincente was becoming interested in Judy for reasons that had nothing to do with how she recited her lines? Exactly what was Minnelli seeing as he gazed through his viewfinder at the twenty-one-year-old Garland?

Just like her director, Judy had been born into show business. Frances Gumm (as Garland was originally named) had been performing since the age of two, appearing with her two sisters in lesser vaudeville houses across the country. Her incomparable voice, sincere delivery, and unique personality had landed her an MGM contract in 1935. Almost from the moment Judy Garland had arrived at MGM, the studio's star-making magicians had been determined to have her problematic figure match her remarkable voice. Chocolate cake was confiscated, and Benzedrine prescribed. There were the unflattering comparisons to studio sirens Lana Turner and Elizabeth Taylor. As a young woman, Judy was made to understand that her extraordinary talents would have to be continuously switched on to compensate for a basic unworthiness.

John Meyer, who befriended Garland in her later years, believes that the vulnerable star had

> a very low self-esteem, which stemmed from her childhood when Louis B. Mayer would call her "the ugly duckling" and "my little hunchback." They tried to bind her chest so she wouldn't develop breasts, and they capped her teeth. The message was that there always seemed to be something wrong with her. It's satirized in *A Star Is Born* where they put her through that whole studio makeover process that James Mason then reverses. That kind of thing always stuck with her. That was the root of the problem. The substance abuse and the drinking—that was almost superficially on top of the root cause of it all.[14]

Like Garland, Minnelli had been frequently and cruelly reminded of his physical shortcomings. By this time, it had been deeply impressed upon him that the only beauty he would ever be associated with was the kind that he could cinematically manufacture. Metro's wunderkinds may have been kindred spirits, but they were also different enough to keep things interesting. Garland's outgoing, gregarious personality stood in sharp contrast to Minnelli's more reserved, introspective nature.

As shooting progressed on *St. Louis*, Minnelli and his leading lady finally seemed to be hitting it off. But exactly what kind of relationship was developing? Vincente gazing adoringly at his star through his viewfinder was one thing—most of the gay members of the Freed Unit were accustomed to worshipping at the temple of Judy Garland—but Minnelli actually *romancing* Judy was another matter entirely. Didn't either one of them realize what they were letting themselves in for? Hadn't Judy heard the rumors about Vincente—hardly the boy next door with an alleged affinity for green eye shadow? And like others at the studio, Minnelli must have heard the whispers about Garland's pharmaceutical dependency. How was it possible that these two hugely talented misfits could be legitimately attracted to one another?

"She surely must have known he was gay," June Lockhart says of MGM's odd couple, echoing the sentiments of virtually everyone on the lot. "I mean, I heard that when Minnelli first got to MGM, they had to ask him to stop wearing make-up to work everyday." Some observers believe that Vincente's "artistic flair" (as Judy termed it) had given everybody the wrong idea. Meredith Ponedel once broached the subject of Minnelli's sexuality with her Aunt Dottie: "We talked about it once and Dottie said, 'Nothing doing. He wasn't gay.' I mean, big deal, so he was in touch with his feminine side. And thank god, because look what he was able to produce. He was in touch with the feminine part of himself and not afraid to work with it. I mean, he probably had more courage than anybody else there." Or, as frequent Minnelli collaborator Hank Moonjean puts it: "He was 98 percent woman and 2 percent man. I mean, the way he walked. The way he dressed. The way he smoked. He was just very feminine. But I never saw him make a gay movement or gesture or proposition to anybody. Ever."[15]

Nevertheless, virtually everyone around them, from Roger Edens to the guard at the gate, registered surprise that Minnelli and Garland were now a studio-sanctioned item. But they most certainly were, and they didn't care if the whole world and Louella Parsons knew it, too. In a town known for its unlikely alliances (Orson Welles and Delores Del Rio) and questionable couplings (Cary Grant and Randolph Scott), Vincente and Judy trumped them all.

"I'll tell you one thing, for the people that worked at MGM when I was there, it made no sense for Judy Garland and Vincente Minnelli to be together at all," says Darryl Hickman, who appeared in *St. Louis* and Minnelli's *Tea and Sympathy*. "Nobody ever understood it. It didn't make a lot of sense. I think Judy was a sensitive, lovely person but she was really used and misused by the studio. . . . The fact that she would reach out to Minnelli or that he would reach out to her was just a weird combination. I think they were probably both in their own way hurting on some level and they reached out to one another. They were some kind of consolation for each other for awhile."[16]

Nineteen years older than Judy, Vincente was another example—though a decidedly more avant-garde one—of the more mature father figure that Garland coveted. First husband David Rose, the professorial, pipe-smoking composer of "Holiday for Strings," was studious, sexually conservative, and by all accounts obsessed with electric trains. Director Joseph L. Mankiewicz, whom Judy started seeing before the start of *St. Louis*, was fiercely intelligent, well read, and equipped with the kind of edgy, vitriolic Addison DeWitt–style humor that Garland found wholly irresistible. In later years, the Harold Arlen song "Happiness Is a Thing Called Joe" (first heard in *Cabin in the Sky*) would become a fixture in Garland's repertoire. Although most fans assumed Judy was singing the poignant tune with her youngest child, Joey Luft, in mind, others close to her believed that she carried a torch for Mankiewicz for the rest of her life.

But there was something about Vincente's gentle, soft-spoken manner that she couldn't resist. And Minnelli seemed to relish the idea of playing Henry Higgins to Judy's Eliza. Several Metro veterans recall that Garland, tutored between takes in the MGM schoolhouse and a graduate of Hollywood High, seemed eager to intellectually better herself by seeking out older, erudite mentors such as Mankiewicz and Minnelli. These sophisticated men of the world could provide her with a kind of finishing school by association. What's more, Vincente treated his star with a courteousness she hadn't been accustomed to.

"He came in with great respect for Judy," says Garland historian John Fricke. "As the legend goes, he treated her as 'Miss Garland' and not as the thirteen-year-old girl that everybody had seen grow up at MGM. . . . And I think he saw it to his great advantage to present her as glamorously as possible within the confines of a role."[17]

While *St. Louis* was still in production, MGM's formidable senior editor, Margaret Booth, sent Minnelli an interoffice memo that expressed the thoughts of many studio veterans working on the picture: "I haven't written you for a number of days but the dailies have been wonderful and the photography is the most beautiful I've ever seen. Judy has never been more beautiful or as sweet, to my way of thinking."[18]

As Booth and her assistants ran Minnelli's footage over and over again, it appeared that the only thing wrong with *Meet Me in St. Louis* was that it was too much of a good thing. It would have to be cut. Before one of the preview screenings, Arthur Freed announced that Margaret O'Brien's nightmarish Halloween sequence would have to go. But that scene was the very thing that had attracted Vincente to *St. Louis* to begin with.

Irving Brecher recalled,

> The day of the sneak preview, Minnelli came in crying. Actually crying. His eye make-up was running and he said, "The son of a bitch wants to leave out the Halloween sequence for the preview." I said, "You've got to be crazy!" Vincente said, "He thinks it stinks. Please go in and talk to him. Maybe he'll listen to you." I said, "He doesn't like me." Minnelli said, "Please! Go!" I did. I went to Freed's office. I said, "Arthur, I understand you're dropping the Halloween stuff from the preview." He said, "What about it?" I said, "It's a preview. Why don't you preview it and see how it goes?" He said, "Mind your own fucking business. I'm the producer, not you. Get the hell out of here." That night at the preview, the sequence was in the film. He had second thoughts. It was the biggest thing in the picture. He never acknowledged that he was wrong. He was not that kind of man.[19]

Tootie's trick-or-treating tour de force was spared the editor's shears, but other scenes weren't so fortunate. The Rodgers and Hammerstein song "Boys and Girls Like You and Me" was excised, as was a lengthy episode in which Garland was seen preparing Mary Astor, in full Gibson girl mode, for a night on the town.

With these deletions and other peripheral alterations completed, *Meet Me in St. Louis* was released in December 1944. The picture grossed a whopping $7,566,000, making it MGM's all-time top moneymaker.

If *Cabin in the Sky* had trumpeted the arrival of a major new directorial talent, *St. Louis* more than made good on that promise. While roundly applauding Garland, O'Brien, and the trio of songs by Martin and Blane, the critics zeroed in on Minnelli's sumptuous visuals and the evocation of a more carefree era. "Vincente Minnelli has staged the original Sally Benson story craftily, wisely concentrating on the details of the script and the colorful backgrounds," wrote Howard Barnes in the *New York Herald Tribune*. *Time*

Esther (Judy Garland) prepares Mrs. Smith (Mary Astor) for a night on the town in a deleted scene from *Meet Me in St. Louis.* Margaret O'Brien's unforgettable Halloween sequence nearly suffered the same fate.
PHOTO COURTESY OF PHOTOFEST

famously reviewed the picture as "a musical even the deaf can enjoy," and in the *New York Times*, Bosley Crowther (borrowing a phrase from the boy next door) dubbed it "a ginger-peachy show."[20]

When the Best Picture nominees were announced during the 17th Annual Academy Awards, *Meet Me in St. Louis* was not among the contenders. In its place was the interminable *Wilson* and the saccharine victor, *Going My Way*. Astoundingly, *Meet Me in St. Louis*, now recognized as a landmark musical, didn't garner a single Oscar, though it was nominated in four categories. While Otto Preminger's nod for *Laura* and Billy Wilder's nomination for *Double Indemnity* were worthy Best Director candidates, Henry King's nomination for *Wilson* (a pet project of Fox mogul Daryl F. Zanuck) is almost unforgivable, considering that Minnelli was shut out altogether. Musicals—no matter how innovative or inspired—were frothy crowd pleasers and not considered "important" enough to merit Academy recognition beyond the Best Song category. It would take another seven years and eight films before Oscar would wink at Minnelli with an overdue nomination. In the meantime, he could console himself with the rapturous reviews and a phone call from Gene Kelly, who told Vincente and Judy, "Goddamn it, they don't appreciate what a fine thing it is. They don't realize all that went into it."

But there was no time to remind them. For Minnelli, it was on to the next assignment.

9

"A Joy Forever,
a Sweet Endeavor . . ."

IN APRIL 1938, MGM announced that it had acquired the motion picture, radio, and television rights to the title *Ziegfeld Follies*. The studio promised that a screen version of the *Follies* would go into production "shortly." Five years later, Arthur Freed, Roger Edens, and a small army of assistants were still poring over the mountainous stacks of material that Metro had amassed concerning showman extraordinaire Florenz Ziegfeld, whom MGM producers seemed single-mindedly obsessed with.

By 1944, virtually every writer, composer, and designer on the lot found themselves contributing to what was regularly being touted in the trades as a "colossal super production." The Freed Unit's *Follies* was so spectacular and sophisticated that it had no use for anything as pedestrian as a conventional plot. Like one of Minnelli's Shubert revues, the *Follies* would forego story in favor of high-toned style. Such an opulent extravaganza would also provide irrefutable proof that MGM really did have "more stars than there are in the heavens," as studio publicists liked to boast.

As Freed and his minions envisioned it, *Ziegfeld Follies* would showcase every star in Metro's lustrous galaxy. Fred Astaire, Gene Kelly, Judy Garland, Lucille Ball, and Lena Horne would be featured in the musical sequences. Fanny Brice, Red Skelton, and Keenan Wynn would handle the comedy sketches. William Powell, who had snagged an Academy Award nomination for MGM's gargantuan 1936 biopic *The Great Ziegfeld*, would re-create his role as the flamboyant impresario, only this time he'd do it in luscious Technicolor.

Minnelli's screen credit for MGM's "super spectacular" *Ziegfeld Follies*. Many promising sequences were cut from the film: Fred Astaire's "If Swing Goes, I Go, Too," Avon Long serenading Lena Horne with "Liza," and Fanny Brice whooping it up as the incorrigible Baby Snooks.
PHOTO COURTESY OF PHOTOFEST

Powell's Ziegfeld would mastermind Metro's *Follies* from his heavenly boudoir. "Just because I moved up here, did the *Follies* have to die, too?" muses a nectar-sipping Ziegfeld as he gazes down upon Culver City.

Billed as "the screen's biggest picture," *Ziegfeld Follies* was such a massive undertaking that it proved to be too much for George Sidney, who vacated the director's chair after helming several sequences.* By May 1944, Minnelli had officially succeeded Sidney as director, though the movie was so big that directorial chores were ultimately divvied up among Robert Lewis, Lemuel Ayres, Roy Del Ruth, Norman Taurog, and Merril Pye. As a result, there would be a noticeable variance in the quality of the sketches. Some routines dazzled, others fizzled. To Minnelli fell the plum-star turns, including several elaborate production numbers featuring the most graceful star in Metro's firmament: the inimitable Fred Astaire.

A pair of Astaire showcases in which the forty-five-year-old hoofer was effectively teamed with twenty-two-year-old Lucille Bremer (fresh from *Meet Me in St. Louis*) immediately captured Vincente's imagination. Dipping into his file of illustrated clippings for inspiration, he would lavish these sequences with the same inventiveness and visual ingenuity that had distinguished his work on the Broadway stage.

---

* Three sequences that George Sidney directed remain in the release print of *Ziegfeld Follies*, including Virginia O'Brien's "Bring on Those Wonderful Men," Red Skelton's "When Television Comes," and Fred Astaire, Cyd Charisse, and Lucille Ball in the eye-popping opener, "Here's to the Girls." A number of other sequences—including Fred Astaire's "If Swing Goes, I Go, Too" and Avon Long serenading Lena Horne with "Liza"—would wind up on the cutting-room floor.

"This Heart of Mine: A Dance Story" was fashioned around a song featuring a lilting melody by Harry Warren and overripe lyrics by none other than Arthur Freed ("And then quite suddenly I saw you and I dreamed of gay amours. At dawn I'll wake up singing sentimental overtures."). The scenario was pure fairy tale: On a summer evening in 1850, a ball is in progress inside a glittering pavilion that resembles a gigantic wedding cake. The guests include Astaire, sporting a monocle and an expression of ne'er-do-well, and a tiara-topped Bremer, looking très distingué in a luxurious chinchilla wrap. In this gloriously artificial setting, Astaire's suave imposter pilfers Bremer's diamonds, though she doesn't seem to mind, as he's also stolen her heart. The "story" may have been slight, but who cared? As glamorous spectacle, the sequence achieves some kind of Freed Unit nirvana.

If all that weren't enough, "This Heart of Mine" also marked the first teaming of Minnelli and designer Tony Duquette, who created some of the exquisitely over-the-top trappings for the sequence. "Vincente and Tony were very close," says designer and one-time Duquette assistant Leonard Stanley:

> The first movie Tony worked on with Minnelli was *Ziegfeld Follies*, which was done in 1944 but never released to the public until 1946. It was really made during the war when Tony was in the army and stationed at Long Beach or somewhere near the coast. He would occasionally go off by himself because he was doing these sketches for Vincente for *Ziegfeld Follies*. . . . One day, these two MPs saw him sketching. They actually thought he was a spy sketching the military layout of the camp that Tony was stationed at. But it was really all of these designs for Vincente's movie. Tony—*a spy*! That just broke me up.[1]

Astaire and Bremer's second teaming, "Limehouse Blues," was inspired by the haunting Gertrude Lawrence tune of the same name and Lillian Gish's silent classic *Broken Blossoms*. The critics were all in accord that this sublime "dramatic pantomime" was the highlight of Freed's *Follies*. Appearing in Oriental make-up, Astaire is Tai Long ("in his shifty slouch, one detects the characteristic movement of the outcast"). Tai inhabits a seedy waterfront world of streetwalkers, sailors, and drunken vagrants. Minnelli had a field day filling up his frame with all of the necessary types from Central Casting: a wizened Chinaman smoking an opium pipe, some overeager trollops, a band of raucous buskers, and a transient pushing a Victrola in a baby carriage.

Out of the London fog appears Bremer's Moy Ling ("to look into her eyes is to look into the solemn depths of a cathedral"). Clad in retina-arresting canary yellow, Moy is the only spot of brightness in Tai's colorless existence. He is immediately entranced and begins following her. After observing Moy as she admires an Oriental fan in a shop window, Tai is mistaken for a robber and shot. On the brink of death, he falls into a hallucinatory delirium—though even in his fantasy, Tai's search for the elusive Moy continues. Now in possession of the fan she once coveted, Moy uses it to lure Tai into the darkened depths of his subconscious. When he finally reaches Moy and touches the fan, all is suddenly light—and chinoiserie. They dance together and achieve the sort of harmonious union that wasn't possible back in the real world. "Limehouse Blues" would be hailed as "the finest production number ever poured into a screen revue," and Minnelli considered the end result "a total triumph."[2] The sequence is not only a visual stunner but also achieves something distinctly Minnelli: taking the viewer inside an unreality (Astaire's dream) within a "reality" (MGM's version of old Chinatown) that was itself a nonreality to begin with.

"One of the things that I always remember about the mise-en-scène of 'Limehouse Blues' is that it's really disorienting in terms of 'film space,'" says Freed Unit scholar Matthew Tinkcom:

> You're moving through all of these different kinds of dream-like layers and smoke and camera movement. As you're watching, there comes a moment when you say to yourself, "I'm not in any kind of space of realism . . ." because in that sequence, we're moving through psychological space. We're into a landscape of the mind and fantasy and desire. What's amazing about it is that it's very atypical of Hollywood continuity. The thought about continuity was always "Do not disorient the spectator . . ." but here it's done in a really powerful way. It's about the Astaire character's shock and grief over the loss of his own fantasy and being forced to leave the realm of the fantastic. . . . It's really the same thing with Minnelli, who always wants to get back into the mental landscape because that's so much richer and more interesting.[3]

Although Norman Taurog or Robert Z. Leonard could have directed these *Follies* episodes in a more than capable manner, Minnelli managed to invest even the most stylistically fixated material with an unusual power and an undercurrent of emotionality that other directors on the studio payroll wouldn't have considered. In other hands, Astaire and Bremer's unrequited romance in old Chinatown would have been tossed off as cutesy pastiche, whereas Vincente takes his fantasy very seriously. Or as William Fadiman once observed, Minnelli "was a man who could honestly believe in make-believe."[4]

"Limehouse Blues" introduced a theme that would resurface time and again in Minnelli's movies. A protagonist in search of romance, a more ad-

George Murphy, Minnelli, Fred Astaire, Arthur Freed, and Lucille Bremer welcome gossip columnist Louella Parsons to the set of *Ziegfeld Follies*. Astaire and Bremer are in costume for the extraordinary "Limehouse Blues" sequence.

PHOTO COURTESY OF PHOTOFEST

venturous way of life, or an authentic self must go within in order to find it. While the outside world will inevitably disappoint, the inner world will uplift, heal, and complete.

Fred Astaire had performed "The Babbit and the Bromide" on Broadway, but for the version of the number included in *Ziegfeld Follies*, he was paired with Metro's other dancing virtuoso, Gene Kelly. "They were completely different," Minnelli would say of his two stars. "Fred Astaire is very elegant, high up in the air. . . . Gene is very athletic and down-to-earth. . . . In *Ziegfeld Follies*, when they worked together, we thought they'd never finish, because they would upstage each other. One would say, 'Well, now, suppose we try this step. . . .' They Alphonse'd and Gaston'ed each step because they had so much respect for each other."[5] "The Babbit and the Bromide" serves as something of an extended "Coming Attraction," as later in his career, Vincente would bounce back and forth between Astaire and Kelly vehicles.

At one point, Judy Garland had been scheduled for "The Babbit and the Bromide," along with virtually every other *Follies* sequence. "I Love You More in Technicolor Than I Did in Black and White" was to have reunited Garland with her frequent costar Mickey Rooney. When Rooney was drafted into the army, the sketch was shelved, and his reteaming with Garland would have to wait until 1948's *Words and Music*. Judy ultimately ended up in a dynamite *Follies* sequence—one that had been cast aside by another star. The Freed Unit's wunderkinds, Kay Thompson and Roger Edens, had conceived "The Great Lady Has an Interview" as a sort of self-parody for Greer Garson. The devastatingly witty number would offer Metro's Oscar-winning grand dame an opportunity to let her hair down and spoof her own noble image.

The irresistible sketch concerns a self-adoring star who comes complete with a butler named Fribbins and a prominently displayed portrait depicting her humble, barefoot beginnings. During a staged press conference, "the glamorous, amorous lady" sings the praises of her forthcoming biopic, "Madame Crematante"—a paean to the inventor of the safety pin.

Upon hearing the piece, which one critic would later pronounce "as wholesome as a slug of absinthe," Garson demurred. It was just as well, as by now the musical content of the sketch required the services of a legitimate showstopper. Enter Judy Garland. As Arthur Freed noted, "Judy loved doing sophisticated parts like 'The Interview' sequence . . . but mind you, that particular number was not one of her biggest successes, except with a certain group." Of course, the group that Freed was referring to was the most fanatical and fiercely devoted component of Judy's fan base—the gay men who were instrumental in forming the Garland cult. As biographer Christopher Finch observed, "Hard core Garland aficionados swooned over Madame Crematon [*sic*]. This was the Judy they had hoped for, the Judy of their most cherished dreams—a camp Madonna."[6]

Film historian David Ehrenstein recalled attending a screening of *Ziegfeld Follies* at a Greenwich Village retro house, and as the title card announcing Garland's sequence appeared, the audience became especially attentive. "I remember there were these two guys sitting next to me and one of them said to the other, 'Okay, here comes "The National Anthem."'" It's hilarious and it's deeply hip at the same time. . . . There's this wonderful combination of intense sophistication and naiveté of material in the Freed Unit musicals."[7] And more than a touch of lavender. The handsome newsboys who receive Our Lady of Culver City on bended knee and dance into the star's sanctuary, linked arm in arm, could be charter members of Garland's own fan club.

Dancer Bert May, who plays one of the reporters in Garland's sketch, made one of his first film appearances in *Ziegfeld Follies*: "I was only a teenager and here I am in a movie with Fred Astaire, Gene Kelly, and Judy—I like to say I started at the top and worked my way down."* May remembered that it was actually Chuck Walters who staged and choreographed Garland's "Interview." Though Walters had carefully planned the sequence, Freed decided that Minnelli should shoot it. "Every bit of action in that number was mine. I almost cried," Walters revealed.[8] It wouldn't be the last time that Minnelli and Walters would "collaborate" on a picture.

Vincente and Judy were reunited for "The Interview"—but only while the cameras were rolling. After *Meet Me in St. Louis*, there had been a romantic detour. "Judy had left me," Minnelli remembered. "She'd been seeing another man before we started going together. He was tortured and complicated and very much the intellectual. She simply gravitated back to him." Of course, the deep-thinker in question was Joe Mankiewicz. Minnelli may have worshipped Garland's star quality, but Mankiewicz was able to completely relate to Judy as a woman: "I remember her as I would an emotion, a mood, an emotional experience that is an event."[9]

---

* Bert May turns up in several Minnelli movies. In *The Clock*, he is the assistant to the judge who marries Judy Garland and Robert Walker. In *The Band Wagon*, he doubled for Cyd Charisse as "Mr. Big" in "The Girl Hunt Ballet." The versatile May also appeared with Barbra Streisand and Larry Blyden in "Wait Till We're Sixty-Five," an elaborate production number ultimately deleted from the release print of *On a Clear Day You Can See Forever*. (Bert May, interview with author.)

The Clock: Minnelli directs Garland in MGM's version of Central Park, 1944.
PHOTO COURTESY OF PHOTOFEST

10

"If I Had You"

"I PRODUCED *The Clock* to give Judy a kick. She wanted to do a straight picture," Arthur Freed recalled—though at first, the producer didn't think allowing his greatest musical star to appear in a nonmusical film was such a smashing idea. The moviegoing public knew and adored Judy Garland as a singing star, and they paid good money to see her musicals, buy her records, and snap up the sheet music of songs from her movies. The bottom line was that there was plenty of profit to be made whenever Judy Garland belted them out.

After giving her all in one elaborate MGM musical after another, though, Garland longed for the opportunity to appear in a more modestly scaled production that would allow her to display her dramatic talents (which radio listeners had already been treated to, courtesy of broadcasts of *Morning Glory* and a nonmusical version of *A Star Is Born* several years earlier).

Paul and Pauline Gallico's unpublished short story "The Clock" had caught Freed's eye. It concerned a lonely, wide-eyed corporal from Mapleton, Indiana, on a forty-eight-hour furlough in New York City who meets a secretary one fateful Sunday afternoon. After a courtship that redefines whirlwind, the couple marries before the soldier ships out again. It was charming. It was timely. There were no big production numbers. And in the form of New Yorker Alice Maybery, Judy had found her first dramatic screen role. Robert Nathan and Joseph Schrank (who had scripted *Cabin in the Sky*) were tasked with adapting the Gallicos' poignant story.

Designing Woman: Minnelli's former fiancée, costumer Marion Herwood Keyes and his
future wife, Judy Garland look over wardrobe designs on the set of *The Clock*.

Robert Walker, who had already spent plenty of time in uniform, courtesy of MGM's *See Here, Private Hargrove*, and *Thirty Seconds over Tokyo*, would play the lovestruck soldier. Jack Conway, the man who directed Metro's first talkie (*Alias Jimmy Valentine* in 1928), was originally announced as the director of *The Clock*, but in June 1944, while shooting process shots on location in New York, he fell ill. Production was temporarily halted. When it resumed, Fred Zinnemann was at the helm. Almost immediately, it became apparent that although Zinnemann was a completely capable director, he was not suitably matched with the star.

"I don't know—he must be a good director but I just get nothing. We have no compatibility," Judy reportedly told Freed.[1] Others close to the production confirm that the lack of chemistry between director and star was an issue from the outset, though some believe that what also concerned Garland was the fact that the rushes revealed that Zinnemann had failed where Minnelli had triumphed. The luminous Judy of *Meet Me in St. Louis* was nowhere to be found in Zinnemann's footage. Under Minnelli's indulgent eye, Garland had blossomed as Esther Smith. On Zinnemann's watch, her Alice Maybery was rather dull and ordinary. "The rushes came in and Judy said it looked like something out of *The Search*," remembers Garland confidant John Meyer.[2] Zinnemann's semi-documentary style may have worked for that postwar drama, but it seemed far too somber for an MGM love story. Clearly something would have to be done. Just because Garland was going legit and playing a nonsinging secretary didn't mean she had to sacrifice every ounce of her newfound glamour. Judy made up her mind: "One day, I went to the officials and told them I knew what the picture needed . . . Vincente Minnelli."[3]

While Freed stopped *The Clock* yet again, Garland summoned Minnelli to a lunch meeting at The Player's Club, the site of countless off-the-lot conferences. Offering Vincente a preview of her dramatic abilities, Judy prevailed upon the same man that she had recently spurned. Her pet project was in jeopardy, and she would do anything to keep it afloat—even if it meant putting personal feelings aside and asking Vincente to take over the picture.

Minnelli quickly realized that this was a working lunch and that his meeting with Judy had more than likely been orchestrated by Arthur Freed. Already a studio-savvy diplomat, Vincente agreed to take on the rescue mission, but only if he could talk to Zinnemann first and under the condition that if he did restart *The Clock*, he would be granted complete creative control. Minnelli conferred with Zinnemann, the future director of such four-star classics as *High Noon* and *From Here to Eternity*. The Austrian-born auteur vented about Judy's unreliability but gave Vincente his blessing to carry on.

And, really, who better to direct a New York love story than Metro's own Greenwich Village refugee? Freed was also shrewd enough to realize that what they were after wasn't so much New York "realism" but a back-projected facsimile of it—coated with a thick veneer of Metro gloss. Whatever cinema verité flourishes Zinnemann had hoped to introduce went the way of his aborted footage. This would be a wartime romance produced by Arthur Freed and directed by Vincente Minnelli, and any resemblance to actual urban realities was purely coincidental. The producer was hopeful that what Minnelli had done for turn-of-the-century *St. Louis*, he'd be able to do for Culver City's version of the Big Apple.

With Garland garnering inordinate attention for appearing in a nonsinging role, nearly everyone overlooked the fact that *The Clock* would be Vincente's dramatic debut as well. Recognizing this as an opportunity to display his versatility, Minnelli was determined that the picture had to stand out. Before diving in, he looked into whether there was anything worth salvaging from Zinnemann's efforts.

When it was pieced together, Zinnemann's footage evidenced none of the dramatic effectiveness of his recent Spencer Tracy vehicle *The Seventh Cross*. As Minnelli observed, "Each scene from the two [*sic*] weeks of footage shot thus far looked as if it came from a different picture. It was very confusing. I could see why Metro's executive committee had canceled the project."[4] Although a minimal amount of material was retained from Zinnemann's version, it was clear that Minnelli would have to start from scratch.

"We tackled the script," Vincente recalled. "We kept all the parts we felt were good, and tried to alter the rest. . . . I decided at once to make New York itself another character in the story and I introduced a number of crazy people." In overhauling the script, Minnelli irked screenwriter Robert Nathan, who complained to Freed, "I still feel very strongly that when a director departs from the instructions in the script, he ought to—if only in politeness—discuss that departure with the writer *before* rather than *after* the scene is shot." According to Vincente, much of what was removed from Nathan's script were "sticky spots," such as a sequence in which Robert Walker befriends a precious young lad in Central Park. "It was all terribly 'darling,'" Minnelli would later remark. "Instead, I made [the boy] kick Walker and that made him more real, more human."[5]

Elsewhere, Minnelli attempted to give the script more atmosphere and local color, and for this he dipped into his own big city experiences: "I tried to remember everything about New York. I set out to create an unexpected gallery of people whose lives might conceivably touch that of the boy and

"Every Second a Heart-Beat . . .": Corporal Joe Allen (Robert Walker) and Alice Maybery (Judy Garland) share a tender embrace in *The Clock*. "The thing was to tell the story of two people who couldn't be alone," Minnelli would say of the film's young lovers.
PHOTO COURTESY
OF PHOTOFEST

girl."[6] For Vincente, New York had meant getting the job done amid constant distractions. While mentally fashioning an extravagant Josephine Baker ensemble in his head, a preoccupied Minnelli was often jolted back to reality by a boisterous cab driver or too inquisitive waitress. In other words, New York was about trying to accomplish something while 38 million other people have very different ideas.

"The thing with *The Clock* was to tell the story of two people who couldn't be alone," Minnelli noted. "There was no possibility of privacy for those two people."[7] Despite their developing intimacy, Alice and Joe are never really by themselves—they are constantly distracted by Minnelli's colorful parade of interlopers: Alice's hyper-conversational roommate Helen (played by Vincente and Judy's friend Ruth Brady), an eavesdropper eating pie à la mode, Keenan Wynn's philosophizing drunk, and a scene-stealing eccentric delectably played by Angela Lansbury's mother, Moyna MacGill.

To all involved, it became immediately apparent that although Zinnemann's grittier authenticity was forfeited, a romantic warmth and charm were regained once Minnelli was in the director's chair. Though Garland doesn't sing a note, in Vincente's hands *The Clock* plays like a musical with the numbers excised.* A charming scene in which Joe scrambles after Alice's 7th Avenue bus almost comes off like a mini-sequel to "The Trolley Song." And George Bassman's beautiful underscoring and his use of the haunting British ballad "If I Had You" add another layer of poignancy to this wartime romance.

It was during the filming of *The Clock* that Minnelli and Garland's own love story reignited. As many at the studio shook their heads in disbelief, Judy and Vincente were once again an item, and this time they were more open about their feelings.

"When I was shooting, she only had eyes for him," actress Gloria Marlen says of Judy's obvious affection for her director. "She was constantly following him around and trying to look through the camera to see what he was shooting. They were not married or anything at the time but it was kind of cute, you could see that she had a real crush on him." Marlen has a memorable bit in the film as a young lady who receives a corsage from a serviceman ("Here's something to top you off . . ."). This inspires Joe to buy one for Alice. Of her director, Marlen remembers that "he was very patient but noncommittal. I mean, Vincente never said a word. He was very business-like in his approach. He gave very little direction and he assumed a lot with me because it was only my second film and I didn't know beans about it. . . . I never knew if I had done what he wanted or not."[8]

The Clock opened at New York's Capitol Theatre in May 1945, and the critics devoted as much column space to praising the film's director as its stars. *Time* raved: "[Minnelli's] semi-surrealist juxtapositions, accidental or no, help turn *The Clock* into a rich image of a great city. His love of mobility, of snooping and sailing and drifting and drooping his camera booms and dollies, makes *The Clock*, largely boom shot, one of the most satisfactorily flexible movies since Friedrich Murnau's epoch-making *The Last Laugh*."[9] And Manny Farber observed: "*The Clock* is riddled, as few movies are, with carefully, skillfully used intelligence and love for people and for movie making and is made with a more flexible and original use of the medium than any other recent film. . . . Minnelli's work in this, and in *Meet Me In St. Louis*, indicates that he is the most human, skillful director to appear in Hollywood in years."[10]

---

* *The Clock* was a favorite of composer Stephen Sondheim's: "I so wanted to make a musical out of it at one point. I persuaded one of the secretaries at MGM to sneak a script out of a vault for me over a weekend so that I could type a copy for myself." But after writing an opening number, he gave up on the idea. Sondheim's 1964 Broadway musical *Anyone Can Whistle* appeared to contain a clever homage to Minnelli in the form of the number "Me and My Town," in which Angela Lansbury's haughty mayoress meets the press in a manner reminiscent of Judy Garland's "Interview" in *Ziegfeld Follies*.

The constantly interrupted romance on screen in *The Clock* was mirrored by Vincente and Judy's own relationship. Life on the lot—especially for two of the studio's brightest talents—was the ultimate gold-fish-bowl experience. As gossip columnists shared every tender Minnelli-Garland glance with readers around the world, there was no hope for any real privacy. When Judy moved into Vincente's elegantly appointed house on Evanview Drive in the Hollywood Hills, the couple did everything possible to keep their cohabitation out of the columns. "At that time, there was Louella and Hedda," Minnelli recalled of the era when all-powerful gossip columnists Louella Parsons and Hedda Hopper reigned supreme. "So we had to keep it very quiet. But it leaked out because somebody's legman lived right across the street."[11] Before long, studio insiders knew that Judy had moved in with Vincente. There were even rumors that the couple intended to marry.

Minnelli studies the script of *Yolanda and the Thief*, 1945.
PHOTO FROM THE AUTHOR'S COLLECTION

11

Dada, Dali, and Technicolor

AS MARRIAGE RUMORS SWIRLED, Minnelli began preparing his next film, *Yolanda and the Thief*. This would be a lavish musical based on a whimsical fable by *Madeline* creator Ludwig Bemelmans and Jacques Thery that had appeared in the July 1943 issue of *Town and Country*. The story concerns a slick swindler who sets his sights on an outlandishly wealthy but spiritually attuned heiress. The con man gets closer to Yolanda's fortune by posing as her guardian angel. In some ways, the plot resembled Fred Astaire's "This Heart of Mine" vignette from *Ziegfeld Follies*, and that sequence may have given Freed the idea to cast Astaire as *Yolanda*'s suave charlatan, Johnny Riggs. Freed and MGM's front office were also banking on *Yolanda* to imitate the success of *You Were Never Lovelier*, the 1942 Columbia triumph that had paired Astaire with Rita Hayworth and that featured a somewhat similar storyline.

As with virtually every musical announced by MGM, Judy Garland was at one time slated to play Yolanda Aquaviva, the most beloved resident of the mythical South American country of Patria—"the land of milk and money." Despite her interest in appearing in *Yolanda*, Garland would ultimately be assigned to *The Harvey Girls*, a pet project of her mentor-arranger Roger Edens. In March 1944, the studio next announced that Lucille Ball, fresh from her triumph in Metro's *Best Foot Forward*, would play the wide-eyed heiress. Ultimately, the role was given to Freed's comely protégé, Lucille Bremer. After receiving positive notices as a result of her memorable pairing with Fred Astaire in *Ziegfeld Follies*, Bremer was being groomed for Garland-sized superstardom. For *Yolanda and the Thief*, Bremer's name would be billed after Astaire's but above the title, a signal to audiences that there was a new star in Metro's firmament.

Many on the lot were surprised that Bremer rose through the ranks as swiftly as she did. "She came out of nowhere," says former contract dancer Judi Blacque. "We certainly never thought that she would become a major star. Don't misunderstand me. She was very nice. Very attractive. And she could dance. But when you look at what was available in Hollywood at that time, it was incredible that she got as far as she did."[1]

After the unqualified success of *Meet Me in St. Louis*, Freed felt that he could confidently turn to screenwriter Irving Brecher to translate the Thery-Bemelmans prose into a screenplay that retained the original story's childlike innocence while managing to keep war-weary audiences awake. "The story was nothing," Brecher admitted decades later. "I didn't like it. But Freed wanted to make it . . . and to star Lucille Bremer, who had been in *Meet Me in St. Louis*, and, if she was not having an affair with Arthur Freed, was at least being coveted by Freed. In any case, I didn't want to work on *Yolanda*. Nothing was happening with it, and I didn't think there was a picture in it that I could do that would be worth anything."[2]

Whereas Brecher's screenplay for *Meet Me in St. Louis* had contained universal situations and humor that anyone with a slightly off-center family could relate to, *Yolanda* occupied more rarefied territory. Minnelli would later boast that *Yolanda* contained "the first surrealist ballet ever used in pictures." Bold and Dali-esque in design, Astaire's "Dream Ballet" was certainly striking, but including a surrealistic ballet in an already fanciful musical was not unlike piling a hot fudge sundae on top of a banana split. Everything in Yolanda's world—from her baroque bathtub to her singing servants—was the stuff of absurdist, off-the-wall fantasy. As Noel Langley, one of the screenwriters of *The Wizard of Oz*, once observed: "You cannot put fantastic people in strange places in front of an audience unless they have seen them as human beings first."[3]

There is nothing earthbound about *Yolanda*, which is both part of its charm and part of its problem. A prime example of Minnelli at his most uninhibited and self-indulgent, the movie showed what could happen when Vincente sacrificed story to style. As would occur later with *The Pirate*, the stylistic excesses of *Yolanda* would delight Minnelli fans but confound mainstream audiences expecting a more conventional musical-comedy outing.

Bremer, while not untalented, was miscast as the pious, convent-bred Yolanda—though, to be fair, even Judy Garland's trademark sincerity would have been taxed with lines such as, "I'm not the only one who's happy tonight. . . . The man in the moon is smiling." It also doesn't help that in the

Taking the plunge: Yolanda Aquaviva (Lucille Bremer) in her luxurious, baroque bathtub in *Yolanda and the Thief.* *Yolanda*'s coauthor Ludwig Bemelmans had high hopes for the film's leading lady. As he told Arthur Freed: "It is so nice and so exciting to sit at the birth of what will be a great star." PHOTO COURTESY OF PHOTOFEST

early scenes, Bremer is noticeably older than her convent classmates, who, in their pinafores and picture hats, seem to have emerged directly from the pages of *Madeline*. Although *Yolanda* has its fiercely devoted partisans, there was only one sequence in the film that seemed to please everybody— the justly celebrated "Coffee Time." Freed from their arch dialogue and contrived situations, Astaire and Bremer were finally allowed to do what they did best: dance. During this one number (choreographed by Eugene Loring), Minnelli's movie suddenly and all too fleetingly sprang to life.

In the end, not even this exhilarating sequence could save *Yolanda* from its fate. To wartime audiences accustomed to the likes of *Four Jills in a Jeep*, *Yolanda* must have seemed as accessible and inviting as a Jackson Pollock canvas. "*Yolanda* is such an interesting failure because it has got these amazing flights of imagination," says writer Clive Hirschhorn. "I mean, 'Coffee Time' is just wonderful and the color scheme throughout the film is simply breath-taking, but the film as a whole just doesn't work because it doesn't really invite you in. It's almost too experimental. Too clever."[4]

As Astaire recalled, "We all tried hard and thought we had something, but as it turned out, we didn't. There were some complicated and effective dances which scored, but the whole idea was too much on the fantasy side and it did not do well."

Edwin Schallert's mixed review in the *Los Angeles Times* seemed to sum up the general consensus: "'Not for realists' is a label that may be appropriately affixed to *Yolanda and the Thief*. It is a question, too, whether this picture has the basic material to satisfy the general audience, although in texture and trimmings it might be termed an event."

But, as usual, it was Judy Garland who nailed the entire experience with a devastating one-liner. After a cooly received sneak preview of *Yolanda*, it became clear that despite Freed's best efforts, Bremer lacked genuine star appeal and Minnelli's musical was something of a misfire. As Garland passed a dispirited Arthur Freed, she quipped: "Never mind, Arthur, Pomona isn't Lucille's town."[5]

"The picture made money," Minnelli would assert in his autobiography, but the MGM ledgers told a different story, estimating a net loss of $1,644,000 (in 1945 dollars). Despite the paltry box-office returns and the lukewarm reviews, *Yolanda and the Thief*, like several of Vincente's later efforts, retroactively achieved cult status, attracting a devoted following of fans who found the film's bizarre mélange of Dada, Dali, and Technicolor irresistibly appealing. Among the faithful were MGM arranger Kay Thompson and her *Eloise* illustrator Hilary Knight, who both embraced the inspired lunacy that is *Yolanda*.

"We were always talking about things that we liked or Kay's experiences at MGM, which were hilarious but usually not very kind to the people involved," Knight remembers. "We also talked about things that we loved about movies and we both agreed that we loved *Yolanda*"—and especially Mildred Natwick's scatterbrained, chihuahua-toting Aunt Amarilla, who spouts the movie's most delectable lines. At one point, the pixilated Amarilla turns to a devoted servant and imperiously demands, "Do my fingernails immediately . . . and bring them to my room!"

In addition to delivering the film's wittiest zingers, the veteran character actress also had an opportunity to observe Freed and Bremer in close proximity. While the studio rumor mill would inextricably link the producer and his reluctant star, there was at least one colleague who thought otherwise. "Natwick told me that she thought Lucille had never succumbed to Arthur," Hilary Knight reveals. "Lucille's mother was always with them, even on the set . . . always protecting her baby from Arthur."[6]

***

"ABSORBED . . . DIRECTOR VINCENTE MINNELLI studies the script of *Yolanda and the Thief*, oblivious of the cameraman snapping his picture," read the caption accompanying a publicity photo of Minnelli on the set of

Vincente and Judy's wedding day, June 15, 1945. Best man Ira Gershwin, Minnelli,
Garland, Louis B. Mayer (who gave the bride away), and studio publicist Betty Asher
(Judy's maid of honor) pose for photographers. The ceremony took place at
Judy's mother's house in Beverly Hills.
PHOTO COURTESY OF PHOTOFEST

his latest production. The rare glimpse of Judy Garland's husband engrossed
in his work was officially approved by Hollywood's Advertising Advisory Council on June 25, 1945, just ten days after the much-discussed Minnelli-Garland
nuptials had taken place at Judy's mother's house in Beverly Hills. It was an
intimate ceremony with none of the customary Hollywood hoopla that usually
attended a celebrity wedding, though MGM was well represented—by Arthur
Freed, publicity chief Howard Strickling, and even Louis B. Mayer, who
gave the bride away.

Now that Vincente was married to one of MGM's most important assets,
the studio would carefully scrutinize any images of him that would be seen
by the public. If Minnelli was not exactly the kind of strapping All American
Boy that Judy's legions of fans would have envisioned her blissfully wed to,
at least the studio could filter out any questionable examples of Vincente's
"artistic flair." After all, it was one thing for Minnelli to go full tilt flamboyant
with a *Ziegfeld Follies* production number, but altogether another matter for
him to appear in public bedecked in a turban as he escorted Judy and their
friend Joan Blondell to dinner at Romanoff's. Vincente and Judy's friends
were happy that the two had formed such a close, supportive bond. And
many hoped that mild-mannered Vincente might have a calming influence
on his high-spirited wife. But even so, they couldn't help but wonder . . .
What kind of marriage was it exactly?

"I admired him before I ever played in one of his pictures," Garland said of her director-husband. Judy told Hedda Hopper: "He's one of the hardest working people I've ever seen. Players like him. They feel he's giving his best, so that brings out their best, too."
PHOTO COURTESY OF PHOTOFEST

The gossip ran the gamut: Garland was attempting to "fix" Minnelli—as in "all he needs is the love of a good woman to make things right." Or the union was a studio-arranged marriage of convenience that would allow both partners the freedom to pursue extramarital affairs (both heterosexual and homosexual). The more cynically minded observers believed that Minnelli, for all his gentlemanly ways, was a shrewd opportunist hitching his wagon to the studio's brightest star. But maybe it was the most improbable scenario of all that contained the real truth: Two extravagantly talented, sensitive people turned to one another seeking sanctuary from their intensely pressured lives. What's more, each could complete the other's fantasy. "I remember Vincente saying about Judy, 'She is a great actress and a great star and I will direct her in important parts,'" recalls singer Margaret Whiting, who had befriended Garland years earlier. "I mean, it was obvious that he was interested in her as a director, but I just don't know what that marriage was all about."[7]

In later years, Vincente would describe his New York honeymoon with Judy as a blissful summer idyll complete with heartwarming episodes that might have been deleted sequences from *The Clock*. Three months in Manhattan and away from the confines of Culver City seemed to work wonders for Garland as she interacted with adoring fans on the street, organized a search for Minnelli's "neurotic" poodle, experienced live theater, and attempted a new beginning. "Judy gave me a cherished gift—a silent promise," Vincente remembered. "We were walking in a park by the river. 'Hold my hand,' she said softly. I did. It was then that I noticed a vial of pills in her other hand. . . . She threw the pills in the East River. She said she was through with them. But the minute we got back [to Hollywood], anything that would happen at the studio, she would take the pills."[8]

* * *

IN THE MID-'40S, largely owing to the success of James Cagney's spirited portrayal of George M. Cohan in *Yankee Doodle Dandy*, all-star musical biographies of America's top tunesmiths were suddenly hot properties, even if they weren't entirely factual. Warner Brothers presented Cary Grant as a heterosexual Cole Porter in *Night and Day*, while Metro countered with Mickey Rooney as a heterosexual Lorenz Hart in *Words and Music*. When it came time to dramatize the life of *Show Boat* composer Jerome Kern in *Till the Clouds Roll By*, screenwriter Guy Bolton knew this posed something of a challenge. A confidant of Kern's, Bolton stood in awe of his friend's considerable talents, but he also knew that the songwriter's private life wasn't remotely cinematic.

Though it was true that Kern had cheated death by not sailing on the ill-fated *Lusitania* (his alarm clock didn't go off), most of the "biography" in the film was pure hokum—including Kern looking after the self-absorbed daughter of a fictional writing partner. To compensate for the lack of dramatic action, the film would be laced with continual references to the theatrical luminaries of the past—a sort of cinematic name-dropping. MGM's stable of stars would portray some of these fabled legends of yesteryear.

The role of Broadway's Marilyn Miller was reserved for Metro's even more beloved answer: Judy Garland. While June Allyson, Lena Horne, and Angela Lansbury would have to make do with dance director Robert Alton,* Garland's sequences were entrusted to Minnelli, now considered Judy's own personal auteur. Of course, Vincente was well versed in the legend of Marilyn Miller, and he was eager to re-create some of her best-loved numbers—including "Look for the Silver Lining" and "Who?"—on screen. In 1925, Miller had one of her greatest successes with *Sunny*, the saga of a circus bareback rider. The stage show was fondly remembered for its splashy, big-top setting. MGM,

---

* Richard Whorf directed the narrative sequences in *Till the Clouds Roll By*. The musical numbers—except for those featuring Judy Garland—were helmed by Robert Alton.

of course, was expected to outdo the original production, and Minnelli's Technicolored circus made Barnum and Bailey look positively sedate.

At one point, the script indicated that during the *Sunny* sequence, Judy was to hurl herself onto the back of a prancing show pony. Obviously, the services of a stunt double would be required, not only because of the risky acrobatic maneuvers involved but also because several months earlier, Judy had discovered that she was pregnant. At age forty-two, Vincente was about to become a father. There was no time to celebrate, as the pressure was on to speed through Garland's numbers (in a mere two weeks) before the star became too visibly expectant to photograph.

Originally, the *Sunny* episode was to have included Judy's rendition of Kern's winsome "D'Ya Love Me?" Despite Garland's heartfelt delivery, the number was deleted from the release print of *Clouds*—and it's a good thing. The surviving footage reveals an oddly uninspired and barely choreographed number. Flanked by a pair of listless clowns, Garland looks uncharacter-istically ill at ease. Her comedic grimace when the playback concludes speaks volumes.

In sharp contrast, the mounting of the buoyant "Who?" was a cinematic bull's eye. Minnelli encircles Garland, who is gowned in vibrant canary yellow, with a bevy of top-hatted chorus boys in tails. As the star twirls and taps her way through the number, Vincente's camera keeps pace—an active and fully engaged participant in the proceedings.

Bob Claunch, one of the pompadoured dancers appearing alongside Gar-land, recalled that working with the frequently tardy star was always worth the wait. "Naturally, I had heard things about her," Claunch says:

> The dancers would talk about their associations with her because they had worked on other films of hers. They knew that she was sick a lot but at that time, nobody really knew what was going on with her. There was a lot of waiting around. I thought to myself at one point, "Where the hell is Judy Garland? She's supposed to be the star of this. . . ." Finally, Garland came in. And just from seeing [dance instructor] Jeanette Bates do the routine one time, that's all Judy needed. She did the dance without a rehearsal or anything. We did a master shot. And she left. It was remarkable. I still can't believe it.[9]

As expectant parents, both Minnelli and Garland were endlessly amused by the spectacle of a visibly pregnant Judy rushing up to one dashing chorus boy after another and confronting each one with the leading question, "Who?" As Judy and Vincente prepared for the birth of their child, the father-to-be surely experienced a great complexity of emotions. Only a few years earlier, gossipers on the lot had whispered that Minnelli was "not marrying material," let alone cut out for fatherhood. In fact, around the studio Judy's pregnancy had been dubbed "The Immaculate Conception." Still others in Minnelli's circle—even those who "knew the score"—believed that Vincente's quiet demeanor, gentle personality, and fondness for fantasy would make him an excellent father.

Till the Clouds Roll By opened in December 1946. The musical would garner much praise for the latest Minnelli-Garland collaboration. Judy's sequences in the film are imbued with such vitality and presented with such panache that Minnelli's portion effectively upstages the rest of the movie. In later years, he would helm sequences for other director's movies (*The Bribe, The Seventh Sin, All the Fine Young Cannibals*) and usually do so without credit. Nevertheless, a Minnelli moment, whether anonymous or not, had a way of standing out, not only in terms of artful composition but also in the way a scene "felt."

Till the Clouds Roll By would clean up at the box office as almost every MGM musical did in the 1940s. For millions of Americans, going to the movies was a must. The dazzling images of luxurious glamour and double-feature doses of fantasy provided "those wonderful people out there in the dark" with a kind of vital emotional sustenance. You may be broke, knocked up, or limp wristed, but there is always hope for you at the movies. Panty hose may be rationed, but just look at Lucille Bremer decked out in a stunning Sharaff ball gown. At home, the roof is leaking, the rent is late, and nobody understands you. But who cares? Fred Astaire is dancing on the ceiling and Gene Kelly is singing in the rain. An MGM musical was better than a sermon on Sunday for those true believers seeking salvation.

For Vincente Minnelli, the creation of this kind of rarefied fantasy fulfilled the same psychological and emotional need. While real life had provided the suffocation of a small town, a developmentally disabled brother, and not nearly enough color, the movies—even for the man directing them—possessed the power to transport.

12

Undercurrent

"I'M SURE WE'LL GET ALONG," Katharine Hepburn announced to Minnelli prior to the start of shooting on *Undercurrent*. According to Vincente, "It sounded like an order and a threat. Never had I met anyone with such self-assurance. She made me nervous. And here was I, theoretically the captain of the ship, being made to tiptoe through my assignment."[1]

The assignment was an unusual one for Minnelli—one of those noirish women's pictures like *Mildred Pierce, Nora Prentiss,* or *The Two Mrs. Carrolls* that were in vogue both during and just after the war. Broadway's Edward Chodorov based his screenplay on a three-part *Woman's Home Companion* serial by Thelma Strabel entitled *You Were There*. In some ways, both Strabel's story and Chodorov's adaptation seemed to be emulating Alfred Hitchcock's similarly themed but infinitely more satisfying *Suspicion*, in which a terrified Joan Fontaine suspects that suave husband Cary Grant is a murderer.

The soft-spoken Fontaine was one thing, but would audiences believe the fiercely independent Hepburn as a damsel in distress? Producer Pandro S. Berman thought so. While at RKO, Berman had shepherded some of Hepburn's more memorable vehicles (*Sylvia Scarlet, Stage Door*) into production. By the 1940s, both the well-respected producer and his star of choice were in residence at MGM. Berman was convinced that the offbeat combination of Hepburn, Minnelli, and a glossy thriller based on Strabel's novelette would result in a box-office knockout. With Robert Taylor and Robert Mitchum mixed into the batter as Hepburn's hunky costars, how could *Undercurrent* miss?

Minnelli Goes Noir: Robert Taylor and Katharine Hepburn in the 1946 melodrama *Undercurrent*. The film features a trio of stars cast against type, some brilliantly moody photography by Karl Freund, and plenty of subtext.
PHOTO COURTESY OF PHOTOFEST

With all of the principals in place, Hepburn stepped into character as Ann Hamilton, a spunky, self-reliant New Englander. Although Ann is a whiz assisting her scientist father (Edmund Gwenn) in his laboratory, she becomes a floundering fish out of water once she marries affluent industrialist Alan Garroway (Robert Taylor). As Ann soon discovers, her volatile husband is harboring some dark secrets about his half brother, Michael (Robert Mitchum), who has mysteriously disappeared.

While Robert Taylor is effective in a refreshing change-of-pace role as the "smooth as patent leather" husband with sinister shadings, both Hepburn and Mitchum are miscast. As Minnelli recalled, "[Mitchum] was never comfortable in the role of the sensitive Michael."[2] Which is hardly surprising given that the character—a pipe-smoking devotee of Robert Louis Stevenson's poetry and Johannes Brahms's *Third Symphony*—seems more appropriate casting for Clifton Webb than the tough-talking, reefer-toting Mitchum.

Adding to Mitchum's discomfort was the fact that Hepburn, who wielded contractual approval of her costars, seems to have only begrudgingly accepted him, though, decades later, the heavy-lidded actor contradicted the oft-repeated stories that Hepburn was openly hostile toward him. "Mr. Mitchum, don't let them muck you about like that," Hepburn told her costar when she noticed that the lighting for their final scene favored her but left him in the dark. Hepburn ordered the crew to rearrange the lighting so that Mitchum would be photographed to best advantage.

If Mitchum benefited from the formidable Hepburn's take-charge approach, *Undercurrent*'s director was not so fortunate. "I thought she was very mean to Vincente," recalls Jayne Meadows Allen, cast in the supporting role of Sylvia Lea Burton, a glamorous socialite:

> I remember that right after we finished some scene that she didn't like, she said something about how terrible *The Clock* was. She said to him, "My advice to you, my dear, is that if you do another movie like that, you'll be on the train back to New York so fast. . . . And I don't mean the Super Chief. I mean you will be run out of town." I didn't know what she was talking about because I had never seen *The Clock*, but I knew Judy [Garland] was the star of that picture and Judy could never do anything bad. Judy was a better actress than Katharine Hepburn could ever hope to be. I was shocked. I mean, attacking a director in front of everybody while we were shooting a scene! And to do this to Vincente, who never said a mean thing to anybody. He was the sweetest, kindest, dearest man and a wonderful director.[3]

If Hepburn was an imposing, commanding presence on the set, her take-no-prisoners personality also seeped through to her performance. As a result, one never quite believes Hepburn during her character's supposedly vulnerable moments. There's also a jarring disconnect between the supremely confident Ann Hamilton glimpsed in the film's opening moments and the hopelessly inept newlywed who emerges just a few scenes later. After witnessing Ann dominating her father's household and trading zingers with a handsome suitor, one can only wonder . . . Would a woman this self-assured be cowed by anyone, let alone a group of cocktail-party dowagers? It's to Hepburn's credit that in several key scenes, she manages to be moving in a part that doesn't really suit her.

With two leads thrust into awkward roles and a director thoroughly intimidated by his leading lady, *Undercurrent* is off kilter from its first frame. If Minnelli's first dramatic picture, *The Clock*, had played to his strengths, his second nonmusical feature exposed some of his weaknesses as a director: Varied decor and costume changes are substituted for authentic character development, and at times the melodrama veers toward over-the-top histrionics. On the surface, *Undercurrent* seems the least likely of Minnelli's movies to provide any kind of self-referential insight. And yet, here is Hepburn as an uncomfortable outcast, unhappily married to a socially acceptable spouse while her subconscious craves a more suitable soul mate—one who will understand her completely and embrace the same romantic ideals that she does.

Ann is "haunted" by her husband's brother, who for most of the movie exists only as a disembodied kindred spirit—someone she has practically willed

Katharine Hepburn, Minnelli, and Robert Taylor break for cake while shooting *Undercurrent* in February 1946. A month later, Vincente would celebrate the birth of his first child.
PHOTO COURTESY OF PHOTOFEST

into being. "I think he's my obsession," Ann admits. "Wherever I go, there he is. I want to forget him. I want to drive him away . . . I must." But Ann is compelled to locate the mysterious Michael Garroway, as tracking him down also means finding the deepest, most authentic part of herself.

"I know it was a studio assignment at the beginning of his career but it seems to me, there's a lot of real Vincente Minnelli meaning in that film," notes film scholar Jeanine Basinger:

> He had a feeling and an affinity for it. It's about the choice between two men. It's also about the choice of the woman who doesn't fit. She's a plain woman, unprepared for the glamorous world she's thrust into. Like so many of his films, it's about trying to be who you really are. If someone knew who you *really* were, would they still appreciate you? It's also about repressing natural instincts and it's about undercurrents and that's what his whole life really was. . . . Sometimes in the films that get dismissed, that's where you can find the most truth, oddly enough.[4]

Or, as Mitchum reminds Hepburn in one of the film's best scenes, "You can't always see that undercurrent, but it's there."

Most critics would take Minnelli to task for serving up what they regarded as a stylish but hollow suspense yarn. As *Time* noted, "The indigestible plot, full of false leads and unkept promises, is like a woman's magazine serial consumed at one gulp."[5] Despite mixed reviews, the picture was a certified hit when it was released in November 1946. *Undercurrent* would also prove to be the first of a half dozen highly profitable collaborations for Vincente and producer Pandro Berman.

Though his latest picture had moviegoers lining up at the ticket window, Minnelli was much prouder of another production—one that had debuted months earlier on March 12, 1946. "I remember one day when we were shooting, a secretary came out from Vincente's office to say, 'Mr. Minnelli, we've just had a phone call from the hospital. You have a baby daughter,'" recalls Jayne Meadows Allen.[6] The baby would be named Liza after the Gershwin song.

Decades after they worked on *Undercurrent*, Allen reminded Katharine Hepburn of this momentous occasion while both were backstage during "The Night of a 100 Stars" gala. "We were talking about the day Liza Minnelli was born," Allen remembers:

> I said, "I shall never forget you, Miss Hepburn—your emotion. . . . You were practically in tears and you said, 'Oh, Vincente, how beautiful that must be. Having a child must be the greatest joy in the world. . . .' And I never forgot it after all these years." Well, Kate denied everything. She said, "I have no recollection of that. I don't feel that way at all. I don't believe I ever said that. . . ." I mean, Katharine Hepburn was the most eccentric woman that was ever a star, in my opinion.[7]

<{13}>

Voodoo

AS MR. AND MRS. VINCENTE MINNELLI made the rounds of cocktail parties and dinner parties and post-premiere parties (parties were a large part of the job in Hollywood), Judy was inevitably asked to sing. In fact, a social occasion couldn't truly be considered a success until MGM's resident belter took her place at the piano. Judy also ranked high on every hostess's invitation list for another reason: She was, without question, one of the wittiest women in Hollywood. In sharp contrast to the conversationally challenged Minnelli, Garland was an extraordinary raconteur who could captivate a roomful of seasoned veterans with her outlandish anecdotes or a devastating Marlene Dietrich imitation. According to Minnelli, it was Judy's affinity for the absurd that first triggered the idea for a film version of *The Pirate*.

S. N. Behrman's comedy had opened on Broadway in 1942 starring the great theatrical couple Alfred Lunt and Lynn Fontanne. The plot had been lifted from the German play *Der Seeruuber* and concerned a rakish actor masquerading as a notorious seafarer as he attempts to win the heart of the mayor's wife. "There was nothing subtle about it," Hilary Knight recalled of the Lunts' version of *The Pirate*. "It looked like a musical, although it wasn't one. . . . It was all decor and style and no more successful than the movie was."[1]

Scenic designer Lemuel Ayres, who had worked on the theatrical version of *The Pirate*, suggested to Arthur Freed that Behrman's play might make for a blockbuster screen musical. Freed, Minnelli, and Garland were all excited by the idea—Judy, especially, as the material would allow her to display her largely untapped talent for sophisticated comedy.

A musical set in the picturesque West Indies would inspire Minnelli to conjure up the kind of lush tropical paradise that he had fantasized about as a boy back in Delaware. He would go to incredible lengths to make certain that MGM's versions of exotic nineteenth-century Calvados and neighboring Port Sebastian were painstakingly thorough in terms of period authenticity. At the same time, this would be the kind of highly stylized Freed Unit utopia where pirates in snug buccaneer briefs, crucifix-sporting señoritas, and African American circus tumblers would all blissfully coexist.

With Garland in the lead, the obvious question became . . . Who would play the hammy actor passing himself off as the dashing pirate? "I never thought of anyone but Gene Kelly for the part of Serafin," said Minnelli, believing that Kelly's knock 'em dead charisma and athleticism were a perfect match for the part. Like Judy, Gene was enthusiastic about the project as it would let him display another facet of his remarkable talents: "I wanted the opportunity to do a different kind of dancing, a popular style with a lot of classic form, acrobatics and athletics."[2] Tongue firmly planted in cheek, Kelly would also pay tribute to the screen's legendary swashbucklers, such as the dashing Douglas Fairbanks Sr., in what would prove to be one of his best roles.

With two of Metro's brightest stars in place, Minnelli turned his attention to the script. Although the basic framework of the Lunt-Fontanne version was retained, much of the stage material would require revamping. On Broadway, Fontanne's Manuela was married to the oafish mayor Don Pedro Vargas while carrying on with Serafin. That scenario could never be sanctioned by either the Breen Office or Louis B. Mayer. For MGM's adaptation, Garland's Manuela Alva would be engaged to the mayor, and she would be less worldly and Catholicized. However, the character would retain her wide-eyed romanticism and penchant for embarking on "mental excursions," a facet of the story that immediately appealed to Vincente. When Manuela finally abandons her repressive surroundings to join Serafin's theatrical troupe, this seemed to refer back to Minnelli's own story: *I was saved from Delaware, Ohio, by the bright lights of show business.*

One writer after another (including Judy's former flame Joseph L. Mankiewicz) would take a crack at the screenplay, but none of these scripts were judged correct. Freed then turned to Anita Loos and Joseph Than, but their version of *The Pirate* would prove to be the most unacceptable by far. In the Loos-Than treatment, the original premise was turned upside down, with the Kelly character becoming a singing-dancing pirate pretending to be an entertainer. This would never do. It was husband-and-wife writing team

Albert Hackett and Frances Goodrich who came to the rescue. Within two months, they had cranked out a zesty, witty screenplay that achieved the right balance between sophisticated farce and whimsical fantasy.

In terms of the score, Freed had initially thought of Hugh Martin, who had come through with three of the finest movie songs ever written for *Meet Me in St. Louis*. "When I came out of the army, I was so anxious to get back to Hollywood that I didn't go see Arthur, which was really wicked of me because he had given me the best opportunity of my life," Martin recalls. "He said, 'I'm really sorry you didn't come to see me because I wanted you to write *The Pirate* and when I thought you were still in the army, I got Cole Porter.' I would have loved to have done it and I felt awful. And I've been feeling awful for about fifty years."[3]

Even for those only casually acquainted with the world of musical comedy, the name Cole Porter was synonymous with unmatched lyrics, sparkling wit, and the best double entrendres in the business. Coming off the failure of his Broadway musical *Around the World in Eighty Days*, Porter was also eager to take on *The Pirate*. The composer admired Garland and marveled at what he described as her "prodigal voice." However, Porter seemed to start off on the wrong foot when the first few songs he submitted were deemed unsuitable by Freed, who sent the composer back to his piano. "Cole wasn't happy with his contributions," Minnelli remembered.[4] Though the score would eventually include such lyrical acrobatics as rhyming "schizophrenia" and "neurasthenia" (in Kelly's "Nina") and the raucous show-business anthem "Be a Clown," Porter prophesized correctly that the score would not yield a single commercial hit.

The long, strange, and at times torturous production of *The Pirate* began in February 1947. What originally seemed like a Freed Unit dream project soon morphed into the kind of nightmare that only legitimately talented people can create. On a good day, Garland would arrive promptly at 11:45— for an 8:00 call. On other days, she wouldn't show up at all. For those who had worked with Judy through the years, this was almost expected. They knew that when she did appear, she would be letter perfect and have everyone breaking up between takes. But during the making of *The Pirate*, a number of unresolved conflicts and psychological torments began to overwhelm the fragile star.

Garland had recently renewed her contract with MGM and she was already having second thoughts. The idea of being locked into another five years of back-to-back film projects, seemingly unrelenting demands, and studio politics dampened her usually exuberant spirits. With her uncanny theatrical instincts, Garland may have been the first to realize that *The Pirate*, for all its stylishness and sophistication, would probably not appeal to the average moviegoer—the kind that had been thoroughly enchanted by her simple, unaffected Esther Smith in turn of the century *St. Louis*.

According to Minnelli, it was while shooting *The Pirate* that Garland "began to feel that she wasn't functioning and turned again to the pills that had sustained her during past crises."[5] Almost before she realized it had happened, Judy was once again caught up in the self-destructive pattern she had valiantly tried to break free from. Now she was back on the treadmill, which meant day after day of having to be that girl up on the screen that everybody loved. There was the constant pressure of having to please studio chiefs, stockholders, producers, costars, cameramen, choreographers, and, most importantly, her fiercely devoted legions of fans. Through it all, America's sweetheart was permanently switched to one setting: on. Nobody ever had as much riding on stardom as Garland did. As a toddler, it had been ingrained in Baby Gumm that her net worth was calculated by how well she had put over a number, how completely she had pleased her audiences—how much love she had managed to summon up for an hour or two.

At times, just the thought of getting out of bed (after yet another angst-ridden, sleepless night) and starting the whole process over again was debilitating. She couldn't even face the day. "For Judy, her talent was like breathing, and I think that was also part of her great insecurity," says Garland historian John Fricke. "She'd wake up in the morning and think, 'Oh, God . . . I've got to do it again. I don't know how I'm doing this. How can I do it?' She would psych herself into sheer terror about not being able to be Judy Garland."[6]

Although the presence of the studio's most valuable asset was essential—if not downright crucial—to the success of a production as star-driven as *The Pirate*, Vincente did his best to film around (and around) his immobilized wife. "It was as if she could sense the exact number of days that the studio could shoot around her," Minnelli observed. But this time Judy miscalculated. All totaled, she would miss ninety-nine days of work on *The Pirate*, a picture that required her to be front and center in virtually every frame. "Now, for the first time, she had failed her substitute fathers, the men at the studio," Vincente recalled. "The shooting schedule had to be extended. . . . She had been to psychiatrists in the past. It was again suggested that she turn to them for help."[7]

With Judy appearing more frequently on her analyst's couch than before the cameras, Minnelli turned to Garland's robust costar for both personal and professional support. Remembering Judy's generosity and kindness to him when he made his first film (*For Me and My Gal*) with her, Gene Kelly was willing to do anything to help. He even played sick for a week to give Garland additional time to pull herself together.

The intimate collaboration between Kelly and Minnelli may have been so creatively harmonious because it was a meeting of polar opposites: the effete, mild-mannered director teamed with an athletic, hyper-masculine daredevil. Oftentimes their creative thinking went in completely different directions, and yet a combination of their ideas could produce stunning results. During Garland's extended absence, Kelly's role in the film may have been beefed up so that the company would have something to shoot. When Judy did return, she thought she noticed some significant changes. Didn't it seem like Minnelli's camera set-ups favored her costar? What's more, Gene's lighting was better, his costumes were sexier, and his close-ups far outnumbered her own. It wasn't long before Judy accused Vincente of having an affair with Gene.

"Judy, in her paranoia, became jealous of the time Gene and I were spending together," Minnelli would politely put it years later. As Garland biographer Christopher Finch noted, "Some hint of Judy's mental state at the time can be found in the fact that she became irrationally jealous . . . going so far as to interrupt one work session with a violent scene, accusing [Minnelli and Kelly] of using the picture to advance themselves at her expense."[8]

In his autobiography, Minnelli cautiously recounts this whole episode, only obliquely referring to Judy's "damning accusation." Nearly thirty years after the fact, Vincente diplomatically defended his relationship with Kelly by explaining that it was all strictly business: "We'd been so concerned with getting the choreography right, that we excluded [Garland] from our discussions. I felt it wasn't necessary for Judy to have to deal with such problems, but she felt neglected."[9] Although Minnelli is careful to never name the specific accusation that his wife leveled at him, one didn't have to be Hedda or Louella to guess that in Judy's eyes, Vincente had been doing entirely too much *choreographing*.

In the midst of all this behind-the-scenes intrigue, Minnelli received word that his father had died in Florida at the age of eighty-four. Vincente arranged a brief leave and attended the funeral in St. Petersburg alone. Upon his return to MGM, production of *The Pirate* (already countless days over schedule) resumed with the mounting of the most elaborate sequences in the picture.

Cole Porter had written a cryptic yet haunting dirge entitled "Voodoo" that included nonsensical lyrics such as *"Voodoo, whisper low from above . . .*

Voodoo, what's this mystery called love?" Although one of the weakest links in a score that was hardly Porter's best work to begin with, "Voodoo" was called into service as the film's musical centerpiece, forming the basis for the inevitable Minnelli excursion into the surreal. After being hypnotized by Kelly, Garland's demure Manuela sheds her inhibitions and suddenly reveals all of the repressed longings and erotic passions buried in the depths of her subconscious. Or, as John Fricke puts it: "Kelly sees Judy not only lasciviously but as if he were Sid Luft in training. You know, with a kind of hungry look that says *'This is somebody who can make me a lot of money.'*"[10]

There was no end of problems with "Voodoo." To begin with, Kay Thompson's eerie, atonal arrangement of the song was genuinely unnerving. And the choreography by Gene Kelly and Robert Alton really pushed the envelope for an MGM musical. "We were doing a little bit of over-groping," Gene Kelly remembered. "It was a sensual and sensuous sequence—both words are applicable."[11] The number was so hot, in fact, that only a god-fearing, flag-waving, mother-loving studio mogul could put out the fire. As John Fricke notes:

> Halfway through the filming of the "Voodoo" number, Ida Koverman breaks into a board of directors meeting and drags Louis B. Mayer out and says, "You've got to see the rushes of the number that Garland and Kelly did yesterday." Louis B. Mayer took one look and said, "Burn the negative! If that gets on any screen we'll be raided by the police!" After Mayer called Gene on the carpet, they toned down the staging for "Voodoo" and the number was still in the film when it went to preview.[12]

When it came time to shoot the sanitized version of "Voodoo," Vincente encountered another problem. Garland appeared on the set overmedicated, wild-eyed, and extremely agitated. After getting a look at a small fire that was being prepared for the number, Judy screamed, "Somebody help me! They're going to burn me to death!" Approaching the assembled extras, she began asking each one, "Do you have some Benzedrine?" Dissolving into hysterical sobs, Garland was carried off the set as the cast and crew looked on in stunned disbelief. When the number was reattempted several days later, Judy was once again in full command.[13]

After *The Pirate* was previewed in October and November 1947, Minnelli bowed to studio pressure to shorten the film to MGM's preferred running time of one hour and forty-two minutes. There was also a concerted effort to recut the picture with an eye toward making it more palatable to mainstream audiences. During this editorial overhaul, "Voodoo" was deleted, as

Judy, Gene Kelly, and
Minnelli during the
tumultuous production of
The Pirate, 1947.
PHOTO COURTESY
OF PHOTOFEST

was a portion of Kelly's stirring "Pirate Ballet." Retakes were ordered, and
these were completed in November and December. Garland's "Mack the
Black" was restaged and presented in a more up-tempo rendition. The num
ber became one of the most scintillating moments in the finished film.

With all that occurred on Vincente's watch during the tortured production
of *The Pirate*, it's a wonder that the film that emerged is as consistently
watchable as it is. "One of the most delightful musicals to hit the screen in
a month of Sundays," *Newsweek* decreed. Considering everything that happened during the epic shoot, it's not surprising that *The Pirate* is both boldly
brilliant and wildly uneven: Minnelli's musical seems to be in the throes of
an identity crisis as it unreels.

"You can't get around how problematic *The Pirate* is," says film scholar
Richard Barrios:

Part of it is the way they kept tinkering with it. I remember the first time I
saw the movie, I just thought "There's something incomplete about this. . . ."
And the truth of it is, it's not incomplete. It's been overly completed. They
went over and over it so many times that they probably cut out whatever vitality

it would have had. I don't think it would have ever been totally coherent, but it would have more snap than it has now. . . . But you can still sense so much of Minnelli's personality in that movie. With all of the tropical stuff, it's almost like *Yolanda* was sort of a tryout, in a way, for *The Pirate*. He probably envisioned that he would be refining it and perfecting it, but there were just too many things that were beyond his control.[14]

Minnelli was characteristically diplomatic when reflecting on the film for *Cahiers du Cinéma*: "I was very pleased with the way the film turned out. Judy gave one of her best performances and the Cole Porter songs were excellent. Unfortunately, the merchandising on the film was bad and it failed to go over when it was released."[15] Gene Kelly was far more candid:

Vincente and I honestly believed we were being so dazzlingly great and clever that everybody would fall at our feet and swoon away in delight and ecstasy as they kissed each of our toes in appreciation for this wonderful new musical that we had given them. Boy, were we wrong! About five and a half people seemed to get the gist of what we had set out to do. . . . Whatever I did just looked like fake [John] Barrymore and phony [Douglas] Fairbanks. . . . The sophisticates grasped it, but the film died in the hinterlands. It was done tongue in cheek and I should have realized that never really works.[16]

It's a tribute both to Minnelli's dedication and to Garland's showmanship that her performance bears little evidence of her tormented condition throughout the making of the film. Occasionally, a tense, edgy Judy seeps through Manuela's wide-eyed innocence, but this is offset by Garland's flawless comedic timing in other scenes, which revealed that she was a gifted comedienne capable of handling the most urbane material. Teamed with Kelly for the spirited "Be a Clown" finale, Judy is joyously carefree on screen. The final images of her in *The Pirate* could make anyone forget that this was a woman with very real problems.

Vincente, of course, was all too aware of the extent of Garland's illness. For all his gentlemanly diplomacy, understanding, and support, he may have been at least partially responsible for Judy's crisis. As Hollywood legend had it, arriving home after an exhausting day at the studio, Garland was shocked to discover Minnelli in their bed and in a compromising position with another man, usually described in retellings as "a domestic." A distraught Judy locked herself in the bathroom and reportedly began slicing at her wrists with a sharp object. Minnelli rushed to Judy's aid, and the unidentified domestic presumably fled. If Garland had wondered if there was any truth to the rumors about her husband, this episode could have left no doubts in her mind.

Not long after the incident, Vincente learned that his wife's new psychiatrist had advised Arthur Freed that Minnelli should be removed from the forthcoming production of Irving Berlin's *Easter Parade*—a highly anticipated project that was originally to have reunited Garland, Kelly, and Minnelli. However, it was suggested that Garland harbored "a deep-seated resentment" of authority figures. Being directed by Minnelli during the day and then returning home with him at night would simply be too much for her. According to Minnelli, the disappointing news was relayed to him by Arthur Freed. Garland never said a word.

Before production began on *Easter Parade* (which would be helmed by Chuck Walters), Judy checked into a psychiatric clinic in Las Campanas favored by many in the Beverly Hills community. It was left to Vincente to explain to two-year-old Liza that "Mama went away for awhile. . . . But she'll be back very soon."[17] For Garland, withdrawal from her pharmaceutical enslavement was a wrenching and often frightening experience, but, true to form, the self-deprecating star would find a way to laugh at her own misfortune.

Judy loved to tell friends the story of her arrival at the sanitarium: "It was very dark that night. . . . These two burly attendants met us at the car and walked me across the grounds. Suddenly, I tripped. They picked me up. I tried to walk but I kept stumbling. When I woke up the next day, I looked out the window. I noticed this nice, green lawn. Then I saw why I kept falling. . . . I'd been tripping over the croquet wickets."

After all of the turbulence and emotional upheaval that Minnelli had weathered, both during and following production of *The Pirate*, there was suddenly a lull. While Judy was whisked from one project to the next, Vincente found himself idle. Unaccustomed to sitting still, he grabbed at whatever assignments were available. "I seem to have directed every screen test filmed at Metro during 1948," he recalled. Just when he thought he'd spend the rest of his career testing every "next Norma Shearer" who wandered onto the lot, the phone rang. Was he interested in bringing a certain literary masterpiece to the screen? "God, yes! When can we start?"

14

"I Am
Madame Bovary"

"I THINK THIS PICTURE is going to be great, and you are going to be great for it," Dore Schary, MGM's new vice president in charge of production, told Minnelli. The picture he was referring to was *Madame Bovary*. And Schary was right. Minnelli was, without question, the perfect man for the job. He'd be helming an adaptation of Gustave Flaubert's immortal novel, which had created quite a stir when it was published in 1857. Public officials had branded the novel obscene and it would be called the "monstrous creation of a degenerate imagination." The story concerned Emma Bovary, the unfulfilled wife of a provincial doctor. Emma yearns for a more glamorous existence and has an insatiable appetite for romantic passion and a life of luxury. As a result, she engages in adulterous affairs, has dealings with an unscrupulous moneylender, and finally commits suicide. Flaubert's novel was widely considered a masterpiece; by the 1940s, *Madame Bovary* had already been filmed twice before, though not successfully in either case.

Many believed Jean Renoir's 1934 French version of the story had been damaged by the miscasting of Valentine Tessier in the title role. With this in mind, Minnelli and producer Pandro Berman carefully considered the actresses under contract to MGM at that time. They hit upon the "audacious" idea of casting the studio's sultriest sweater girl, Lana Turner, as the heroine who had been called "a disgrace to France and an insult to womanhood." While the studio immediately saw dollar signs, Joseph L. Breen's censorship office saw things differently. A Breen office administrator cautioned that the coupling of the screen's most scintillating sexpot with an allegedly obscene novel was too erotically potent for conservative, postwar America. "You could make it easier to stay within the code if you used an actress with more dignified appeal, like Greer Garson or Jennifer Jones," he informed Berman and Minnelli.[1] Metro executive Ben Thau initiated the negotiation process to borrow the Oscar-winning Jones from her very proprietary husband, producer David O. Selznick.

In terms of the various screen adaptations of Flaubert's story, Robert Ardrey's treatment for MGM's version was surprisingly sympathetic to its doomed heroine, and much of this can be directly attributed to Minnelli: "*Madame Bovary* has always been one of my favorite novels. . . . I developed an attitude about the character that I wanted to convey."[2] In Vincente's reading of the novel, Emma is not simply greedy or sexually rapacious but desperately attempting to manifest the dream image of herself that she's harbored since her youth.

"I am Madame Bovary," Gustave Flaubert reportedly said of himself in later years, but such a revealing admission might have come directly from Metro's house director. In fact, *Madame Bovary* would emerge as one of Minnelli's most personally revealing films. In the early scenes, in which Emma Rouault is glimpsed in her farmhouse bedroom, Vincente's camera lingers over the illustrations torn from the pages of *Les Modes* decorating the walls. These are "images of beauty that never existed," images that "taught a lonely girl to live within herself." This is the first clue that Minnelli, an inveterate collector of beautiful images, has aligned himself with his main character; beneath the sudsy surface of a Jennifer Jones melodrama, there lies a poignant autobiography in code.

"My point of view is that she wanted everything to be as beautiful as possible, yet everything that touched her was ugliness. But she never lost her desire to have beauty around her," Vincente would say of his discontented protagonist.[3] According to film scholar Drew Casper, the director could have been talking about himself:

It's very self-reflexive, his work—in that he was a man for whom the outside world was always not to his liking. He always wanted to thrust his own inner world out there. And there was a good deal of oppression in the outer world. . . . The projects the studio wanted him to make, his own homosexuality and having to appear straight, the challenges with Garland . . . all of this kind of stuff. What Minnelli did was he went inside himself to create his own world . . . the way the world should be. That was what movies represented to him—a way to present his own vision. The film itself was this other reality that he had created and it was an escape from his own reality.[4]

Jennifer Jones and Vincente welcome three-year-old Liza Minnelli to the set of *Madame Bovary*. The title role was originally slated for bombshell Lana Turner but the censorship office warned that the combination of the screen's most scintillating sexpot and an allegedly obscene novel was too erotically potent. Jones was cast instead.
PHOTO COURTESY
OF PHOTOFEST

Or, as Flaubert wrote of Emma Bovary:

As for the rest of the world, it was nothing, it was nowhere, it scarcely seemed to exist. Indeed, the nearer things were, the more her thoughts turned away from them. Everything in her immediate surroundings, the boring countryside, the imbecile petits bourgeois, the general mediocrity of life, seemed to be a kind of anomaly, a unique accident that had befallen her alone, while beyond, as far as the eye could see, there unfurled the immense kingdom of pleasure and passion.[5]

Just as Emma is forced to hide her financial dealings with the unscrupulous moneylender Lheureux (the magnificent Frank Allenby), she must also keep secret her pursuit of illicit passion. For some observers, direct parallels can be drawn between the scandalous Emma and a director constantly whispered about and branded as sexually suspect. "Look at what society felt about her and Minnelli didn't care because she managed to realize her inner self," says Drew Casper. "The fact that she wants to escape that humdrum life that she was living with the kid and the doctor. . . . In the end, Minnelli puts it in this framework, which exonerates Flaubert for writing this story. What Minnelli is saying is that none of what she's done is immoral."[6]

It's not surprising that the most memorable moment in Minnelli's third melodrama is a musical one. "The waltz in *Madame Bovary* is terribly important because that's the biggest scene in the book," Vincente told interviewer Richard Schickel. "The waltz itself is her one moment of gratification. Things are the way she expects them to be." In staging this elaborate sequence, Minnelli created one of his most sublime, transcendent set pieces. Working closely with composer Miklos Rozsa and choreographer Jack Donohue, he designed the waltz so that it matched Flaubert's vivid description in the novel: "Everyone was waltzing. Everything was turning around them . . . the lamps, the furniture, the paneling, the parquet floor, like a disc on a spindle."[7]

The mood achieved is so deliriously giddy and exhilarating that it's obvious that Madame Bovary isn't the only one enjoying a transportive experience. One can feel Minnelli's rapture whenever a scene he was directing allowed him an opportunity to unleash some deeply held belief or an emotion he may have been too accustomed to keeping in check. In *Madame Bovary*, it is the sequence Minnelli dubbed "the neurotic waltz" that radiates with that peculiar power, signifying that the director was not only fully engaged with the scene but living it right along with the characters.

While the waltz brings out the best in both Minnelli and star Jennifer Jones, they are aided immeasurably by Miklos Rozsa's masterful score. "Minnelli was a sensitive artist and director and he made a masterpiece of *Madame Bovary*," the Hungarian-born composer recalled:

> Flaubert describes the waltz in detail and Vincente wanted to recreate it accordingly. . . . I was able to write the music to match and in a spirit of dedication, knowing that in this instance the camera would be following my music, not my music following the camera. Minnelli was so excited by the waltz that he asked his wife, Judy Garland, to come over to hear it. There is a sudden modulation in the piece where the big tune lurches into an unexpected key, and at that moment, Miss Garland gasped in thrilled amazement and goose pimples appeared on her arms. Always the actress![8]

Rozsa's waltz is so electrifying that it was later recycled for *The Seventh Sin*, but it was never used more effectively than it was in *Bovary*.

Thankfully, Minnelli and Pandro Berman did not succeed in casting Lana Turner in the lead, as Jennifer Jones is unusually well suited to the title role. Restless and a bit neurotic off screen, Jones had left her husband, actor

Robert Walker, for producer David O. Selznick. The detail-obsessed Selznick seemed almost single-mindedly determined to turn Jones into a star of the highest magnitude. It was exactly the kind of Faustian exchange that Flaubert would have appreciated. *The Song of Bernadette* may have netted Jones the Oscar as Best Actress, but her Madame Bovary is a much better fit: the half-mad gleam in her eye during the waltz; her look of supreme disgust as the town clock strikes "the death of another hour;" her agonized expression as her lover's carriage rides off without her. *Time* said: "Miss Jones, in her best picture to date, manipulates Emma's moods and caprices with sensitive dexterity. Hardly ever out of sight of the cameras, she gives a performance that is hardly ever out of focus, a feat that even the finicky Flaubert could admire."[9]

And what would the author of *Madame Bovary* have thought of Minnelli's sympathetic take on his heroine? "You could argue that the film is not really Flaubert," says historian John Fitzpatrick. "Though it's a good film on its own terms. In many ways, Minnelli has this very florid and romantic sensibility, whereas Flaubert is very often ironic and distant. The tone of the film is really quite different from Flaubert's tone. It's not that Minnelli gets it wrong, it's just that it all came out rather differently."[10]

Even so, most of the critics would praise Vincente's direction. As the *New York Times* noted in a review: "The high point of his achievement, indeed, is a ballroom scene which spins in a whirl of rapture and crashes in a shatter of shame. In this one sequence, the director has fully visualized his theme."[11]

***

IN MAY 1949, Judy checked into Peter Brent Brigham Hospital in Boston, where she would undergo treatment for her dependency on prescription medication. She had just been suspended by the studio after failing to make it through her latest picture, *Annie Get Your Gun*. Although Arthur Freed had purchased the rights to Irving Berlin's Broadway smash with Garland in mind, his would-be Annie Oakley was in no condition to headline another mammoth musical. As Minnelli recalled, Judy was down to a dangerously thin 90 pounds. As she struggled to make it through yet another production that was totally dependent on her for its success, she appeared wild-eyed and manic one day, practically sleep walking the next. Her addiction, coupled with exhaustion from years of overwork, had managed to immobilize the ordinarily unstoppable Judy Garland.

The weeks Judy spent at the hospital offered her an opportunity to completely decompress. This was the first time she'd had to unwind since she and Vincente had honeymooned in New York four years earlier. While at

Peter Brent, Judy would endure the agonizing nightmare of withdrawal, and by June she could proudly report to the press that she was "learning to sleep all over again." Within a few weeks, Judy's doctors had guided her back to a regular sleeping and eating routine, but it was her visits to a neighboring children's hospital that proved to have the most therapeutic effects. "If I was cured at Peter Brent Brigham, it was only because of those children," Judy would later say. "They were so brave, so darling."[12]

Once her appetite and health were restored, Judy traveled to New York, where she was reunited with three-year-old Liza, who was accompanied by a nurse. Vincente had remained in California, though he called regularly. He was thrilled to hear that Judy was on the mend but concerned that his marriage—which had been rocked by recent events—would not recover so neatly.

"A Few Words
About Weddings . . ."

"IT'S A COMEDY-DRAMA about a man whose heart breaks because he loves his daughter and is about to lose her. It's not a joke. The laughs come out of sadness and reality. We could never do it with Jack." So said producer Pandro Berman as he attempted to dissuade Dore Schary from casting comedian Jack Benny in *Father of the Bride*.

Schary, who would soon succeed Louis B. Mayer as MGM's production chief, had offhandedly promised Benny the lead in MGM's screen version of Edward Streeter's bestseller. The comic novel concerned the father of a bride-to-be. Stanley T. Banks is overwhelmed by the seemingly endless preparations for his daughter's wedding as well as his own feelings as he realizes he's losing his beloved "kitten" to holy matrimony. As Minnelli and Berman immediately realized, with Benny in the title role, *Father of the Bride* might be an entertaining diversion, but it wouldn't be infused with the warmth and dimension that a legitimate actor could bring to it.

Minnelli shot a screen test of Benny as Stanley Banks out of professional courtesy to "the world's oldest thirty-nine-year-old." "It was a fine test and technically correct," Minnelli pronounced. "It had only one failing. His reading lacked the conviction underneath, that only a highly gifted actor like Spencer Tracy could supply."[1] And who better than Spencer Tracy to play the hapless head of the Banks household? Husband and wife screenwriting team Frances Goodrich and Albert Hackett (who had scripted *The Pirate*) admitted that they had nobody but Tracy in mind when they were working on their adaptation. And yet, the word around the lot was that the actor wasn't interested in the part.

After Minnelli pleaded his case to Katharine Hepburn, a dinner was arranged. Vincente put his cards on the table, telling Tracy, "With you, this picture could be a little classic of a comedy. Without you, it's nothing." As Minnelli later recounted to Richard Schickel, this very personal appeal made all the difference. "Well, [Tracy] blossomed like a rose. . . . He had heard that we were testing people and had other people in mind and he was just one of the boys, and that hurt his ego. . . . He simply wanted to be wanted, and loved the project and agreed to do it. It was as simple as that."[2]

Without question, Tracy was the perfect embodiment of Streeter's aisle-shy patriarch who comes to discover that he's fonder of his first born than he realized. Throughout the relatively stress-free shoot, Minnelli found Tracy to be "an inspiration," and he wasn't the only one who was impressed. Others who worked on the picture recall that Tracy was both accessible and unfailingly professional.

One of them was contract player Carleton Carpenter, who can be glimpsed throughout *Father of the Bride*, first appearing as a "be bop hound" in a delightful montage featuring Elizabeth Taylor's rejected suitors. "All told, I have an elbow or an ear lobe in every other shot in the picture," says Carpenter, who managed to make an impression on the film's legendary star. "I only had one little scene with Spencer Tracy but he was very nice to me," Carpenter recalls. "At one point, he said, 'You're from New York, aren't you, Carp?' And I said, 'Yeah . . .' and Tracy said, 'I could tell. You don't seem like a movie actor. You seem like a stage actor.' And I thought that was very sweet. It just started things off in the right way."[3]

Russ Tamblyn made one of his first film appearances in *Father of the Bride* as Tracy's youngest son. "It was an incredible experience," Tamblyn says of being part of an ensemble that included Tracy, Elizabeth Taylor, Joan Bennett, Billie Burke, and Leo G. Carroll. Though duly impressed with the star power, Tamblyn says he was unaware of the stature of their director. "I was so young, I really didn't know who he was." Though even as a teenager, Tamblyn recognized that there was something different about the man at the helm: "He seemed to pay unusually close attention to details—the way a suit looked on an actor and that sort of thing. What I remember about Vincente Minnelli is that he was very gentle, very quiet, very calm. . . . I guess he'd have to be, being married to Judy Garland." Four years after the release of *Father of the Bride*, Tamblyn would star in *Seven Brides for Seven Brothers*, directed by

Stanley T. Banks (Spencer
Tracy) about to lose daughter
Kay (Elizabeth Taylor) to
holy matrimony in *Father of
the Bride*. Minnelli's movie
made the *New York Times*
Ten Best List for 1950 and it
was in the running for
Best Picture but lost to
All About Eve.
PHOTO COURTESY
OF PHOTOFEST

Stanley Donen, MGM's other important director of musicals. Tamblyn noted
that Metro's preeminent pair seemed to have more than just a studio in common: "Both had an effeminate side that I wondered about, quite frankly."[4]

The film was a turning point for third-billed Elizabeth Taylor, seventeen
at the time and transitioning to more adult roles. If the plots of Taylor's
movies often seemed to mirror her off-screen exploits, *Father of the Bride*
was no exception. On May 6, 1950, just days before the premiere of the
movie, Taylor would marry hotel heir Nicky Hilton in a star-studded ceremony
that seemed executive-produced by MGM's front office. Taylor's screen
mother, Joan Bennett, remembered: "The whole more-stars-than-there-are-
in-the-heavens crowd was out . . . and you'd jolly well better show up, because
the studio sent out invitations, promoting *Father of the Bride*."[5]

Though the first of Taylor's many marriages would fail, the movie was the
kind of gargantuan hit that studio executives sell their mothers for. In its
initial release, *Father of the Bride* earned $4,150,000, making it one of the
top grossers of the year. The picture ranked third on the *New York Times*
"Ten Best Films of the Year" list. And for the first time, a Vincente Minnelli
production was nominated for a Best Picture Academy Award (though it
would lose to the more cynical and sophisticated *All About Eve*). Spencer

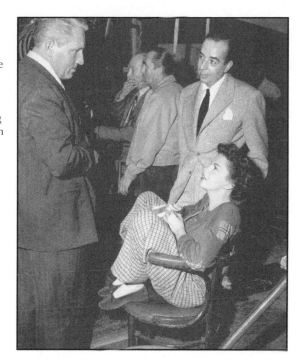

Spencer Tracy and Vincente receive a visit from Judy Garland on the set of *Father of the Bride*. At the time, Garland was shooting *Summer Stock*, her final film for MGM.
PHOTO COURTESY OF PHOTOFEST

Tracy was nominated as Best Actor for a role that he had initially resisted (he lost to José Ferrer's bravura turn in *Cyrano de Bergerac*).

Boxoffice bestowed its "July Blue Ribbon Award" on the film and gushed: "As blithe and breezy as spring itself is this comedy which goes with the season like orange blossoms and tulle." Entitled "Gay Occasion," Otis L. Guernsey Jr.'s review summed it up nicely: "The occasion is well ordered, the people charming, the lapses not serious and the end achieved before the conviviality is exhausted."[6]

Those who regard MGM as a factory that cranked out motion pictures the same way that General Motors made Frigidaires would scoff at the notion that a domestic comedy like *Father of the Bride* could have been attempting to "say" anything. But for Minnelliphiles, who believe his work is layered so that it can be appreciated on many different levels, Spencer Tracy's separation anxiety goes deeper than "Who giveth this woman?"

From the moment Kay Banks announces her engagement, her hapless father is simultaneously pulled along and shut out of the preparations for her impending nuptials. Stanley Banks is lost—and not only in terms of his encounters with caterers and prospective in-laws: He is suddenly displaced within his own family.

As the father of the bride, Stanley is asked to do his bit in carrying off many time-honored traditions, even though the role he's been thrust into seems alien and uncomfortable to him. While his wife and daughter are actively engaged in planning the wedding, Stanley is a detached observer, playing a role that is as ill-fitting as his twenty-year-old cutaway. Stanley even has a nightmare (complete with surrealist imagery straight out of German Expressionism) in which he single-handedly destroys his daughter's wedding. He's late, doesn't know his lines, and isn't as well rehearsed as the rest of the wedding party. In Streeter's novel, Banks is jeered by his friends and relatives: "How could a man like that have such a beautiful daughter? They say she isn't his. It's a joke. He's a joke." There in the midst of a wedding ceremony—one of society's sacred rituals—Stanley T. Banks is revealed as a fraud.

"I think there's probably a Minnelli autobiography in every one of his films," says film scholar Beth Genne:

> Every movie probably contains incidents and bits and pieces from his life but I think in *Father of the Bride*—that was a life he really didn't know at all. You can say that there's a certain kind of yearning for that. It's like what MGM did with [the] Andy Hardy [series]—Wouldn't it be nice to be part of a family where things went well every single minute? It's really interesting what he does in *Father of the Bride*. First, he suckers you into that comfortable little world. He wants to make you feel good. He also wants you to laugh at human foibles. Then he springs that nightmare on you. And it's the nightmare that everybody has—of making a fool of themselves in public. Through the style, he tells you about the real horror of the situation. I love that sequence because it's so human. And that's what comes through in that film and in all of his films—his empathy. What Minnelli had was an artist's empathy. I think that's what the greatest artists always have—an empathy for people.[7]

***

THE MOST ELABORATE Hollywood production that Vincente Minnelli and Judy Garland collaborated on was not *Meet Me in St. Louis* or *The Pirate* but their own marriage. Surely the screen's brightest star and MGM's most gifted director would be able to create a life together that was as spectacular and stunning as anything they had produced on the screen.

Their union may have been completely improbable, but as any screenwriter worth his salt knew, an unlikely love affair sold more tickets than Buck Rogers, Deanna Durbin, and Charlie Chan combined. Judy may have hoped that, as Vincente had helped her to blossom on film, he would aid her off-

Vincente and Judy in the
late 1940s.
PHOTO COURTESY
OF PHOTOFEST

the-lot transformation as well. Courtesy of "the Minnelli Touch," Mayer's "hunchback" would disappear and a stylish and sophisticated woman of the world would emerge. And with a wedding ring on his finger and a precocious daughter who regularly turned up on his sets, perhaps Vincente was convinced that he would at last silence all the whispers about him. The marriage had been designed to save both of them, but in the end, it proved to be the one MGM production that was missing the studio's essential component: a happy ending.

"Looking back on it, I think that marriage was just too much for both of them," says MGM publicist Esme Chandlee:

Of course, Minnelli was not the strongest figure in the world. Judy was tempestuous. He wasn't. Though in some ways, you had two personalities that were so completely alike because they were both terribly nervous people. You could always sense the nervousness about Minnelli when you were talking to him. I think maybe Minnelli was "both ways" and that really tolled on him. It was always kind of odd that he got married and had a child to begin with. And with all that was going on with Judy, I don't think that marriage was the happiest time of his life, either. Though I never heard one of them ever say a bad word about the other. Ever. I think they respected one another—both professionally and as people—but eventually, they realized that being married to each other just didn't work.[8]

Given his introverted nature and a need to frequently escape into his own inner world, Minnelli found himself overwhelmed by the torrent of emotion and expectation that his wife sent flowing in his direction every day. Despite Judy's incomparable talents and widespread acclaim, Minnelli would recall that "her desire for constant approval was pathological."[9] How could Vincente ever provide all of the validation and reassurance Judy required? At times, it seemed as though Minnelli was tasked with undoing the years of psychological and emotional damage that had been done to Garland—by her mother, Mayer, the studio, and the vagaries of a life lived in the glare of the spotlight. No matter how much tenderness, support, and understanding Vincente could have offered, it would never be enough.

Eventually, both husband and wife were harboring deep-seated resentments. To Minnelli, the fact that Garland lied to her psychiatrists (according to Vincente, she had seen as many as sixteen) was unforgivable. "Our relationship was drastically damaged," he recalled.[10] To Judy, the fact that Vincente seemed to side with the studio during her battles with Metro's front office offered damning evidence that Minnelli wasn't really married to her but to his own career.

16

The Time
in His Mind

IT STARTED WITH A TITLE. "Ira, I've always wanted to make a picture about Paris," Arthur Freed said to Ira Gershwin one night in November 1949 after a pool game. "How about selling me the title *An American in Paris*?" Ira agreed, but only if the picture attached to the title contained exclusively Gershwin music. "I wouldn't use anything else, that's the object," was Freed's response.[1] At that point, the producer wasn't certain whether his next musical would star Fred Astaire or Gene Kelly, but one thing was certain—with wall-to-wall Gershwin music, this latest Freed Unit endeavor was virtually a guaranteed success even if Bela Lugosi ended up belting "I've Got Rhythm."

In terms of the score, the Gershwin songbook offered an embarrassment of riches. "During early meetings on the project with Arthur, Vincente, Gene and Alan [Jay Lerner] around the piano at my house, somewhere between 125 and 150 songs were played and studied as possibilities," Ira Gershwin remembered.[2] Among those tunes that would make the final cut were such standards as "'S Wonderful," "Love Is Here to Stay," and the rollicking "By Strauss," which Vincente had introduced in *The Show Is On*.

The story, however, didn't come as easily. Ira Gershwin was reportedly disappointed with *Rhapsody in Blue*, the highly fictionalized, song-studded biopic of 1945 featuring Robert Alda as an ersatz George Gershwin. Taking a lesson from this well-intentioned Warner Brothers extravaganza, Freed decided that *An American in Paris* should not attempt another version of the George Gershwin saga set to the composer's own work. An original story that somehow referred to the title was required.

Both Freed and Kelly would later claim credit for discovering a *Life* magazine article about artists on the G.I. Bill of Rights who stayed on in Paris to paint after the war. The expatriate concept also melded nicely with the fact that in the 1920s, George Gershwin had studied art in Paris—his years there inspiring his immortal tone poem *An American in Paris*, which he described as "a rhapsodic ballet." Gershwin musical plus the art world could only equal Minnelli, and in February 1950, MGM officially announced that Vincente would helm the production, which would star Gene Kelly, whose presence would be felt in practically every facet of the film's development.

"I think it was in the late spring of 1949 when Arthur Freed first mentioned *An American in Paris* to me," Alan Jay Lerner recalled. "It must have been some time in November when I finally got some notion of what I was going to do. And that was *a kept man falls in love with a kept woman*. That was the problem that I started with and tried to develop."[3] Fresh from penning Metro's effervescent *Royal Wedding*, Lerner was now tasked with creating his second original screenplay. During a Palm Springs retreat, he hammered out the first forty pages of what critics would later describe as a "wafer-thin story," which focused on the romantic entanglements of Kelly's brash American painter Jerry Mulligan.

Residing on the Left Bank, above the quaint Café Hugette, Mulligan spends his days painting, trading quips with neighbor Adam Cook (the "world's oldest child prodigy"), and supplying Parisian moppets with American bubble gum. An ex-G.I. from Perth Amboy, New Jersey, Mulligan is torn between his chic benefactress, the mink-lined Milo Roberts, and pixyish Parisienne Lise Bourvier. Initially, he doesn't realize that Lise is already engaged to his best friend, showman Henri Baurel, who selflessly cared for the orphaned l'enfant throughout the occupation.

With Kelly in place and Gershwin confidant Oscar Levant essentially playing himself in the form of acerbic pianist Adam Cook ("the only Adam in Paris without an Eve"), Minnelli and company next focused on filling the role of the sprightly nineteen-year-old ingenue who immediately captivates Mulligan. Contract players Cyd Charisse, Vera-Ellen, and Marge Champion were all briefly considered, but Freed was adamant that an actual Parisian mademoiselle be cast as the enchanting gamine who is "not really beautiful and yet has great beauty." After viewing tests of French music-hall headliner Odile Versois and a teenager from the Ballets des Champs-Elyssées who had been featured in Roland Pettit's *Oedipus and the Sphinx*, it was decided that the younger candidate possessed the freshness and spontaneity that the part demanded. She was eighteen years old, and her name was Leslie Caron.

"I never thought this was serious," Caron recalled of the studio's interest in casting her as the thirty-eight-year-old Kelly's love interest. "I thought, 'Oh, well, I won't say no to doing a test if they really want me to . . .' and then I promptly forgot it. I didn't see why I needed to go to Hollywood." In fact, Caron had never even seen Kelly, her hypothetical leading man, on the silver screen.

Caron was not only a demure newcomer struggling with English as a second language but also a self-described "odd bird." And one suddenly transplanted to a place as disorienting as Hollywood. Even so, the young actress received virtually no guidance from her tongue-tied director. "Vincente is not somebody who talks to actors very easily," Caron observed. "In fact, I can't remember him giving me more than one piece of direction in three films that we made together. . . . He stutters and puckers his lips until you try exactly what he wants, but he's not going to tell you, he's incapable of it." According to Caron, Vincente's only intelligible bit of direction to her throughout the entire filming of *An American in Paris* was, "Just be yourself, darling."[4]

Yves Montand was initially considered for the role of the dapper cabaret star Henri Baurel, but the actor was disqualified because of what technical adviser Alan A. Antik described as Montand's "communistic tendencies." Minnelli and Freed next hoped to persuade sixty-two-year-old Maurice Chevalier to accept the role as Caron's fiancé. Chevalier passed, as his character didn't wind up with the girl at the final fade out. Besides, the French crooner was "persona non-grata," as there had been reports that he had performed for Nazi sympathizers during World War II. Ultimately, the more age-appropriate Georges Guetary won the role and one of the film's showstoppers, "I'll Build a Stairway to Paradise."

In casting the pivotal role of Milo Roberts, the competition again boiled down to two contenders: Nina Foch and Celeste Holm, the latter having just snared a Best Supporting Actress Oscar nomination for her role in Joseph L. Mankiewicz's blistering bitchfest *All About Eve*. After hearing Foch read the scene in which Milo tells Mulligan that her family "is in oil— suntan oil," it became obvious that no further testing was necessary. "It was decided that Nina had just the right amount of *savoir-faire*, worldliness, sweetness and bitchiness," Gene Kelly would later observe.[5]

"I'd already been a small-time movie star at Columbia," Nina Foch recalled. "I was under contract and I made one picture after the other." On the way up, the cool, patrician Foch had endured such low-grade schlock as *The Return of the Vampire* and *Cry of the Werewolf*:

Milo Roberts (Nina Foch) hovers over her handsome, multitalented protégé Jerry Mulligan (Gene Kelly) in *An American in Paris*. According to Foch, some of her best work wound up on the cutting room floor.
PHOTO COURTESY OF PHOTOFEST

I hadn't been happy at Columbia. I didn't like the people. I didn't like the movies. I didn't know what the hell I was doing there. Most of the stuff you do, you do because you're in the profession. I mean, all of this crap we talk about movies after we've made them. . . . Usually we're trying to figure out something clever to say to the press that's after you. Half of the time, we've made it up and then by the time we've said it twenty-seven times, we start to believe it. That's not true about *An American in Paris*. That was an honor to be in. The Arthur Freed Unit, you know. This was a very classy thing. At the time, I knew I was in something special but I had no clue as to how special.[6]

Musical supervisor Saul Chaplin, on the other hand, was all too aware of how unique Production #1507 was. "All I can say is that I never worked on any score that I had more respect for, and that I did so carefully," said Chaplin, who combed through countless compositions in the Gershwin catalog, not only selecting numbers for musical sequences but also themes for the film's underscoring. All the while, Chaplin was conscious of the specter of George Gershwin hovering over the project, "I must have chosen 50 songs that absolutely *had* to be in the picture. . . . I was careful and I was worried. I was careful because I wanted to make sure it came out to the best of my ability, to see if I could match the master. And worried that I might be doing something wrong."[7]

Chaplin said that he "considered George Gershwin 'God,'" a reverence shared by Minnelli, Levant, and virtually everyone connected with the film. It almost went without saying that as a cinematic tribute, the climactic *American in Paris* ballet would have to be extraordinary. There had been ambitious, even groundbreaking ballets featured in Metro musicals before—Astaire's surrealist spin in *Yolanda and the Thief*, Kelly's memorable "Slaughter on Tenth Avenue" in *Words and Music*—but in retrospect, those efforts would seem like elaborate dress rehearsals for what would ultimately be proclaimed "MGM's masterpiece."

"We had no definite plan for the ballet all the while we were shooting the book," Minnelli told author Donald Knox:

> We knew in a vague way that it had to incorporate parts of Paris that artists had painted, but we had no time to figure this out until Nina Foch came down with chicken pox. There was nothing left to shoot whatsoever, so Irene Sharaff, who I had hired to design the costumes, and Gene Kelly and I locked ourselves in my office for hours and hours and hours on end. We worked out the entire ballet during those days. It was the luckiest chicken pox I've ever known.[8]

At first, an all-too-literal Parisian ballet was proposed. Kelly would romp through the City of Light's most enchanting boulevards in a variation on his on-location ramble through Manhattan in *On the Town*. To Freed, this seemed redundant. And to Minnelli and his colleagues, it was clear that something more *psychological* was in order—which is what George Gershwin appeared to have in mind to begin with: "The individual listener can read into the music such as his imagination pictures for him," Gershwin said of his orchestral tone poem, which had debuted at Carnegie Hall in 1928.[9] For Minnelli, reading into the music resulted in plenty of pictures—all of them by the Impressionists. Cued by the varying moods of the music, each section of the ballet would feature settings, costumes, and styles of dance inspired by masterworks by Henri Rousseau, Raoul Dufy, and Vincent van Gogh.

Having settled on the visual look of the ballet, Minnelli and company next turned to the matter of theme. "Gene thought you had to have a story," Vincente remembered. "I said, 'You can't have a story because if it's a new story, that's bewildering. . . . I said, 'It has to be something to do with *emotions*, the time in his mind, the way he feels having just lost his girl, and a whole thing about Paris.' Everything had to become a jumble in his mind, a kind of delirium because Leslie's leaving him hits him so hard."[10]

Once the production team convinced themselves that their idea for an Impressionistic ballet was sound, they had to turn around and sell it to the powers that be. As Gene Kelly recalled, "Dore Schary had now taken over Mayer's job as head of production, so we brought all the sketches to him and gulped and cleared our throats and said, 'You know, we want to do this ballet . . .' and I described it. He finally said, 'Wait a minute. Wait a minute! I don't understand one word that you're all talking about but, you know something, it looks good and I trust you people. . . . Get out of here and go and do it.'"

For the reunited team of Minnelli and Kelly, the division of duties that existed on *The Pirate* continued through *An American in Paris*. For Kelly, as both star and choreographer, the film—and particularly the ballet—provided an opportunity for the kind of virtuosic tour de force that he'd been building toward since his debut in *For Me and My Gal* nearly a decade earlier.

Whereas other directors would brook no interference from *some actor*, Minnelli was smart enough to know when to let a collaborator do what he or she did best for the benefit of the picture. As Alan Jay Lerner expressed it, "Vincente doesn't try to do your creating for you. . . . Vincente knows the direction, but he will let you drive."[11] Relinquishing the reins to Kelly was also a practical necessity, as Minnelli was contractually obligated to direct *Father's Little Dividend*,* the pleasant though pedestrian sequel to *Father of the Bride*, at the same time.

Dividing his attention between a routine vehicle that failed to inspire him and a Gershwin-scored ballet that paid homage to his Impressionist idols was the sort of situation that would reemerge later in Minnelli's career. To some extent, it was also the kind of psychological predicament that Vincente struggled with on a daily basis. Reality, like some colorless, uninspired screenplay, always seemed to be tugging him back from a place he'd much rather be—namely, wandering through his own mind, the ultimate MGM musical.

***

"MY FIRST DAY ON *An American in Paris*, I looked around and I thought, 'Wow! This is a really good group,'" says dancer Marian Horosko, who appeared in the ballet:

----

* Ironically, it was *Father's Little Dividend*—one of Minnelli's least inspired efforts—that won him some long-overdue industry recognition. Minnelli received the Director's Guild of America Award for helming the comedy, which was also named the Best-Written American Comedy of 1951 by the Writers Guild of America.

Gene Kelly and Leslie Caron in the ballet from *An American in Paris*. Minnelli decreed: "It has to be something to do with *emotions*, the time in his mind, the way he feels having just lost his girl, and a whole thing about Paris. . . ."
PHOTO COURTESY OF PHOTOFEST

You could tell that this was not your cute little Hollywood number. . . . I remember Gene Kelly had a sweetness about him that you would just do whatever he wanted. He was your baby brother. He was jazzy and he had a good sense of humor and he sometimes looked concerned but not worried. The constant worrier was Vincente Minnelli. He always had a frown on his face and a twitch around his mouth and you wondered, "Does he hate us? . . . Are we all going to get fired?" Some of his physical tics were off-putting but if you could see through that, you found that he was a very intelligent man and his involvement was thorough. It was not just a director directing. He used fewer words than any director I've ever known except Balanchine. . . . He was always thinking and shaping things in his mind.[12]

As the ballet was taking shape, it was easy to forget that there was another world going on beyond the one that had been carefully manufactured on the set, though every now and then reality would intrude. As Horosko recalls:

Underneath the joy and happiness and the good work, there was this undercurrent of unease with the House Un-American Activities. That whole business with the McCarthy investigations. You know those big gates that they have at

MGM? They would close the gates at lunch time and Louis B. Mayer would come out and say, "If you know anybody who's not loyal to the United States, come to my office. We understand these things and just come and talk to us about it." And I thought, "Oh, boy!" To me, that was pure Nazi stuff. I came back to New York fast enough.[13]

The ballet would include some of the most indelible imagery in the entire Minnelli canon. The long, slow dissolve from the Dufy-inspired Place de la Concorde to the Renoir-styled flower market ("Marché aux Fleurs") at dawn is gracefully synched to Gershwin's music. The shot of Kelly and Caron intertwined on the Greutert fountain as John Alton's *fumata* cascades over them is undoubtedly one of the most unapologetically erotic moments in all of Minnelli. As Kelly and Caron jump up and down on the fountain during the euphoric climax, their exuberance is not only about finding one another but about willing such a beautiful moment into being. For Vincente, the sequence was both a daunting challenge and the realization of many fantasies— suddenly his cherished art-book images were vibrantly alive, as they had been for so many years in his mind.

As the ballet dominated the second half of the picture and extended its running time, a number of deletions were deemed necessary. Although it was Kelly's favorite of his own numbers, "I've Got a Crush on You" was excised from the release print along with two Guetary solos, "Love Walked In" and "But Not for Me." However, the most poignant cutting-room floor casualty belonged to Nina Foch.

"I had a wonderful scene at the end of the movie where I sat with Oscar Levant and I was complaining and crying about losing Gene," Foch recalls. "I think it's one of the best pieces of acting I've ever done. I'm just buzzing, about to be a weepy drunk, half-laughing, and suddenly up comes this truly lonely, lonely little girl whose daddy never loved her." Milo's big moment was to have taken place in the midst of the black and white ball and included a brilliant bit of improvisation when a piece of confetti tumbled into Foch's champagne glass—she retrieved it and knocked it back as though it were a pill. "Everyone who had seen it talked to me about that scene," remembers Foch. "I got a letter from Arthur Freed afterwards saying, 'We're sorry we cut that wonderful scene out. We all loved it, but it made Gene look bad.'"[14]

Though studio insiders were already buzzing about how outstanding the picture was, one of the most important endorsements was phoned in from New York. "I've seen your little picture," Judy told Vincente. "Not bad. Only a masterpiece." And most of the critics would concur. "Brilliant is the word for MGM's *An American in Paris*," raved the *New York Journal American*. "Here's a musical that's out of the very top of the top drawer. . . . Its direction by Vincente Minnelli sets and sustains a sparkling tempo."[15] In *Compass*, Seymour Peck quipped, "Who knows, it may even put Paris on the map."

***

MARCH 20, 1952. OSCAR NIGHT. Vincente's "little picture" had been nominated for eight Academy Awards. Despite the fact that Arthur Freed was producing the 24th annual Academy Awards ceremony, *An American in Paris* seemed very much the dark horse in the Best Picture race as it was up against such dramatic heavyweights as *A Streetcar Named Desire* and *A Place in the Sun*. "There is a strange sort of reasoning in Hollywood that musicals are less worthy of Academy consideration than dramas," Kelly told the press.[16] His point was underlined by the fact that the last musical to snare the top prize had been Metro's *The Great Ziegfeld* in 1936.

For the first time in his career, Minnelli was nominated as Best Director, an honor many in the industry felt had been deserved as far back as *Meet Me in St. Louis*. When the envelopes were opened, *An American in Paris* would not only prevail as Best Picture but collect six other Academy Awards. Arthur Freed would be honored with the prestigious Irving Thalberg Award, and Gene Kelly received an honorary Oscar "in appreciation of his versatility as an actor, singer, director and dancer, and specifically for his brilliant achievements in the art of choreography on film." The film's director, however, would go home empty-handed. "How could anyone vote for [*An American in Paris*] as Best Picture of the Year and not recognize Vincente's obvious contribution?"[17] Saul Chaplin would ask, echoing the feelings of many who had observed how tirelessly Minnelli had worked.

Years later, Vincente seemed to even the score in his autobiography. Despite the fact that Lerner was solely responsible for the script, the Gershwins had furnished the score, and Kelly and his assistants handled the choreography, Minnelli assigned credit where he thought it was due: "Though I don't minimize anyone's contributions," he wrote, "one man was responsible for bringing it all together. That man was me."[18]

***

"I GREW UP WHERE EVERYBODY'S PARENTS were movie stars," Liza Minnelli once said of her Beverly Hills upbringing—though even in the land of Lanas and Hedys, Liza's household was unique. For "Mama" was Judy Garland, "Daddy" was Vincente Minnelli, and everything they did kept Leo the Lion

Party Girl: "The Oscar for Best Birthday Given by a Parent went to Vincente Minnelli for Liza's sixth," said actress Candice Bergen, a childhood friend of little Liza May. Two years earlier, for Liza's fourth, Judy and Vincente gave the birthday girl a puppy.
PHOTO COURTESY OF PHOTOFEST

roaring. After school, most kids rushed home for milk and cookies. Not so for Liza Minnelli, who raced over to her own personal playground, which the rest of the world knew as Metro-Goldwyn-Mayer. It was here that she rode the boom with her father, mesmerized by the sight of Gene Kelly being pursued by a bevy of Sharaff-styled furies as Gershwin pored over the play-back machine. And even after Daddy called "Cut!" the magic didn't end. For at home, Vincente was aiding and abetting the creation of a mini movie star.

As Liza remembers it: "I would stand there and he would create these costumes on me, just with safety pins and crepe paper. And I could watch and see myself becoming this Spanish dancer. And he would watch me dance for hours. He was just wonderful because he fed my imagination."[19] And then some. If Mama attempted to play disciplinarian, Daddy encouraged Liza's incredible flights of fancy. Well versed in the art of wish fulfillment, Vincente understood the need to dream. And nobody dreamed bigger. In Hollywood, over-the-top occasions were standard, but Liza May's star-studded

birthday parties were so extravagantly lavish that they could have been produced by Arthur Freed.

"Most seemed to agree that the Oscar for Best Birthday Given by a Parent
went to Vincente Minnelli for Liza's sixth given at Ira Gershwin's house in
Beverly Hills," remembered actress Candice Bergen, who, along with Mia
Farrow, was one of Liza May's childhood playmates. According to Bergen,
Vincente made sure that Hollywood's crowned princess was dressed appropriately for the part: "I remember always asking to go to Liza's to play dress
up because in her closet hung little girl's dreams. Vincente Minnelli had
seen to that. In her dress-up closet glowed tiny satin ball gowns embroidered
with seed pearls, wispy white tutus. . . . You could choose between Vivien
Leigh's riding habit from *Gone with the Wind* or Leslie Caron's ballerina costume from *An American in Paris*."[20]

It's no wonder that Liza considered Vincente her own personal Wizard of
Oz. He was the master magician who could transform her into a can-can
dancer or a pint-sized Cyd Charisse. While others in the movie colony turned
their children over to overburdened nannies so that someone else could do
the entertaining, Vincente seemed to revel in the fantasy as much as his
daughter did.

Although Liza and her chums were thoroughly enchanted with such exquisite make-believe, actress Nina Foch thought Minnelli had gone too far:

> One thing he did that I didn't like was when he asked Irene Sharaff to make
> Liza little copies of all of Gertrude Lawrence's costumes from *The King and
> I*. And she did. It was this incredible, unbelievable set of costumes. They
> even came in this little Siamese trunk. I chastised him for that. I said, "Jesus,
> Vincente, you shouldn't be giving this little girl all of this stuff. She'll grow
> up thinking the entire world works this way. It's entirely too much. You'll
> have a child who doesn't have a proper set of values." It's not that they weren't
> simply incredible, beautiful things. They were. . . . It was the thought of giv-
> ing this small child a completely distorted view of life. But I guess you still
> have to hand it to him in a way. . . . He may have spoiled her, but he did it
> to *perfection*.[21]

***

TOWARD THE END OF JUDY GARLAND'S long and often stormy association with
MGM, the Hollywood trade papers seemed to be constantly reporting that
the increasingly fragile star was being replaced in one elaborate production
after another: *The Barkeleys of Broadway* (Ginger Rogers would reteam with

Fred Astaire instead of Judy), *Annie Get Your Gun* (Betty Hutton took over the title role after the studio suspended Garland), and *Royal Wedding* (Judy filled in for an expectant June Allyson until Jane Powell had to fill in for Judy). Though she made it through *Summer Stock*, MGM began to view Garland, once their most valuable asset, as an increasingly costly liability. Whereas Mayer may have buckled and given Judy another chance in a smaller-scale Joe Pasternak production, Dore Schary was apparently not as forgiving. On September 29, 1950, the studio announced "with reluctance and regret" that Judy had requested a release from her Metro contract, and that they had given in "with a view to serving her own best interests."

A few months later, another noteworthy separation was announced. On December 21, 1950, the world received the news that the marriage of Vincente Minnelli and Judy Garland appeared to be over. "Climaxing a turbulent two years of career and personal problems, actress Judy Garland announced through the William Morris Agency that she and her director husband, Vincente Minnelli, have separated," the Associated Press reported.[22] Flying in the face of countless rumors, the separation was termed "an amicable arrangement." In the wake of some of Judy's very public calamities, press sympathy seemed to lie with Minnelli. "Perhaps Vince was too easy and too gentle with her," mused Louella Parsons.

Minnelli seemed to agree: "I'd been too sympathetic, too ready to see it her way, when I should have been more assertive," he wrote. Ever the gentleman, Vincente attempted to end his marriage to Judy on a dignified note: "I was glad she was happy and functioning, and would do nothing to cause her a moment's concern. Peace and freedom was something we both wanted."[23] Decades after the divorce (which became final in April 1952), Garland's friend June Allyson was more matter-of-fact about the demise of one of Hollywood's more unconventional marriages: "It was no surprise that it couldn't work out. He was wrong for Judy. Totally wrong."[24]

***

AT LEAST ON THE WORK FRONT, things were looking brighter for Minnelli. Arthur Freed was interested in reviving an ambitious project that he had launched back in the '40s and then abandoned: a musical version of *Huckleberry Finn*. Freed considered Mark Twain's classic "the best book ever written in America," and the impressive array of talents the producer had initially lined up for the project said plenty about his level of commitment. From the beginning, there seems to have been a conscious attempt to recapture some of the magic of *Meet Me in St. Louis*. Freed had hired Sally Benson, the author of the original *St. Louis* stories, to transport Twain's enduring book to

the screen. He had also hired *St. Louis* songwriters Hugh Martin and Ralph
Blane to compose the score for *Huckleberry Finn*. It was Freed's hope that
the songs Martin and Blane whipped up for Twain's riverfront waif would
be as memorable as the ones they had written for Garland's lovestruck teenager. Although everything about the project seemed promising, by the mid-
'40s Freed's plate was brimming over—the producer was readying several
elaborate musicals for the screen, including Minnelli's *The Pirate*. With
Freed unable to give *Huckleberry Finn* the attention it needed, the project
was temporarily shelved.

Freed started over in the '50s with a whole new creative team: writer Donald Ogden Stewart, lyricist Yip Harburg, and composer Burton Lane. At the
height of the Red Scare era, left-leaning progressives Stewart and Harburg
were suddenly deemed unsuitable and ousted. Alan Jay Lerner was then assigned to both book and lyrics. "Alan had a great love for *Huckleberry Finn*,"
says Lerner's assistant Stone Widney. "He thought the book was one of the
seminal works in American literature. He really, desperately wanted to get
that made and he and Burton Lane wrote about five or six songs." (They included "I'll Wait for You by the River" and "The World's Full O'Suckers.")
"Alan had very high hopes for that project," Widney added. In fact, Lerner
would refer to the material he created for *Huckleberry Finn* as "some of the
best stuff I've ever written."[25]

In early script conferences, it was decided that Metro's musical version
of *Huckleberry Finn* should not attempt to dramatize every episode in Twain's
sprawling saga. Instead it would focus primarily on wily orphan Huck Finn's
adventures with Jim, a runaway slave. But it would also reserve a considerable
amount of screen time for a pair of scene-stealing supporting characters,
two vagabond gamblers known as the Duke and the Dauphin. These roles
would be tailored to the talents of Gene Kelly (also on board as choreographer) and Danny Kaye (on loan out from Samuel Goldwyn). In large part,
the project would also be dependent on the star power of Kaye and Kelly to
lure moviegoers into theaters.

In March 1951, Minnelli was announced as director. Rehearsals began
and Kelly found himself working on *Huckleberry Finn* in the morning and
then dashing off to codirect his other important picture in production, *Singin'
in the Rain*, in the afternoon. Things seemed to be progressing smoothly
when suddenly the studio pulled the plug. "MGM announced that it will
postpone production of *Huckleberry Finn* until next year," the *Independent
Film Journal* reported in October. "This was made necessary because of the
impossibility of completing rehearsals and filming in time for Danny Kaye
to report back to the Samuel Goldwyn Studios [to begin shooting *Hans*

Christian Anderson] by December 15. Gene Kelly, Kaye's costar, still has work remaining on his current film, *Singin' In The Rain*, until Oct. 15th."[26]

The need to honor preexisting commitments was the official reason given for shutting down Minnelli's latest production, though it's been suggested that Kaye may have felt that his role as the Dauphin ("son of Looy The Sixteen and Marry Antonette") was simply not substantial enough. According to Kelly, "Danny quit the picture because he wasn't enthusiastic about it. He saw that the two vagabonds were not as important as Huck and Jim. . . . He was delighted to leave it."[27]

There may have been another reason behind the studio's decision. Even before Vincente had shot a single frame, *Huckleberry Finn* had already garnered the wrong kind of publicity. As the Associated Press reported, the Independent Progressive Party had loudly protested the inclusion of a blackface sequence in the musical: "Party officials said a blackface dance number with Danny Kaye and Gene Kelly 'tends to degrade and vilify the role of the American Negro and to portray them in a vicious, stereotyped manner.'"[28]

But as Vincente remembered it, the abrupt shutdown had more to do with money: "A provision in the federal tax law then permitted an American to avoid paying taxes if he spent eighteen calendar months working outside the country. . . . Gene would be allowed to take advantage of this provision for his contributions to *An American In Paris* and the up coming *Singin' In The Rain*." Whatever the case, not long after *Huckleberry Finn* was scrapped, Kelly set off for England to work on his pet project *Invitation to the Dance*.

After months of preparation, *Huckleberry Finn* was permanently shelved.[*] Minnelli gamely attempted to rise above the disappointing developments: "These were the breaks of the profession and not worth moping over," he wrote.[29]

***

ALICE DUER MILLER'S 1933 BESTSELLER *Gowns by Roberta* became Jerome Kern's Broadway musical triumph *Roberta*, which introduced such evergreens as "Smoke Gets in Your Eyes," "Lovely to Look At," and "Yesterdays." In 1935, RKO filmed *Roberta* with an all-star cast. The exuberant Fred Astaire and Ginger Rogers dance sequences upstaged the flimsy plot, which concerned

---

[*] In February 1953, Louella Parsons reported that a 3-D version of *Huckleberry Finn* (!) was going into production with Minnelli at the helm and Danny Kaye on board once again, but this version of the project never materialized either. In 1974, Hollywood finally got around to a musical version of *Huckleberry Finn*—this one directed by J. Lee Thompson with a score by Richard and Robert Sherman of *Mary Poppins* fame. "It transforms a great work of fiction into something bland, boring and tasteless," said the *Illustrated London News*.

Randolph Scott as an all-American halfback turned couturier romancing Irene Dunne.

In November 1948, the *Los Angeles Times* published an item trumpeting MGM's plans to remake *Roberta* featuring four of its top stars: Judy Garland, Gene Kelly, Frank Sinatra, and Betty Garrett. Nothing ever came of it. Then, in 1950, producer Jack Cummings announced that he would produce his own version of *Roberta*. Retitled *Lovely to Look At*, the now familiar story was redressed in more contemporary couture and billed as "MGM's Technicolor Spectacle." This refurbished *Roberta* would feature a stellar array of Metro contract players: Kathryn Grayson ("thrills you with her golden voice!"), Howard Keel ("his romantic singing!"), Ann Miller ("gorgeous stepper!"), and the studio's answer to Fred and Ginger—Marge and Gower Champion. If all that weren't enough, *Lovely to Look At* also marked the film debut of Miss Hungary of 1936, the irrepressible Zsa Zsa Gabor.

Despite the fact that he was best known for gritty action flicks like *Little Caesar* and *I Am a Fugitive from a Chain Gang*, Mervyn LeRoy was asked to oversee this tune-filled remake. Although LeRoy was the credited producer on *The Wizard of Oz* and would go on to helm a splashy, widescreen adaptation of *Gypsy* in 1961, lavish musicals weren't really the director's bag.

Early into production, it was decided that although LeRoy would direct the majority of the picture, he would relinquish the directorial reins in at least two instances. Fred Astaire's choreographer of choice, Hermes Pan, would direct the Champions as they swirled amid a starry, ethereal backdrop to the tune of "Smoke Gets in Your Eyes." For the climactic fashion-show finale, it was abundantly clear that the services of a director more intimately familiar with organdy were required. Enter Vincente Minnelli. "He came on because Mervyn LeRoy said, 'I know how to direct Edward G. Robinson but I don't know how to direct a fashion show,'" recalled Marge Champion. "He turned it right over to Vince Minnelli and to the brilliant Tony Duquette."[30]

With *Huckleberry Finn* stalled and *The Band Wagon* still a year away, it seemed the perfect time to take on a project that was not epically scaled or too demanding. "I was between pictures and it sounded like a nothing assignment," Minnelli would later remark. In tapping Vincente for his runway expertise, LeRoy very shrewdly downplayed the amount of work involved: "It's just a little show. Shouldn't take you longer than three days."[31]

Minnelli, of course, was constitutionally incapable of doing anything halfway. LeRoy's "three days" ballooned into three weeks. What had been a pleasant though pale musical for its first eighty-five minutes suddenly metamorphosed into something quite spectacular in its final fifteen minutes. In

terms of pictorial composition, the transition from LeRoy's bland settings to
Minnelli's ravishing set pieces is almost jarring.

"You have to cast directors almost the same way that you cast actors,"
Champion says. "Mervyn was an absolute darling but I remember when he
was shooting a scene, his only direction to us was, 'Let's have a lovely scene.'
Well, we were all very happy to have a lovely scene but [MGM's resident
dramatics instructor] Lillian Sidney had coached us in that same scene for
weeks before we did it. . . . With the fashion show, we really needed something more."[32]

Adrian, the celebrated costumer of everything from Garbo's *Camille* to
the winged monkeys' stylish bell-boy attire in *The Wizard of Oz*, was pressed
back into service after a decade-long absence from MGM. The bill for the
forty-two costumes that Mr. Janet Gaynor designed for *Lovely to Look At*
was a then impressive $100,000. The expense paid off handsomely. The
fashion show is so sumptuously styled that the sequence could be an overdressed outtake from *Ziegfeld Follies*. The eye isn't dazzled so much by the
fashions themselves as by the way every extravagant ensemble is showcased.
With Duquette's harlequins and living chandeliers standing guard, each of
the costumes, models, and performers is allowed to have a runway "moment."
Almost everyone emerges from a dramatically lit "tunnel of louvers," a technique Vincente had employed to great effect on stage in *At Home Abroad*.

"The fashion show did credit to the picture," Minnelli would modestly
observe.[33] In fact, it was singled out by most of the critics as the most noteworthy aspect of an otherwise uninspired movie.

***

"THERE WAS A THING HE DID that drove some people crazy," remembers Farley
Granger, who starred in Minnelli's portion of the glossy, three-part episodic
drama *The Story of Three Loves*:

> He would stand right next to the camera and watch you while you were doing
> the scene and mouth every line of dialogue right along with you. I think he
> was doing it to try and infuse you with the feeling that he wanted from the
> scene. At first, I thought it was going to drive me mad and then I got used to
> it and I found it charming. . . . It was all a result of his passion and enthusiasm,
> really. To find a director who is that passionate and enthusiastic about what
> he's working on was unusual.[34]

Vincente's sequence was entitled "Mademoiselle," a mini-fantasy in which
a preadolescent Ricky Nelson, tired of being tutored by French governess

Leslie Caron, enlists the aid of a benevolent witch to turn him into an adult. As a result of that special brand of wizardry that only Hollywood could conjure, Ricky Nelson isn't only transformed into a grown man but an eye-filling Adonis in the form of Farley Granger.

The assignment seemed made to order for Minnelli. And the director was genuinely inspired by the presence of theatrical grand dame Ethel Barrymore on the set. Playing the pivotal though relatively minor role of the sorceress Mrs. Pennicott, Barrymore nevertheless prepared for the part as though she were reprising her celebrated turn in *The Lady of the Camellias.* Vincente was awed and treated Barrymore like some dowager empress.

However, Minnelli wasn't nearly as formal with actor John Angelo, who played a bellhop in scenes that were ultimately deleted from the "Mademoiselle" sequence. "He pinched me," Angelo says of his director's quite literal "hands-on" approach. "We were both Italian and he thought he was in Rome, I guess. . . . He cruised a lot of people, now whether they went with him or not, I don't know. I wasn't interested really. People said he was gay and yet he married four times. He kept his gayness in the shadows, I think. But he was always very nice to me. I never said 'Yes' to him . . . but I did get pinched."[35]

Minnelli's segment of *The Story of Three Loves* was originally envisioned as the centerpiece of the film. All of that changed, however, in the cutting room. "Much to Vincente's dismay and mine, ["Mademoiselle"] was cut mercilessly by Gottfried Reinhardt, who produced the film and directed the other two segments," says Farley Granger. "We were very disappointed."[36]

What remained of the sequence was charming, but slight—Minnelli in miniature, as it were. Compared with other 1953 releases, such as *From Here to Eternity* or *Pickup on South Street,* *The Story of Three Loves* seems to have been produced on some very fey planet. As a result, the public stayed away, and the MGM ledgers showed a loss of $1 million.

The critics weren't exactly swept away either. One reviewer wrote:

The Story of Three Loves is episodic by design and inconclusive by lack of it. . . . Earnestly directed by Gottfried Reinhardt and Vincente Minnelli and painstakingly produced by Sidney Franklin, the whole project suffers from pretentiousness and self-consciousness. Dragging out meaningless clichés beyond all endurance and relying heavily on MGM's usual super-production, they have attempted to make drama without creating real character, authentic situations or believable narration. Artificial respiration does not bring the picture to life.

17

Tribute to
a Bad Man

"CERTAINLY THE MOST UNEXPECTED and hottest teaming of 1952 (so far) will be Lana Turner and Kirk Douglas pitching woo in *Tribute to a Bad Man* at MGM," wrote Louella Parsons in her syndicated column of January 28, 1952. The droning gossip columnist wasn't the only one salivating over the project. As producer John Houseman noted, there was a "heady atmosphere of success that surrounded us from the first day of shooting; it also related to the amusement we all derived from so much 'inside' material—full of private and not so private jokes and references."[1]

The juicy insider references originated with a short story by George Bradshaw entitled "Memorial to a Bad Man" that appeared in the February 1951 issue of the *Ladies' Home Journal*. Bradshaw's ruthless protagonist, Gil McBride, is a dead ringer for irascible theater impresario Jed Harris, of whom it was said: "If Jed thought his mother was wrong for a part, and her life depended on it, he would still fire her." Bradshaw's description of his antihero—"He was admired, worshiped, adored—any superlative you can think of for his abilities in the theater, but for himself he was hated"—was worthy of both fictional counterpart and real-life prototype.

While Bradshaw's *Rashomon*-style story and characters were certainly compelling, by the early '50s there had been many memorable movies concerned with backstage intrigue, including Gregory La Cava's *Stage Door*, George Cukor's *A Double Life*, and Joseph L. Mankiewicz's recently released *All About Eve*.

Determined to avoid becoming a cinematic cliché, Houseman wisely decided to shift the story's setting from Broadway to Hollywood. There may have been another reason for this transition, too, and it was called *Sunset Boulevard*. Billy Wilder's sardonic masterpiece had copped three Oscars in 1950, and although Louis B. Mayer would berate Wilder ("You befouled your own nest"[2]), he and every other executive in town were keenly aware of how much acclaim the self-reflexive saga of Norma Desmond had garnered. Houseman assigned screenwriter Charles Schnee to rework "Memorial to a Bad Man." In addition to making the story more cinematic, Schnee would also work in plot elements from Bradshaw's similarly themed *Cosmopolitan* novelette "Of Good and Evil."

When Schnee's script was ready, Houseman summoned Minnelli to lunch at Romanoff's. As Vincente later recalled, "The screenplay fascinated me. It told of a film producer who uses everyone in his rise to the top. . . . It was a harsh and cynical story, yet strangely romantic. All that one loved and hated about Hollywood was distilled in the screenplay."[3]

What's more, Minnelli recognized that the characters (now more Schnee than Bradshaw) would register as more authentic if they were patterned after real-life models: First there was Jonathan Shields, the unscrupulous producer who rose from the B-movie junk heap. Shields seemed to be a clever composite of *Cat People* producer Val Lewton and Louis B. Mayer's former son-in-law, the fanatically involved David O. Selznick. Then there was Georgia Lorrison, the boozy has-been who deifies her dead father and scrapes her way to stardom, reportedly modeled on John Barrymore's daughter Diana. Henry Whitfield, a British director with a taste for the macabre, could have been either Alfred Hitchcock or James Whale. The even more exacting auteur Von Ellstein seemed reminiscent of Fritz Lang or Erich von Stroheim. All of these roles were camouflaged just enough to keep everyone guessing with a general "Wait a minute, *Is that supposed to be? . . .*" effect permeating the entire picture—exactly the kind of illusion-on-an-illusion that Minnelli and Houseman had hoped to achieve.[*]

In December 1951, Hedda Hopper had announced to her readers that MGM hoped to entice Clark Gable to play Jonathan Shields. When that casting didn't pan out, producer and director had only one other actor in mind for the wily, backstabbing heel you love to hate: Kirk Douglas.

---

[*] R. Monta of MGM's legal department expressed concern that some of the thinly veiled characters weren't cloaked quite enough. In an interoffice memo, Monta wondered if the character of George Lorrison—glimpsed only in photographs—resembled John Barrymore too closely. Monta cautioned: "The actor should wear the type of hat entirely unlike any kind of hats Barrymore was known to wear." (MGM memo, n.d.)

Tribute to a Bad Man: Ruthless producer Jonathan Shields (Kirk Douglas) cops the Oscar in a sequence deleted from the release print of *The Bad and the Beautiful.* Douglas said of his director: "He was a genius and for whatever reason, that has never been properly recognized."
PHOTO COURTESY
OF PHOTOFEST

"I was the teacher's pet," Douglas says of working with Minnelli on the first of their three pictures together:

We seemed to be on the same wavelength. We were so different but we seemed to understand each other very well. He told me something and I got it the first time. I never had such gratification making a movie than I did with Vincente Minnelli. You know, he was an unusual guy. He was always humming and he was always rearranging the props all over the set but he really knew what he was doing. He was a perfectionist—without question. And he was always annoyed with everybody but me. He would smile at me with approval and then he would snap at someone else. Sometimes he could be very impatient and irritable with incompetence in an actor. But we never had a problem.

In his own way, I think Vincente had a tremendous sense of humor, which would come out in some of the most unusual ways. . . . I liked him so much. He encouraged me in everything that I did and, as an actor, I think that I blossomed under his direction. He was a genius and for whatever reason, that has never been properly recognized.[4]

As Douglas began shaping his performance, Minnelli suggested that the actor soft-pedal his trademark intensity and "play it for charm." The suggestion worked so well that Douglas, like his character, was charm personified. "Kirk's behavior was exemplary," Houseman would recall, refuting rumors that the photogenic leading man could be prickly and hot headed. "He was up on the lines of his huge role—indefatigable, intelligent and receptive to Minnelli's direction."[5]

Another surprise was leading lady Lana Turner, who campaigned for the role of Georgia Lorrison. After her latest outings, *The Merry Widow*, *Mr. Imperium*, and *A Life of Her Own*,* all tanked at the box office, Turner knew that her career was desperately in need of rehabilitation. The role of the gin-soaked starlet who rises to fame seemed like just the ticket. "When the script reached me, I knew right away that I understood the character—a film star who is seen at first as a soggy mess and then is resuscitated by an unscrupulous producer," Turner said. "I could believe in her. Moreover, the screenplay was a much better one than those I usually received."[6] And how.

For once, Turner's costume changes would not be substituted for legitimate character development. This would be the "sweater girl's" meatiest role since her memorable turn as the white-turbaned femme fatale in *The Postman Always Rings Twice* in 1946. And Minnelli was determined to extract a real performance from Turner—one that, ironically, called for her to strip away her movie star veneer in order to play a movie star. For her first scene in the picture, Turner is present only as a disembodied voice (as Georgia lurks in the shadows of Crow's Nest, her late father's decaying mansion)—a legitimate challenge for an actress accustomed to relying on her physical gifts to make an impression.

Metro veteran Walter Pidgeon convinced Minnelli that he could check his Brooks Brothers persona at the door and play the penny-pinching producer Harry Pebbel, who only wants "pictures that end with a kiss and black ink on the books." Originally, Barry Sullivan was cast as southern novelist James Lee Bartlow and Dick Powell was scheduled to play director Fred Amiel. Powell (who was still an important marquee draw at that time), immediately realized that the gentrified novelist was a better part, and he asked Minnelli and Houseman to cast him as Bartlow and reassign Sullivan as the director. They complied. The one and only Gloria Grahame (she of the insolent pout and bee-stung lips) was cast as the writer's wife, "a modern day Southern

---

* In July 1949, MGM had announced that Minnelli would direct Lana Turner in *A Life of Her Own*. However, by the time the sudsy melodrama went before the cameras, George Cukor was at the helm.

Kirk Douglas, Paul Stewart, Vanessa Brown, Barry Sullivan, and singer Peggy King in a
party sequence from *The Bad and the Beautiful*. King's bit part was inspired by Judy
Garland's impromptu vocal performances at Hollywood parties.
PHOTO COURTESY OF PHOTOFEST

belle," at the suggestion of Houseman, who said of the actress: "She had an
instinctive talent complicated by a number of peculiar aberrations—including
a taste for facial surgery that she did not need."[7]

Even with his formidable line-up of stars in place, Minnelli continued
casting—supporting roles, bit players, and walk-ons. In a Vincente Minnelli
production, there was no such thing as a small part. "I was doing a cameo
in the picture but he directed me as if it was the most important scene in
any film he ever directed," says singer Peggy King, who performs the haunting
ballad "Don't Blame Me"* in a party sequence. "It was very strange being a
starlet at Metro in those days. Everybody was doing stuff behind everybody
else's back. But not Vincente. He was so wonderful. He treated me as if I
were on an equal footing with Kirk and Lana and the other stars. . . . Wasn't

---

* Written for the 1932 musical revue *Clowns in Clover*, "Don't Blame Me" was apparently a Minnelli favorite. After
Peggy King's performance in *The Bad and the Beautiful*, Minnelli had Leslie Uggams reprise the song in *Two Weeks in
Another Town*. Minnelli also requested that Jack Nicholson croon the Dorothy Fields–Jimmy McHugh standard during
his audition for *On a Clear Day You Can See Forever*.

I lucky that if I was going to do a cameo in a picture that it turned out to be that one and with Minnelli as the director?"[8]

Houseman fought to have the film photographed in color and to retain the story's original title, but he lost the battle on both counts. With Turner receiving top billing over Douglas, it was suggested that a more romantically attuned title was in order. MGM's chief publicist, Howard Dietz, suggested *The Bad and the Beautiful*, and despite Houseman's very vocal objections, it stuck. Production began on April 9, 1952.

Musicals aside, *The Bad and the Beautiful* would contain some of the most indelible images that Minnelli would ever capture on film, including Shields paying off the mourners-for-hire at his despised father's funeral ("He lived in a crowd, I couldn't let him be buried alone . . .") and Georgia's ascent to superstardom, which Minnelli accomplishes in one magnificently fluid transition: After capturing Georgia's performance on the set, the camera sails all the way up to the soundstage rafters, where several seen-it-all grips and electricians are beaming with pride: a blazing arc light that one of them is operating morphs into a blinding klieg light on the eve of Georgia's big premiere. The star trip in shorthand. This is followed by Lana's gloriously over-the-top vehicular nervous breakdown, which critic Tom Shales would salute as "one of the great melodramatic arias ever staged for a film."[9] And who can forget character actor Ned Glass as a grizzled wardrobe man peddling some unintentionally hilarious cat suits ("lots of character in the tail . . .") for Jonathan's low-budget horror flick *The Doom of the Cat Men*.

"If you look at the cat man sequence in *The Bad and the Beautiful*, nobody else would have done that in quite the way he did that," says writer and Minnelli enthusiast Sir Gerald Kaufman:

> Or that scene at the end with all of them clustering around the telephone, listening to what was being said by Jonathan Shields on the other end—I can't imagine another director staging it that way. Despite the difficulties of the Hollywood studio system, it's perfectly clear in my mind that Minnelli put an enormous amount of himself into his films. I can't think of another Hollywood director, except, say, John Ford or Alfred Hitchcock, whose films were theirs in the same way that Minnelli's films were his. I mean, let's face it, MGM was there to make films to make money. . . . They wouldn't have kept him as long as they did or allow him to make all kinds of films—a western like *Home from the Hill* or a comedy like *The Long, Long Trailer*—if they didn't have enormous confidence in him. He wasn't just a journeyman director. He was a totally unique director. And you can see that in every frame of *The Bad and the Beautiful*.[10]

Film audiences of the day may have relished what appeared to be a privileged glimpse of the world behind the screen, but it was "real life," according to Metro-Goldwyn-Mayer. Composer David Raksin, who would furnish the film with one of the most haunting themes in movie history, summed it up perfectly: "This is no mere photograph of Hollywood but rather a romantically diffused look into a mirror. . . . When it looks at scars and wrinkles, it is with a lover's eye."[11]

The sweet and sour tone sustained throughout *The Bad and the Beautiful* does feel authentic, and who better to direct a study of driven careerists in the business of manufacturing illusion than Minnelli, who by that time had seen more than his fair share of bad and beautiful. Although Vincente is adept at handling the cynical tone, it is the cynicism of a die-hard romantic who still believes in happy endings, Hollywood style.

On September 18, 1952, *The Bad and the Beautiful* was previewed in Pacific Palisades. Of the 160 preview cards returned, 44 audience members rated the film "outstanding" and 67 thought it was "excellent," though many patrons grumbled about the film's length. As a result, some footage was excised—including an elaborate Peter Ballbusch "star-seeing" montage—before the picture was released in January 1953.

"Let's say that any resemblance to persons living or dead is hardly a coincidence," wrote Josh Rosenfield in his *Dallas Morning News* review. "The picture is a directorial feat for Vincente Minnelli, who shows imposing stature. He holds all the strands of a complicated story in tight rein. He gives the whole a treatment of unexpected twists."[12]

Nominated for several Academy Awards (including a well-deserved Best Actor nod for Douglas), *The Bad and the Beautiful* would ultimately earn statuettes for Charles Schnee's screenplay, Robert Surtees's moody cinematography, the art direction by Cedric Gibbons and Edward Carfagno, Keogh Gleason's set decoration, and the costume design by Helen Rose—and Gloria Grahame's brief but unforgettable turn as the doomed Rosemary Bartlow copped the Best Supporting Actress Oscar. Among the nominees for Best Director were Cecil B. DeMille, John Ford, and John Huston—but not Vincente Minnelli. But the overworked auteur barely had time to notice the oversight. Freed was already nudging his favorite director toward his next production.

18

New Sun
in the Sky

IN 1931, THE NEW AMSTERDAM THEATRE had staged a new revue by future MGM publicity chief Howard Dietz and Arthur Schwartz entitled *The Band Wagon*. The headliners had been Fred and Adele Astaire. Two decades later, Freed decided that a film built around the Dietz-Schwartz songbook (which included such standards as "Dancing in the Dark" and "By Myself") had hit potential—especially with Mr. Astaire back on the *Wagon*. As they had done with *Singin' in the Rain*, Betty Comden and Adolph Green were ordered to fashion a story around a preexisting collection of songs.

Apart from the title,[*] Fred Astaire, and a trio of tunes, there was little else that Comden and Green were able to retain from the original 1931 production. "That was a revue in the real sense of the word," says Comden. "There was no plot. There were just some wonderful performers and charming numbers but it was not a musical that had any kind of linear story that you could base anything on. It was just a revue. Needless to say, we had our work cut out for us."[1]

Eventually, they came up with a story about a washed-up movie star on the comeback trail. Hoofer Tony Hunter heads to Broadway to make a name for himself on the stage only to get mixed up with avant-garde artiste Jeffrey Cordova. Suddenly, Hunter's unassuming little show has morphed

---

[*] In June 1952, Hedda Hopper reported that Fred Astaire, Cyd Charisse, and Nanette Fabray were set to star in Vincente Minnelli's *Strategy of Love*, which, along with *I Love Louisa*, temporarily served as the title of Comden and Green's script before it reverted back to *The Band Wagon*.

into an overproduced musical version of *Faust*—complete with a classical ballerina as costar, a role that almost seemed tailor-made for Freed Unit favorite Cyd Charisse.

As always, Minnelli was very present during story-development sessions. "I discussed every inch of the script with Betty and Adolph," Minnelli remembered. In fact, it was Vincente who encouraged Comden and Green (who were not married) to pattern the characters of Lester and Lily Marton (*The Band Wagon*'s wedded writing partners) on themselves. "Vincente was very involved in all of the details of our work," Comden recalled. "We would write sections and then read them to him and he would make suggestions. I think he liked very much what we were doing. He was very brilliant, had some wonderful ideas, and almost everything he suggested to us ended up in the movie."[2]

Apart from Minnelli's core crew (which included dozens of Freed Unit veterans), some new talents would also climb aboard *The Band Wagon*. Clifton Webb passed on the role of flamboyant theater impresario Jeffrey Cordova but suggested British music-hall star Jack Buchanan for the part. This proved to be an inspired bit of casting. Buchanan was wonderfully versatile—able to spoof José Ferrer at his most megalomaniacal, match Astaire's elegance, and even carry a tune. Choreographer Michael Kidd had made a splash on Broadway with his inventive dance direction for *Finian's Rainbow* and *Guys and Dolls*. Minnelli asked Kidd to make the numbers for *The Band Wagon* "believable as theatre" yet "cinematic." It was a tall order for a Hollywood newcomer, who was also tasked with teaching the master a few new tricks. As Kidd remembered it, "Astaire was at first suspicious of me—even though he requested me—because I represented an entirely different kind of work."

The Band Wagon is so much fun to watch that it's almost shocking to discover that one of the most joyous and exuberant musicals in cinema history was abject misery to create. "It was one of the most unpleasant things I think I've ever done," Nanette Fabray would say of her experience on the film:

> It was a very cold atmosphere. . . . Astaire's wife was either ill or had died. He was very aloof. He wasn't being unfriendly but he was just not in a position to take anybody on as a friend. Oscar Levant had just gotten out of a mental hospital and he was a real pain in the neck. I mean, he had nobody to pick on. He picked on me. Every day he kept saying, "Oh, I'm having a heart attack . . ." Nobody paid any attention to him but it turned out he really was having little mini heart attacks, but because he was such a nut nobody paid much attention to him. Most of the time, Jack Buchanan was out having his

Jack Buchanan, Fred Astaire, Nanette Fabray, and Oscar Levant belt out the show business anthem "That's Entertainment!" in *The Band Wagon*. One of the most joyous and exuberant musicals in cinema history was abject misery to create.
PHOTO COURTESY OF PHOTOFEST

teeth fixed. He came to America to have his teeth done. Of course, Judy was so ill that Minnelli was in no shape whatsoever to be friendly to anybody. He just came in and did his work and that was it. . . . So, it wasn't that anybody was being mean to me except Oscar, it's just that nobody was in an emotional position to reach out.[*]

It had been fifteen years since Fabray had appeared opposite Bette Davis in *The Private Lives of Elizabeth and Essex*. Fabray had found the formidable Davis to be surprisingly helpful; the same could not be said of the director of *The Band Wagon*. "It was a very, very stressful time and I got no help from Minnelli at all," Fabray says. "I didn't get any sort of mean attitude from Minnelli, it's just that I don't know that he even recognized that I needed help. He was there to do his job and that's what he did."[3]

Dancer James Mitchell, who had appeared in the original Broadway production of *Brigadoon* and made one of his earliest film appearances in the

---

[*] By the time *The Band Wagon* was in production, Minnelli and Garland were already divorced. (Nanette Fabray, interview with author.)

Maria Montez cult extravaganza *Cobra Woman*, also encountered a cast of highly accomplished yet profoundly unhappy professionals. "It wasn't a pleasant experience," Mitchell says. "Minnelli kind of trod on Cyd. I don't know why but he wasn't pleasant with her. He left Cyd in tears for no good reason. I have to say, I don't remember him very kindly." Although *The Band Wagon* is wall-to-wall production numbers, Mitchell—a protégé of choreographer Agnes De Mille—was never called upon to do what he did best. "I didn't have much to do in the picture, really," Mitchell says ruefully. "I didn't dance. I wasn't in any of the numbers. I mean, what do you do with Astaire in a film . . . *dance around him?*"[4]

Despite the strained atmosphere on the set, *The Band Wagon* is sheer movie joy. The musical offers up one unforgettable sequence after another—the kind of pulse-quickening moments that cinema buffs live for: Astaire, Fabray, and Buchanan as squabbling toddlers in the delightful "Triplets"; the spellbinding "Dancing in the Dark" with Astaire and Charisse in crisp summer whites, whirling through Central Park while accompanied by Conrad Salinger's sweepingly romantic arrangement; "I Guess I'll Have to Change My Plan," presenting Astaire and Buchanan—all easygoing elegance in top hat and tails—before Oliver Smith's minimalist backdrop; and, of course, "A Shine on Your Shoes," in which Astaire's newfound exuberance is matched by the vibrant attractions he discovers in a Times Square penny arcade—including dancing partner LeRoy Daniels.

One of the most talked about sequences in *The Band Wagon* was shot last and in only seven days: "The Girl Hunt Ballet."* In this hilarious, visually inventive spoof of pulp mysteries, Vincente Minnelli meets Mickey Spillane. Astaire is gumshoe Rod Riley, a distant cousin to Sam Spade and Mike Hammer. "I wrote Fred's voice-over narration to the action," Minnelli claims in his autobiography, taking credit for such howlers as "She was scared . . . scared as a turkey in November," and "She came at me in sections. More curves than a scenic railway."[5] Given the specificity (and hilarity) of the language, it's more probable that Minnelli supplied a thematic outline for the ballet before enlisting the aid of one of his sharpest collaborators to supply Astaire's tongue-in-cheek dialogue. According to Hugh Fordin,

> Alan Jay Lerner was at the studio working on *Brigadoon*. He had lunch with Freed, and Minnelli joined them. Looking very pointedly at Lerner, Minnelli

---

* In their book *Film Noir: An Encyclopedic Reference to the American Style* (New York: Random House, 1984), authors Alain Silver and Elizabeth Ward wrote, "Minnelli asserted himself in an unexpected musical context with 'The Girl Hunt Ballet,' which says more about film noir in ten minutes than *Undercurrent* does in two hours."

said, "We need a narration in *The Band Wagon.*" For ethical reasons Lerner was very reluctant, after all this was Comden and Green's picture; but Freed and Minnelli gently pressured him. "No conditions, no money—I'll do it for fun," Lerner said. Minnelli even promised he would claim to have written it himself.[6]

True to his word, in the years following the film's release, Minnelli took full responsibility for authoring the Spillane spoof—though now he seemed to have convinced himself of his sole authorship as well. When MGM Records released an abbreviated version of the original soundtrack from the film, "The Girl Hunt Ballet" was credited to Lerner and Roger Edens. Displaying what Judy Garland had once described as his "dago temper," Minnelli demanded that Metro recall the soundtrack and redistribute the record with his own name replacing Lerner's on the album jacket.[*] It was the kind of backstage backbiting that seemed to come straight out of *The Band Wagon.*

Nevertheless, "The Girl Hunt Ballet" is an exhilarating knockout, thanks largely to Minnelli's scenic effects and Michael Kidd's imaginative choreography. Kidd borrowed Jimmy Cagney's trademark shoulder-hitches and twitchy mannerisms and gave them to his dancing gangsters. The result is the most highly stylized swagger the screen has ever seen. And in Cyd Charisse, Astaire found a dancing partner even more ideal than Ginger Rogers—for Charisse is really Astaire's female equivalent: elegant, graceful, and beamed direct from Planet Flawless.

Production wrapped in January 1953, and for most of the principals, the end came not a moment too soon. During post-production, it was decided that *The Band Wagon* needed to be trimmed. Along with a portion of "The Girl Hunt Ballet," several production numbers were deleted. The most intriguing of the excised sequences was Charisse's "Two-Faced Woman," a lavish dance number built around one of Minnelli's favorite themes—the exhilarative effects of a split self. "*Someday I will wake up, find out what is wrong . . . With my dual make-up, I don't belong . . .*" trills India Adams, the voice double for Charisse. As Cyd obliges with one sultry pose after another, a flock of chorus girls flit by—one half in virginal white, another brigade decked out in Minnelli red.

Dubbed "The Manic Depressive's National Anthem," the sizzling "Two-Faced Woman" may have been a casualty for *The Band Wagon*, but a

---

* To make matters worse, the original one-sheet poster for *The Band Wagon* contained a legendary mix-up. Arthur Freed is credited as the director of the film while Minnelli is listed as the producer.

powerhouse Adams vocal backed by a superb Roger Edens–Conrad Salinger arrangement was too good to dispose of entirely. A year after the release of *The Band Wagon*, Joan Crawford starred in Chuck Walters' *Torch Song*, a film that practically defines camp. At one point, Crawford appears in a night-club sequence in "tropical make-up" and a carrot-colored wig, lip synching along to the resuscitated "Two-Faced Woman" audio track. The spectacle is so gloriously over-the-top and unintentionally hilarious that it could have been masterminded by Jeffrey Cordova himself.

Reviewing *The Band Wagon* in *The Nation*, Archer Winsten summed up the feelings of many when he concluded his unqualified rave by declaring Minnelli's movie "the best musical of the month, the year, the decade, or for all I know of all time." Reviewing a reissue of the film decades later, even the hard-to-please Pauline Kael conceded that "there have been few screen musicals as good as this one." While applauding Buchanan's "rosy-ripe way with the lines" and the fact that Levant was featured "in one of his best movie roles," Kael also noted that "when the bespangled Charisse wraps her phenomenal legs around Astaire, she can be forgiven everything, even her three minutes of 'classical' ballet and the fact that she reads her lines as if she learned them phonetically."[7]

For those who horde their Playbills, worship Carol Channing, and have blazing marquee lights permanently reflected in their eyes, Minnelli's movie radiates with the soul of showbiz. "The movie is timeless in the way it depicts show business," says entertainer Michael Feinstein. "When Vincente watched the film, he was just beaming with pride. He was not critical. He was just enjoying it. . . . I never heard him say, 'Gee, I wish I had done that better or done this better.' But evidently, he got everything he wanted on the first try, and that's the way you leave a legacy."[8]

***

IN 1951, CLINTON TWISS PUBLISHED *The Long, Long Trailer*, a bestselling rib-tickler that chronicled the author's misadventures tooling across the country in the company of Mrs. Twiss and an enormous "twenty-eight foot aluminum whale of a trailer."

With its raucous slapstick episodes, *The Long, Long Trailer* seemed custom built for television's first couple of comedy, Lucille Ball and Desi Arnaz. The stars of the phenomenally popular CBS series *I Love Lucy* had conquered the small screen but a feature-film success remained elusive. After Arnaz read an abridged version of the Twiss novel in *Reader's Digest*, he attempted to acquire the rights to the property but found himself outbid by MGM producer Pandro Berman (rumored to have been a Ball beau back in her starlet days at RKO).

Berman was convinced that the story had the makings of another *Father of the Bride*–sized smash and went to work assembling much of the same team that had brought *Bride* to the screen. The inevitable Frances Goodrich and Albert Hackett would handle the adaptation, while Vincente agreed to direct. Ball and Arnaz signed on to star, preparing to shoot *Trailer* while on summer hiatus from their series. Everything had fallen into place, with one exception: MGM was dead set against the idea of a Lucy-Desi movie.

I Love Lucy was a weekly must-see event for virtually everyone in America with a television, but Metro executives didn't think people would leave the comfort of their living rooms (where they could enjoy Lucy and Desi's zany antics for free every Monday night) to pay to see them at the local movie house. But Berman was banking on the fact that Ball and Arnaz, then at the height of their unprecedented popularity, would make for "boffo boxoffice," and he ultimately persuaded the studio to see things his way. Television's Lucy and Ricky Ricardo morphed into *Trailer*'s Tacy and Nicky Collini.

Once Lucy and Desi had signed on, MGM's initial trepidation about casting the couple evaporated. The studio rolled out the red carpet for Ball and Arnaz, both returning to the studio they had called home as contract players a decade earlier. In addition to their combined $250,000 salary, the couple were showered with star perks. Lucy would be occupying Lana Turner's former dressing room (rumored to have been the busiest on the lot), while Desi would make himself at home in Clark Gable's old quarters.

For Minnelli, guiding Ball and Arnaz through a widescreen variation of their weekly sitcom shouldn't have been too taxing. After all, he had just helmed one of the most memorable musicals of all time and skewered his own industry in the film preceding it. And yet, Ball recalled that as filming began in June 1953, Minnelli was "a basketcase." According to Ball, it wasn't the logistics of the shoot that were agitating Vincente but an especially bad case of ex-wife: "He was a great director. It was Judy who was making him crazy. Judy made *everybody* crazy. They were already divorced. But Judy was going through one of her crazy times. God, that woman was impossible. He was trying to take care of Liza and Judy wanted her, but Judy was so drunk and full of pills that he didn't want Liza to be with her. Jesus, it was a mess."[9]

When Ball offered to take seven-year-old Liza in to live with the Arnaz clan, Vincente was beyond grateful. "He grabbed my hand and just kept saying, 'Will you? *Will you?*'" recalled Ball, who would play surrogate mother to Liza for nearly a year.

Nicky and Tacy Collini (Desi Arnaz and Lucille Ball) and the forty-foot monster that comes between them in *The Long, Long Trailer*. Tacy's Aunt Anastacia happens to reside on the *Meet Me in St. Louis* street and her cousin, the painfully shy "poor Grace," was based on Minnelli's Aunt Anna.
PHOTO COURTESY OF PHOTOFEST

With his domestic situation settled—at least for the time being—Minnelli could concentrate fully on the film. Despite all of the chaos on screen and some rigorous shooting on location in Yosemite National Park, Vincente would recall the shooting of *The Long, Long Trailer* as "painless." Even Ball, who in later years would gain a reputation as a hard-nosed taskmaster, seemed to be enjoying the ride. "I didn't find her controlling at all," says Perry Sheehan Adair, who appeared in the film as one of Ball's bridesmaids. "In fact, she seemed quite nice. I think she and Minnelli really clicked on that picture, too. They brought out the best in each other and it really showed on screen."[10]

Only two months after the movie started shooting, it was previewed at the Picwood Theatre in West Los Angeles. Among the raves, there were some dissenting votes: "Minnelli has lost his touch," read one comment card. "Acts very similar to the weekly TV show," griped another. And most pointed of all: "This is a television team primed for a half hour of experienced laughs. Arnaz is not movie material. Lucille Ball is movie material. Let her co-star with someone else. Let Desi lead a band."

Though many Minnelli disciples tend to write off *The Long, Long Trailer* as soulless studio fluff and nothing more than an elongated *I Love Lucy* episode, others believe that it has been dismissed unfairly. "There are these statements that Minnelli is making about consumerism and obsession with surface details," says film scholar Richard Barrios:

In a way, he's almost getting back at the people who attack him for just being absorbed with surfaces. . . . That whole set up when Lucy takes Desi to the auto show and she falls in love with the trailer and then it becomes the third

character in the movie is really wild. And Minnelli doesn't just use the trailer
as a prop. In a way, it's the *deus ex machina* and it's the villain and it tries to
break up the marriage. Vincente's absorption with textures and surfaces is so
perfect because that's what this story is all about—it's really the embodiment
of a consumer nightmare. . . . There's so much mythology with Lucy and Desi
that it's easy for people to overlook who directed it and how important Minnelli
is to the way it works.[11]

And it certainly worked. In its initial release, the film raked in an estimated
$4.5 million and ranked among the top grossing pictures of the year. As Arnaz
liked to boast, for years *The Long, Long Trailer* held the title as the most
commercially successful comedy ever released by MGM. The critics were
generally agreeable, with *Time* observing: "Director Vincente Minnelli, as
skilled a comedy hand as Hollywood employs, has a way of letting the story
babble on absently between solid banks of common sense until the audience
is lulled in smiles."[12]

Almost Like
Being in Love

WHEN GEORGETTE MAGNANI was introduced to Vincente Minnelli by composer Vernon Duke, she was in her early twenties, newly arrived from France, and almost always referred to as the "Sister of Miss Universe of 1953," Christiane Martel. Georgette had come to California to look after her sister, who even at the tender age of seventeen didn't seem in dire need of an escort. After her beauty-pageant triumph, Christiane was being courted by Universal Pictures. She was engaged to marry Ronnie Marengo, heir to the Marengo department store fortune. Being constantly referred to as an appendage of Miss Universe may have prompted the equally photogenic Georgette to attempt to forge her own identity—one that had nothing to do with her much-discussed sister. Suddenly items about "Christine's Sis" began appearing in print. Columnists described Georgette as though she were the Second Coming of Sophia Loren: "She's the same height as Christine [*sic*]— 5 feet, 6 inches. Other statistics: waist 23, bust 35, hips 35." Va-voom.

Beyond the vital stats, Minnelli maintained that he was attracted by Georgette's "open manner" (the same quality he said had drawn him to Judy), her "Latin temper," and her French-Italian ancestry, which (more or less) matched his own. After they began a whirlwind courtship, rumors were circulating that Judy Garland's ex was preparing to tie the knot again. When queried about his matrimonial intentions, Vincente told columnist Harrison Carroll, "We aren't definite on our plans. . . . It's highly probable. We see a lot of each other and she's a wonderful girl."[1]

All speculation ended on February 16, 1954, when Vincente and Georgette wed in a Riverside ceremony termed a "surprise marriage" by the press. For many in the Hollywood community, the phrasing could be interpreted in more than one way. Cyd Charisse changed out of her *Brigadoon* costume long enough to be Georgette's matron of honor while dapper French actor Claude Dauphin served as Vincente's best man. The couple's honeymoon was postponed as production resumed on Minnelli's latest musical extravaganza.

***

BRIGADOON. THE VERY NAME was meant to conjure up images of rolling hills, sable skies, and, of course, the inescapable heather on the hill. If ever a movie cried out for open air, scenic vistas, and local color, it was Production #1645. Expectations were through the roof for MGM's widescreen version of the triumphant Broadway musical about a pair of American malcontents who stumble upon a mythical Scottish village that springs to life for a single day every hundred years. When the original stage production opened at "the house of hits"—the Ziegfeld Theatre—in 1947, *Brigadoon* was showered with rapturous reviews ("All the arts of the theatre have been woven into a singing pattern of enchantment," said the *New York Times*[2]). The musical racked up 581 performances, netted the New York Drama Critics Circle Award, and solidified the reputations of musical-comedy's new dynamic duo, Alan Jay Lerner and Frederick Loewe. The talented team was now being touted as the best thing to happen to the American musical since Jerome Kern and Oscar Hammerstein.

It seemed a good omen when Lerner was tapped to adapt his own libretto for the screen. And given the fact that the property was a lush musical fantasy, Minnelli seemed a very natural choice as director. After all, *Brigadoon*'s lovers-in-a-race-against-time scenario was essentially *The Clock* in kilts. If the saga of MacConnachy Square could succeed within the confines of a New York theater, surely the movies could make a good thing even better by souping it up with what the ads trumpeted as "Breathtaking CinemaScope" and "Gayest Color." MGM was fully confident that its production of the musical would improve upon the stage show by featuring popular stars whom the paying customer out in Omaha had actually heard of.

In March 1951, it was announced that Gene Kelly and Kathryn Grayson—the stars of *Anchors Aweigh* in 1945—would be reunited in *Brigadoon*. With Kelly in the lead, it became immediately apparent that Lerner and Loewe's enchanting score (which included "The Heather on the Hill" and "Almost Like Being in Love") would take a backseat to the star's fancy footwork. "It

Vincente married his second wife, Georgette Magnani ("The Sister of Miss Universe"), in 1954.
PHOTO COURTESY OF PHOTOFEST

became a dancing show instead of a singing show," says Lerner's longtime assistant Stone Widney. Exit Kathryn Grayson. Enter Moira Shearer. The striking, flame-haired ballerina had delivered a star-making performance in Michael Powell and Emeric Pressburger's *The Red Shoes*. Whereas Grayson hailed from Winston Salem, North Carolina, Shearer was an authentic Scottish lass. As fate would have it, Shearer's ballet company was reluctant to release its star for the length of the film's shooting schedule, however, and Metro finally settled on someone closer to home: contract player and Freed Unit favorite Cyd Charisse.

"I was excited about being in it, but it started off badly," Charisse recalled. "That was because Kelly wanted to film it on location, in Scotland, while the studio said no, that was impractical because of the weather there, and insisted it be done in Hollywood. Minnelli preferred shooting inside a soundstage, so tons of earth were moved onto several soundstages and it was all shot inside."[3] The heathered hills of *Brigadoon* were brought to life with a gargantuan 600-foot-long matte painting that encircled the entire set. The blatantly artificial environs would remain a sticking point with Gene Kelly.

If Minnelli and Kelly couldn't agree on *where* the film should be shot, they were also at odds regarding *how* it should be shot. "Vincente and I were never in synch, I must confess," Kelly admitted. Minnelli envisioned the movie as "more of an operetta"—the type of "theatrical artifice" that was less like *An American in Paris* and more like *The Pirate*. Kelly, however, saw *Brigadoon* as "a Scottish Western"—Arthur Freed meets John Ford. When the entire production veered more in Minnelli's direction, the star-choreographer was unhappy, and it showed. Minnelli later said he "had many talks with [Kelly], trying to impress on him the need to show exuberance in the part."[4] But the star remained remote and grim-looking.

Although he had been overruled on location and approach, Kelly would get his way in another matter. "Minnelli was named as the director but Gene seemed to be doing everything," remembers Michael Maule, a former New York City Ballet dancer who was initially cast as *Brigadoon*'s bridegroom, Charlie Chisholm Dalrymple. "I must say that I was very suspicious because there was this stand-in for me. A nice-looking young man. Gene would say, 'Let whatever-his-name-was run through the scene for you. You just take it easy and let him do everything for you.' And he kept doing this. Never giving me a chance to play a scene myself. I was very suspicious but everybody was so nice." One day, after a run-through, Maule was abruptly dismissed:

> They fired me. Minnelli didn't say much. It was Gene who said, "I'm sorry. I just didn't have time to work with you." I think that what happened was that they had signed me in New York without Gene being told. And he wanted to show them who was boss. I was heartbroken. I must have cried for about half an hour. . . . Later, I called up Vincente Minnelli's office and I said, "Could I have an appointment to see you?" And he said, "Yes, certainly." I went in to see him and put in a complaint about what had happened. I said, "I just want to tell you the way I feel and I think it was a dreadful thing to do." And Minnelli agreed with me. He was terribly nice and he said, "I'm so sorry but, you know, I'm really powerless to do anything." I really believe Minnelli had nothing to do with it. . . . I think Gene was hot for my stand-in.[5]

Principal photography got underway in December 1953. Adding to the already palpable tension on the set was the fact that once the performers finally managed to produce whatever effect their exacting, nonverbal director was looking for, they were obliged to do it all over again. As beleaguered costar Van Johnson recalled,

> They were going from widescreen to CinemaScope, so when we got a take, Vincente would say, "Now we're going to do one for CinemaScope. . . ." So I watched him. It took another 45 minutes to put this big camera on and relight

Van Johnson, Cyd Charisse, and Gene Kelly in Minnelli's adaptation of Broadway's
Brigadoon. Vincente wanted to shoot it in Scotland but was overruled. Kelly envisioned it
as a "Scottish western," while his director saw it as "more of an operetta." To top it all off,
the musical was shot simultaneously in two versions: widescreen and CinemaScope.
PHOTO COURTESY OF PHOTOFEST

and widen the thing. So, finally, I said, "I'm shooting two pictures!" I went to
see Dore Schary and I said, "I'm shooting two movies. I should have two
salaries . . ." but Dore said, "Yes, you're shooting two versions. That's right.
And you're getting one salary, Van, and be glad that you're getting it . . ." and
I walked out very meekly. I never did that again.[6]

Minnelli would later praise Lerner's fantasy as "ingenious" and the score
as "melodic and haunting." However, according to Gene Kelly, Vincente was
never in love with *Brigadoon*, and this seems to be borne out in the claus-
trophobic, airless feeling that permeates parts of the film. Occasionally, the
musical manages to free itself from its soundstage shackles and soars. "The
Heather on the Hill" is a glorious sequence, which succeeds because of the
gracefulness of Kelly and Charisse and the inspired arrangements of Conrad
Salinger.

At first glance, *Brigadoon* appears to contain all of the makings of a Minnelli classic: It's a musical in which a restless soul traverses the pathways
between an unsatisfying everyday existence and a far more enchanting dream
world. Yet, a frustrated Minnelli, a "curiously remote" Kelly, and the drudgery

of repeating every shot a second time in the name of CinemaScope added up to a 108-minute disappointment for some observers. "I told him I thought it kind of sucked and particularly a lot of Vincente's work," Stone Widney says of a postscreening autopsy he conducted with Alan Jay Lerner. "It had lovely touches in various places but clumsy staging, though Alan didn't want to hear that and I think he was probably kind of in denial about that. As long as the show gets on and it has big stars and it makes money, I think Alan felt that it was a success."[7]

Fifty years after its initial release, *Brigadoon* is dismissed by some, championed by others. "I think *Brigadoon* is an underrated film," says film and dance scholar Beth Genne:

> For one thing, I think that they were quite successful in transferring it to film. Some of the compositions are really beautiful, like the opening scene where the village comes back to life. . . . But I think there's a prejudice against it because when [the stage show] first appeared, the sophisticated New York critics said—as they did with *Oklahoma!*—that it was corny. There was also this feeling that *Brigadoon* was "twee," which means something that goes beyond cute. Like when you go to "Mrs. So and So's Kozy Komfort Inn" and she's got too many ribbons on everything and a few too many scented candles. . . . After awhile, you just can't handle it. It's overdone. I don't think *Brigadoon* is overdone but it's maybe just a little bit twee. But even so, there are some marvelous things in it.[8]

Despite some of *Brigadoon*'s redeeming features, most of the critics took aim: "The whimsical dream world it creates holds no compelling attractions," said Penelope Huston in the *London Times*. "Hollywood can still put its worst foot forward in the classic manner," griped *Newsweek*.

Farley Granger, who had remained friendly with Vincente after *The Story of Three Loves*, remembered that he and designer Oliver Smith were visiting with Minnelli when the reviews of *Brigadoon* were phoned in to the film's mortified director.

> I remember that Vincente was on the phone all the time that we were having drinks. Liza, who was a little girl at the time, kept running in and out in these incredible costumes. We could hear the phone conversations coming from the other room. . . . *Brigadoon* had opened in New York and it had gotten roasted, and we could hear Vincente saying, "Were they that bad?" and "That bad . . . *really?*" Oliver Smith, who had a very funny, dry sense of humor, would raise an eyebrow and giggle, and in would come Liza as Little Bo Peep.[9]

20

Cobwebs

ALONG WITH *Alice in Wonderland* and *The Catcher in the Rye*, W. H. Hudson's 1904 fantasy *Green Mansions* was on the short list of great books best left unfilmed. Although it ranked alongside the Bible and the dictionary on the all-time bestseller list, Hudson's classic was considered "too special" to be adapted for the screen. Set in "the forbidden forests beyond the Amazon," the novel concerned a disillusioned political refugee who retreats into the jungle, where he encounters Rima, the ethereal Bird Girl who captures his heart. The revolutionary joins Rima on a trek to find the lost civilization of Riolama, but their journey ends in tragedy.

As several frustrated producers would discover, attempting to transfer *Green Mansions* to the screen was a daunting prospect. Even a semi-faithful adaptation would demand stunning on-location photography, a barrage of special effects, and a leading lady who could be believable speaking "bird" and flitting about in cobweb couture.

In the early '30s, *King Kong* director Merian C. Cooper attempted to bring *Green Mansions* to the screen for RKO (which had acquired the rights to Hudson's book in 1932). A Technicolor camera crew was dispatched to South America to shoot atmospheric location footage, and costumer Walter Plunkett was commissioned to create a smock of spider webs for exotic beauty Dolores del Rio, who was a shoo-in to play Rima. Everything seemed to have fallen into place when a regime shift at RKO spelled the end of Cooper's *Green Mansions*—but that didn't stop other filmmakers from trying. In 1945, MGM acquired the screen rights to Hudson's allegory of eternal love. A steady stream of press releases announced everyone from Peruvian folk singer Yma Sumac to the far too earthy Elizabeth Taylor as Rimas-in-waiting, but still *Green Mansions* defied the cameras.

In October 1953, the *Los Angeles Times* reported that Metro was taking a "new whack" at the property: "MGM still thinks it can lick the *Green Mansions* problem—i.e., how to get a movie out of W. H. Hudson's classic. . . . Present solution: To turn it over to Alan Lerner, writer; Vincente Minnelli, director; and Arthur Freed, producer—a trio endowed with comparative taste and intelligence—with permission to shoot the works."[1]

Despite the participation of Minnelli, Lerner, and Freed, none of them had any intention of making *Green Mansions: The Musical*. It would be a drama, though music would play an important part in the production. In fact, Brazilian composer-orchestrator Heitor Villa-Lobos was engaged to create a "Bird Symphony" for the film. This would be part of what Minnelli hoped would be a "mystical score" based on authentic birdsongs.

In February 1954, Alan Jay Lerner reported that he was "cruising up the Orinoco," with twenty-five pages of his *Green Mansions* screenplay completed. "I am resisting desperately the temptation to write 'charm' and 'local color,'" Lerner explained to Arthur Freed. "I feel very keenly that it must never look like a fantasy. . . . I am also trying to write it economically, not only to preserve the mood and narrative flow, but also so that there will be adequate room for the visual."[2]

As usual, the visual was very much on Minnelli's mind as he flew off to Peru, Panama, British Guiana, and Venezuela to scout locations for *Green Mansions* that June. Like Lerner, Minnelli realized that the last thing Hudson's fairy tale needed was a studio-manufactured South America. The more naturalistic the setting, the more believable the story—though once Vincente was en route to the rain forests, he may have wished he was back in Culver City: "I was in this one motor plane with Indians and their babies who vomited in the aisles, goats and hound dogs. . . . I never thought we'd get there in one piece," he said of the trip.[3] In the jungles of Venezuela, Minnelli and company were hampered by incessant rain, primitive conditions, and oppressive heat. After a week of waiting around for the torrential rains to subside, Minnelli, art director Preston Ames, and a skeleton crew managed to shoot some stunning 16 millimeter images.

Meanwhile, the search for the perfect Rima continued. *Life* magazine, on orders from MGM's powerful publicity chief, Howard Strickling, pushed for demure, Italian-born Pier Angeli in the role: "She is a strong contender but hasn't been promised anything. Our idea is to have her audition for the part for *Life*'s camera and let her show why she ought to have it. . . . Pier

feels she was born for the role and says she'd wear brown trunks, bra of flowers and wear her hair long and wild as she flies through the forest."[4]

In October, Minnelli prepared to shoot one of the most elaborate screen
tests in Hollywood history on MGM's Stage 15. Pier Angeli (minus bra of
flowers) would try Rima on for size, and handsome newcomer Edmund Purdom would play the lovelorn fugitive. As though he were mounting a full-
fledged feature, Vincente ordered up a lush jungle paradise complete with
an artificial lagoon. Branches left over from *Brigadoon* were strewn with cob-
webs. No less than Joseph Ruttenberg would photograph the mini-spectacle.
It took two weeks and $130,000 to shoot.

Although all eyes were on Angeli, Minnelli noted that the proceedings
were "as much a test of us—to see how we would approach the picture."[5]
After viewing the footage, Arthur Freed concluded that there was no sense
in proceeding any further, as nothing about the test was persuasive. Pier Angeli was not entirely convincing as Rima, but then again, what actress would
be? Once again, plans to bring *Green Mansions* to the screen were scrapped.
In 1959, Hudson's tale would finally reach the screen, with Audrey Hepburn
(as believable as anyone could be as the Bird Girl) and a miscast Anthony
Perkins as the rugged revolutionary. The movie, directed by Hepburn's then
husband, Mel Ferrer, was both a commercial and critical disappointment.
The film's failure proved Freed right. *Green Mansions* belonged on a book
shelf, not the silver screen.

***

"THE TROUBLE ABOUT THE LIVING-ROOM DRAPES . . ." ignites an interoffice
Armageddon in William Gibson's engrossing 1954 debut novel *The Cobweb*.
The novel is set at the Castle House Clinic for Nervous Disorders, a psychiatric care facility that Gibson patterned after the Austen Riggs Center in
Stockbridge, Massachusetts (where Judy Garland had once received treatment). The self-absorbed wife of the head doctor purchases drapes for the
clinic's common room, and this seemingly insignificant act sparks several
simmering rivalries among the staffers, who make the patients look perfectly
sane by comparison.

For a decor-obsessed director like Minnelli, being handed a story in which
interior furnishings play a pivotal role must have seemed like a gift from the
cinematic gods. "*The Cobweb* was a psychological story that appealed to me
greatly," Vincente said. "The thing that attracted me was that it wasn't about
the inmates, although the inmates happen to be strange. It was about the
doctors and the foul-ups in their lives. . . . It was so rich in possibilities that
I volunteered to direct."[6] Although he didn't say so, Minnelli may have also

responded to the material for another reason. With an institutionalized brother and an ex-wife who had been attended by several psychiatrists, he must have realized that *The Cobweb* hit awfully close to home.

Minnelli and producer John Houseman weren't satisfied with screenwriter John (*The Wild One*) Paxton's initial attempts at adapting *The Cobweb*. Motion Picture Production Code restrictions had forced Paxton to either eliminate or tone down some of the novel's more daring themes (homosexuality and adultery being the obligatory offenders), but that wasn't the only problem; it seemed as though any sense of drama had been lost in translation.

"They were having trouble with the script and I could smell it," says William Gibson:

> And I thought it would be interesting to see how movies are made. So, I wrote John Houseman a note and he called me up and said, "Do you want to come out and work with us?" and I said, "Sure." First they sent me this unsatisfactory script by John Paxton, a well known and well paid screenwriter of the day. I read it on the plane. I thought it was miserable. . . . When I got out there, I sat with Minnelli and Houseman for eight long hours just talking about that script. . . . I then returned to the cottage I was staying in, which was owned by one of Freud's disciples. I worked there and Houseman would pick up my pages every morning. . . . We only had about three weeks before the cameras began.[7]

Though he may have been the author of the original novel, Gibson was untested as a screenwriter. Fortunately, he would prove to be a gifted dramatist, as his later plays, *The Miracle Worker* and *Two for the Seesaw*, demonstrated. In his hands, a revamped version of *The Cobweb* might amount to something.

While Gibson went to work overhauling the screenplay,[*] Minnelli and Houseman turned their attention to casting. Houseman suggested using Warner Brothers' smoldering new star, James Dean, in the role of Stevie Holte, an antisocial though artistically gifted patient contemptuous of authority figures. "I would hear a sharp roar of his motorcycle outside the Thalberg Building," Houseman recalled of the visits he received from Hollywood's resident hell-raiser, James Dean. "He would sit on the floor of my office and we would chat for hours. I took him over to Minnelli, who was delighted by him and began to develop our boy's sequence with James Dean in mind."[8]

---

[*] Regarding authorship, the final screen credit on *The Cobweb* reads: "Screenplay by John Paxton. Additional dialogue by William Gibson, based on the novel by Gibson."

Without question, Dean would have been ideal casting. The young rene-
gade came equipped with an unnerving intensity and a sexual ambiguity—
qualities that were perfect for such a conflicted character. "Jimmy Dean had
a lot of color and Houseman was absolutely right to be thinking in that direction," Gibson says.[9]

But a James Dean performance in a Vincente Minnelli production was
not to be. "Suddenly we ran into trouble—typical Hollywood trouble," Houseman recalled. "Dean had a contract with Warner Brothers at a modest salary,
which following his success in *East of Eden*, he and his agent were trying to
raise. He had the right to make one outside film—which would be ours. His
agent's strategy was to use the salary we would pay Jimmy for *The Cobweb*
as the basis for his revised salary at Warner's."[10] Once executives at MGM
and Warner Brothers got wind of Dean's scheme, however, Minnelli's movie
was out one death-defying thrill-seeker.

After searching for a suitable replacement, Minnelli and Houseman settled
on twenty-four-year-old John Kerr, who had garnered good notices playing
a similarly tormented character in Elia Kazan's acclaimed stage production
of *Tea and Sympathy*. In the shift from Dean to Kerr, one crucial element
was forfeited. Whereas the rebel from Fairmount, Indiana, had sex appeal
in spades, Kerr was the very image of the clean-cut Ivy Leaguer—and about
as alluring as balsa wood.

In terms of the film's other pivotal players, MGM first announced the
photogenic trio of Robert Taylor, Grace Kelly, and Lana Turner as the stars
of *The Cobweb*. As script revisions dragged on, however, the studio realized
that replacements would have to be found. Ultimately, Richard Widmark,
Lauren Bacall, and Gloria Grahame—three of the busiest actors of the Eisenhower era—would star as the clinic manager, his burgeoning love interest,
and his love-starved wife, respectively. But it was the casting of the boozy,
philandering Dr. Douglas Devenal that was the cause of a major rift between
director and producer. "I thought Charles Boyer would be an offbeat choice
but John didn't see it," Minnelli noted. Houseman countered: "[Boyer's] sophisticated, accented charm seemed to me to give a false twist to the entire
plot. . . . I gave in—and bitterly regretted it."[11] For the role of the asylum's
waspish administrator Victoria Inch, Minnelli and Houseman hit the bull's
eye, casting silent-screen legend Lillian Gish.

In Gibson's novel, the character known only as "Capp" is flamboyantly
gay, but as Vincente noted, "at that time you couldn't do homosexuals and
Oscar [Levant] had called and wanted to be in the picture, so I patterned
the character after Oscar himself [with the] same kind of hang-ups that he

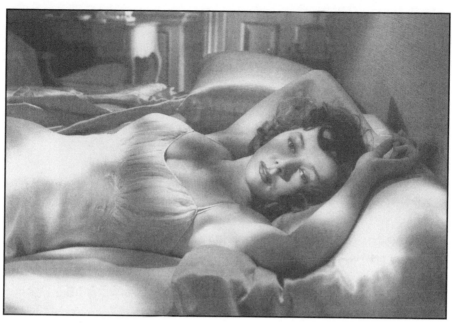

The Cobweb: The love-starved Karen McIver (Gloria Grahame)
seems to have more on her mind than changing the drapes.
PHOTO COURTESY OF PHOTOFEST

had. And he was awfully good in that."[12] Even so, Capp on screen wasn't
nearly as interesting as Capp on the page.

Minnelli began shooting *The Cobweb* in December 1954. William Gibson
recalled:

> When I turned up on the set, [Richard] Widmark told me, "You're very lucky
> to get Minnelli. There are only two directors who could handle this material—
> Kazan and Minnelli." I thought that overrated Minnelli's gift because Kazan
> was a real theatre person coming out of the Group Theatre and he had been
> an actor. I never saw Minnelli either in our conferences or on the set doing
> anything that was corrective of an actor. He had an excellent pictorial sense
> but he was not really an actor's director. He was all visual.[13]

Lauren Bacall found this out the hard way:

> On *The Cobweb*, I'd arrive on the set and there he'd be up on the boom, zoom-
> ing up to the drapes, and I thought to myself, "He's really in heaven now." The
> bloody drapes. It was all about the goddamned drapes in *The Cobweb*. I loved

Vincente and we were friends, but I used to joke with Oscar Levant about Vincente's direction because he was so totally involved with what everything looked like. . . .

I will never forget, when we were rehearsing this one scene, I was sitting on a sofa between Lillian Gish and Oscar Levant, and I had my left leg crossed over my right and I was just sitting there. Vincente was walking back and forth in front of us while we were rehearsing and he's humming the whole time, "*Hmmm Hmmm Hmmm*, . . ." and he suddenly walked over to me and lifted my left leg and put it on the floor and then picked up my right leg to cross over my left leg. What that meant to him I'll never know. But Oscar and I laughed about that for quite awhile, let me tell you.[14]

On the first day of principal photography, Houseman invited Gibson to come and observe:

So, I went on the set and that's when I realized that a lot of the dialogue that I had taken out of the script was suddenly back in because Houseman and Minnelli were apparently writers also. I remember Houseman said to me, "It doesn't matter who holds the pencil. . . ." Now that's the key to the entire operation out there. In my life, the man who holds the pencil is named Shakespeare. It's not part of the concept there. You just become part of the machinery. . . . Then I saw things like Lauren Bacall walking in front of the camera, in a scene where she's crossing a field, and there she was swinging her ass very sexily and I thought, *Has she not read the part?* This character has just lost her husband and her child. She's in a state of mourning. She's not swinging her ass. But nobody cared about that.[15]

The scene Gibson witnessed would wind up on the cutting-room floor along with a sizable chunk of the movie. Vincente's original cut of *The Cobweb* ran two and a half hours, unusually long for a Metro release. Minnelli and Houseman clashed bitterly over excisions that Houseman felt were necessary in order to bring the picture in at a manageable length. "Our worst time was during the editing of the film, which came out far too long—by artistic and commercial standards," Houseman remembered. "Yet Vincente obstinately refused to lose anything—even after the previews. . . . When I ran it for him after hacking close to half an hour out of the film, including entire scenes he had shot with loving care, he made a violent, lachrymose scene in the projection room, accusing me of insensitivity and treachery. I offered to let him recut the film, but he refused."[16] It was an unpleasant scene that Minnelli would find himself replaying frequently throughout the latter half of his career.

Even at a significantly reduced running time of 124 minutes, *The Cobweb* still seems ponderously paced, a fact that was not lost on the critics: "A select minority among filmgoers may find the even-keeled clinical study interesting, but there's not enough contrast between its dramatic highs and lows, nor sufficiently developed sympathy for the characters to attract the entertainment fancy of the majority," *Variety* decided. *Film Daily* noted, "The picture is on the cerebral side, lacking the impact and mood which would have made for more emotional appeal." The most memorable review belonged to Philip T. Hartung, who famously dubbed the picture "The Drapes of Wrath."

And as for the author, William Gibson says, "I found it totally boring." And what's more, he was finished with Hollywood. "I thought . . . this is not where I want to spend my life. It's a choice between their money and my words and I think I'll go home and live with my words." Gibson was so turned off by his experiment in movie-making that even when Minnelli and Houseman dangled a plum assignment before him, he could not be moved. "On my last day, they offered me the chance to write their next movie. I said, 'No, I'm going back to Stockbridge to work on a play of my own. They kept talking about this movie they were going to make about van Gogh, *Lust for Life*. Minnelli said to me, 'I think it can be a masterpiece.'"[17]

21

Stranger
in Paradise

IF MINNELLI COULDN'T WAIT to get to *Lust for Life* and explore the tormented psyche of Vincent van Gogh, he couldn't have been less interested or more uninspired by *Kismet*, which was standing in his way. Although Vincente had turned down Arthur Freed's invitation to direct a lavish screen version of the Broadway show, Dore Schary simply wouldn't take no for an answer. "We need you desperately for *Kismet*," Schary implored. "You could direct it before you go to Europe for *Lust for Life*."[1] Although the studio chief reached out to Vincente in the form of an impassioned plea, there was an implicit ultimatum behind Schary's words—if Minnelli didn't direct *Kismet*, there would be no *Lust for Life*.

At the height of a 1953 newspaper strike that deprived several Broadway shows of some well-deserved accolades, *Kismet* got lucky. Thanks to good word-of-mouth, audiences flocked to this "musical Arabian night." With its Robert Wright–George Forrest score adapted from Alexander Borodin's music, the show produced two hit songs that would become piano bar staples, "Stranger in Paradise" and "Baubles, Bangles and Beads." Alfred Drake was roundly applauded for his bravura turn as Hajj, the street poet—though even as the actor was taking his curtain calls, theatergoers were already wondering who would end up playing Drake's part when Hollywood mounted its own version of the show.

Of course, Broadway's *Kismet* was only the latest interpretation of the shop-worn tale of a poetic beggar who ascends the social ranks to become Emir of Baghdad. Edward Knoblock's operetta had debuted in 1911. And by the time Minnelli found himself saddled with it, there had already been three film versions of *Kismet*. The most memorable incarnation had arrived in 1944 and featured Ronald Colman in the lead. This exercise in exotica was best remembered for the indelible spectacle of Marlene Dietrich writhing seductively in a "dance" sequence, her legendary legs coated in gold body paint.

On May 23, 1955, production began on Minnelli's *Kismet*. Stars Howard Keel, Ann Blyth, and Dolores Gray were initially enthusiastic about bringing the Broadway smash to the screen, though, from the outset, their director exhibited impatience with nearly everything concerning the production. It was readily apparent to both cast and crew that of all the films Vincente had helmed so far, *Kismet* was the one project that failed to engage him on any level. "*Kismet* was doomed from the start. Nothing planned fell into place," an embittered Howard Keel remembered.[2]

Minnelli gritted his teeth and soldiered on, but he proceeded with greater haste than ever before. The quiet, infinitely patient auteur of *Meet Me in St. Louis* was suddenly replaced with a tyrannical, Otto Premingerish alter ego. Vic Damone, fresh from warbling Sigmund Romberg in Stanley Donen's bloated biopic *Deep in My Heart*, had to contend with an openly hostile Minnelli. As Keel remembered it, "Vincente was terrible to Vic. Instead of trying to help him, Minnelli berated him at every opportunity and in front of everyone."[3]

And Minnelli wasn't the only one throwing tantrums. "I was on the set of *Kismet* and I witnessed a nasty scene that Dolores Gray made," recalled artist Don Bachardy, nineteen at the time and an unpaid assistant to Tony Duquette, who designed the costumes. "Arthur Freed was forcing her to be photographed by daylight. Seeing her in daylight, I couldn't help but understand her objections. She had a bad complexion and daylight is just murder for that. Especially with make-up over her face . . . and a bad nose job besides."[4] Gray's sizzling renditions of "Not Since Nineveh" and "Rahadlakum" more than made up for the actress's display of temperament, and her scintillating delivery manages to liven things up on screen.

When Gray is not around, there is always the decor—plus Tony Duquette's outré Arabian apparel. As Don Bachardy remembered it, Minnelli and Duquette strove to improve upon the work of their predecessors: "I think they were in total agreement about the art work on the previous MGM version of *Kismet* with Dietrich. I think they both agreed that the art work in it was pretty awful." Determined to outdo Cedric Gibbon's uninspired settings, Minnelli decided on a monochromatic Mesopotamia but also one that was "like Olsen and Johnson in Baghdad . . . very beautiful and chic."[5] Duquette

Dolores Gray in Minnelli's screen version of *Kismet*. As the alluring Lalume,
Gray enlivens the film and her sizzling rendition of "Not Since Nineveh" is a knockout.
The showstopper also kept things hopping off screen as well.
PHOTO COURTESY OF PHOTOFEST

let his imagination run wild, conjuring up enough colorful Arabian finery to
satisfy a thousand and one nights.

"Vic Damone looked prettier than the girls in that movie," recalls assistant
director Hank Moonjean, referring to the outlandish ensembles that the former Vito Farinola found himself tarted up in:

> The Tony Duquette clothes were something else. Even the dancers couldn't
> dance in their costumes. Jack Cole's dancers had to twirl and spin around a
> lot but the girls were wearing these huge, elaborate headpieces and every time
> they spun around, their head gear fell over. Finally, they had to get rid of all
> those heavy hats and start over. You know, it was my first musical and I re-
> member it in great detail. I couldn't believe movies were made this way but I
> learned very quickly.[6]

Despite the palpable tension on the set, dancer Nita Bieber remembered
that Vincente enjoyed a harmonious working relationship with the equally
exacting choreographer Jack Cole: "Minnelli really listened to him because
Jack Cole had real insight into what was going on with that story and how

the dancers could help bring the whole thing to life. . . . There may have been other problems going on but as I remember it, Minnelli and Jack worked together very well."[7]

Others felt that on *Kismet*, Vincente was anything but a team player. When Keel observed Minnelli reviewing plans for *Lust for Life* on *Kismet*'s clock, Metro's booming baritone lost all patience with the director's supreme disinterest. Keel went to Freed and issued an ultimatum. "If Minnelli is on the set tomorrow morning, I'm not on it. So, pull whatever strings you have and get someone else. I am not finishing this picture with Vincente."[8] Minnelli obediently disappeared, and the equally talented Stanley Donen inherited the project for ten days.

Despite CinemaScope, Eastmancolor, and the talents of Tony Duquette, *Kismet* is an ill-turned rarity: an uninviting Vincente Minnelli musical. As Keel duly noted, much of the blame for the lackluster quality of the picture must rest with Vincente. If Minnelli's work was indeed the story of his life, *Kismet* would rate only a telegraphic footnote. In fact, in the director's autobiography, discussion of the film is relegated to a few dismissive paragraphs with a sobering moral included: "The experience taught me never again to accept an assignment when I lacked enthusiasm for it."[9]

***

ON MAY 20, 1955—three days before Minnelli began shooting *Kismet*—his second child was born. Liza now had a half sister named Christiana Nina, who would later be called Tina Nina. Her formative years would coincide with the busiest period of Minnelli's career. When Liza was growing up, virtually all of Vincente's films had been shot on MGM's Culver City soundstages. During Tina Nina's childhood, Minnelli was frequently being whisked away to film on location (landing everywhere from Paris, France, to Paris, Texas). Although Vincente obviously loved Tina Nina, and indulged her in much the same way he had Liza, his time with his youngest would be limited.

"Liza was much more at ease, much closer to daddy than I was," the adult Tina Nina recalled. "She had her mother, [and] although Judy had her ups and downs, Liza had her on a pedestal. But daddy was her stability and Liza was practically in love with him. She worshipped him and he worshipped her. He didn't have a family, other than an aunt. All he had was Liza. . . . He was alone and she was alone. They only had each other."[10]

The bond between Vincente and Liza was so strong and so special that Tina Nina, like Georgette before her, may have felt like an intruder at times. How could Minnelli's "other" daughter ever hope to compete with Liza, who was not only a multimedia goddess in the making but, without question, the center of attention in Vincente's life. Sure, Tina Nina would slip into Liza's miniature Metro ensembles and attempt a Cyd Charisse–style pirouette, but this was just "play time." It almost certainly didn't fulfill the same need that it did for her older sister—or their father, for that matter. Vincente and Liza were dependant on the fantasy as a means of psychological escape, whereas Tina Nina, the daughter of practical, down-to-earth Georgette, was simply having a bit of fun.

Vincente made every attempt to make Tina Nina feel loved, and he went out of his way to bring his two daughters together. After Judy married third husband Sid Luft in 1952, Liza didn't seem to mind sharing her mother with half-sister Lorna or half-brother Joey. But sharing her beloved father with another child was another matter entirely. As Tina Nina recalled: "Daddy and Liza were so close that she would get jealous when I arrived. Sometimes she pretended to be sick. Then daddy rushed into her room and comforted her. I remember her lying in bed and crying, 'Daddy, you don't care about me. You only care about Tina Nina. I'm jealous of Tina Nina.' I felt so guilty."[11]

Vincente would remember Tina Nina as "the brightest spot" in his four-year marriage to Georgette. While an introvert like her husband, The Second Mrs. Minnelli was grounded and pragmatic. Vincente, on the other hand, was dreamy, restless, and detached. At times, it seemed as though their daughter was one of the few things they had in common.

22

Maelstroms
and Madmen

IF MINNELLI HAD SPED THROUGH the filming of *Kismet* with nearly complete disinterest, *Lust for Life* would engage him on every level. "It was the most thrilling and stimulating creative period of my life," Vincente would later say of the production.[1] The director's affinity for his subject, Vincent van Gogh, would result in one of Minnelli's most moving and psychologically intimate films. While it may be something of a stretch to draw parallels between Vincent van Gogh's postimpressionist innovations and Vincente Minnelli's unconventional filmmaking techniques, artist and director clearly had more in common than their first names.

Although van Gogh's fiery, volatile temperament could not have been more dissimilar from Minnelli's dreamy passivity, spiritually the two would appear to be working from the same palette. Van Gogh's *Wildflowers* and *Starry Night* radiate with an almost tangible electricity and intensity of feeling, and Minnelli's *Lust for Life* is alive with the same kind of passion, sensuousness, and mastery of color.

The ultimate nonconformist in Minnelli's long line of iconoclasts, van Gogh was profoundly talented, operatically tortured, and, like the director, chronically frustrated by his attempts to communicate his artistic intentions to others. "It is practically always so painful for me to speak to other people," van Gogh wrote to his brother Theo in 1883.[2] Instead, he communicated on canvas, and the messages he left behind are hopeful, mystical, and heart breaking.

Virtually all of Minnelli's movies had been influenced by painting to some degree or patterned after the works of specific artists. *Meet Me in St. Louis* paid tribute to the paintings of Thomas Eakins. *An American in Paris* and its climactic ballet allowed Vincente to honor the Impressionists. A Minnelli movie might contain a reference to Goya or a nod to Caravaggio. But never before had Vincente been so determined to present "art"—spelled out in reverent capital letters—on the screen. In a complete reversal from his calamitous approach to *Kismet*, Vincente's total immersion in van Gogh's story proved contagious. Despite the objectionable presence of CinemaScope (which practically screamed lurid spectacle), everyone involved sensed that this would be an inspired, faithful account of the last twelve years of van Gogh's life. No *Naked Maja* was this *Lust for Life*.

Pointing to the success of John Huston's Toulouse-Lautrec biopic, *Moulin Rouge*, Minnelli and Houseman sold Dore Schary on the idea of adapting Irving Stone's semifictional 1934 van Gogh biography for the screen. And not a moment too soon. As a property under option, *Lust for Life* had been languishing on the studio shelf since 1946.

"They were in danger of losing their option," screenwriter Norman Corwin recalls:

> The studio's ownership of that property was due to expire in a couple of months. So, this was a last-ditch effort. When John Houseman called me and asked if I would be interested, he told me they had struck out on two previous screenplays and would I like to see them? I said, "No, I'd like to read the book, however." Let me confess that I was disillusioned somewhat by the book *Lust for Life* because there seemed to me to be areas of brilliant writing followed by some pretty plain Jane prose. I decided to turn to the letters of Vincent, which were beautifully written. I felt that if we based the picture on the letters rather than the book, we'd be on safer ground. Houseman agreed with me. So, the picture ended up drawing upon Vincent's letters more directly than the book.[3]

Even as a secondary source, Irving Stone's biography posed problems. Metro's legal department had discovered that the studio's ten-year option would expire in nine months. Stone was unwilling to grant an extension, so the race was on. From casting to cutting, *Lust for Life* would be an example of grace under pressure.

Two years earlier, Kirk Douglas's production company (the Bryna Company) had announced that Jean Negulesco would direct Douglas in its own van Gogh biopic. That project never materialized, and when Schary greenlighted *Lust for Life*, it was clear that the Russian-born Douglas, who bore an uncanny resemblance to Dutchman van Gogh, was ideal casting.

Van Gogh's friend and rival Paul Gauguin had been convincingly played by George Sanders in *The Moon and Sixpence* in 1942. However, in bandying about casting suggestions for *Lust for Life*, Minnelli and Houseman decided that their Gauguin should be earthier, more physically imposing, and exhibit a smoldering sexuality. Paging Anthony Quinn. The Mexican-born actor had already copped an Oscar for his role as Marlon Brando's brother in *Viva Zapata*. After casting Quinn as Gauguin, Houseman dubbed him "perfect in looks and manner," though the actor's seemingly endless Method preparations would later exasperate the producer.

If Minnelli had lost the battle to shoot *Brigadoon* on location, he was not going to make the same mistake twice. Director and producer convinced the studio that in the name of authenticity, a film biography of an immortal European artist must be photographed in a more naturalistic setting than Stage 29. Miraculously, permission was granted.

With production on *Lust for Life* limited to basically five months, the shooting schedule redefined breakneck. Minnelli landed in France on a Saturday and cameras were expected to roll on Monday. The rigors of commanding an ambitious, on-location production—and one barreling ahead at warp speed—immediately agitated Minnelli. According to Houseman, even before shooting a single frame, the director was already "exhausted, harassed and vile-tempered."[4]

In some ways, the whiplash-inducing pace of the picture harkened back to Minnelli's frenzied days at Radio City Music Hall. Or perhaps even further back than that. As the crew dashed from one location to the next with an array of costumes at the ready, Vincente likened the experience to "the travels of a third-rate repertory company."[5] It was the Minnelli Brothers Mighty Dramatic Company all over again, and everything Vincente had learned about redressing reality back in Delaware would prove invaluable as the company sped from one picturesque location to another.

As Minnelli later revealed, "Houseman and I had the script but when we saw the real settings, we changed everything in response to them": "We went to Paris, Arles, St. Remy and Belgium. We shot in Amsterdam and in the actual coal mine in which van Gogh worked."[6] Along the way, Minnelli, Freddie Young (later to become David Lean's cinematographer of choice), and Russell Harlan captured some breathtaking images: Upon his arrival in Arles, Vincent throws open his shutters to reveal an orchard with row upon row of fruit trees in full bloom. Van Gogh, sporting a straw hat rimmed with illuminated candles, captures the shimmering waters in *Starry Night over the Rhone*, the fierce autumn winds stirring up the crimson-colored brushwood—and Vincent's restless psyche.

On location, Minnelli
prepares Pamela
Brown for a scene in
Lust for Life.
PHOTO COURTESY OF
PHOTOFEST

When he wasn't protesting the rearrangement of his script, Norman Corwin had an opportunity to witness much of the shooting in progress as well as to observe collaborators Houseman and Minnelli up close. "I knew John Houseman from the Mercury Theatre days. He had a patrician quality. He had very expressive nostrils and he used them to good effect. An unusual intellect. Perhaps the best intellect of any film producer of his time, in fact."[7]

While Corwin remembered Minnelli as an "impeccable" director, he also glimpsed the overworked auteur in a less composed moment. "I would say Vincente was punctilious to a point of distress at times. For example, I heard him roundly ball out a routine actor who was playing a small part. My sympathy is always with the man who is trying. This poor guy shriveled under Minnelli's attack. But then I realized that Minnelli was a perfectionist. If something didn't go well, he looked around for a target to blame." As for Minnelli's rapport with the French-Anglo crew, "he drove them half-mad with his exacting and often unreasonable demands," Houseman noted. Usually they caved into the director's requests but when Vincente ordered that a standing bridge be razed and then reconstructed elsewhere, they drew the line.[8]

Just as there had been a friendly rivalry between van Gogh and Gauguin, so there seemed to be some professional competitiveness between the actors inhabiting those roles. "Ever since I've arrived here, I've been hearing nothing but how great Kirk is," Quinn lamented to Minnelli. "I'm beginning to feel like Gauguin must have felt when he came to Arles."[9] It wasn't long before Quinn claimed to be communicating with the spirit of Gauguin, who made a point of letting the actor know he was holding the paintbrushes all wrong.

Minnelli's leading man had some hair-raising encounters of his own. "I evidently have a marked resemblance to van Gogh," says Kirk Douglas:

> One day, when we were shooting in Amsterdam, I went to the van Gogh Museum and the room was filled with self-portraits. I was made up as van Gogh and looking at all those paintings. Suddenly, it seemed very still and I turned around and about a hundred people were just quietly watching me. It startled me because they were all just staring at me. They said I had this uncanny resemblance to van Gogh. . . . When we were at Auvers-sur-Oise, where Vincent van Gogh committed suicide, there was an old lady there. When she saw me she said, "He has come back!"
>   I began to have an experience on that picture that I've never had in my life and that was where I felt that the character had completely taken me over. In acting, you should be taking the character over, but Vincent was such a powerful figure and such a mythic guy and so poignant and his life was so sad that it really took hold of me completely. You know, when I finished the movie, it was hard to watch it. I never had that kind of experience with any other movie.[10]

Is it any wonder that Minnelli couldn't wait to get to *Lust for Life*? *An American in Paris* aside, this was Vincente's first real opportunity to explore the life of a painter. Since he had picked up Whistler's biography in Paul Stone's studio, he had been completely intrigued by the lives of the artists he idolized. Even as he was being proclaimed the master of the Broadway musical, Minnelli had admitted to a reporter that he "would rather paint one good canvas than have his name above the show title of the smash hit of the season."[11] Through van Gogh's story, Minnelli would be allowed to say what making art meant to him.

In *Lust for Life*, the creative process offers refuge from disappointing relationships, spurned affections, and a world that would never really understand. But the struggle for artistic expression is actually a secondary theme in *Lust for Life*. The main theme is loneliness and social alienation, a leitmotif Minnelli would turn to repeatedly throughout the '50s. In addition to van Gogh's story, there would be Sinatra's conflicted novelist in *Some Came Running* and John Kerr's frustrated folk singer in *Tea and Sympathy*. Simply by being who they are, Vincente's characters are in immediate opposition to the world around them. The eventual exile that a Minnelli protagonist endures is often self-imposed, as each extraordinary misfit instinctively knows that he or she must ultimately turn inward to attempt to heal themselves and achieve some kind of life-altering liberation.

Table for One:
Kirk Douglas as
lonely outcast
Vincent van Gogh in
Lust For Life.
PHOTO COURTESY OF
PHOTOFEST

It's no accident that iconic pictures about rebels, loners, and mavericks emerged in the 1950s, a period described by screenwriter Jay Presson Allen as "an era of such towering dullness."[12] It's also no accident that Vincente Minnelli would be pressed into service to direct movies about people who were naturally nonconformist. Who better to explore the world of the extraordinary outcast than a man whose very being had been in question all the way from Delaware, Ohio, to the Director's Guild of America?

Despite some last-minute studio tinkering (including the removal of several scenes that Minnelli had begged Dore Schary to retain), the director was confident that *Lust for Life* contained some of his best work. "I didn't need any critics to tell me it was a great film," Minnelli boasted. "It looked and smelled right. We'd pulled it off."[13] Even if he didn't need the critical reassurance, it was there. "Two hours of quite shattering and exciting entertainment," raved Alan Dent in the *Illustrated London News*. "Hollywood's most profound exploration of the artistic life," said *Newsweek*. "One of the most beautiful films ever made," gushed the *New York Times*.

When the Oscar nominations were announced, Douglas and Quinn found themselves contenders in the Best Actor and Best Supporting Actor categories, respectively. Although Douglas would go home empty handed (though still in character), Quinn copped the Best Supporting Actor prize for his nine-minute turn as Gauguin, prompting rival Mickey Rooney to turn to fellow nominee Robert Stack and lament, "We wuz robbed."[14] Of course, the real injured party was *Lust for Life*'s director. Despite all of the critical approbation, Minnelli hadn't even been nominated as Best Director. Once

Self-Portrait: Kirk Douglas as
van Gogh in *Lust for Life*.
"He directs like a madman,"
Douglas said of Minnelli.
"If you don't know him,
he can drive an actor crazy.
But what comes out is
beautiful."
PHOTO COURTESY
OF PHOTOFEST

again, he had been passed over in favor of some dubious contenders. Having
an opportunity to pay tribute to one of his idols had proved to be the real re-
ward: "I felt a great affinity for van Gogh. . . . He was too much for anybody.
Nobody could live with him for more than a couple of weeks without going
mad. Because he gave too much, he wanted too much. And this is the kind
of character that is inconsistent and therefore I think brilliant to work out."[15]

23

Sister Boy

"IT HAS NOTHING to do with homosexuality," Robert Anderson would say of his best-known work, *Tea and Sympathy*. Though others would beg to differ. "*Tea and Sympathy* is definitely about being homosexual," says film historian Richard Dyer. "It's about curing homosexuality and the signs of homosexuality are effeminacy." This echoed the feelings of many who felt that Anderson somehow missed the point of his own story. The author, however, remained insistent: "It's about a false charge of homosexuality . . . but that is not a gay play."[1]

Tea and Sympathy, which opened on Broadway in 1953, is set in a prestigious New England prep school. Tom Lee, a sensitive, artistically inclined "off horse," is assumed to be gay and shunned by his classmates. While the real men on campus are out playing handball or climbing mountains, Tom thinks nothing of getting gussied up in drag to play Lady Teazle in *The School for Scandal*. As if the chintz curtains hanging in his dorm room aren't bad enough, seventeen-year-old Tom has no interest in becoming a businessman like his father but instead intends to ply his trade as a folk singer who performs "long-hair music."

The vulnerable outcast is also more comfortable in the company of women, especially Laura Reynolds, the motherly wife of the burly headmaster. Tom harbors a crush on Laura and feels connected to her as a kindred spirit. Observing how Tom is ostracized and tormented by the other students (all "regular fellows"), Laura befriends him, believing that he is a nice, sensitive kid who doesn't even know the meaning of the word "queer." Just before the

curtain falls, in a moment of supreme self-sacrifice, Laura offers herself
(body and soul) to Tom with the immortal line, "Years from now . . . when
you talk about this . . . and you will . . . be kind."

It was steamy stuff for 1953. Therefore, it came as no surprise to anyone
that MGM, which acquired the rights to the play (for a then impressive
$150,000), would not have an easy time convincing Production Code ad-
ministrators Joseph Breen, Geoffrey Shurlock, and Jack Vizzard that its screen
version of *Tea and Sympathy* would be sufficiently sanitized to receive the
censor's stamp of approval. From the moment Minnelli and producer Pandro
Berman were assigned to the picture, there were countless discussions regarding how such verboten themes could be presented in a mainstream film.
As Vincente recalled, "[Berman said] that if the play had actually been about
homosexuality, the motion picture code wouldn't have permitted us to do
it."[2] Robert Anderson, who was adapting his own work, was prepared to make
changes to placate the censors. In a creative trade-off, the author was willing
to downplay any elements in the script that smacked of "sexual perversion"
as long as Tom and Laura's adulterous affair remained.

The first compromise involved the elimination of a pivotal character in
the play. David Harris, "a good-looking young master," is forced to resign
after his students complain to the dean that the instructor and Tom were
discovered together, cavorting "bare-assed" in the dunes. Although the David
Harris character appears only once, in the first act, his presence is key.
Branded "a fairy" by Laura's husband, Harris is an all-too-real reminder of
what the effeminate, impressionable Tom Lee might eventually morph into.
Harris is also the physical embodiment of *Tea and Sympathy*'s real villain:
homosexuality itself. The gay threat is more palpable in Anderson's play than
in Minnelli's film. As Deborah Kerr, who starred in both versions, noted,
"The crucial point of the play, that [Tom] had been swimming with a master
everyone assumed to be homosexual, had to be omitted altogether. The boy
was so innocent he would not even have known what that meant—he went
with the man because he was nice to him—and that was all there was to
it."[3] Needless to say, Leo the Lion could never roar before a film containing
such blatant homoerotic overtones. In life as in the play, Harris would have
to go.

Then there was the matter of Laura's act of erotic charity. According to
the Motion Picture Production Code's restrictions, the very married den
mother could assist the effete protagonist in unleashing his manhood, but
she'd have to be punished for it. The Production Code insisted that it be
made clear to audiences that although Laura's mission was a "noble" one,

there would be devastating consequences as a result of her philanthropic infidelity. Anderson was forced to tack on a contrived prologue and epilogue. It was now revealed that the headmaster's wife was banished from her marriage and the school and was last known to be residing "somewhere near Chicago"—a fate worse than death in the eyes of MGM and the Legion of Decency.

Yet another serious Production Code violation involved Tom's misguided effort to prove his manhood by visiting the town whore, Ellie Martin. "The element of the boy's attempt to sleep with the prostitute is thoroughly unacceptable as written," proclaimed Joseph Breen. Clearly any filmmaker intent on bringing *Tea and Sympathy* to the screen had his work cut out for him.[*]

"Persistence has paid off for Metro-Goldwyn-Mayer in the case of *Tea and Sympathy*," the *New York Times* reported in September 1955. "The Production Code Administration was prepared to resist its filming. Homosexuality, or rather the suspicion of such that motivates the play, and adultery are proscribed by the Code . . . but Dore Schary, head of the studio, and Pandro S. Berman believed there was a way to resolve the problem."[4] Although Berman assured the *Times* that Minnelli's movie would "retain all the essentials" of the play, it was clear that *Tea and Sympathy* could push the envelope—but only so far. Episodes and overt dialogue ("All right, so a woman doesn't notice these things. But a man knows a queer when he sees one . . .") that had been acceptable in Elia Kazan's Broadway production would never pass muster in a feature produced by a major Hollywood studio.

Deborah Kerr had won raves on Broadway as Laura Reynolds and she was enthusiastic about recreating her role on film under Minnelli's direction. The censors had her worried, however, as she revealed in a letter to Vincente: "Adultery is o.k.—impotence is o.k. but perversion is their bête noir!! . . . It *really* is a play about persecution of the individual, and compassion and pity and love of one human being for another in crisis. And as such can stand alone I think—without the added problem of homosexuality. But above all— it needs a sensitive and compassionate person to make it—and that is why I'm so thrilled at the prospect of your doing it."[5]

Were the words "sensitive" and "compassionate" Kerr's way of suggesting that there was more than a touch of Vincente Minnelli in Tom Lee? And

---

* Letter from Joseph I. Breen to Columbia Pictures Chief Harry Cohn, October 20, 1953. Production Code representative Jack Vizzard met with *Tea and Sympathy*'s stage director, Elia Kazan, and author Robert Anderson to discuss the obstacles involved in transferring the play to film. As Vizzard reported, "We secured from Mr. Kazan a statement that, in his opinion, this play should never be made into a motion picture, and as far as he was concerned it would not be." (Production Code memo by Jack Vizzard, October 29, 1953 [the meeting with Elia Kazan and Robert Anderson took place on October 28 at the Waldorf-Astoria], from "Hollywood and the Production Code—Primary Source Microfilm Series: Selected Files from the Motion Pictures Association of America Production Code Administration Collection.")

what did Minnelli think about directing a story that was so undeniably similar to his own experience that it practically bordered on documentary? The scenes of Tom Lee being bullied and persecuted for his effeminacy must have dredged up some unhappy memories of Delaware and Minnelli's own years as a playground pariah. Laura giving herself to Tom so that he can prove his manhood and convince himself that he's unquestionably heterosexual seemed to many Hollywood insiders to be a page right out of the Minnelli-Garland wedding album. What's more, *Tea and Sympathy* is all about people performing—not in a theatrical milieu but in everyday life. Tom Lee actually rehearses the role of "regular fellow" to avoid being taunted; Laura's husband, Bill, is playacting his way through a conventional marriage; and even Tom's brawny roommate, Al Thompson, admits that despite his locker-room swagger, he's never been alone with a girl. All the world's a stage, even in a Minnelli melodrama.

There's no evidence that Vincente ever resisted the project because he felt that Tom Lee's story hit too close to home. Instead, the most Minnelli would allow—at least publicly—was that "ostrich-wise, the censors refused to admit the problem of sexual identity was a common one."[6]

As production began in March 1956, Minnelli may have felt like an outsider on his home turf. Along with Deborah Kerr, several members of the stage production had been retained for the film. During the Broadway run of *Tea and Sympathy*, the actors had not only bonded with one another but with Kazan, whom they revered. John Kerr (who had appeared in Minnelli's *The Cobweb*) would reprise his role as the hero in touch with his feminine side, and Leif Erickson would again play Bill Reynolds, Tom's burly housemaster—a character Vincente suggested was "perhaps a latent homosexual himself."[7]

Broadway's Dick York was unavailable to reprise his role in the film as Tom's roommate. Jack Larson, forever identified as Jimmy Olsen of *The Adventures of Superman* series, met with Minnelli to discuss the part. "He had eyes like Bette Davis was supposed to have," Larson recalls. "I found him effeminate. I guess they would have politely called it *epicene*. He was very courteous to me. He could have been a Noel Coward leading man but he wasn't handsome at all. There was nothing attractive about him and there was a languor to him. I sat with him in his office, which was very fancy. Everything was in very good taste. . . . There weren't any little Greek statues around."[8] Minnelli was impressed with Larson, but at Robert Anderson's urging the part was ultimately awarded to Darryl Hickman, who years earlier had appeared in *Meet Me in St. Louis*.

"Minnelli could be so prissy. I mean, he would drive me nuts," Hickman says. "I remember going in to shoot the 'walking' scene with John Kerr, who

Man Power: Tom Robinson Lee (John Kerr) asks his roommate Al (Darryl Hickman) to help him perfect his manly stride in 1956's *Tea and Sympathy*. "I don't think he was that secure about himself," Hickman says of his director. "I think he made up for whatever lack of self-confidence he may have had as a person in his work. . . . I would say that he had a very important inner world that the films represented."
PHOTO COURTESY
OF PHOTOFEST

never talked to me. I remember standing there from nine o'clock in the morning until noon because we went to lunch without ever having rehearsed the scene." The infamous "walking" scene, in which Al teaches light-in-his-loafers Tom Lee to walk like a man, was one of the most mind-blowing sequences in the film and later a highlight of the 1995 gay-themed documentary *The Celluloid Closet*.

According to Hickman, Minnelli obsessed endlessly over the visual details in the scene. Valuable production time was eaten up as Vincente returned to his window-dressing roots with a vengeance. The director arranged various props on the set (including a bust of Beethoven) so that they were *just so* and maneuvered his actors as though they were Marshall Field mannequins. "It looks artificial to me when I watch myself doing it," Hickman says of his Minnelli-dictated delivery:

He had me doing things with my arms, my hands, and with objects, and it was so precise. You know, if you're a real actor's director, you don't do that to an actor. It makes you very self-conscious. It makes you feel like a robot. And a really good actor's director like George Cukor would never do something like that to an actor. I don't think Minnelli, with all of his success and with all of his wonderful work that he did in films, was ever really an actor's director. First of all, if you're a really good actor and you have the stature, you say, "Go fuck yourself . . . I'm going to do this the way I want to do it." I mean, he certainly didn't tell Deborah Kerr what to do.[9]

Kerr, who would go on to star in *The King and I* and *An Affair to Remember*, endeared herself to director, cast, and crew. Although she was the consummate professional, Kerr didn't take herself as seriously as some of the other grandes dames on the Metro lot. Even the cluster of rising young actors playing Tom Lee's tormentors were surprised by the leading lady's approachability. As costar Don Burnett recalls, "Deborah Kerr used to call us 'H.B.'s,' which means 'Horny Bastards.' She'd say, 'O.K., all you H.B.'s, come on . . .' She would say things like that but she was so regal and wonderful. You wouldn't dare use bad language in front of her, and then she'd come out with something like that."[10]

While Hickman found Deborah Kerr "one of the most charming, sensitive and warm coworkers," the same could not be said of *Tea and Sympathy*'s remote director. "I don't ever remember seeing Vincente Minnelli laugh," says Hickman:

He wasn't an easy man to be around on a set. He wasn't outgoing. You know, it sounds strange to say this but I don't think he was that secure about himself—*personally*, not professionally. Maybe it came out in his painstaking perfectionism because he felt that he had to live up to some standard that he set for himself. I think he made up for whatever lack of self-confidence he may have had as a person in his work. . . . I would say that he had a very important inner world that the films represented.[11]

If one is searching for clues in Minnelli's own films regarding how the director may have grappled with his own conflicted sexuality, one need look no further than *Tea and Sympathy*. As the only film in Vincente's canon that openly (at least for 1956) addresses gay oppression, *Tea and Sympathy* can be "read" as Minnelli's own confessional: *Take a look at what happened to me. I, too, was a flaming creature until Delaware, Ohio, Louis B. Mayer, and the Legion of Decency made me wash off the mascara, get married, and walk like a man.*

Like the play, the film is very definitely a work of its era. On the one hand, Robert Anderson's drama seems to be pleading for tolerance and understanding for those who are miserably lonely, misunderstood, or "off the beam." On the other hand, *Tea and Sympathy* makes it clear that the same kind of support and compassion should not be extended to an individual if he actually is homosexual. Throughout the film, various characters assure "Sister Boy" Lee that "we can lick this thing," as though his effeminacy were akin to heroin addiction or smallpox. It's understood that tea and sympathy can only be offered if one is willing to conform, butch up, and sleep with the headmaster's wife. If you get naked in the dunes with your swishy instructor and you actually enjoy it, then God help you. As Anderson himself asserted, "The crux of the whole play" was "THE BOY WAS ALL RIGHT AND GOT MARRIED."*

After a sneak preview of the film, producer Pandro Berman found himself in a dramatic showdown with the Legion of Decency over proposed prerelease alterations. In order to receive the Legion's approval and escape the dreaded "C" (for "Condemned") rating, MGM was being asked to excise some scenes and overdub several lines of dialogue that the Legion found especially offensive. "Am terribly disturbed at news of our capitulation on *Tea and Sympathy*," Berman cabled Arthur Loew in MGM's New York office. "We are being treated badly and taken advantage of. The last reel of this picture will be ridiculous and in my opinion, should be laughed at by audiences. I think we have made ourselves fair prey for all future contacts with the legion. . . . It is a sad state of affairs when they not only can tell us what to say but how to say it and can write propaganda in their language for us to disseminate for them."[12]

Although he was already immersed in preparations for his next effort, *Designing Woman*, Vincente applauded Berman's uncompromising stance. "I want you to know what admiration I have for the courageous stance you have taken on *Tea and Sympathy*," Minnelli wrote in a memo to Berman. "I know the pains that were taken to satisfy the representatives of the Code . . . and to treat this subject in a manner which would not offend their standards, while still not distorting or cheapening a fine and distinguished play."[13]

As the film was being readied for general release, studio executives remained nervous that *Tea and Sympathy* would be too much for audiences in

---

* Letter from Robert Anderson to Vincente Minnelli, June 24, 1956, archived in the Minnelli collection at the Margaret Herrick Library, Academy of Motion Picture Arts and Sciences, Beverly Hills, California. Robert Anderson revealed to Mike Wood, "I get letters all of the time from people saying, 'Wasn't [Tom Lee] at least bisexual?' I say, 'The whole point of the play was a false charge.' It was the McCarthy period, you know." (Robert Anderson, interview with Mike Wood, February 22, 1994, William Inge Center for the Arts, available at http://www.ingecenter.org/interviews/robert andersontext.htm.)

the Eisenhower era. After all, the closest moviegoers got to "sexual perversion" in the '50s was either a Tennessee Williams adaptation or the finicky Tony Randall character in an innocuous Doris Day–Rock Hudson romp. However, as the reviews rolled in, it looked as though Minnelli had come through for Metro yet again.

"Everybody said it would be impossible to make a movie of *Tea and Sympathy*," wrote William K. Zinsser in the *New York Herald Tribune*. "But the movie has been made—and made with good taste. It's emphasis has been changed slightly, but the spirit of the play remains intact. . . . Vincente Minnelli's direction is quiet and compassionate and he has caught many subtle shadings of love and pain."[14]

While generally praising the film and its performances, other critics took exception to the way Anderson's play had been tampered with. As Justin Gilbert noted in the *Daily Mirror*, "A significant line uttered by Deborah Kerr, 'If this is going to come out, let it come out in the open,' which was one of the more challenging lines in the play, seems almost insignificant in the movie." Leo Mishkin of the *New York Morning Telegraph* concluded that "the changes . . . are enough, in a sense, to destroy much of the impact of the work."[15]

Decades after the film's release, its creators would acknowledge that the various concessions and compromises they had been forced to make had succeeded in diluting *Tea and Sympathy*'s central theme. "The picture didn't come off as we had hoped," Robert Anderson admitted. "We had to make too many changes for censorship. We kept fooling ourselves that we were preserving the integrity of the theme, but we lost some of it." Of the film's director, Deborah Kerr noted, "He was extremely sensitive to the subject. . . . The only thing that might have diffused it a little was that his great talent for making movies beautiful pictorially might have softened it and lushed it up a little."[16]

Others contend that Vincente's pictorial effects managed to make evident aspects of the story that the Production Code and the Legion of Decency had attempted to wipe off the screen. "For Minnelli, the mise-en-scène is very significant in terms of how he gets around what can't be said in the narrative," says film scholar David Gerstner. "What can't be said must be *shown*. This is how a director like Minnelli—working in Hollywood with the Production Code in effect—could still make visible whatever was hidden or had to be hidden."[17] Gerstner points to settings, costumes, and even the use of color as key elements that Minnelli employed to smuggle the story's taboo themes back into the movie.

In the "walk like a man" sequence, for example, Minnelli places Tom Lee and his roommate Al in their school's music room, which is something of an aesthetic refuge for Tom. Surrounded by musical instruments and busts of classical composers, Al attempts to show Tom how to act more manly. He even offers a demonstration of his hyper-masculine locker-room swagger. "It is at this moment in the film that masculine anxiety, confronted with its own ridiculous construction, can no longer support itself," notes Gerstner. "Al, pressed within and against the mise-en-scène of the Minnellian text and finally caught in the vestiges of masculinity, can't understand why walking a particular way is more manly than any other."[18]

Years after its initial release, *Tea and Sympathy* would resurface in theatrical resissues and on television. Many of Minnelli's fans were curious to know whether the director thought his once controversial melodrama still had something meaningful to say to audiences in a post-Stonewall world. While fielding questions from journalists at the Athens International Film Festival in 1978, Minnelli announced to the press corps: "I made the first homosexual picture while I was at MGM. That was *Tea and Sympathy*."[19] And he said it with what sounded like enormous pride.

24

"There'll Be
Some Changes Made"

IF MGM'S PUBLICIST, Howard Strickling, was the keeper of the studio's darkest secrets, Metro's house designer, Helen Rose, was privy to what many leading ladies considered far more privileged information. Rose, who had costumed Minnelli's *Father of the Bride* and *The Bad and the Beautiful*, knew which bras required significant padding or if an Oscar-winning waistline had suddenly expanded. From three-piece suits to birthday suits, Rose had certainly seen it all. As film historian David Chierichetti recalls, "Helen said Cyd Charisse was the only woman who looked as good naked as she did dressed."[1]

Like her better-known rival, Edith Head, Rose had a talent for accentuating nature's gifts and downplaying the defects. In 1953, the two-time Oscar winner put down her measuring tape long enough to submit a simple yet irresistible scenario for a movie: Fashion maven weds sportswriter. Although Rose's *Designing Woman* seemed to bear more than a passing resemblance to the Katharine Hepburn–Spencer Tracy vehicle *Woman of the Year*, studio chief Dore Schary was so taken with the concept that he decided to produce the movie himself. Metro executives agreed that a lighthearted comedy would offer a refreshing change of pace from Schary's deadly earnest, socially conscious "message pictures," such as *The Red Badge of Courage* and *The Next Voice You Hear*.

Screenwriter George Wells fashioned a slickly witty script from Rose's original scenario. The paper-thin plot concerned the connubial collision of chic fashionista Marilla Brown (caught up with her fittings and fall collections) and avid sportsman Mike Hagen (whose Runyonesque world is populated by punch-drunk middleweights and guys with names like "Charlie the Sneak").

In terms of casting, Schary's initial idea was to reunite the stars of Hitchcock's *Rear Window*—Jimmy Stewart and Grace Kelly—as the squabbling newlyweds. Joshua Logan was slated to direct. However, when Kelly abdicated her Hollywood throne in favor of the real thing by marrying the Prince of Monaco, Schary's production was suddenly without its *Designing Woman*. Minus her majesty, the project didn't seem as appealing to either Stewart or Logan and both bowed out. The directorial chores were then shifted to Minnelli, fresh from *Tea and Sympathy*. It seemed that the director couldn't completely shake his high-minded exploration of gender roles, though, and some of that "sister boy" stuff would spill over into *Designing Woman*'s riotous battle of the sexes.

Gregory Peck, who inherited the role of the newspaperman, had contractual approval over his costar. He green-lighted Minnelli's choice: Lauren Bacall. Though Humphrey Bogart's better half had displayed her comedic abilities in *How to Marry a Millionaire*, the sultry star usually found herself cast in dramatic roles. There had been a string of hard-boiled, noirish dramas at Warner Brothers. But by the mid-'50s, even those were hard to come by. "My career had come to a dead stop," Bacall remembers. "No one offered me anything. . . . So I called Dore, told him I could play it, wanted to, and when I cut my salary in half, he finally said yes."[2]

The supporting cast would include two *Kismet* survivors: Dolores Gray as Peck's brassy former paramour Lori Shannon, and choreographer Jack Cole, in a rare before-the-cameras turn, as dancer Randy Owen, a flamboyant friend of Bacall's uptown girl. The initially reticent Cole was persuaded to take the role by his analyst. "He told me this might help bring me out of myself," Cole said.[3]

Shooting began in September 1956 and both leads eagerly threw themselves into their work. Since *Roman Holiday*, Peck had subsisted on a steady diet of somber dramas (*Night People*, *The Purple Plain*, *The Man in the Grey Flannel Suit*). The stalwart leading man relished the opportunity to flex his comedy muscles and he marveled at Minnelli's "wonderful sense of pacing . . . of not letting things get boring, keeping it dancing along."[4]

Bacall was coping with the failing health of her real-life husband, Humphrey Bogart (who would die of throat cancer the following year). The virtually carefree set of *Designing Woman* proved to be the perfect refuge. "The whole experience for me was absolute heaven," Bacall says:

Choreographer Randy Owen (Jack Cole) gets inspired as squabbling newlyweds Marilla (Lauren Bacall) and Mike (Gregory Peck) realize how very different their worlds are in *Designing Woman*. Back in the '30s, Minnelli and Cole had worked together at Radio City Music Hall.
PHOTO COURTESY OF PHOTOFEST

I love that movie. Greg Peck, of course, became one of my dearest friends. We had a funny, wonderful script to work with. I had never played a part like that before, which I adored. And then we had Vincente as our director. . . . He was always very sure of what he wanted. I remember there would be a cigarette box on the table and he would come over and move it about an eighth of an inch to the left or to the right. I mean, he was cuckoo about that kind of thing. But even that was funny. He had his own idiosyncrasies but there was nobody like him. He wouldn't let anyone run over him. Not that anyone ever tried. I certainly never tried.[5]

Like *The Long, Long Trailer*, *Designing Woman* was the kind of lighthearted romp that didn't demand much of Vincente. He realized that he was there to shepherd his good-looking leads through a frothy comedy, and without complaint, he did exactly that—though just beneath the glossy veneer of *Designing Woman* is the kind of slyly cutting-edge, ahead-of-its-time exploration of gender roles that gets film scholars and academics salivating. And yet the yin-yang dynamics of the story aren't exclusively concerned with a marriage of opposites.

Jack Cole's character, Randy Owen, is the furiously theatrical ringleader of Marilla's "show crowd," which she describes as "a pretty neurotic bunch." Randy is so flamboyantly effeminate that he makes *Tea and Sympathy*'s Tom Lee look like a Navy SEAL by comparison. Inspired by the notion of staging an undersea ballet, Randy offers a preview of his best seahorse. Marilla and her friends are delighted by the wild exhibition, though Mike and his Wednesday-night poker pals are speechless.

Later, when Randy overhears Mike questioning his manhood ("Is that guy for real?"), he immediately whips out photos of a wife and three sons and offers to beat both of Mike's ears off. Randy can be considered something of a spokesperson for Minnelli, who was, as film historian Stephen Harvey diplomatically put it, "a somewhat suspect figure as well."[6]

At first, the very presence of Randy Owen in *Designing Woman* seems rather daring (for 1957), but after the revelation regarding the wife and kids, it becomes clear that it's all just another misunderstanding. As attentive audiences should have learned from *Tea and Sympathy*, appearances can be deceiving. Just because something looks one way doesn't mean that it is that way. Randy Owen, like Vincente Minnelli, would appear to be the victim of his own artistic flair. Or maybe the character, like the director, needed the photos of the wife and kids to convince himself.

"That whole dimension of Vincente's life interested me," says writer William Gibson. "It did in John Houseman, too. Houseman had a reputation of being homosexual also. And yet, both of them were married and the fathers of young children. On the surface, everything was standard, but it was curious because you felt that there was also a need to display this picture of a young, happy family. . . . I had the impression that both guys were trying very hard to live a 'normal' American life."[7]

Designing Woman opened in January 1957, and the picture was generally well received. As *Time* noted, "Director Vincente Minnelli plays his game of pseudo-sociological croquet with the careless good form of a man who does not have to worry about making his satiric points. He plays for the box office score instead, working the sex angles and the big names and the production values—yum-yum Metrocolor, flossy furniture, slinky clothes—with the skill of a cold old pro."[8] Thanks largely to its A-list star power, *Designing Woman* returned $3,750,000 to the MGM coffers.

There was also a surprise in store. When the Oscar nominations were announced for the 1957 ceremonies, *Designing Woman* netted a nomination for "Best Story and Screenplay Written Directly for the Screen." In something of an upset, the George Welles script was awarded the Oscar over such strong contenders as *Funny Face* and *I Vitelloni*. As Welles accepted his statuette, he noted that "the suggestion for the screenplay came from one of our industry's most designing women . . . Helen Rose."

***

"THERE'LL BE SOME CHANGES MADE," Dolores Gray belts out in *Designing Woman*, and by the time the picture was released, she could have easily been referring to the major transitions that had occurred in MGM's front office. After a controversial eight-year reign as the studio's production chief, Dore Schary was fired. "Dore Schary was a writer and a picture maker and he didn't any more know how to run a studio than fall through the roof," says MGM publicist Esme Chandlee. Schary was replaced by Joseph Vogel, who immediately set the tone for the new regime by announcing his plans to remake the 1927 silent epic *Ben-Hur*.

Meanwhile, Minnelli was involved in a takeover of his own. He was summoned to replace director Ronald Neame on *The Seventh Sin*, an updating of the 1934 Greta Garbo vehicle *The Painted Veil*, which had been adapted from the Somerset Maugham story of the same title.

"The enterprise was sour from the beginning," Minnelli recalled in his autobiography. "The company didn't get along with each other and the producer and director were having battles royal with the front office. They'd struggled through most of the filming when matters finally became untenable."[9]

Fifty years after he walked off the troubled production, Ronald Neame wasn't forthcoming about why his set had become such a fierce battleground, but he remained grateful to Vincente for stepping in and wrapping up the rest of the picture.

If walking on to a contentious set was not something Minnelli relished, at least he wouldn't have to be there for long. With most of the picture in the can, Vincente would only have to shoot some retakes and a few additional scenes. Although most of *The Seventh Sin* belongs to Neame, the finished film contains some distinctive Minnelli flourishes. The opening scene begins with ravenous close-ups of shoes, silk stockings, and jewelry—all obviously shed in the midst of an adulterous interlude. When the nervous lovers, played by Eleanor Parker and Jean Pierre-Aumont, are first glimpsed together, they're posed before the inevitable Minnelli mirror. A later sequence features a sweeping boom maneuver; the camera sails up to Parker's bungalow and then right through an open window. Must be Minnelli. The visual ingenuity distracts from the low-budget look of the film and lines such as, "I've never been to an epidemic before. I hope it'll be fun." And just in case audiences weren't hip to the fact that Parker's character was a slave to her own desires, Miklos Rozsa recycles his *Madame Bovary* waltz to tip everybody off.

Regardless of which moments were attributable to Neame and which to Minnelli, the critics could find little to praise in *The Seventh Sin*, with the reviewer for *Cue* noting that the picture "meanders after Maugham but never quite catches up with him."[10]

25

Unacceptable, Objectionable, and Unclean

"WHY DOES ARTHUR *want to make a picture about a whore?* . . ." That question was reverberating through the executive boardroom of Loew's, Inc. The assembled suits, though not a prudish group by any means, were nevertheless dumbfounded. Why did Arthur Freed, the esteemed producer of such family-friendly fare as *The Wizard of Oz* and *Meet Me in St. Louis*, want to sully his cinematic reputation with a movie about a young girl groomed to be a perfectly mannered prostitute? After the disappointments of *Brigadoon*, *It's Always Fair Weather*, and *Kismet*, naysayers were already wondering if Freed was losing his touch. Or had that enigmatic collector of Roualts and prize-winning orchids discovered a diamond in the rough in the form of the semi-scandalous *Gigi*?

"You know, basically, it is awfully good," Minnelli would say of Colette's original short story. "She wrote it as a kind of throwaway. She never considered it one of her major works, like *Cheri*. But it's the one that has endured."*

For all its wistful charm and Gallic whimsy, *Gigi* was written in the midst of agony and despair. During the French Occupation, a sciatica-plagued seventy-year-old, Colette, tormented by the Gestapo's arrest of her Jewish husband, produced what many consider to be her most unapologetically romantic work. *Gigi* was inspired by the real-life May–December marriage of

---

* In 1963, Minnelli was approached about directing a film version of Colette's *Cheri*, which would have starred Alain Delon and Simone Signoret. The project never got beyond the preliminary discussion stage. In 2009, Michelle Pfeiffer starred in a cooly received widescreen adaptation of *Cheri*. (Richard Schickel, *The Men Who Made the Movies* [New York: Atheneum, 1975].)

Yola Henriquez and the much older Henri Letellier, editor of France's popular daily *Le Journal*. In 1926, Colette had an opportunity to observe Yola and Henri together as the novelist and the newlyweds happened to be staying in the same hotel on the French Riviera. Colette discovered that the proprietors of the hotel were two aging courtesans who had raised Yola and tutored the young woman in the fine art of snagging a millionaire. All of this formed the basis for the story that ultimately became *Gigi*.

Although inspired by more contemporary events, Colette pushed the setting of her story back to the more picturesque Paris of 1899 or *La Belle Epoque*. The saga of a courtesan-in-training created quite a stir when it was published as a novelette in 1944. Seven years later, there would be a Broadway incarnation starring a luminous twenty-two-year-old newcomer named Audrey Hepburn, hand-picked to play the title role by Colette herself. Though the Anita Loos adaptation was judged "slight but diverting," Hepburn was acclaimed as "the acting find of the year." In November 1953, Hepburn's *Gigi* was staged in Los Angeles, and among those in attendance were Arthur Freed and Vincente Minnelli. While Freed was charmed, Minnelli dismissed the production as "too farcically played" and, Audrey aside, "not very good."[1]

Nevertheless, Freed decided to submit Colette's story (and the Loos script) to Geoffrey Shurlock and the Motion Picture Production Code office. Freed knew full well that Colette's courtesans would have the censors swarming, but he was curious to know how many code commandments *Gigi* was actually breaking. Did a prospective producer have any hope whatsoever of getting the property passed? The initial response was not encouraging. Joseph Breen made it more than clear that the story of a "kept woman" was unacceptable, objectionable, and unclean: "This play is so basically opposed to everything the Code stands for, that any attempt to bring it around to conformity with the Code would prove futile," he cautioned in his response.

A year passed as Freed turned his attention to other projects. Then he received a telegram from Anita Loos. The playwright responsible for putting Colette's characters on stage now wanted to turn *Gigi* into a big-time Broadway musical. Would Freed be willing to let Loos see the censor's report, so that she'd have some idea of what she was up against? The Loos inquiry reignited the producer's interest in the property. A musical version of *Gigi* . . . of course. It almost seemed tailor-made for Minnelli.

For two years, Freed and the censors went back and forth on *Gigi*. The one element the code office most strenuously objected to was the fact that the story seemed to glorify the "system of mistresses" that existed in Gigi's family. Metro's story editor Kenneth MacKenna argued that despite her family's notorious history, Gigi herself is a moral girl "who simply wants no part of this shabby way of life." Code administrators stood firm. The story put "an illegal relationship in the same class as marriage."[2]

Freed and his team then made all sorts of suggestions regarding how the story might be sanitized in order to obtain code approval. Instead of a "grand cocotte," what if Gigi's Aunt Alicia had been a former chorus girl? Or perhaps Gigi was not descended from a line of courtesans, but instead, her family operated a matrimonial bureau that introduced middle-aged men to "lonely women"?

Eventually, Freed and his associates seemed to wear the censors down. By July 1957, MGM's scripted version of *Gigi* (then titled *The Parisians*) met "the basic requirements of the Production Code." After hurdling that obstacle, Freed found himself facing another challenge. After Colette's death in 1954, her widower, Maurice Goudeket, had sold the musical adaptation rights to *Gigi* to *both* MGM and the Broadway-bound team of Anita Loos and producer Gilbert Miller. When the studio trumpeted its forthcoming production of *Gigi*, Loos and Miller cried foul. It would cost Freed a pretty penny (some $87,000) to prevent *Gigi* from lighting up the Great White Way.

With code administrators at last appeased and would-be competitors paid off, Freed could finally turn his attention to artistic matters. Although Minnelli had been unimpressed with the stage version of *Gigi*, he greatly admired Colette's work, and the prospect of bringing turn-of-the-century Paris to life with musical accompaniment was irresistible. He signed on to direct. Freed and Minnelli agreed that their *An American in Paris* collaborator Alan Jay Lerner (who owed Metro another script as part of a three-picture commitment) would be the ideal choice to handle the adaptation.

In February 1956, Freed surprised Lerner by turning up backstage during the Philadelphia tryouts for the composer's new show, *My Fair Lady*, starring Rex Harrison and Julie Andrews. Freed wanted to discuss the composer's next assignment for MGM. Although Lerner expressed interest in scripting *Gigi*, he initially resisted the idea of furnishing lyrics as well.

A month after Lerner's meeting with Freed, *My Fair Lady* landed on Broadway. It would be hailed as one of the finest achievements in the history of the American musical theater—a triumph and then some. As a result, Lerner was now in a position to make a few demands. First, he did not want to write *Gigi* in some cramped cubicle in a corner of the MGM writer's building. He wanted all of Europe. Freed agreed. Next, Lerner insisted that Minnelli's movie must include some kind of substantial role for his idol—the ever-debonair

Maurice Chevalier.[*] Freed agreed to this condition as well. Lerner also re-quested that the studio engage Cecil Beaton to design the sets and costumes for *Gigi*, as Beaton had graced *Fair Lady* with one outlandishly elegant, as-tonishingly beautiful design after another. Like Minnelli, Beaton expressed himself visually, and his unique talents were perfectly suited to an opulent Impressionist fable.

The only item that writer and producer disagreed on was the crucial casting of the leading lady. Lerner preferred Audrey Hepburn, who was now one of Hollywood's most beloved (and bankable) stars. Freed favored Leslie Caron, who had played Gigi in an unsuccessful 1956 production in London's West End. When Hepburn declined the offer to recreate her acclaimed charac-terization on film, Caron was handed what would become her signature role.

In the summer of 1956, Lerner started writing. Although the essence of Colette's story and much of her dialogue were retained, Lerner made some significant changes for the screen. The character of Gigi's mother, which Minnelli had found to be too present in the stage production, was reduced to an off-screen voice, while a passing reference to another character was built up into a pivotal supporting player. Colette had only hinted at a youthful romance between Gigi's grandmother, Madame Alvarez, and an "elder Lachaille." From this suggestion, Lerner created the character of Honore Lachaille, the charismatic uncle of Gigi's millionaire suitor, Gaston Lachaille. The graying roué would offer his nephew advice on affairs of the heart and also serve as the story's narrator and "master of ceremonies." The role prac-tically screamed Chevalier.

As the screenplay began taking shape, Lerner realized that his *Gigi* was more than slightly reminiscent of *My Fair Lady*. Both musicals offered a sharp-eyed social critique in the form of a sumptuous Cinderella story. There were also some unmistakable similarities in terms of the plot: Both Eliza Doolittle and Gigi undergo a stunning transformation—from gamine to god-dess. And in each story, the central character, who is groomed to find a better way of life, goes a step further and finds herself—to the astonishment of her more mature love interest. Lerner began second-guessing himself, recognizing that there was more than just a passing resemblance between the two prop-erties. "Stop trying to be different," Arthur Freed reportedly told Lerner. "You

---

[*] Minnelli was a great admirer of Chevalier's 1932 musical *Love Me Tonight*, directed by Rouben Mamoulian: "I'm only interested in musical stories in which one can achieve a complete integration of dancing, singing, sound and vision," he wrote. "I would often look at *Love Me Tonight* as it was such a perfect example of how to make a musical." (John Kobal, *Gotta Sing, Gotta Dance: A History of Movie Musicals* [New York: Exeter Books, 1983].)

don't have to be different to be good. To be good is different enough."[3] The *My Fair Lady* connection would become even more pronounced when Lerner agreed to write the lyrics and convinced his initially reluctant *Fair Lady* partner, Frederick Loewe, to sign on to write the music for *Gigi*.

In Leslie Caron, Freed had found an authentic Parisian star, but one who was anything but eager to work with Minnelli again. Throughout the production of *An American in Paris*, Caron had struggled with Vincente's cryptic communication style (which Judy Garland had described as "Burmese hieroglyphics"). In January 1957, Caron wrote to Freed, expressing her preference for a real talker, such as George Cukor. Unmoved, Freed backed Minnelli all the way. The other members of Caron's on-screen family would be played by two venerable British actresses: Hermione Gingold as Madame Alvarez, Gigi's overprotective grandmama, and Isabel Jeans as the imperious Aunt Alicia (who gets to deliver one of the film's most memorable lines: "Bad table manners have broken up more households than infidelity.")

With Gigi and her family finally in place, the search was on for an actor to play Gaston, the dashing heir to Lachaille Sugar. "It takes considerable style and skill to play a bored man and not to be boring," observed Alan Jay Lerner, who believed that nobody could do the bored bit better than Dirk Bogarde.[4] The British leading man was seriously considered for the role but he belonged to producer J. Arthur Rank, who would not release the actor.

Then someone suggested Louis Jourdan, who had worked with Vincente nearly a decade earlier on *Madame Bovary*. Sauve and exuding a distinctly cosmopolitan air, Jourdan matched Colette's description of Gigi's well-heeled suitor as "a man accustomed to champagne and baccarat." Initially, Jourdan turned down the role, as he was concerned about the vocal demands involved. After being assured that he could "talk-sing" his numbers in the film (as Rex Harrison had done so effectively in *My Fair Lady*), Jourdan signed on. Besides, Lerner and Loewe's score—which included "The Night They Invented Champagne," "I Remember It Well," and the title tune—practically sang itself. Unless you happened to be Leslie Caron, that is.

Caron believed that she would be doing her own vocalizing in *Gigi* until the day she showed up at a studio recording session, ready to lift her voice in song, only to be informed by conductor-arranger André Previn that she would be dubbed (by Betty Wand). According to Alan Jay Lerner, Caron was "furious and doubly so because she had not been forewarned." Apparently Arthur Freed had neglected to inform his star that all of her musical numbers would be handled by a professional singer (despite the fact that Caron had already made prerecordings of her songs with Previn). "I'm surprised she took it so hard," Freed shrugged.*

In April 1957, Minnelli flew to Paris, and on this trip, more than his art books went along for the ride. Vincente was accompanied by Georgette, her parents, and two-year-old Tina Nina. It was one of the rare occasions that the entire family was together. "Working day after day, long into the night, cut drastically into our domestic life," Minnelli would say of his conspicuous absence from the sprawling residence on Crescent Drive that they had recently moved into. As Georgette was more often than not home alone, it was as though her marriage to Vincente was in name only, which many in the Hollywood community assumed anyway.

With Minnelli shooting an elaborate period musical on location and under pressure, the highly charged atmosphere didn't seem at all conducive to bringing an already distant couple any closer together. And as usual, work won out. Said Minnelli: "If you're going to do a musical and have it linger with people awhile, then I think you have to put as much thought and sweat and intelligence into it as a dramatic picture." The sweat would be easy to come by, as Paris was hit with what Caron remembered as "The worst summer in twenty years."[5] Hot enough to blister. That didn't deter the film's unstoppable director, however. Minnelli was already consumed with resurrecting an entire bygone era. And no detail was too minute to escape his attention.

Just as 5135 Kensington Avenue had been a central "figure" in *Meet Me in St. Louis* and New York had become a third character in *The Clock*, the locations in *Gigi* were not just scenic backdrops but a vital part of the story. Lerner observed, "Paris was as much a character as Gaston and Gigi themselves."[6] As Gigi's Aunt Alicia understood and appreciated the difference between a marquise-shaped diamond and a yellow diamond of the first quality, Minnelli knew that each of the film's locations was like one of those multifaceted gems—every setting would create a distinct mood and illuminate the characters in different ways.

Shooting began in August. "It was a battle of the queens," says former second assistant director Hank Moonjean, who would witness the converging of several outsized egos on the set. "Beaton thinks the most important thing about the movie are the dresses. The camera man thinks the most important

---

* Lerner, *The Street Where I Live*. In this memoir, Lerner erroneously credits Marni Nixon as Caron's voice double. Nixon provided the singing voice for Audrey Hepburn's Eliza Doolittle in the 1964 film version of *My Fair Lady*, which may account for the confusion. Wand did Caron's singing in *Gigi* (though that's Caron herself handling the verse on "The Night They Invented Champagne"). Wand would later dub some of Rita Moreno's Anita in the 1961 film of *West Side Story*.

thing is the camera work. The make-up man thinks the most important thing is the make-up. And Sydney Guilaroff thinks the most important thing in the movie is the hair. . . . It wasn't an easy shoot."[7] Vincente seemed oblivious to it all. With *Gigi*, he was bound and determined to create his most breathtaking canvas yet.

The film would open and close with Chevalier crooning "Thank Heaven for Little Girls" in the Bois de Boulogne. In the opening sequence, Chevalier's boulevardier introduces himself, the youthful Gigi, and the risqué notion that in Paris, "there are some who will not marry and some who do not marry." The opener would also set the visual tone for the film. Throughout the picture, Minnelli would pay tribute to France's greatest artists, particularly the caricaturist Sem, though it was the work of watercolorist Constantin Guys that served as the inspiration for the look of the Bois. In these initial images in the film, the luxurious fairy tale that is *Gigi* begins to cast its spell. Though on the set, the mood was decidedly more nightmarish.

The heat was punishing. Tightly corseted cocottes fainted dead away. Freed's beleaguered assistant, Lela Simone, seemed to be extinguishing a dozen fires at once. And all was not right according to Minnelli's unerring eye. For starters, the Bois de Boulogne wasn't nearly verdant enough. Vincente called for a small row of trees to be planted so that the location would more closely resemble the paintings of Constatin Guys. But it seemed that the moment one problem was solved, another emerged.

When Minnelli took a good look at the rented costumes the assembled extras were wearing, he pronounced them "disasters." In an attempt to salvage the offending ensembles, Beaton and his dutiful assistants scurried over to each actor, affixing ribbons, plumes, and other eye-catching accessories to each outfit. When Beaton was finished, the eyesores had been transformed into the last word in turn-of-the-century chic.

Every day was a race to create a little magic while the weather, wilting trees, exasperated extras, fading light, and constrained budget got in the way—to say nothing of the Parisian notion of "coffee breaks." According to Hank Moonjean, "The French crews have a bottle of wine at lunch. Let's just say that things after lunch are not as good as they are before lunch."[8]

Officials at the Department of the Seine were dumbfounded when Vincente informed them that he wanted to shoot at the Palais de Glace, the cavernous ice-skating rink. Not only did this crazy American auteur want to photograph ice in August, but he wanted to do so at the crumbling old démodé ice palace, which was anything but ready for its close-up. After Minnelli and Beaton worked their magic, however, the dilapidated relic was restored to a convincing version of its former glory.

Actress Monique Van Vooren, whom Cecil Beaton described as "a tall blonde with a Mae West figure and a personality of equal proportions," remembered that Minnelli spent considerable time in the Palais de Glace, although much of his work wound up on the cutting-room floor: "We had a lot of scenes in the ice-skating rink, but so much of it was cut. It's too bad because I was a great skater. . . . I came into the production rather late. They had already cast everyone. But I think Vincente liked me very much and he agreed to put me in the picture. He was very gentle, endlessly patient, and somehow managed to observe every little detail."[9] Except one.

Richard Winckler, the actor originally cast as Eva Gabor's unusually attentive ice-skating instructor, was forced off the picture when Gabor decided she preferred to be drilled by the devastatingly handsome Jacques Bergerac instead. The actor was summoned, and when he finally appeared, a new costume had to be fitted (Bergerac was taller than his predecessor). It was only after Minnelli called "Action!" that Bergerac admitted that he didn't know how to skate.

Several of *Gigi*'s most memorable sequences were shot at the legendary Parisian eatery Maxim's (Freed had convinced the owners to close for a few days to accommodate the shooting). In the finished film, the scenes at Maxim's are a delirious swirl of luscious color and sparkling orchestrations— the best kind of sensory overload. One can feel Minnelli's exhilaration as his camera swoops in and soaks up all of that art nouveau atmosphere. Beaton's gossiping cocottes are done up like vibrantly plumed, exotic birds. Like the rest of their score, Lerner and Loewe's "She Is Not Thinking of Me" is expertly interwoven with the dramatic content of the scene. As Gaston fumes over the inattentiveness of his lady love, his witty interior monologue is heard on the soundtrack: "In her eyes tonight, there's a glow tonight, they're so bright they could light Fontainbleau tonight. . . . She is not thinking of me."

As Maurice Chevalier and Eva Gabor glide by in their giddy waltz, it's hard to believe that the effervescent joie de vivre displayed on screen is the ultimate grand illusion. For shooting in the restaurant's cramped quarters and in such sweltering heat that even the walls were perspiring was a living hell. "All I can remember is that it was so damned hot in that Maxim's," says Hank Moonjean. "*It was so damned hot*. Everyone's make-up is going and all the actors are in heavy period costumes and it was congested. It was a miserable, miserable shoot, and of course, Minnelli would be going up to take 30, take 35 . . . take 40. And the extras were getting tired. Everyone was just anxious to get the hell out of there." Temperatures soared and tempers flared. "I saw Arthur Freed and Minnelli go at it . . . you know, like they're going to kill each other any minute," Moonjean remembers. "On movies, it's sort of standard that producers fight with directors and all that but this was fierce. . . . You know, they were probably friendly enemies, they were together for so many years."[10]

Fidgety and easily agitated even on the back lot in Culver City, Minnelli was all jangled nerves on location. While he was pushing himself, the cast, and the crew to the limit in the oppressive heat, a series of calamities befell the overburdened director. Vincente's omnipresent boom smashed through the tinted glass ceiling at Maxim's, and somewhere between shooting the skating sequence at the Palais de Glace and Eva Gabor's illicit rendezvous in Montfort-l'Amaury, Minnelli contracted whooping cough. Then, while shooting the title number in the Jardin de Bagatelle, the director was bitten by one of the swans he had painstakingly "auditioned" for four days.

Back in Hollywood, Metro executives were equally frazzled. Although Elvis Presley was setting the box office on fire with *Jailhouse Rock*, many of the studio's other recent releases had tanked. For the first time in the studio's history, MGM lost money, sinking some $455,000 into the red. At the end of August, Ben Thau summoned Minnelli and company back to Culver City. In an effort to curtail expenditures and keep a closer eye on Vincente's extravagant endeavor, angsty executives insisted that the rest of the picture would have to be completed on the lot.

The only thing remaining in Paris was Georgette Magnani. She had decided that her marriage to Vincente was over. At this point, it had to have been perfectly clear to her that she would always be competing with something for her husband's attention: his latest picture, the studio, Judy's enormous shadow, Liza, a thick volume on Leonardo da Vinci, or any number of Vincente's other romantic interests. Even on the rare occasions when the couple were actually in the same room, Minnelli could still be pretty hard to find. "Vincente was in another world. He was a dreamer," Magnani would later remark.[11]

Shooting resumed in California in September. Venice Beach, which usually played host to body builders and bohemians, stood in for France's Trouville. For the scenes depicting Gigi and Gaston's carefree weekend by the sea, Minnelli hoped to emulate the style of French landscape painter Eugene Boudin—or at least what he thought was Boudin. Taking his cue from Vincente, Cecil Beaton outfitted the actors and extras in dark shades like the ones on display in Boudin's 1869 painting *Bathers on the Beach at Trouville*. When Minnelli saw the results, he was aghast. The director had envisioned his seascape in bright pastels. Of course, that kind of palette was more in league with the Impressionists (Renoir, Manet), but Beaton didn't bother to argue. Instead, he doled out colorful clothing and accoutrements in an attempt to give Vincente the Impressionist effect he wanted.

Beaton, for one, believed that artifice was winning out over authenticity. "All the scenes that were taken in Hollywood were very damaging," the designer remarked. "To me, the whole success of the film was the Parisian flavor and that was created by making it in France. As soon as we had a swan on the back lot, it looked like the back lot."[12]

Chuck Walters, who had made contributions to Minnelli's *Ziegfeld Follies* and had helmed Leslie Caron's 1953 sleeper *Lili* (which Vincente had declined to direct), was called in to choreograph the exuberant "The Night They Invented Champagne," one of the few musical numbers in *Gigi* that features dancing. Minnelli had graced the picture with a stately elegance, but it was Walters who added a welcome ingredient: energy. Throughout the film, the principals often perform their songs while seated. In a refreshing change of pace, Walters gets everyone up on their feet and moving.

In the three months between the official end of production and the initial preview, *Gigi* was the cause of much in-house intrigue. Minnelli had been so entranced with the atmosphere at Maxim's that he had favored long shots while shooting there. But what about close-ups of Louis Jourdan during "She Is Not Thinking of Me"? These were needed to reinforce the notion that the viewer was eavesdropping on Gaston's private thoughts. At great expense, close-ups of Jourdan would have to be shot in Hollywood with a carefully reconstructed set doubling as Maxim's. Another mad scramble ensued. After assisting with this and countless other emergencies, Freed's overwhelmed assistant Lela Simone finally threw in the towel after years of dedicated service.

The rest of the team soldiered on, including editor Adrienne Fazan, who was tasked with putting all the pieces of *Gigi* together. At one point, Margaret Booth, the venerable grande dame of the MGM editing department, was brought on to assist with cutting the picture. But in Fazan's eyes, Booth butchered the film, hacking out the very heart of the story: "She cut all the warmth out of it—with Chevalier, Caron, Gingold, everybody!"[13]

It was this version of *Gigi* that was first previewed on January 20, 1958, at the Granada Theatre in Santa Barbara. The reception the film received reminded its creators of Howard Dietz's comment to Arthur Freed upon hearing Lerner and Loewe's score for the first time: "Arthur, this will be the most charming flop you ever made."[14] MGM's upper echelon was reasonably satisfied with the audience's reaction to the picture, but the composer and lyricist did not share their optimism. For Lerner and Loewe (and especially

Gigi (Leslie Caron) and
Gaston Lachaille
(Louis Jourdan) come to terms.
Gigi must have been one of the
films that director Billy Wilder
had in mind when he said,
"I don't shoot elegant pictures.
Mr. Vincente Minnelli,
he shot elegant pictures."
PHOTO COURTESY
OF PHOTOFEST

Lerner), there was something missing. Although the film was visually spec-tacular, the warmth and intimacy of Colette's story only occasionally found its way to the screen. Pacing was another problem—some scenes overstayed their welcome, while others (such as Caron's "The Parisians") seemed to flit by without making any impression. The orchestrations, according to Lerner, were "too creamy and ill-defined." The team that had galvanized Broadway with *My Fair Lady* left the preview feeling that their *Gigi* had somehow slipped away. "To Fritz and me, it was a very far cry from all we had hoped for, far enough for both of us to be desperate," Lerner said. "The ride home from Santa Barbara was not unlike the ride home from any funeral."[15]

After some tightening and fine-tuning, there was a second preview, which to Lerner and Loewe seemed as uninspiring as the first. Clearly, something would have to be done. "We were determined that the picture not be released the way it was," Lerner recalled.[16] However, recalling the actors, reshooting entire sequences, and arranging for additional scoring would come with a hefty price tag. It seemed highly unlikely that the studio would open its checkbook for a production that had already gone over budget. Besides, Min-nelli was already back in Paris preparing his next film, *The Reluctant Debu-tante*. Nevertheless, Lerner and Loewe insisted on changes.

"They wanted a lot of work to be done on the picture," says Lerner's former assistant Stone Widney. "As Alan tells it, it was going to cost three hundred grand to do the retakes. Vincente had already gone on to another movie and wasn't available. But Alan and Fritz stuck to their guns and offered to buy the print back from the company themselves and finish it. . . . I think the scoring was totally incorrect as far as Fritz was concerned, even though André Previn had done it. Fritz felt that it was way overboard."[17]

In a desperate ploy, Lerner and Loewe offered to buy "10 percent of *Gigi* for $300,000." Later, they upped their offer to $3 million for the purchase of the film's negative (even though they didn't have that kind of money). The elaborate ruse worked. Metro executives Joseph Vogel and Ben Thau were so impressed with Lerner and Loewe's commitment that they agreed to lavish an additional $300,000 on the picture—anything to make *Gigi* perfect. Although Minnelli would not be involved in the retakes on *Gigi*, Lerner felt an obligation to play messenger and relayed the news to the absentee director, who noted: "When you're in another country and you hear that the picture you made didn't go over well and that parts of it are being reshot, you tend to believe that the picture couldn't have been any good," Minnelli said.[18]

Chuck Walters was called back to oversee nine days of reshoots. "Gaston's Soliloquy" was reattempted; Caron marched through "The Parisians" yet again; Hermione Gingold uttered her final line, "Thank heaven . . ." with the quiet contentment that Lerner was looking for. Now it was up to editor Adrienne Fazan to sort through the miles of footage and make some attempt at patching together the best of Minnelli and Walters, just as she had pieced together Paris and Culver City. Fazan found herself in a race against time as she attempted to incorporate innumerable changes (most of them Lerner-dictated) into the final edit.

At last, on May 15, 1958, *Gigi* was ready to make her grand entrance, and Freed made sure it was a luxurious red-carpet affair. Radio City Music Hall simply wouldn't do for a cinematic event this prestigious. Instead, Broadway's Royale Theatre would have the honor of presenting *Gigi* as though it were a legitimate theatrical attraction—white tie and hard ticket included. In Hollywood, splashy premieres were par for the course, but this was something unique. And the critics knew it. "*Gigi*, the delectable musical film that opened last night at the Royale, is a triumph of style over matter," declared the *New York World-Telegram*'s William Peper: "Director Vincente Minnelli has taken his CinemaScope and color cameras on a ravishing whirl through Paris. And with the help of a refreshingly witty screenplay by Mr. Lerner, he has given the film a pace and sparkle that belie its tiny plot." The *New York Times* saluted *Gigi* as the "Fair Lady of Filmdom," with critic Bosley Crowther

"Thank Heaven for Little Girls": Oscar night, 1959. Minnelli receives an Academy Award for his direction of *Gigi*. "It's about the proudest moment of my life," Vincente declared in his acceptance speech. The presenter is actress Millie Perkins.
PHOTO COURTESY OF PHOTOFEST

noting, "Vincente Minnelli has marshaled a cast to give a set of performances that, for quality and harmony, are superb."

Variety would describe Leslie Caron as "completely captivating and convincing in the title role." Although the actress was ably assisted from all corners, it is her endearing performance that is the centerpiece of the film: her mischievous expression as she reveals that the one thing she wants most is a "Nile green corset with rococo roses on the garters"; her maturing tone as she says, "It's silly. . . . It's absolutely silly" in response to the fuss over one of Gaston's impulsive outbursts; her look of quiet command as she throws open the doors of her bedroom and emerges as a Beatonized bird of paradise.

But if the film really belongs to anyone it is Minnelli. "I don't think of it as an MGM movie," says writer Ethan Mordden. "It seems to be in its own style entirely." The sumptuousness serves the story in a unique way. Scenes are so masterfully composed, they are like oil paintings come to life. All of this and an endearing message about trying one's wings and flying against the flock.

***

IT WAS OSCAR NIGHT, APRIL 6, 1959, at the RKO Pantages Theatre, and after performing "Thank Heaven for Little Girls," Maurice Chevalier was presented with his honorary Oscar by an admiring Rosalind Russell. Then it was time for Gary Cooper and Millie Perkins to announce the nominees for Best Director. Along with Minnelli, the contenders included Richard Brooks and Stanley Kramer, both nominated for provocative fare—*Cat on a Hot Tin Roof* and *The Defiant Ones*, respectively. "And the winner is . . . Vincente Minnelli."

Vincente (who attended the ceremonies with Ginger Rogers) made his way to the podium and addressed his colleagues:

> Ever since *Gigi* was written years ago by Colette, it's been produced through the years in many mediums and many versions and many languages and it has a history of bringing wonderful things to the lives of people connected with these productions. I know personally of a great many of them and I'm sure there are a great many more. And it's brought wonderful things to us connected with this movie and to me tonight. It's about the proudest moment of my life. I want to give my deepest gratitude to you and to *Gigi* for this great honor.

As eloquent and heartfelt as Minnelli's acceptance speech was, the audience was distracted by the fact that he picked an unusual moment to scratch his eye—with his middle finger. For a director so attuned to visual minutiae, it seems odd that Vincente didn't realize how this would appear on camera. Or was this Minnelli's own special tribute to all of the exasperating MGM executives he had tangled with over the years?

26

A
Glittering Tiara

WHEN IT OPENED AT THE Cambridge Theatre in London in 1955, William Douglas Home's play *The Reluctant Debutante* seemed to be the answer to the question most frequently asked by MGM executives: "Where can we find another *Father of the Bride*?" At first glance, Home's very British high-comedy appeared to offer the same satisfying mix of good-natured satire with an endearing father-daughter relationship at its center. The high-society London setting succeeded in camouflaging the familiar plot just enough so that it didn't seem too familiar.

Metro acquired the rights to *The Reluctant Debutante* and even financed the 1956 Broadway production of the play, but the studio decided that before its property reached the screen, it needed to be anglicized so that American audiences wouldn't be put off by the ritzy tea-and-crumpets tone. *Father of the Bride*'s screenwriting team, Frances Goodrich and Albert Hackett, were initially offered the opportunity to adapt Home's play, but they passed, feeling that the scenario was in some ways too similar to the domestic predicament faced by Spencer Tracy and his brood.

As Debbie Reynolds was being considered for the debutante of the title, MGM next turned to one of the authors of Reynolds's 1955 crowd-pleaser, *The Tender Trap*. Julius G. Epstein and his brother Philip had not only scripted the immortal *Casablanca* but had also been responsible for transplanting two of Broadway's most inspired comedies, *Arsenic and Old Lace* and *The Man Who Came to Dinner*, to the screen. Julius (sans Philip) was tapped to work the same magic with *The Reluctant Debutante*, but his *An American in London* approach was ultimately deemed wanting—and then some.

"We wouldn't play one word of that lousy script!" prospective star Rex Harrison barked at producer Pandro Berman. The irascible "Sexy Rexy" and third wife Kay Kendall (also set to star) were none too pleased with Epstein's fish-out-of-water scenario, in which an American father and daughter find themselves in the thick of London's high season. Minnelli also found the Americanized approach contrived and "off kilter." Epstein was out and William Douglas Home, author of the original play, was in. Home would crank out a completely new screenplay at breakneck speed even as cameras began to turn in February 1958. Due to the Harrisons' complicated tax situation, the picture would actually be filmed in Paris, with a mere two days spent immersed in authentic London fog. Debbie Reynolds was replaced with Sandra Dee, and Angela Lansbury joined the cast as catty Mabel Claremont.

Although Rex Harrison was his usual impossible-to-please self ("He didn't give a damn whom he offended," Home observed), everyone—including Minnelli—fell in love with his vivacious new bride and the picture's leading lady, Kay Kendall.[1] Unbeknownst to Vincente, the crew, and even Kendall herself, the star was battling myeloid leukemia (but led to believe by Harrison and others that she was grappling with an iron deficiency). "Kay was really, really ill, having transfusions almost every day," remembers Angela Lansbury:

> I was with them a great deal during that period. We were living in the same hotel in Paris and I'd have dinner with them almost every night. It was extraordinary how she kept up her spirits and her energy. I don't know how she did it. She was so lovely and such a dear, funny person. Rex adored her and took great care of her over that period, which was a new thing for Rex. He had such a rakish reputation with his amours and his failed marriages. With Kay, he really came into his own.[2]

Kendall was such a thoroughgoing professional that the effects of her illness were never evident during production, despite a physically demanding role.

In a sense, the glittering high-society swirl depicted in *The Reluctant Debutante* was not that far removed from the Holmby Hills cocktail-party circuit that Vincente knew all too well. In fact, Minnelli may have been a little too enchanted by the overdressed socialites he was supposed to be sending up in *Debutante*: Where the comedy should be biting (à la Cukor's *The Women*), it is polite.

Lansbury also found her director well-mannered yet remote:

Kay Kendall, Angela Lansbury, and Rex Harrison in the thick of the London season in 1958's *The Reluctant Debutante*. In reviewing this frothy comedy of manners, the *Evening Standard* said "Vincente Minnelli's direction glitters like a tiara."
PHOTO COURTESY OF PHOTOFEST

Vincente simply sat back and watched and waited. He didn't interfere with an actor's approach to how to play a character. His whole view was that of the picture that he was going to encapsulate in his film. And it was us in relation to the flowers on the table or the way the set was dressed and what we were wearing—all of those things. . . . I felt he was such a hesitant person. He didn't exactly stutter but he was certainly very, very slow in framing his sentences. You know, there was nothing immediate about him. He had to think about it. He talked with his hands a lot and he visualized with his hands. I think that he was probably far more definite with the people that he was working with in the arts department than he was with the actors. As far as the acting was concerned, he did leave that to us.[3]

And it is the performances that make *The Reluctant Debutante* worthwhile. Kay Kendall is a madcap delight, twittering hypertensively and flitting about in her Pierre Balmain feathers, and Angela Lansbury is great fun as the acid-tongued Mabel. Despite the presence of teeny-bopper icon Sandra Dee, the picture was not the *Father of the Bride*–style cash cow the studio had hoped for. The reviews, however, offered some consolation: "Vincente Minnelli's direction glitters like a tiara," said the *Evening Standard*. "Lighter than air, entertaining as all get out," *Newsweek* chirped.

Just before *The Reluctant Debutante* went before the cameras, Minnelli was served with divorce papers. In her statement to the court, Georgette charged Vincente with "mental cruelty." During the hearing, she testified that "he said he was sorry he ever met me because he liked being alone better."[4]

The sister of Miss Universe would emerge victorious. Georgette was awarded custody of three-year-old Tina Nina and a property settlement that provided her with $4,325 a month in alimony for fifteen months and an additional $1,700 a month as long as she remained single (according to Georgette, Minnelli's MGM contract entitled him to $4,250 a week). When pressed for a statement about the proceedings, Vincente had no comment.[5]

27

Some
Came Running

MADISON, INDIANA, may have been thrilled to see Frank Sinatra coming, but the feeling wasn't exactly mutual. The city, which had once been selected as "the typical American small town" by the Office of War Information, was a far cry from the Chairman of the Board's natural habitat. It certainly wasn't The Sands in Las Vegas, where one could order hookers as easily as waffles from room service. If Madison was too low rent for Sinatra (he told the press it reminded him of skid row in Los Angeles), it was the perfect Parkman, the fictional Midwestern town of *Some Came Running*. In this sprawling character study, Minnelli would confront '50s conformism and small-town repression head on. The cast, which included Sinatra, Dean Martin, and Shirley MacLaine, descended on Madison (population 10,500) in August 1958.

Although Vincente was thoroughly well versed in dealing with temperamental talent, Sinatra was in his own category. From the get-go, the working relationship between director and star was bound to be strained. Sinatra was a firm believer in getting his performance down in the first take. "If you want a second take, print the first one again," the unpredictable star had informed one of his dumbfounded directors. Minnelli, the plodding perfectionist, had been known to proceed beyond take thirty in pursuit of some elusive effect—usually visual—that he wasn't able to name. Although he was as much of an iconoclast as Sinatra, Vincente's taffeta personality didn't click with his male leads.

Sinatra and Martin "thought he was too precious and pursed his lips too much," Shirley MacLaine recalled. "The two of them could dislike people because of small things that personally offended them."[1] With his tics, fidgety mannerisms, and Noel Coward-ish way with a cigarette, Minnelli gave them plenty of ammunition.

Despite all of his idiosyncrasies, however, Minnelli was clearly the man in charge. "When he would walk onto the set, there was almost like a hush," says Peter Woodburn, who had a bit part in the film. "You'd hear people whispering, 'Mr. Minnelli's here. Mr. Minnelli's here . . .' and that was from the crew and that sort of spilled over to all the extras. Everybody straightened up when he came on the scene."[2]

With so many strong personalities on board, the company braced for fireworks as the cameras began to turn. They weren't disappointed. When hapless assistant director William McGarry interrupted Sinatra's 'tini time with a reminder that they were behind with the shooting schedule, Ol' Blue Eyes decided to make everybody's life a little easier—by ripping out a twenty-page chunk of the screenplay. "There, pal," Sinatra said, "Now we're on schedule."[3] It wasn't as though the story couldn't have used a little pruning. The original James Jones novel weighed in at over a thousand pages—an epic length to tell the story of the prodigal Dave Hirsh returning to a hometown rife with hypocrisy ("Dave was back and the whole town knew that trouble—and women were close behind!").

An ex-serviceman and frustrated novelist, Dave Hirsh is one of Minnelli's most conflicted protagonists. Although his duffle bag is well stocked with William Faulkner, John Steinbeck, and Thomas Wolfe, Dave spends his days playing poker or getting loaded at Smitty's bar. Complex and unpredictable, Sinatra's character even comes complete with polar-opposite love interests.

Martha Hyer's Gwen French is a frigid, buttoned-up schoolteacher who prefers engaging with Dave in affairs strictly literary; Shirley MacLaine's amiable floozy, Ginny Moorehead, is a cheap souvenir Dave picked up at Gilly's Green Room in Chicago. Throughout the film, Ginny is described as "a pig," "a pushover," and "a nobody," though she is just about the only character in the film who is truly herself. Like night and day, the two women in Dave's life embody his own identity crisis. Hirsh is torn between the cultured life of the intellectual and a neon-tinted world of bars, booze, and broads.

Accustomed to studio hacks or autocrats such as Otto Preminger, Sinatra seems to have been thrown by the have-it-your-own-way freedom that Minnelli offered his actors. For Sinatra, shaping his own portrayal may have allowed some familiar emotions to rise to the surface. His schizoid mix of brutality and sensitivity, his Madonna-whore complex regarding the women in his life, and his need to occasionally park his machismo and artistically express himself were all very much a part of his character.

Frank Sinatra, Shirley MacLaine, and Dean Martin in *Some Came Running*. Film scholar Joe McElhaney hails the 1959 melodrama as "one of Minnelli's great films, perhaps even his masterpiece." *Variety* noted: "The most impressive thing about Minnelli's direction is his ability to hold a concept of the picture as a whole. . . . The story never wavers nor diffuses its intensity."

PHOTO COURTESY OF PHOTOFEST

Sinatra's costars seemed to flourish under Vincente's hands-off directorial approach. "For me, Vincente Minnelli was an excellent director, simply because he didn't direct much," Shirley MacLaine observed. "He 'let' us actors find our own characters and our own way. Dean thrived on the freedom he felt with Vincente—one reason his character of Bama was the finest of his career. But Frank was threatened by this way of working because the freedom of choice exposed him too much."[4]

Like MacLaine, Martha Hyer would emerge from *Some Came Running* with an Oscar nomination. If Sinatra was left to his own devices, Hyer was kept under close surveillance: "I loved working for Vincente Minnelli. His direction was personal, sensitive. He was a perfectionist and even suggested how the character might stand or move in a certain way. A lot of actors don't like that kind of direction. I do."[5] Other cast members admitted that they needed all the help they could get.

"I didn't know what I was doing," says actor Denny Miller, who appeared in *Some Came Running* a year before landing the title role in MGM's *Tarzan, the Ape Man.* "Even though I rehearsed my two or three lines about 738,000 times, I'm sure I made Mr. Minnelli's life miserable for a few hours, but I was frightened to death and a misplaced basketball player from UCLA."[6]

Miller was witness to a mind-boggling incident that has passed into the annals of Minnelli lore:

> We were to work from sundown to sunrise on the carnival scene and the guys that were in charge of putting up the Ferris wheel had just finished it. Everything was ready to go. There were hundreds of extras standing around waiting. . . . Mr. Minnelli came out and looked at the Ferris wheel and studied it from several angles. He then told his assistant director to tell the crew to take the whole thing down and move it a foot. When Sinatra and Dean Martin showed up on the set and heard about that, they rented a Lear jet and flew home. We didn't do any work that night. It took Minnelli at least an hour to convince the crew that he was not joking. After they realized he was serious, they took it down and moved it.[7]

It seemed an extraordinary indulgence, even for Minnelli. But he had been saving himself for this. If Vincente had exercised admirable restraint in terms of the visual composition of the rest of the picture, he would make up for it with the climactic carnival sequence. "I said it should be like the inside of a jukebox," Minnelli remembered telling the crew.[8] As Steven Peck's deranged Raymond Lanchak stalks Sinatra and MacLaine with a loaded gun, the film's naturalistic colors turn lurid. Elmer Bernstein's score is suddenly shrill and foreboding. Bill Daniels's camera races to keep up with Dave and Ginny while being barraged with bright lights and revelers in every direction. Editor Adrienne Fazan's cuts come fast and sharp. Shots of boys taking aim at a shooting gallery are intercut with glimpses of the armed madman surveying the frenzied scene from an upstairs window.

From Spencer Tracy's nightmare in *Father of the Bride* to John Kerr's bonfire initiation rite in *Tea and Sympathy*, Minnelli's movies throughout the 1950s had been building up to this moment of almost operatic hysteria. "*Some Came Running* is certainly one of Minnelli's great films, perhaps even his masterpiece," says film scholar Joe McElhaney:

> It comes at the end of a year of enormous creative intensity for him, with a major work in each of the three genres at which he excelled—the musical [*Gigi*], the domestic comedy [*The Reluctant Debutante*] and the small town family melodrama [*Some Came Running*]. Each of these films deals with frag-

mented families who are the products of mesmerizing, decadent, hypocritical worlds—worlds that continue to observe certain rules of social conduct and ritual, regardless of whether these make anyone happy or not. For me, there are few sights in cinema more moving than the final shot of *Some Came Running*. The camera slowly tracks around a small group of mourners for Ginny before it ultimately moves toward a clearly devastated Bama Dillert as he finally removes that sacred hat of his, a gesture of respect toward a woman he had called "a pig" only a day or two earlier. . . . The camera ultimately tracks past him, past all of the human beings gathered there, and opens out onto a shot of the Indiana landscape in the background, with the stones of the cemetery visible in the bottom foreground and a statue of an angel at the far left of the frame—an image of hope and despair.[9]

28

"Minnelli's Texas"

VIRTUALLY EVERYONE IN THE INDUSTRY agreed that *Gigi* and Vincente Minnelli had been the perfect union of sumptuous subject matter and inspired direction. It appeared that anything MGM threw at Vincente, from musicals to melodramas, turned to gold—though the owner of the Academy's 31st Best Director statuette would later concede, "Many things I'm not right for. I don't think I could do a Western, though lots of people think *Home from the Hill* is one. . . . I liked the *Home from the Hill* story right away because it was about people."[1] Minnelli may have responded so strongly to the people in *Home from the Hill* because, all references to "Westerns" aside, the characters are actually far more Tennessee Williams than Louis L'Amour.

At first glance, the story's small-town Texas setting, wild boar hunts, and bastard-son subplot seemed better suited to tough guy directors John Ford or Howard Hawks than to an auteur more accustomed to turning out Judy Garland in Victorian lace. Nevertheless, only a few days after his triumph at the Academy Awards, Vincente found himself on location in Oxford, Mississippi, preparing to shoot a picture that would practically ooze testosterone from every frame. Based on William Humphrey's 1957 debut novel, *Home from the Hill*, was MGM's latest contribution to the neurotic southern-family soap-opera genre (which included *Cat on a Hot Tin Roof*, *Sweet Bird of Youth*, and the unintentionally hilarious *Written on the Wind*).

At the center of *Home from the Hill* is seventeen-year-old Theron Hunnicutt, another of Minnelli's mossy green, soft-spoken misfits with his manhood in question—a sort of second cousin to Tom Lee in *Tea and Sympathy*.

Theron is caught in the middle of his parents' long-simmering feud. The boy's father, Captain Wade Hunnicutt, is both a red-blooded he-man and notorious ladies' man who is as well known for his extramarital exploits as he is for bagging the last wild boar in northeastern Texas.

Wade's long-suffering wife, Hannah, distances herself from her husband after his "poaching on the preserves of love" results in his siring several illegitimate children. After this betrayal, Hannah devotes herself to Theron, raising him to be a mild-mannered, sensitive young man (note the butterfly collection adorning his bedroom wall). As a result of Hannah's coddling, Theron is nothing like his father. The youngster is derided as a "mama's boy" until Wade agrees to take his son under his wing and tutor him in the fine art of manliness.

With *Home from the Hill*, Minnelli would once again present a character torn between two sharply contrasted worlds: the cultured, civilized realm of the mother, and the almost savage universe inhabited by the father. Divided right down the middle, Theron is in conflict over which side he should surrender to. "What every man hunts out there is himself," Wade proclaims before Theron embarks on his journey of self-discovery.

Husband and wife writing team Harriet Frank Jr. and Irving Ravetch (who would later share an Oscar nomination for scripting *Hud*) crafted a screenplay with "almost Biblical simplicity," according to Vincente, who judged their work flawless. "Minnelli was a gentleman but he was remote from us on this project, not by design but by circumstance," says Frank, who recalls meeting with Minnelli only once before the director was whisked away on location.[2]

Left to their own devices, Frank and Ravetch shifted the story's setting from the 1930s' Depression era to the 1950s. Wade's several illegitimate offspring in Humphrey's novel were blended into a composite character: the faithful yet forsaken Rafe. All of this met with Minnelli's approval. "I'm pleased and flattered that he approved of our work, but if you asked me what my favorite films of mine are, that one would not be first and foremost," Frank says.[3]

Though the final film would prove to be something of a disappointment for its authors, the chain smoker in the director's chair made a favorable impression. "All I can say is that Minnelli was gracious," says Frank. "I hear people say things to the contrary but with us, he was a very mild-mannered man. He was pleasant to talk to but our meeting didn't have that—what shall I say?—the heated exchange that sometimes happens with directors or even an imposed point of view. . . . It sounds condescending but he was a *nice man* and I think he had a kind of tenderness for the projects that he chose for himself." Stetsons and sulphur bottoms aside, it's no surprise that Minnelli would gravitate toward *Home from the Hill*. A poignant coming-of-age tale with an outcast at its center was by now as much of a Vincente Minnelli specialty as a lavish musical.

For the part of Theron, Minnelli was instrumental in casting handsome newcomer George Hamilton. The eternally tan heartthrob had recently signed a seven-year contract with MGM but so far had only one prior film to his credit. Hamilton would describe his director as "an autocrat" who micromanaged every aspect of his performance—from lightening his hair to dictating his line readings. "If he could have wired you up and put you on remote control, he would have been much happier," George Hamilton says:

> I learned the trick to Minnelli and that was to watch him, not watch myself. Not study the part but study Minnelli. You had to figure out what it was that he was trying to articulate—get it and do it quickly. And he'd give you plenty of takes to get it. . . . I learned fast because he was a mentor and he wanted me to deliver and he was incredibly helpful to me, but you had to get over the ego because he was a tyrant on the set. If you're a sensitive actor and you didn't give him what you wanted, you felt like you had just committed suicide and Minnelli's at your funeral. You'd be wondering . . . *What have I done wrong?*[4]

It was clear that the character of the uber macho Wade Hunnicutt required an actor who could be commanding, complex, and sexually charismatic without breaking a sweat. Robert Mitchum, anyone? The actor (who quipped that the title of the film should be *Minnelli's Texas*) signed on after Clark Gable proved unavailable. More than a decade had passed since Robert Mitchum had swapped banalities with Katharine Hepburn in Minnelli's *Undercurrent*. In the intervening years, the heavy-lidded actor had become a bona-fide movie star and tabloid staple, but his unfailingly professional, fuss-free approach to acting hadn't changed.

Like Gene Kelly and Kirk Douglas, Mitchum had an alpha male persona that meshed surprisingly well with Minnelli's nervous-Nellie aestheticism. "He loved Mitchum for what he was," George Hamilton says. "Mitchum was this Mount Rushmore and all Vincente wanted him to do was be in the middle of the action, deliver his lines, and then [Minnelli] could do the whole ballet around it. He loved that force of Mitchum. It was a power for which other things could vibrate. You can't create that. You couldn't have added menace or power to Mitchum. Mitchum was Mitchum. And Minnelli loved that about him."[5]

The sailing wasn't as smooth with third-billed newcomer George Peppard. A graduate of the Actor's Studio, Peppard would be making one of his first important screen appearances as Mitchum's illegitimate son, Rafe. "Minnelli had big problems with George Peppard because George was this Method actor," remembers George Hamilton:

> He had to *arrive* at his performance. He kept asking about motivations and reasons for this and that and finally Vincente went up to George and said, "I know inside you're a seething volcano with lava about to pour out but trust me, nothing is happening on your face." And Peppard just lost it. He could never be the same after that . . . and Minnelli just couldn't compromise. He had a vision. He was painting it. And people just got in the way of it all.[6]

Both Georges—Hamilton and Peppard—were awed by industry veteran Mitchum, who could not have been less impressed with his own legend. As Hamilton remembered it, when Mitchum wasn't tanked or toking up, he'd be "ramming away at a lovely townie whom he had splayed over a chair." When Peppard clashed with Minnelli regarding the way the final cemetery sequence should be played, Peppard took his complaint to Mitchum. Expecting sympathy from the screen's iconic rebel, Peppard announced that he planned to walk off the picture. "It'll be a very expensive hike," Mitchum cautioned. "I'm certain that it will be your last job. I'm sure the studio can sue you. Even though you think Minnelli is wrong, do it his way."[7] Peppard complied.

Doing things "his way" applied not only to the performances but to even the most microscopic elements of the production. George Hamilton vividly recalled the day Vincente pointed toward some leafy underbrush and informed a slack-jawed assistant, "I want more of this." As tactfully as possible, the assistant attempted to explain, "But Mr. Minnelli, that's poison ivy." "Plant it!" Minnelli commanded.[8] So what if it was poison? It was pretty and it fit with the picture that Minnelli was painting in his head.

For Minnelli, the decor helped shape the story as much as the dialogue or action—even in a "Western." "I spent ages on that room. I'm a great furniture mover," Vincente said of designing Mitchum's over-the-top hunter's den.[9] Surrounded by bear-skin rugs, bloodhounds, and mounted trophy heads, Theron is carefully framed by Minnelli as though he's about to become his father's next prey. As the camera pans across Mitchum's lair, one can sense Vincente's delight in decorating a room in such a flagrantly barbaric style. And there's no way to miss the point that Theron is about to be indoctrinated into the world of Real Men.

Three's Company: George Hamilton shares a blanket with co-star Luana Patten and
director Minnelli on location for *Home from the Hill*, 1959.
PHOTO COURTESY OF PHOTOFEST

Is it purely coincidental that *Tea and Sympathy*, *Some Came Running*, and
Home from the Hill all focus on men grappling with what might be termed
"male identity issues"? Those who consider studio system directors like Minnelli nothing more than factory foremen would dismiss the similar storylines
as pure happenstance—the sort of thing that was "in the air" at the time.
Auteurists, devotees of *Cahiers du Cinéma*, and Minnelli disciples prefer to
see the links as part of a grander plan. It would appear that Vincente was
seeking out and shaping properties that explored his theme of choice: a repressed misfit, unable to seek solace from his family or from the world around
him, must go within in order to heal himself. This would be the sort of thing
writers David Siegel and Scott McGehee would describe as "the peculiar
sub-genre of the Minnelli Male Melodrama. . . . Perhaps it is something
about the weird genre/gender conflict of a man telling a story about men in
this particularly feminine idiom that gives these films their disturbing and
psychotic beauty."[10]

For everything that works in *Home from the Hill* (Mitchum, Bronislau
Kaper's moving score), there are key elements that do not (the contrived

storyline is simply too much, and there's a tendency toward pop-eyed melo-dramatics). Although Minnelli's direction is assured and he's clearly inter-ested, it takes an awfully long time—150 minutes, in fact—to tell a story that could have easily been wrapped up at the two-hour mark. But this South-ern Gothic soap opera seemed to encourage Vincente's penchant for excess.

"Under Vincente Minnelli's direction it is garishly overplayed," wrote *New York Times* critic Bosley Crowther, who dismissed *Home from the Hill* as "aimless, tedious and in conspicuously doubtful taste," while *Commonweal* found Vincente's staging throughout the film "particularly uneven." "Some scenes," wrote the reviewer, "are straight overacted melodrama, and then again, some, like the hunting and chase sequences in the woods . . . are done with extraordinary strength and beauty."[11] Despite the mixed reception, *Home from the Hill* would prove to be the last Minnelli movie to turn a re-spectable profit ($5,610,627).

Better Than
a Dream

"NOTHING EVER TERRIFIED ME as much as that switchboard," Judy Holliday would recall of her days keeping up with the calls as an operator at Orson Welles's Mercury Theatre. Despite her on-the-job jitters, Holliday's switchboard experience (such as it was) would prove invaluable years later when she opened on Broadway in *Bells Are Ringing*.

The hit 1956 musical was written by Holliday's old friends, Betty Comden and Adolph Green, with music composed by Jule Styne. In a Tony Award–winning tour de force, Holliday starred as Ella Peterson, a kind of answering-service oracle who is everything to everybody. On the front lines at the Manhattan-based "Susanswerphone," Ella not only fields calls and relays messages but serves up a dazzling array of over-the-phone alter egos to keep her subscribers happy. If some mother's little darling refuses to eat his spinach, Ella slips into her most convincing Santa Claus and gives junior a talking to. If playboy playwright Jeffrey Moss is sleeping off a severe case of writer's block, Ella turns herself into the unfailingly supportive "Mom" and makes sure Shakespeare gets his daily wake-up call. But when it comes time for the unconfident Ella to deal with people face to face, it's one wrong number after another.

According to Betty Comden, the idea for the show was inspired by a rude awakening:

> I didn't have an answering service and I asked Adolph what his service was like and he said, "I don't know. Let's find out where it is!" We found out it

was just around the corner from where he lived on East 53rd Street. We pictured that it would be this sort of shiny, stainless steel place with rows and rows of telephones and glamorous girls sitting at them. Instead, it was in this terrible ramshackle building, down a couple of little cellar steps, and it was really depressing as hell. We walked into this incredibly messy room that was unpainted and peeling and in the middle of all of it sat this one very fat lady at a switchboard saying, "Gloria Vanderbilt's residence. . . ." We looked at each other and said, "Now here's an idea for a show!"[1]

Hollywood was notorious for not allowing Broadway stars to recreate their acclaimed stage roles on film—Mary Martin, Ethel Merman, and Julie Andrews had all been passed over when *South Pacific*, *Gypsy*, and *My Fair Lady* turned up on movie screens. Holliday proved to be the exception to the rule as she already had a cinematic track record, having won an Oscar and enormous acclaim for her performance as Billie Dawn in *Born Yesterday*. The film's director, George Cukor, considered Holliday "A true artist. . . . She made you laugh, she was a supreme technician, and then suddenly you were touched."[2] Holliday was highly regarded off screen as well. Many of her colleagues remembered her as an endearing presence and an exceedingly generous performer. Despite her tremendous talent, though, her insecurities and self-doubt could be crippling, and Minnelli was about to experience her neurotic side at full volume.

From the moment she signed a contract with MGM to appear in a Freed-produced, Minnelli-directed version of *Bells Are Ringing*, Holliday seemed to have second thoughts. The comedienne agonized over what she perceived to be some of the weaknesses in the screenplay. In reviewing the stage show, the same Brooks Atkinson who had saluted Holliday and the sprightly score had grumbled about "one of the most antiquated plots of the season."[3] Although Comden and Green had handled the adaptation chores themselves, Holliday felt that in attempting to open up the story for the screen, they'd only succeeded in making the show longer—not more cinematic. Would the flimsy plot become even more conspicuous when it was magnified on a movie screen? This got the slightly overweight star to thinking about how *she* would look on a movie screen—blown up to CinemaScope proportions, no less. With each passing day, Holliday's doubts and fears multiplied.

In a script conference with Minnelli and Freed, Holliday shared her thoughts on how the screenplay might be improved. Although Freed acknowledged that Holliday had "a few good suggestions," he dismissed her concerns as "nothing monumental."[4] Still, the star fretted over the fact that

Judy Holliday and Dean Martin
in conference with their director
on the set of *Bells Are Ringing*.
PHOTO COURTESY
OF PHOTOFEST

little was being done to transform an intimate theater piece into a wide-screen event. As Holliday told *Cosmopolitan*: "Of course, lots of things have to be changed when a stage show is filmed. And should be, I think."[5] Like the leading man, for example.

Reportedly, Holliday had had an affair with her Broadway *Bells* costar, Sydney Chaplin. Despite the positive notices for his stage portrayal, Chaplin would not be invited to re-create his role on film. For one thing, his fling with Holliday had ended badly. But even more important to MGM was the fact that his name meant next to nothing to moviegoers. Instead, Dean Martin was cast as the procrastinating playwright Jeff Moss, or "Plaza O-double-four-double-three," as he's known on the switchboard. As principal photography began in October 1959, Holliday feared that Martin, like Minnelli, was sleepwalking his way through *Bells Are Ringing*—though Dino's laissez-faire attitude certainly suited the character and his easygoing demeanor offered the perfect contrast to Holliday's high-spirited intensity.

Convinced that she was starring in a mediocre retread of her Broadway show, Holliday asked to be released from her contract and even offered to hand back her salary if Minnelli would start over with, say, Shirley MacLaine manning the switchboard. The studio did not take Holliday up on her offer.

She would have to continue. She even made her reservations public, telling reporter Jon Whitcomb: "I've done four pictures with George Cukor, and he's a perfectionist. I'm afraid Arthur Freed and Mr. Minnelli are very easy to please. They don't mind okaying things that strike me as only half right. If anybody knows the values in this play, I do. After living in it for three years, I'm the final authority on what lines ought to get laughs and how to get them."[6]

As Holliday biographer Gary Carey noted, "Vincente Minnelli was surprised to find he couldn't gain Holliday's confidence. . . . Minnelli did his best to reassure her, but he failed to win Judy's confidence simply because she was convinced that the entire concept of the film was hopelessly, irredeemably wrong." As outrageously talented and insecure as that other Judy, Holliday also shared Garland's susceptibility to illness—either real or imagined. Over the course of a tense production, Holliday suffered from laryngitis, bursitis, bladder problems, and a kidney infection, all of which may have been early indications of the far more serious health problems ahead for Holliday. Or were these physical manifestations of her fears? "I kept reassuring her, but Judy was a constant worrier," Minnelli said of Holliday, likening her to Fred Astaire. Both performers were exacting perfectionists whose work appeared effortless on screen. It was ironic that two of the most talented stars in the business were rarely satisfied with their own efforts.[7]

Wisely, Minnelli lets his camera linger on his leading lady throughout *Bells Are Ringing*. Blessed with undeniable magnetism and unsurpassed comedic timing, Holliday is the heart and soul of the whole picture. Just as *Funny Girl* wouldn't have been much minus Barbra Streisand, *Bells Are Ringing* is totally dependent on its shining star for life support.

Whether belting out the ultimate 11 o'clock number, "I'm Going Back" (". . . Where I can be me at the Bonjour Tristesse Brassiere Company") or poignantly realizing that "The Party's Over," Holliday dazzles with a superlative musical-comedy performance that's charged with a genuine warmth and vulnerability. Although Rosalind Russell or Shirley MacLaine could have played Ella Peterson and come through with an effective comedic performance, the endearingly neurotic switchboard operator is clearly a role that Holliday was born to play. "The picture owes more to Miss Holliday than it does to its authors, its director or even to Alexander Graham Bell," Bosley Crowther declared in the *New York Times*.[8]

Though the film was a personal triumph for Holliday and the Comden and Green score is first rate, some of the star's concerns about the production turned out to be well founded. As the finished film reveals, Minnelli made only marginal attempts to open the story up and liberate it from its theatrical roots. And why was CinemaScope—a process better suited to breathtaking, panoramic vistas—foisted upon an intimate musical comedy set largely indoors and in confined quarters?

None of this phased the *Hollywood Reporter*: "It is a better musical on screen than it was on stage," decided James Powers. "For MGM, 'Bells' will ring loud and long, in the friendly clang of the box office cash register." This proved to be the case when the picture opened at Radio City Music Hall in June. Later that summer, MGM's accountants were able to proudly report: "*Bells Are Ringing* joined an elite company of blockbuster films when it topped the one million dollar mark at the Radio City Music Hall box office."[9]

The picture would be Holliday's last. In 1965, the actress died of cancer at the age of forty-four. *Bells Are Ringing* would not only stand as a testament to Holliday's inimitable talents but was also the Freed Unit's last hurrah— at least musically speaking.

For Minnelli, it was on to the next project, and as always, there was already one waiting for him: an epic remake of Rudolph Valentino's silent classic *The Four Horsemen of the Apocalypse*—though once on board, Minnelli, like Ella Peterson, probably wanted nothing more than to hightail it back to the Bonjour Tristesse Brasierre Company.

30

Apocalypse

IT WAS WHILE VACATIONING in Rome that Vincente met an unstoppable force of nature who would become his third wife: Denise Giganti. Or as some of her detractors referred to her: "Denise, Inc." She wasn't a superstar like Judy, or a knockout like Georgette. Nevertheless, incredible things seemed to happen whenever Denise was around. Or maybe she just grabbed life by the scruff of the neck and made things happen. After all, she had never been shy about going after whatever she wanted, despite the fact that she told Minnelli's old friend Eleanor Lambert: "I don't want a lot of things. Just good and right for me."[1] Even so, Denise seemed to be in perpetual pursuit of *something*. And she was so thoroughly charming—what with that adorable stutter, super-chic sense of style, and trademark braided hair—that one tended not to notice whenever she pounced.

Long before she met Minnelli and took Hollywood by storm, Denise's story seemed ready-made for the movies. It had everything. *An exotic location:* Namely, Belgrade, Serbia, where, somewhere in the vicinity of 1931, Denise—or Danica Radosavljevic, as she was then named—was born. *An unconventional upbringing:* Daughter of a military officer loyal to the monarchy, "Dusica" (as Denise was nicknamed) was raised largely by her grandparents. As Denise would remember it, her own mother had been judged "inappropriate" as her primary caretaker. *Secrets revealed:* During the upheaval of World War II, Denise's grandfather disclosed to her alone the location of the family's hidden stash of gold, which she duly noted. *The daring escape:* After the war, as Tito's Communists solidified their control, Denise fled her homeland by sailing off in a tiny rowboat. Miraculously, she was spotted by a British minesweeper and pulled to safety. The captain of the ship "took a shine to her," and instead of hauling Denise back to Serbia, he deposited her in a refugee camp in Bari, Italy. *Dangerous liaisons:* While working as a model in Rome, Denise caught the eye of Giuseppe Giganti, a considerably older though extraordinarily wealthy Italian mogul (rumored to have had some shady connections), and they were married. Although Denise would later refer to Giganti as her "first husband," it appears that she had been married at least once—possibly twice—before meeting him.* *The moment of truth:* In 1958, Denise walked out on her marriage, but by all accounts, she emerged with mucho lira and a world-class collection of jewels that made the House of Harry Winston look seriously underdressed.

It was quite a saga—more than enough melodrama for three Joan Crawford pictures. In fact, many felt that Vincente should have scrapped plans for his next epic, *The Four Horsemen of the Apocalypse*, and instead turned his cameras on *The Denise Giganti Story*. Now *that* movie would have sold tickets, and everybody would still be talking about it. According to Denise, people couldn't stop talking about her—even if they had only seen her from across the room at a Dior showing or at a Vivien Westwood retrospective: "Over 90 percent of the people who write or talk about me have never met me," she once observed.[2]

Even Hollywood insiders who had met her (and who were all too familiar with larger-than-life personalities) were genuinely intrigued. "Denise would be a fantastic subject for a novel," writer-actress Ruth Gordon told the *Los Angeles Times* in 1967. "She's fiction, right out of Somserset Maugham or Michael Arlen. And I'm sure if she were *written*, she would turn into a real person. Only then could you find out who she *really* is."[3]

As it turned out, Ruth Gordon was right. Denise *was* a fantastic subject for a novel. In Joyce Haber's blistering 1976 bestseller *The Users* (best described as the literary love-child of Rona Barrett and Harold Robbins), the character of "Elena Brent" was reportedly inspired by The Third Mrs. Minnelli.

In Haber's racy roman à clef, the enterprising Elena becomes a Beverly Hills super-hostess after scraping, scheming, and sleeping her way to the top. Her stunning ascent begins when she flees dreary East Berlin after bedding down with a border guard ("She spent half an hour of her last evening in East Berlin in the shack with Helmut, while his friends guarded their privacy.") So, did Denise see any parallels between herself and Haber's scrappy heroine? Not a chance. "You can believe if I had to escape by going to bed with some-

---

* Passport records reveal that Denise traveled under various names in the early 1950s, including "Danica Gay" and "Danica D. Guilianelli."

body, it would be a commander," Denise announced.[4] Still, there seemed to be some striking similarities between the Serbian powerhouse and Haber's wily Elena, who realizes "that sex was something she could use if she had to, without feeling that she had betrayed herself, and that it didn't require love."

By the time Denise divorced Giuseppe Giganti and made her way to America, she had acquired plenty of life experience and some choice baubles, but she was still sorely lacking in the social-standing department. "Denise was a nobody," says designer Luis Estevez. "She arrived from nowhere and with a very sketchy past."[5] But all of that would change. As friends and foes alike would learn, one must never underestimate The Power of Denise. It wasn't long before she had charmed her way into a glittering circle composed of Hollywood's super-elite.

As Luis Estevez recalls, "[Producer] Sam Spiegel and his wife Betty had befriended Denise and introduced her to very sweet, adorable, talented, wonderful Vincente Minnelli . . . who was gay." Denise seemed willing to overlook that particular detail. During production on Vincente's next film, *The Four Horsemen of the Apocalypse*, the couple's relationship blossomed. As Minnelli recalled, "It was very easy for me to begin having serious thoughts about her, and I hope she felt the same."[6]

* * *

IT HAD CATAPULTED Rudolph Valentino to superstardom in 1921. Could a modernized version of *The Four Horsemen of the Apocalypse* do for some swarthy unknown in the '60s what it had done for Rudy in the Roaring '20s? In an attempt to emulate the megahit that was Metro's 1959 remake of *Ben-Hur* (which had also been a silent smash in 1925), MGM was digging deep into the vaults and dusting off any properties—no matter how antiquated— that had once turned a tidy profit for the studio. Valentino's *Four Horsemen* had raked in an estimated $5 million back in the days when Warren G. Harding was still in office. So, even though nobody had asked for it, Metro was going to give a new generation their own *Apocalypse*—only this one, of course, would be bigger and better, in CinemaScope, in Metrocolor, and directed by Vincente Minnelli. Even the World War I setting of Valentino's version and the original Vicente Blasco Ibáñez novel wasn't good enough. A movie this super-colossal required no less a global conflict than World War II. Julian Blaustein, who had produced such historical dramas as *Desiree* and *The Wreck of the Mary Deare*, would mount his most ambitious production to date with *Four Horsemen*. Robert Ardrey, who had scripted Minnelli's *Madame Bovary*, was assigned the daunting task of reworking such musty material and bringing it up to date.

Minnelli immediately voiced concerns about updating the story, though he felt that this was a challenge that could be worked through, especially with The Second Coming of Rudolph Valentino in the lead. But where would MGM's new matinee idol come from? There seemed to be no worthy contenders among the studio's dwindling roster of contract players. Well, maybe one. In March 1960, the *New York Times* announced that George Hamilton was the front runner: "Mr. Hamilton, a poised, dark-haired young man who once spent six months studying bullfighting in South America, is serious about his aspirations to become another Valentino."[7] Montgomery Clift was mentioned. Dirk Bogarde was discussed. Horst Buchholtz was a prime candidate. While vacationing in Rome, Minnelli also met with a stunning up and comer named Alain Delon. The former French soldier turned heads wherever he went, oozed sexual charisma, and would soon be coveted by casting couches of every persuasion throughout Hollywood. Minnelli lobbied for this smoldering star of tomorrow, but Metro's executives were unmoved. Nobody knew (or at that moment cared) who Alain Delon was.

The *Four Horsemen* required a dashing young man to play Argentinean playboy turned Resistance crusader Julio Desnoyers, but MGM needed an established star to carry the picture. What Minnelli ended up with was Glenn Ford. The actor had recently signed a multi-picture deal with the studio, and headlining their newly anointed star in an important period piece seemed the perfect way to trumpet the association. At forty-two, Ford was still photogenic, but he was well beyond his Johnny Farrell peak opposite Rita Hayworth in *Gilda*. Metro may have felt more confident having a bankable star on board, but Ford's presence seemed to immediately age the project. What's more, the supporting cast that had been assembled also included more than a touch of distinguished gray. Some twenty years after *Casablanca*, Paul Henreid once again found himself playing a noble Resistance leader and husband to a wife enamored with another man. *Watch on the Rhine* star Paul Lukas and Minnelli favorite Charles Boyer would play the German and French heads of the Desnoyers–von Hartrott family. A nearly unrecognizable Lee J. Cobb in a white wig and heavy make-up portrayed the blustery, larger-than-life patriarch Madariaga.

In the role of Julio's alluring love interest, Marguerite Laurier, the studio bypassed Hollywood's reigning leading ladies and instead chose Ingrid Thulin, the luminous star of several Ingmar Bergman features. The Swedish-born star of *Wild Strawberries* may have been a consummate actress, but her name meant next to nothing to the paying customer in Bayonne, New Jersey.

When preproduction began in Paris in August 1960, Vincente's doubts about the script mushroomed into major concerns. While ensconced in the George Cinq hotel, he scrutinized the screenplay, becoming ever more convinced that Ardrey's adaptation lacked passion—romantic, political, or otherwise.

John Gay, one of the most prolific screenwriters in the business, received word that his services were desperately needed. "I was working for MGM. I had just finished reworking *How the West Was Won*, and they said, 'Go over to Paris. They're having trouble with this picture,'" Gay recalls:

> They said, "We want you to rewrite the love scene." So, I got the script. I read it on the plane and god, there were about *five* of them and I didn't think *any* of those love scenes worked. So, I was going to go over and be very cautious and ask, "Which love scene do you want rewritten?" When I arrived, the first thing Vincente says is, "How do you like the script?" and I said, "It was . . . all right. Now which love scene do you want rewritten?" That went back and forth. Finally, Vincente turned to Julie [Blaustein] and said, "*I told you.* I told you he didn't like it. I told you it wasn't any good. I told you we have to work on it. . . ." So, right away, I wanted to go home. I mean, here I was working with Minnelli—a great opportunity—and I was hoping he *didn't* like what I turned in because if he didn't like what I was rewriting, then I could go home. But, instead, he said, "This is what I want. . . ." The more I found myself digging deeper and finding trouble with [the script], the more I wanted to get out. Vincente was very tenacious, though. . . . I felt that some things going into it were good, but we never really had enough time to do all the stuff that had to be done. And the money spent on that picture! When you needed four extras, Vincente used a hundred.[8]

As Gay slogged through the seemingly endless rewrites, there were "streams of memorandums flowing" between Blaustein, studio chief Sol Siegel, and a determined but continually undermined Minnelli. Every aspect of the production, from the epic to the minute, was hashed over. Film historian George Feltenstein once digested the 6,000 or so pages contained in the studio files on *The Four Horsemen* and discovered that the trouble had started at the top and trickled down: "Sol Siegel, whom Minnelli had the great success with on *Some Came Running*, had transitioned from being an outside producer to head of production. . . . Siegel was really the one who was forcing all of these changes on Minnelli. There are letters from Vincente, in which he is begging and pleading for them not to do this and not to do that. But they wouldn't listen."[9]

Brian Avery (best remembered for his role as Dustin Hoffman's rival in *The Graduate*), played Paul Lukas's son in *Four Horsemen*. Avery recalled that Vincente made an indelible impression from the very first casting call:

Apocalypse Now: Ingrid Thulin, Minnelli, and Glenn Ford on location for
The Four Horsemen of the Apocalypse in 1961. Pushed to the breaking
point by her director, Thulin walked off the set.
PHOTO COURTESY OF PHOTOFEST

Mr. Minnelli wore these long-sleeved yellow cashmere sweaters and he had
a twitch. Sometimes the sides of his cheeks would kind of twitch when he
talked and he generally had a cigarette. He said to me, "What kind of parts
do you specialize in?" And I said, "Sons." So, he cast me and it was an extraordinarily wonderful experience. I got to spend five weeks on what was then
and may still be the largest soundstage in the world, which was Stage 15 at
MGM.[10]

On that stage, Avery and most of the principal players appeared in a dramatically charged dining-room sequence in which Heinrich von Hartrott
(Karl Boehm) reveals that he is a Nazi and the major conflicts of World War

II are metaphorically played out as domestic drama. Although Avery was be-friended by several of his veteran costars, his on-set experiences also included the inevitable dose of self-absorbed star behavior. "He was a piece of work," Avery says of leading man Glenn Ford:

> Glenn had read his own publicity, I guess. He was not friendly. The entire time I worked on the film—those five or six weeks—and sat across the table from him all day long, he never once greeted me or said, "Hello" or "Goodbye" or acknowledged my existence. Meanwhile, Charles Boyer is treating me like a son, I'm going to lunch with Lee J. Cobb all the time, . . . but Glenn Ford would sit and make jokes with Yvette Mimieux about some dwarf doing each of them under the table.[11]

In sharp contrast, Avery found his director a thoroughgoing professional: "Mr. Minnelli ran the set very well. He was attentive. He was always there if you needed to speak to him about something. He was very interested in the women. I remember when Ingrid Thulin was on the set and he was very, very present to her."[12] Some might say omnipresent.

In late December, a crisis emerged when Ingrid Thulin, perilously close to having a nervous breakdown, walked off the set. Thulin was the latest in a long line of actors who found it difficult to adjust to Vincente's unconventional and often quite literal hands-on approach. In a letter to Thulin's agent, Paul Kohner, the actress's husband, Harry Schein, detailed her miseries—not the least of which was a strained relationship with her director:

> In Sweden, when a director shows an actor how to do a scene, how to act, one feels that either the director or the actor is an amateur. Since Ingrid not only likes Minnelli as a person but also admires his films and certainly knows that *he* is no amateur, she is now convinced that he considers *her* to be an amateur. She feels like a puppet or marionette instead of like the professional actress she is. . . . Ingrid has told me that Minnelli often wants her to look at him while he is showing her how to move, look, stand. She is then so occupied in studying his plastic and mimic movements that she loses not only her memory but also her concept of the scene. . . . Even if working conditions will be improved, I doubt that she will change her mind about her future activities in Hollywood.[13]

On December 31, 1960 (the same day that Thulin's husband wrote his letter), Minnelli was focused on someone other than his beleaguered leading lady. At the Palm Springs home of Joan Cohn (widow of Columbia Pictures

Vincente and the third Mrs. Minnelli, the colorful Denise Giganti. Rex Reed dubbed her "Queen of Group A," the grand empress of Hollywood's power elite. Those less enamored of the lady referred to her as "Denise, Inc."
PHOTO COURTESY OF PHOTOFEST

chief Harry Cohn), a justice of the peace married Vincente and Denise Giganti in a decidedly informal, off-the-cuff ceremony that seemed to recall the rushed nuptials in *The Clock*. Laurence Harvey, who had been considered for Ford's *Four Horsemen* role, served as an attendant.

After returning to Beverly Hills with his charismatic third wife in tow, Vincente resumed work on *The Four Horsemen*. The only element of the film that received as much attention from Minnelli as Ingrid Thulin were the four horsemen themselves. At several points throughout the film, Tony Duquette's andiron statues, representing Conquest, War, Pestilence, and Death, come to life, and the figures can be glimpsed galloping through an apocalyptic void. "All he worried about were the horses," recalls Hank Moonjean, who served as the first assistant director in Paris. "It must have been at least five days to shoot that, maybe even longer, and it was so difficult. And the poor horses—we thought they were going to die. Extremely difficult. I don't think any of that could ever be repeated."[14]

Following a preview in October 1961, substantial changes were made to the picture. "There was so much cutting and reshooting, they had to rerecord the entire score," says George Feltenstein. Alex North's underscoring was tossed and replaced with some stunning new music by André Previn. It was also decided that Ingrid Thulin's soft-spoken delivery and tenuous command of English were causing many of her lines to be lost. The orders came down that the actress would be dubbed, and her voice would be supplied by none other than Angela Lansbury. As Brian Avery remembered, "It was so remarkable that you had a Swede playing a French woman who is dubbed by an Englishwoman."[15]

John Gay believes that studio politics also played a part in the dubbing. "I never had any problems with Ingrid Thulin's voice," Gay says. "Of all the troubles we had going on, I thought Ingrid Thulin was wonderful. She was a terrific actress. I think it was MGM—the big wigs—I don't think they could understand her."[16] In fixating on *The Four Horsemen*'s auditory alterations, MGM seemed to be missing the big picture. For starters, Glenn Ford and Ingrid Thulin appeared to be mere acquaintances throughout the film instead of lovers.

"The only memory I have—without going into anything that is just completely unkind—is my father saying that there was absolutely no chemistry between Glenn Ford and Ingrid Thulin," says Paul Henreid's daughter, Monika. "There are people who are on fire as lovers and you get what they call 'movie magic,' and there are people who play opposite each other and absolutely nothing happens. I think this is just a case where absolutely nothing happened."[17]

Nevertheless, MGM executives seemed to be looking at a completely different movie. "You could have heard a pin drop during the entire showing," Metro executive Bob Mochrie reported to Vincente after a preview screening in late December. "I'm sure the public will be equally impressed and the word of mouth will be terrific. Pictures like this don't come very often and I would like you to know that we will do all in our power to properly launch this great attraction."[18] Mochrie was no prophet.

When it was all over—the 250,000 tons of military equipment, the 15,000 extras, the disembodied voice of Angela Lansbury—this $7 million "great attraction" just seemed to sit there on the screen. In his review for the *New York Herald Tribune*, Paul V. Beckley summed up the opinions of many when he wrote:

Warfare here is tidier than it ought to be, considering the basic point of the film. The prevailing tone is of genteel civility, sleek coiffures, delicately chosen furnishings. . . . Ingrid Thulin, who will be remembered as one of Ingmar Bergman's group, here is over-powdered, over-cosmeticized to the virtual

exclusion of the vivid charm she possessed in the Bergman pictures. . . . I suspect any moviegoer could suggest a dozen films that in recent years have made
the basic point this film undertakes but made it urgently, passionately and
with deep conviction. *The Four Horsemen of the Apocalypse* fails precisely on
this score.[19]

"The whole thing is a mess," says George Feltenstein. "But it didn't have
to be. Had Vincente been able to make the movie he wanted, I think it would
have turned out beautifully."[20]

31

Don't Blame Me

THE DECREE CAME DOWN from MGM's new studio chief, Joseph Vogel: "MGM is now in the business of producing family pictures." As the director of a Roman bacchanal that featured infidelity, attempted suicide, and an orgy, Minnelli had good to reason to be worried. It was unlikely that *Two Weeks in Another Town* would qualify as Vogel's idea of wholesome family entertainment. In fact, Minnelli's movie paled only in comparison to one other holdover from the studio's previous administration: Stanley Kubrick's *Lolita*, in which James Mason harbors an intense erotic obsession with teen-ager Sue Lyon. While Disney had ushered in the '60s with *Pollyanna* and *The Parent Trap*, the MGM lion was now roaring over the likes of *Boys' Night Out*, in which four men (three of them married) maintain a "bachelor pad" that comes complete with Kim Novak—though even that scenario seemed tame compared to Minnelli's excursion into hedonistic excess.

Spurred on by the international success of Federico Fellini's *La Dolce Vita*, which featured egoistic moviemakers squabbling against Roman back-drops, MGM's former regime had pounced on a property with a similar set-ting and attendant freewheeling sexuality: Irwin Shaw's coolly received 1960 novel, *Two Weeks in Another Town*. In Shaw's novel, Jack Andrus—a phys-ically and emotionally scarred NATO adviser—is summoned overseas to supervise the dubbing on a troubled movie that his mentor, Maurice Kruger, is directing in Rome. Once there, Andrus finds himself in the director's chair, and his on-set battles are matched by his clashes with his capricious ex-wife, Carlotta.

After a self-imposed, three-year hiatus, John Houseman was once again producing pictures for MGM, and *Two Weeks in Another Town* seemed like the perfect project to welcome him back. Despite their skirmishes on *The Cobweb* and *Lust for Life*, Minnelli was Houseman's first and only choice as director. *Two Weeks* (which would be shot partially on location in Rome) would reunite Vincente not only with Houseman but also with leading man Kirk Douglas,* screenwriter Charles Schnee, and composer David Raksin. With so much of the *Bad and the Beautiful* team reassembled, comparisons between that film and *Two Weeks in Another Town* were inevitable. In fact, it often seemed like the earlier picture was haunting this latest effort, which was not so much a sequel as a more oregano-flavored remake.

Charles Schnee had worked wonders in terms of fleshing out George Bradshaw's *Tribute to a Bad Man* and transforming it into *The Bad and the Beautiful*. But adapting Irwin Shaw's solemn prose would prove to be more problematic. In early script conferences, it was decided that many of Shaw's plot elements would be altered or streamlined for dramatic effect. It was Metro's head of production Sol Siegel who suggested that audiences should be introduced to a Jack Andrus who has hit rock bottom—recovering from a nervous breakdown in a mental institution. This would prove to be one of the few good ideas a studio executive would have regarding *Two Weeks in Another Town*.

After reviewing an initial draft of the script, Motion Picture Production Code supervisor Geoffrey Shurlock thought Schnee had remained far too faithful to Shaw's text: "The portrayal of free and easy sexual intercourse is so graphically depicted herein that any pretense of presenting it in a moral light would appear to be almost ludicrous," he wrote.[1] And during the Vogel regime, a sequence in which Jack Andrus was the headliner at an orgy would have been about as welcome as a stripper at a church social. Despite the fact that it had taken Schnee almost a year to knock out a treatment and two full drafts of *Two Weeks in Another Town*, he was asked to go back and reshape some of the material with an eye toward refashioning hard-core smut into soft-core smut.

Metro's front office believed that the superlative cast that was assembled might distract the eagle-eyed censors from the plot's tawdrier elements. In addition to Kirk Douglas, *Two Weeks* would feature Edward G. Robinson, Oscar-winner Claire Trevor, Cyd Charisse, and the eternally poised George Hamilton, who immediately felt ill at ease as the picture's resident bad ass, Davie Drew.

---

* As earlier with *The Bad and the Beautiful*, MGM's initial choice for the role ultimately played by Kirk Douglas was Clark Gable.

"The character I was playing was a real bad boy—a cross between James Dean and maybe Warren Beatty," says Hamilton:

I got the role because of Minnelli, but it wasn't really me and it wasn't something that I was terribly comfortable playing. But all they wanted me to do was come to Rome and shoot . . . though they were constantly getting behind. So, they just gave me a Ferrari and a lot of per diem, and I drove around Rome till three or four in the morning because we were doing night shooting and they never called me. They just had me on stand-by all night. So, I didn't get to see much of the shooting in Rome. I was just there and living the life of what was going on . . . the real *La Dolce Vita.*

It was an interesting period because it was Elizabeth Taylor and *Cleopatra* and that whole era. So, I was right in the middle of all of that. But as far as filmmaking goes, I think the picture that Kirk had done earlier with Minnelli [*The Bad and the Beautiful*] was much more on the money than this. [*Two Weeks*] was this kind of almost Fellini-esque movie. And it really wasn't grounded in reality. It wasn't even grounded in movie reality. It was almost like a comment on another era and another time, and that time happened to be *La Dolce Vita.* But it really didn't ring true—our movie. It seemed to me very phony as a film. It had all of that back projection going on. . . . When you have those techniques and the times were changing, all of a sudden, it looked very old-fashioned to me. . . .

So, there we were in Rome, but we were still very much Hollywood at the same time. I never felt as though we were shooting scenes about something real.[2]

Back projection aside, Minnelli's biggest challenge on *Two Weeks* appears to have been competing with himself. For the specter of *The Bad and the Beautiful* hovers over the picture. At one point, Minnelli goes full tilt self-reflexive: Kirk Douglas's Jack Andrus screens clips of Kirk Douglas in *The Bad and the Beautiful.* Later, in a dramatically charged sequence, Jack's reckless driving—with a hysterical Carlotta along for the ride—seems intent on recapturing the effect of Lana Turner's automotive meltdown. And even composer David Raksin can't refrain from appropriating portions of his haunting *Bad and the Beautiful* score for *Two Weeks.*

"They were doing this sort of, kind of like a sequel to *The Bad and the Beautiful.* Could they do it twice? That was sort of the idea," remembers actress Peggy Moffit:

Kirk Douglas in search of a little *La Dolce Vita* in Minnelli's *Two Weeks in Another Town*. The film would find favor with the *Cahiers du Cinéma* crowd and a young film critic named Peter Bogdanovich, who said that Minnelli's Roman bacchanal was "surely the ballsiest, most vibrant picture he has signed."
PHOTO COURTESY OF PHOTOFEST

There was a sequence in *Two Weeks* that was supposed to be a very stylish orgy in Rome. I was friends with John Houseman and he said, "I want you to meet Vincente Minnelli about this part. So I did and was cast. It was a glorified-dress extra kind of thing. . . . It turned out to be a totally soporific scene that does not come off at all. When I look at Vincente's other movies, I'm impressed with how wonderfully staged and thought out they were, but my impression was that he had totally run dry on this one—though everybody was absolutely mesmerized by him and revered him, from wardrobe and make-up to the grips and gaffers. It was like "his holiness." They would do whatever he asked. . . .

I remember Minnelli staring at the cocktail table where Leslie Uggams was sitting and he would twitch away and say nothing. We would be standing there for hours and then he would finally say something to a set decorator and it would be about something he didn't like—like the roses on the coffee table.

He wanted gladiolas. And so, somebody would go scurrying all over the MGM lot to try and find a bunch of fake gladiolas. . . . I walked away thinking, "He's fooled everybody . . . he's got no talent whatsoever."

Well, of course, that's absurd. He had great talent. I think he did great things, but *Two Weeks* was utterly deadly. And so, this idea of debauchery and wild car chases and passion and all of that certainly did not permeate the film—or the set, for that matter. Nobody lit anybody's fire on that one. Trust me.[3]

Whatever sparks may have existed in Minnelli's original cut of *Two Weeks in Another Town* were snuffed out by Joseph Vogel after he screened the film and ordered a drastic re-edit. Considerable cuts were made without consulting either Houseman or Minnelli. After Houseman fired off an angry letter to MGM's legal department, the producer was allowed to reshape the film— but he was only allowed to use Vogel-approved footage. Understandably, Minnelli was outraged that *Two Weeks* had been wrested away from him. In its final form, the story was missing so much meat that the result is not so much a complete movie but 107 minutes of rushes.

"The picture should have been better than it was," Cyd Charisse reflected years later. "When I finally saw it, I couldn't make heads or tails of the story— it was so disconnected— and I'd been in it."[4] The reckless, pre release editing pared away not only wholesale chunks of the narrative but revealing bits of character. In the studio-sanctioned version, Charisse's Carlotta comes off as a soulless, self-absorbed virago. In Minnelli's version, the character had more shading. "Last time I counted, I had over a thousand dresses," Carlotta admits in a deleted sequence. "More than four hundred suits. Including the first suit I ever owned—a hound's tooth gabardine I bought in Macy's basement for nineteen ninety-five. It's a trait of mine. I can't stand to give up anything I've ever owned." With the back story removed, Carlotta's clinging to her ex-husband seems inexplicable and odd—like so much of the film in its truncated form.

"*Two Weeks in Another Town* was a disappointment," Kirk Douglas admitted forty-five years after he made a valiant attempt to rescue the film from the butcher's block:

I wrote to Vogel, even though I was just an actor in it. . . . I argued with him, told him that if he wanted to make a family picture, he should have never made *Two Weeks in Another Town*. I went to [editor] Margaret [Booth], pleaded with her. She agreed with me that what they were doing was wrong, but she

worked for MGM and was frightened of losing her job. She burst into tears. . . .
They cut most of the exciting scenes. I felt this was an injustice to Vincente
Minnelli, who'd done a wonderful job with the film. And an injustice to the
paying public, who could have the experience of watching a very dramatic,
meaningful film. They released it that way . . . emasculated.[5]

Any positive assessments of the film tended to be drowned out by the
vocal majority: "The whole thing is a lot of glib trade patter, ridiculous and
unconvincing romantic snarls and a weird professional clash between actor
and director that is like something out of a Hollywood cartoon," Bosley
Crowther wrote in the *New York Times*.[6]

Two Weeks in Another Town did find some important champions, including
twenty-three-year-old future director Peter Bogdanovich, who reviewed it
for *Film Culture* and saluted it as

a picture of perversion and glittering decay that in a few precise and strikingly
effective strokes makes Fellini's *La Dolce Vita* look pedestrian, arty and hopelessly socially-conscious. . . . It could be said that all the characters are two-
dimensional, but it is such an obvious remark that only an idiot could imagine
that Minnelli didn't know exactly what he was doing: a grand melodrama,
filled with passion, lust, hate, and venom, surely the ballsiest, most vibrant
picture he has signed.[7]

32

Happy Problems

DENISE WAS IN. After only a few years of marriage to Minnelli, she was already being hailed as "Hollywood's Josephine"—as in the guilelessly charming French empress. The comparison suited Beverly Hills' busiest hostess just fine. "My favorite historical personage is Josephine," Denise told *Los Angeles Times* reporter John Hallowell. "She was an elegant swinger, darling. Napoleon, he was ze general; Josephine was the *influence*. And she was not stuffy."[1] Neither was Denise, who could certainly swing with the best of them. She dished with Truman Capote, dined with Vanessa Redgrave, and got the guest room ready for the president's daughter, Lynda Bird Johnson. Denise rubbed elbows with everyone—from Hollywood royalty, such as Jennifer Jones Selznick, to real royalty, such as the Duke and Duchess of Windsor.

The parties she threw were legendary, and the self-described "international nomad" proved to be as adept at assembling an all-star cast as her husband. "I am basically a frustrated David Merrick," Denise admitted. "I don't invite people. I *cast* people for my parties—the players, supporting players, chorus girls and boys, interesting character actors. Every party is like opening night." And there was no mistaking who the headliner was. As columnist Joyce Haber once noted, the supersonic jet-setter was a walking cinematic event, who was "personally dressed by Donald Brooks and Jimmy Galanos, bejeweled by David Webb, arranged by Valerian Rybar, profiled by Rex Reed, photographed by Cecil Beaton and carefully bedecked by everyone who is anyone."[2]

On the arm of an Oscar-winning husband, Denise was A-list all the way. And thanks to his wife, Minnelli was back on the map socially. All of the balls, black-tie events, and blowouts at the Bistro that he attended landed Vincente's name—or at least "The Minnellis," in the columns on an almost daily basis.

"That marriage was very important for both of them because it established her social position in Los Angeles and New York and the rest of the world, which is what she always wanted, and also, she had such an aggressive and powerful personality that she was able to really revive Vincente's career," says one who witnessed Denise's meteoric ascent.[3]

It was Denise who was the driving force behind Venice Productions, the independent production company that she and Vincente founded in 1962 ("Venice" was an amalgam of their names). Three Minnelli movies would be produced under the Venice banner (*The Courtship of Eddie's Father*, *Goodbye, Charlie*, and *The Sandpiper*). Although husband and wife were supposed to be equal partners in the venture, it soon became apparent that one of the participants seemed to have the upper hand where financial matters were concerned—and it was not the director of *Meet Me in St. Louis*.

"Denise demanded things from the studios and she pushed and pushed beyond anything that you can imagine," says designer Luis Estevez. "Although they had a great house right on Sunset Boulevard, Denise knew from the beginning that Vincente was never going to make enough money for her."[4] Even those in Denise's inner circle would blame her for the fact that Minnelli was passed over when Warner Brothers went shopping for a director for their film version of *My Fair Lady*. As the story goes, Denise pressured Vincente to ask for too much money and he ended up outpricing himself. Warners snapped up George Cukor for $300,000, and Minnelli lost his chance to direct what could have been one of the most important films of his career.

But the "hostess par none" wasn't about to miss any opportunities. In the '60s, Denise's socializing hit a peak. As one of her former intimates recalls:

That's when she started on her quest to meet all of the rich and powerful women of Hollywood—the ladies who lunch, shall we say. And Denise knew how to work them right around her finger. She had the fashionable clothes. She knew everybody. She threw these lavish parties and hosted these lunches. And all the while, she was fishing and scheming and turning herself into "Denise, Inc." She had a good vehicle with Minnelli, and, of course, being married to him, she was living in the midst of the most powerful people in Hollywood—where he was very highly regarded and should have been. Later on, when Denise decided it was time to move on, she saw her chance and took it.[5]

***

AFTER THE FULL-BLOWN CATASTROPHE that was *The Four Horsemen of the Apocalypse*, it seemed like some sort of demented kamikaze mission for MGM to reunite the apocalyptic trio of Minnelli, Glenn Ford, and screenwriter John Gay for *The Courtship of Eddie's Father*. Only this time, the forecast was far sunnier.

Whereas *The Four Horsemen* had been overpopulated and epically scaled, *Eddie's Father* was an intimate comedy. The characters were the kind of up-scale Manhattanites that captured Vincente's imagination in ways that *Horsemen*'s underground radicals and resistance fighters had failed to. Also, for the first time, Minnelli was teamed with Joe Pasternak, a producer known for whipping up innocuous crowd-pleasers (*Nancy Goes to Rio, Skirts Ahoy!*) that always came in on time and under budget. If an Arthur Freed film was vintage champagne, a Pasternak production was more like strawberry milk.

John Gay's screenplay was based on a bestselling autobiographical novel by Mark Toby (with an uncredited assist from Dorothy Wilson). It told the story of Tom Corbett, a widowed radio executive coming to terms with his wife's untimely death while caring for his son Eddie, who even at the age of six proves to be an incredibly resourceful matchmaker.

"I really followed that thing. I mean, it was a beauty," John Gay says of Toby's novel. "I didn't want to lose one line. Of course, I had to open up the story a little with New York and the talk show [subplot] and all of that but it was really a dream job, you know? And this time, it turned out to be a perfect part for Glenn Ford."[6] In Minnelli's eyes, Ford would deliver a performance both "touching" and "true" as the Upper West Side's most coveted bachelor father. The character of a single man balancing parenthood and professional obligations was one that Vincente could certainly relate to, having assumed that role in his own life.

There is a genuine tenderness and poignancy to the film's father-son exchanges in school hallways, breakfast nooks, and summer camps. The bond between Tom (Glenn Ford) and his precocious Eddie (Ron Howard) could have been patterned after Vincente's own relationship with Liza. Minnelli usually interacted with his eldest daughter as though she were a pint-sized cocktail-party companion. "While other kids were hearing about Heidi and her goats, I was learning about Colette and her gentlemen," Liza remembered.[7]

Like *Meet Me in St. Louis*, Minnelli's latest effort boasted a bravura performance by a child performer. Eight-year-old Ronny Howard, best known as "Opie" on *The Andy Griffith Show*, would shoot *Eddie's Father* while his hit series was on hiatus. "I was fascinated by Vincente Minnelli," Howard

The Courtship of Eddie's Father featured two future television icons, Shirley Jones and Ron Howard. "I was fascinated by Vincente Minnelli," recalled Howard, who went on to helm his own films. "My first exposure to a crane was Vincente Minnelli up there. The way he could handle that thing—it was just incredible."
PHOTO COURTESY OF PHOTOFEST

would later recall. "I remember that he was photographing *The Courtship of Eddie's Father* a lot differently than the way the Andy Griffith shows were done. . . . My first exposure to a crane was Vincente Minnelli up there. The way he could handle that thing—it was just incredible."[8] While Howard may have been fascinated by his director, the rest of the cast was fascinated by him.

"Ron Howard was never a child," says Stella Stevens, who played Dollye Daly, the wide-eyed masher magnet "picked up" by both father and son. "I think Ron Howard probably came out of the womb acting . . . *Ta da! Here I am! I'm going to sing and dance and work.* He was like an old man trapped in a boy's body. He was great as a child and wonderful to work with. When I see him in that movie, he makes me cry every time, especially when his goldfish dies."[9]

For a light family comedy, there are some unsettling emotions lurking in the shadows of the story. Minnelli's knack for transforming such everyday occurrences as moving out of the neighborhood or the death of a pet into arias of childhood anguish is indelibly displayed in one sequence. Distraught over his mother's death, Eddie loses it when he discovers one of his goldfish has also succumbed. While child actors in other films might shed glycerin tears or set their lower lips to quivering to indicate despair, Vincente encouraged his young performers to completely freak out. As essayist Carlos Losilla has observed, "[Minnelli] understands that one should film not only the body but the psychology of the infantile mind racked by pain."[10]

Eddie's fear of death (his mother has died only days before the story begins) is mirrored in all of the lonely grown-ups he encounters. Every adult in Eddie's universe is attempting to step out of a self-protective shell and forge a meaningful connection with another person. In their search for a surrogate wife/mother, Tom and Eddie meet the Three Faces of Woman (according to the very narrow definition of 1962): saintly nurse (Shirley Jones), sweet sexpot (Stella Stevens), and steely fashionista (Dina Merrill). "We were very lucky. They all turned out to be very good casting," John Gay says of the leading ladies who starred as *Courtship*'s blonde, brunette, and redhead. This talented trio of actresses not only had to contend with a natural scene-stealer in the form of their young costar but also a director who sometimes confused his actors with what Stevens described as "decor de Minnelli."[11]

"He was not necessarily an actor's director," says Shirley Jones, who was cast in *Courtship* fresh from her Oscar-winning turn in *Elmer Gantry*. "He sort of moved you around like a piece of scenery. I found it more difficult to work with Vincente than I had with several other directors that I had worked with earlier. But the result of what he did was always extraordinary. . . . I felt that I needed more direction from him, but that's not the way he worked."[12]

Dina Merrill, cast as Eddie's "skinny-eyed" adversary, Rita Behrens, also recalled that actors weren't exactly a top priority for the scenically obsessed Minnelli. "He was more concerned, it seemed to me, with painting a picture than he was with the performances. You had to kind of go on your own for the performances."[13]

Of the three, only Stella Stevens (singled out for praise in Minnelli's memoir) was completely sold: "I've often said that Vincente was my favorite director. . . . You know, most directors don't pay much attention to the women [in a film] but this man took a long time to talk to me about the part, so that we both understood what I was doing. . . . I would argue with a signpost. I would never argue with Vincente. He knew his stuff. He was a true genius."[14]

Released in March 1963, Minnelli's comedy garnered generally favorable reviews, though *Cue* noted: "The story is too, too familiar; Vincente Minnelli directed it in Panavision and high-glossy Metrocolor, and Joe Pasternak produced. Joe is always happiest when he is making happy pictures about happy people with happy problems. Everybody's happy, except sometimes the audience."

33

Identity Theft

AFTER VINCENTE LOST OUT on his opportunity to direct the highly anticipated screen version of *My Fair Lady*, many of his admirers found themselves
playing the "What if? . . ." game. What if . . . he had directed Audrey Hepburn's Eliza? Or what if Minnelli had helmed *Gypsy* instead of Mervyn
LeRoy? What if his plans for a biopic of bisexual blues singer Bessie Smith
had actually come off? In the latter half of Minnelli's career, there seemed
to be missed opportunities aplenty—such as Irving Berlin's *Say It with Music*.
MGM touted this "super spectacular" as though it were the greatest thing
to happen to movies since the advent of sound.

"When you decide to go ahead on a big picture, go with the pros—and
the .400 hitters," said MGM's vice president, Robert Weitman, at a studio
press conference in April 1963.[1] The heavy hitters Weitman had assembled
included Arthur Freed, Vincente Minnelli, and Irving Berlin. They were join-
ing forces to mount an ambitious, multimillion-dollar musical tentatively entitled *Say It with Music*. The score would include a cavalcade of Berlin
standards and seven new songs by the celebrated composer of "God Bless
America" and "White Christmas." Arthur Laurents was tapped to write the
screenplay. Jerome Robbins was lined up to choreograph a ragtime ballet.
Robert Goulet would star as a globe-trotting lothario who romances beautiful women around the world, including Sophia Loren, Julie Andrews, and
Ann-Margret.

With such a staggering array of talent involved, *Say It with Music* was shaping up as a surefire, can't miss, good old-fashioned Arthur Freed extravaganza.

Too bad it never got made. "Every time they were ready to shoot, the whole management of the studio changed," says Barbara Freed Saltzman. "They would say, 'Well, this is too expensive . . .' or 'We want to do something differently with this. . . .' The people who made the decisions changed. They became much more business oriented and less artistic."[2]

By 1968, Minnelli was out and Blake Edwards was in as director. After countless false starts and a ballooning budget, it looked as though *Say It with Music* was finally hitting the big screen. Edwards's wife, Julie Andrews, was set to star in a 70-millimeter reserved-seat attraction. That is, until MGM was dismantled by its new studio chief, James Aubrey, who seemed far more interested in making real-estate deals than in making movies. Freed's dream project died, and in essence, so did the studio where Vincente had spent more than two decades of his working life.

As the type of grand-scale musicals that Minnelli specialized in began to fall out of favor in the '60s, the director was forced to turn his attention elsewhere and accept whatever projects were being offered to him. Sadly, several of Vincente's later assignments didn't seem well suited to his talents. *Goodbye, Charlie*, for example: George Axelrod's comedy concerned Charlie Sorel, a chauvinistic screenwriter who is bumped off and then reincarnated as the kind of luscious little tomato he used to lust after (or, as the transformed Charlie puts it: "It's as though I've been a gourmet all my life and now, suddenly, I'm a lamb chop").

In 1959—the same year that Axelrod's sex farce hit the Great White Way—moviegoers had lined up for Billy Wilder's *Some Like It Hot*. Marilyn Monroe plus a gender-bending comedy added up to a mega-blockbuster. Hoping to duplicate the phenomenal success that United Artists had with the picture, 20th Century Fox snatched up the rights to *Goodbye, Charlie* with an eye toward developing the property for Monroe, the studio's top star. Fox executives believed that Marilyn in the title role would result in an avalanche of box-office receipts. However, the actress didn't see it that way at all: "The studio people want me to do *Goodbye, Charlie* for the movies, but I'm not going to do it. I don't like the idea of playing a man in a woman's body, you know? It just doesn't seem feminine."[3]

In 1961, Vincente Minnelli's name had appeared on the short list of directors that Monroe had agreed to work with (George Cukor, Alfred Hitchcock, and John Huston were among the others). And it's possible that Fox may have secured Minnelli's services in an attempt to entice Monroe to appear in *Goodbye, Charlie*. But to no avail. The star could not be persuaded,[*] and

---

[*] An addendum to a 20th Century Fox Legal Department document dated May 25, 1961, notes that "20th will not require Miss Monroe to render services in a picture based on *Goodbye, Charlie*."

in August 1962, she died of an overdose at the age of thirty-six. Nevertheless, Minnelli remained at the helm of the picture, and for the first time since his aborted stint at Paramount in the '30s, he found himself working at a studio other than MGM.

If Monroe had been ideal casting, her studio-sanctioned substitute, Debbie Reynolds, was not, though at the time the vivacious Reynolds was considered a theater-owner's dream. Constantly in the headlines as the wronged wife in the Elizabeth Taylor–Eddie Fisher adultery scandal, and fresh from an Oscar-nominated tour de force in Metro's high-spirited musical *The Unsinkable Molly Brown*, Reynolds was, in *Variety* parlance, "boffo box office." While Reynolds virtually guaranteed brisk business at the ticket window, her cutie-pie chutzpah seemed wanting compared to Monroe's triple-threat combination of vulnerability, sex appeal, and offbeat comedic timing.

MGM's legendary acting coach Lillian Burns Sidney had advised Reynolds not to take the role of the gender-confused title character, as she was convinced that *Goodbye, Charlie* was essentially a one-joke story. But Reynolds wanted to work with Minnelli, so she signed on. "When one combines her self-possession with a tendency toward cuteness, you don't get the exact quality I was looking for," Minnelli would say of Reynolds.[4] However, Vincente was about to be reminded that Reynolds, who had survived Gene Kelly's rigorous direction during *Singin' in the Rain*, could be one of the hardest-working troopers in the business. Even if pert, wholesome Debbie was essentially miscast, she was determined to give *Goodbye, Charlie* her all.

Casting concerns aside, Minnelli also hoped to avoid some of the pitfalls of the original theatrical production. For her performance in the Broadway version of *Goodbye, Charlie*, star Lauren Bacall had been taken to task by critic Brooks Atkinson for playing the part of the reincarnated Charlie like "a cross between a female impersonator and Tallulah Bankhead." Minnelli decreed: "The approach, as I saw it, should have been more feminine." As a result, the transformed Charlie would emerge as a glittering glamour girl. Reynolds would be dolled up by Minnelli's fellow MGM expatriates—costumer Helen Rose and hair stylist Sydney Guilaroff (who appears in the film's memorable beauty-parlor sequence). In addition to overseeing the glamorization of Charlie Sorel, Vincente would work diligently with Debbie, dictating bits of physical business and insisting on specific line-readings.[5]

Although Minnelli missed his opportunity to work with Monroe, he did snare her *Some Like It Hot* costar Tony Curtis, who would play Charlie's devoted but disoriented friend George Tracy. "He was one of the better directors that I worked with," says Tony Curtis:

His and Hers: George Tracy (Tony Curtis) counsels the gender-confused Charlie Sorel (Debbie Reynolds) in *Goodbye, Charlie.* "I think the most important thing about [Minnelli's] movies is this notion of 'identity,' and a person's sexuality is, after all, the core of their identity," says Minnelli disciple John Epperson.
PHOTO COURTESY OF PHOTOFEST

He was so sensitive to whatever environment he was in. His sets. The props he used. The actors he used. The lighting. All of these things blending together to give him a mood. I admired him a lot. He was a brilliant man but that brilliance was vitiated, perhaps, by a lot of his personal dilemmas . . . his marriages, the kind of pictures he really wanted to do, the pressures he was under. I don't think he was a particularly happy man as all of these elements had a way of beating him up. He could still do the work, though. Nothing ever got in the way of that.[6]

Rising star Ellen McRae (better known as the Oscar-winning Ellen Burstyn) would remember her director, whom she tagged as "a strange bird," with far less affection: "At this point in his career, he was a bit past his prime, married to a woman named Lee Anderson,* but his manner seemed campy,

---

* Minnelli would marry fourth wife Lee Anderson on April 2, 1980. He was still married to Denise Giganti during the filming of *Goodbye, Charlie.*

if downright androgynous. . . . Minnelli seemed polite to everyone on the set but me. He railed at me, humiliating me at every opportunity." When Burstyn began saying her lines, Minnelli started reciting them along with her. When she stopped, he exploded. "Say the line!" Minnelli bellowed at the frazzled Burstyn. While Farley Granger and other actors had found ways to adjust to this directorial quirk, Burstyn found it extremely challenging. "I just couldn't imagine he wanted me to say the line with him at the same time. But that's what he wanted. Over and over until I had his rhythm and there was nothing left of mine. I was doing his performance of the character."[7]

In only one genuinely hilarious sequence does *Goodbye, Charlie* hint at what might have emerged after half a dozen rewrites. Reynolds's Charlie and her well-heeled, mother-dominated suitor Bruce Minton (a surprisingly not bad Pat Boone) are parked seaside and the trust-funder reveals to Charlie that his Maserati is "one sick little car." The double entendres come fast and furious. "Put an overdrive unit between her differential housings," Charlie suggests. "Have you stripped her? She'll thank you for it." Framed like some wind-swept, romantic interlude from *A Summer Place* and beautifully underplayed by Reynolds and Boone, the scene leaves the viewer wondering why the rest of the movie couldn't be this deliciously sly and restrained. For in the film's early scenes, Debbie Reynolds isn't so much a man reincarnated in a woman's body as an actress possessed by her previous role. With all of the mugging and caterwauling going on, Reynolds seems unable to shake her celebrated *Molly Brown* portrayal. More than once, the star seems ready to burst into a chorus or two of "Belly Up to the Bar, Boys."

A couple of decades after Minnelli's foray into transgendered territory, *Tootsie*, *Victor/Victoria*, and *Yentl* would mine the gender-bending premise for all it was worth, but *Goodbye, Charlie* isn't really about gender politics, it's about schtick, as in the anatomically revised Charlie's self-appraisal: "I don't have to see Brigitte Bardot movies anymore, all I have to do is come home and pull down the shades."

Of course, sexual ambiguity was anything but an alien concept to Vincente, who had been described by his colleagues as everything from "epicene" to "androgynous." Although *Goodbye, Charlie* is an especially broad comedy, it's not too much of a stretch to imagine that Minnelli empathized with his gender-jumbled protagonist. And perhaps there was a moment of genuine recognition for the director when he helmed those scenes in which Charlie realizes that there's still a man buried beneath her couture and cosmetics.

How did Minnelli feel as he set up the sequence in which George tenderly caresses a distraught Charlie until he remembers that his friend may physically be a *she* but in every other way is still very much a *he*. Did the content of that scene—in which George experiences a moment of homosexual panic ("We were practically necking!")—strike a personal chord with the man directing it? "You know, I felt that when I was doing it," recalls Tony Curtis. "It seemed that there was some dilemma between Vincente and the part and then a dilemma between myself and him, which made it possible for both of us to be in tune with each other. . . . It was interesting and it worked."[8]

For many Minnelliphiles, *Goodbye, Charlie* offers an intriguing variation on the director's favorite theme. "I think the most important thing about his movies is this notion of 'identity,' and a person's sexuality is, after all, the core of their identity," says Minnelli disciple John Epperson:

> It's a theme that pops up all the way through the movies, not just *Tea and Sympathy* or the Jack Cole character in *Designing Woman*. . . . *The Pirate* is about people pretending to be what they're not. *On a Clear Day* is about a woman who has many different personalities and facets. It's also what *Bells Are Ringing* is about—she pretends to be all these different people on the telephone. Then we get to Debbie Reynolds in *Goodbye, Charlie*—a man inside of a woman's body and the confusion of the gender identity there. . . .
>
> I don't know if Minnelli consciously knew that he was doing movies about "identity." . . . I mean, when someone like Alfred Hitchcock pitched an idea to the studio bosses, he didn't say, "I'm going to make a movie about the two facets of my personality. . . ." Instead he'd say, "I want to make a movie about a frigid kleptomaniac who is forced to marry a man because he finds her out. . . . It's a sex mystery." So, Minnelli probably never said out loud to anyone, "I make movies about identity," because he might lose his job if he ever said anything that cerebral.[9]

Although *Goodbye, Charlie* wasn't anywhere near Minnelli's best work, *Films and Filming* still liked what they saw: "A director's quality can best be gauged when his material is taxing. . . . Therefore, in any thoroughgoing assessment of Minnelli from here on in it will be impossible to overlook *Goodbye, Charlie*, a victory of décor over dialogue, of pace over pawkiness, and of directorial control over a script that is wild as all get out."

Others were far less forgiving. As Judith Crist noted for the *New York Herald Tribune*, "*Goodbye, Charlie* hasn't lost a bit of its bad taste in transition to the screen. In fact, all the smarmy creepiness and sleazy smuttiness inherent in a comedy about a lecherous man being reincarnated as a sexy female, with his masculine mind making the transmigration intact, has been expanded about as far as it could be—and then a half hour beyond that, as is the wont of today's fun-loving filmmakers."

Upon its release in November 1964, the title *Goodbye, Charlie* proved prophetic, as the comedy quickly disappeared from movie screens. Minnelli's latest was certainly not the *Some Like It Hot*–sized smash that Fox executives had hoped for. Tony Curtis believes that the movie had something to say before audiences were ready to hear it: "It was way ahead of it's time. I really felt that. But if I may be so bold, I've always felt that about the movies I've made. I've always hoped that they would be just a little sharper than the average movie."[10]

34

The Shadow
of Your Smile

"ONE OF THE MOST TEDIOUS, inane and ludicrous films ever made" is how writer Eleanor Perry would sum up *The Sandpiper*. The movie, which Perry christened a "$5.3 million sleeping pill," was supposed to be about a Big Sur bohemian—the conspicuously unwed mother of an illegitimate son—who falls in love with a married minister.[1] Of course, what the movie was really about was Liz and Dick. Like *Cleopatra* and *The VIPs* before it, the entire film seems like an excuse to cinematically eavesdrop on Elizabeth Taylor and Richard Burton and cash in on their monstrous celebrity. How else to explain all those ravenous, can't-get-enough close-ups of the couple? To say nothing of the cinematic ogling of that other, equally famous couple— the heaving, omnipresent Taylor bosom, which throughout the '60s seemed to enjoy a high-profile career all its own.

For sudsy trash, *The Sandpiper* boasted a classy pedigree. Blacklisted writers Dalton Trumbo and Michael Wilson (who had scripted Taylor's magnificent *A Place in the Sun*) were engaged to write the screenplay based on producer Martin Ransohoff's "original" scenario. William Wyler was initially approached to direct, but he wisely turned the offer down and made the Oscar-nominated *The Collector* instead. This left the field open for the Burtons' second choice: Minnelli, who had misgivings but proceeded anyway, knowing that a Taylor-Burton enterprise not only would generate a tidal wave of publicity but virtually guaranteed impressive box-office returns.

It's to Taylor's credit that she attempted to enliven *The Sandpiper* with a bit of nontraditional casting. For the role of her lover-sculptor Cos Erikson,

Taylor suggested Sammy Davis Jr. Although an interracial romance might have perked the picture up considerably, Minnelli and Ransohoff agreed (for perhaps the first and only time) that it would simply be too much. "There was no time to work on the script because all our preliminary time was taken up with whether or not Sammy Davis should play the part of the sculptor," Minnelli recalled in the notes for his autobiography. "I objected to him. It was just a spectacular effect—a bid for trying to fit a black man into a niche not right for him. It put a different onus on the story. He dropped out and Charles Bronson played the part."[2]

The Burtons insisted that the film had to be shot in France so they could receive a tax break. So although production launched in September 1964 with some stunning location work at Big Sur, much of *The Sandpiper* would be filmed at Billancourt Studios in Paris. The highly entertaining Liz and Dick show (which at times seemed like a variation on their roles in *Who's Afraid of Virginia Woolf?*) was performed daily for the supporting cast, crew, and visiting members of the press. There were lover's quarrels, an ever-present entourage, and drinks for everyone. "Wine flowed as if Jesus had turned all the water in Paris into vin du pays," visiting reporter Liz Smith noted.[3] In fact, there was so much imbibing behind the scenes that *The Sandpiper* often looked more like a Metrocolor remake of *The Days of Wine and Roses*.

"Elizabeth and Richard liked to sip champagne all day, which is a nice way of putting it," recalled MGM publicist Robert Crutchfield:

> By lunchtime, they were in pretty good shape. Some of these press people who had lunch with them tried to keep up with Richard . . . and you just don't keep up with Richard. I helped many reporters back to their hotels and took their faces out of the gravy and mashed potatoes. It was an incredible experience because working with [Taylor and Burton], you don't really stay on schedule. I bought my first house with the extra money—the "golden time"—I made on that film.[4]

When not functioning as the production's designated driver, Crutchfield also had an opportunity to observe the lack of chemistry between Minnelli and producer Martin Ransohoff, an unlikely duo whom he describes as "the real odd couple":

> Marty was a great, big Broderick Crawford–type slob that wore sweatshirts with real sweat rings under the arms and he had a piece of hair that he strategically

wrapped around his head so that no one would know he was bald, and of course, he would get nervous and he'd start twirling that hair in his finger, and he'd stand up on the cliff and watch Vincente down there with his long cigarette holder and beret mincing about the beach. Minnelli was brilliant, but he certainly didn't make any attempt to hide the way he behaved. . . .

I remember Vincente was shooting this one scene on the beach and we started losing the light, but he wanted to do it again. And again. Then the water started to fill up the hole that we had dug for the camera to go down in because the tide was coming in. And Marty's up on the hill screaming and hollering that we've got to get this shot and *What the goddamned hell is he doing?* They really were not at all compatible.[5]

With everyone's eyes trained on the bottom line, it's no wonder that what emerged on-screen was, as critic John Simon put it, "straight Louisa May Alcott interlarded with discreet pornographic allusions." Everywhere you turn, *The Sandpiper* is simply bad—though in many ways, deliciously so. "For me, just seeing Elizabeth Taylor holding a brush and palette makes the screen start vibrating," says film historian Richard Barrios. "I kind of liken Liz as a painter to when you see Joan Crawford in her nurse's uniform in *Possessed*. When you see someone who can only be a movie star trying to play some kind of working person, it's ridiculous. . . . With *The Sandpiper*, you can really sense a talented director trying to do his best with what he's been given to work with."[6]

An example of Metro gloss that has hardened into shellac, the movie offers plenty of camp compensations. MGM's idea of a free-spirited beatnik is an ultra glamorous Elizabeth Taylor, stunningly coiffed by Sydney Guilaroff, wrapped in a Sharaff poncho and dwelling in a palatial beach house direct from the pages of *Architectural Digest*. The entire movie follows suit. It's a big, square commercial venture masquerading as 1965's version of hip and cutting edge, complete with clean-cut, mild-mannered hippies sent over from central casting. There isn't much that Minnelli could do with such an overblown "sex-on-the-sand soap opera," except make sure it looked good—and this he did. Cinematographer Milton Krasner (an indispensable member of the expert team that now followed Minnelli from one picture to the next) captured some breathtaking images of the film's two natural beauties: the violet-eyed Taylor and Big Sur.

If only the story was as arresting as the scenery. Taylor's character, atheistic naturalist Laura Reynolds, may be the latest in a long line of Minnelli nonconformists, but she is unquestionably the blandest. It also doesn't help that

"The Shadow of Your Smile":
Laura Reynolds (Elizabeth
Taylor) and Dr. Edward Hewitt
(Richard Burton) go bohemian
in *The Sandpiper*.
PHOTO COURTESY
OF PHOTOFEST

all of the characters speak in beatific platitudes ("Thinking is almost always a kind of prayer . . .") instead of more naturalistic dialogue. It's nobody's best work, but Eva Marie Saint manages one good scene when she tells Burton off. And Robert Webber is a lot of fun as Ward, the creepy swinger who punctuates nearly every sentence with "baby."

Johnny Mandel and Paul Francis Webster's haunting theme song, "The Shadow of Your Smile," may be the only guilt-free pleasure associated with the movie. Recorded by everyone from Barbra Streisand to Pinky Winters, that lovely chart topper would win *The Sandpiper* its sole Oscar.

35

"At Best, Confused"

IN 1932, DEPRESSION ERA AUDIENCES had flocked to see Greta Garbo as the exotic temptress Mata Hari. And forever after, the public would identify "The Swedish Sphinx" with the slinky secret agent. But to Vincente Minnelli, Mata Hari had always been a more complex figure—a question mark. Did the cooch-dancing vamp who called herself Mata Hari betray her legions of French lovers by passing their secrets on to the Germans? When the alluring femme fatale was executed by a firing squad, was she gunned down more for her loose morals than for her spying?

Vincente believed all of the ambiguity surrounding Mata Hari would make for compelling drama. "I wanted the audience to leave the theatre having great doubts about her," Minnelli would say of the central character in the stage production of *Mata Hari* that he ended up directing in 1967. He certainly got his wish. The privileged few who saw her would leave the theater having great doubts not only about the subject but about nearly everything else connected with the show decades after it was staged. *Mata Hari* still ranks as one of the most notorious debacles in theatrical history—Vincente Minnelli's very own *Springtime for Hitler*.

In the beginning, a musicalized *Mata Hari* seemed like a sure thing. A trio of talented collaborators—Jerome Coopersmith (book), Edward Thomas (music), and Martin Charnin (lyrics)—had created an antiwar musical originally entitled *Ballad of a Firing Squad*. It retold the Mata Hari saga from the point of view of one of her lovers, Captain Henry LaFarge of French Military Intelligence. The musical juxtaposed Mata Hari's exploits with

275

scenes in which a character known only as "The Young Soldier" marches off to the front lines. In a haunting song entitled "Maman," the young but no longer innocent soldier sings the contents of a letter he has sent home to his mother: *"He was young, maman. He was small. I was trapped, maman, by a wall. Then he lunged, Maman, and I spun, face to face, Maman, gun to gun. Then and there, Maman, I could see . . . He was me, Maman. He was me. Just a boy, Maman, not a man . . . Can I kill, Maman? Yes I can."*

Although ostensibly about World War I, the show seemed to offer up-to-the-minute commentary on the current political situation—the American occupation of Vietnam. "We were in a time of producing shows that had virtually no contemporary political or social significance," recalls Martin Charnin. "The shows that were going on then were *The Happy Times* and *How Now, Dow Jones?* Stuff like that. We wanted to do something of real substance. . . . We thought that the Vietnamese experience and how ugly and terrifying the war was could be paralleled by virtue of the Mata Hari story."[1] Charnin was slated to direct. All he and his partners needed was a producer willing to roll the dice.

In 1967, showman David Merrick was recovering from several recent failures, most notably a misguided musical version of *Breakfast at Tiffany's* that featured Mary Tyler Moore as a singing, swearing Holly Golightly. This recent catastrophe aside, Merrick's Broadway record spoke for itself: *Gypsy, Hello, Dolly!* and *Carnival.* If anybody could make a musical out of the legend of Mata Hari, it was Merrick. When Martin Charnin pitched the musical to Merrick, he was pleasantly surprised that the unpredictable producer seemed receptive to the concept—even the antiwar theme. What's more, Merrick wanted to move ahead immediately—though with a director more experienced than Charnin (whose mega-smash *Annie* was still a decade away). Merrick believed that it was important to have a big name attached to such an ambitious, epically scaled production.

At that moment, Minnelli was once again a hot commodity in Hollywood, thanks to the announcement that he'd soon be directing Barbra Streisand in a lavishly budgeted screen version of the Broadway musical *On a Clear Day You Can See Forever.* But in terms of Broadway, Minnelli was about as sought after as an Actor's Equity strike. In fact, the sixty-five-year-old Minnelli hadn't directed a theatrical production since *Very Warm for May,* way back in 1938—when Zsa Zsa Gabor was still on her first husband. Despite Vincente's former glories on the Great White Way, selecting him as the director of a piece that addressed the futility of war seemed ill-advised at best. "It was totally Merrick's idea to have Minnelli as the director," Charnin says.

"We were not given a choice. It was sprung on us. It was all about having a name director. Even though the name was a little musty. Even so, there was this gigantic cachet just in terms of Minnelli's name value."[2] Merrick would surround Minnelli with a team of top theater professionals, including designer Jo Mielziner and two transplants from Hollywood whom Vincente knew and respected—choreographer Jack Cole and designer Irene Sharaff.

For the role of Captain LaFarge, an actor with a powerful stage presence and voice to match was required. Yves Montand was offered the role but declined. Pernell Roberts, best known as Adam Cartwright on television's highly rated *Bonanza*, agreed to star.

In terms of the crucial casting of the leading lady, it was not Vincente but Minnelli's wife Denise Giganti who played talent scout. A stunning Viennese-born model regularly appearing in the pages of *Vogue* and *Harper's Bazaar* had caught her eye. "It was Denise, who made the first contact with Marisa Mell," Vincente recalled. "After they met in Rome and lunched together, Denise cabled back, 'She's your girl.'" *Washington Post Times Herald* reporter Eugenia Sheppard, however, noted that "since they spoke in Italian all through the luncheon, Mrs. Minnelli forgot to ask Marisa if she spoke English. She didn't find out, either, whether she could sing."[3]

Although Mell's English was acceptable, many connected with the show recalled that her "singing" was not. In fact, prior to *Mata Hari*, Mell's only musical experience had been a stint in an obscure European touring company of *Kiss Me Kate*. "Marisa Mell was only hired to be the lead because she was having an affair with Denise Minnelli," says Hugh Fordin, who was David Merrick's head of casting at the time.[4] Whether or not the rumors were true, a Broadway musical featuring a lead performer who could neither sing nor dance proved to be the tip of the iceberg.

As Fordin recalls:

I was casting *Mata Hari* for Minnelli and he had the nerve to have Elaine Stritch come in to audition for what turned out to be the Tessie O'Shea role in the second act—a flower girl. Ridiculous. . . . Minnelli turned to me during one of the audition days and said, "Remind me before we start to go into rehearsal, I want to run my movie of *The Band Wagon* for the whole company." And instantly I knew what he was saying was that this was going to turn into that disaster in *The Band Wagon*—the musical version of *Faust*.

Even at the beginning, when I sat in the office to read that script and meet the three guys who created the show, Martin Charnin was not talking to Ed Thomas, the composer, nor was he talking to Jerome Coopersmith, the book

Minnelli rehearses Pernell Roberts and Marisa Mell for the ill-fated *Mata Hari* in 1967.
"Jesus, what a nightmare it was . . ." dancer Antony DeVecchi says of the musical, which
still ranks as one of the greatest debacles in theatrical history.
PHOTO COURTESY OF PHOTOFEST

writer. This was even before Minnelli came in. And I went into Merrick and
told him it was going to be a disaster and he said, "I don't care. It's not my
money anyway. It's RCA/Victor's money."[5]

The record label had ponied up most of the money for *Mata Hari* and planned
to recoup part of the investment with the release of the original Broadway
cast album. As fate would have it, neither the album nor *Mata Hari* on Broadway would ever materialize.

There were signs of the disaster to come early on. Although the cast was
excited to appear in a production helmed by the legendary Vincente Minnelli,
they were dismayed to discover that their director still seemed to think that
he was back on a Culver City soundstage. As dancer Antony DeVecchi
remembered:

We'd all be ready to rehearse and Vincente would be sitting out in the audience,
and he'd yell, "Camera! . . . *Action!*" And we'd say to each other, "What the
fuck is going on?" We were used to direction like "Move downstage left," you
know? We were theater people. But it wasn't his direction that killed the show.
It was the script. It was just a lousy, uninteresting story. It didn't only kill Vin-

cente. It killed all of us. Mata Hari was this nondescript character. Basically, she was a hooker screwing everything she could get. She didn't have a brain. If Mata Hari had just been a supporting character who came in and left and you focused on the Deuxième Bureau, the FBI of France, we would still be running on Broadway.[6]

Others close to the production believed that Minnelli was the show's primary problem. "I think he was lost," says Martin Charnin:

> To me, Vincente was very much living in a fantasy about what he thought the show was about. I mean, we had written a very dark musical, but Vincente was far more interested in whether or not there were enough crinolines in the dresses on stage. I mean, he had more meetings with Irene Sharaff than he had with the writers. Practically from minute one, the *Mata Hari* that we had created began to sink into this frou-frou world, and it never recovered. It was swallowed up by silk and feathers.[7]

Vincente seemed to be approaching the material as though it were a Radio City Music Hall revue circa 1934. "Minnelli made it sexless," writer William Goldman observed. "He had taken a deadly serious anti-war effort and directed it as if it were a Nelson Eddy–Jeanette MacDonald movie."[8] When actress Martha Schlamme asked Minnelli about her motivation in a key scene, the director reminded her that it was of the utmost importance that her Galeries Lafayette shopping bag should be displayed in such a way that the label would be clearly visible to the audience.

Although advance publicity had promised that the show's leading lady would emerge a shining star, *Mata Hari* would prove to be anything but Marisa Mell's *Funny Girl*. Antony DeVecchi befriended the overwhelmed actress and believes that she, like everyone else, was weighted down by the overproduction:

> Marisa knew what she could do and she knew what she couldn't do and she told that to Vincente. She couldn't sing. She couldn't dance. So, in came Jack Cole. In came Irene Sharaff. And she was surrounded by probably the top ten male dancers in the country. She moved very well but she was not trained as a dancer. On top of all that, Irene would put her in a costume and it was made of gold-plated chains. The costume weighed seventy-five pounds. It took almost three of us to lift her. I mean, you could put Pavlova in that thing and she's not going to move.[9]

Before its Broadway opening, which was scheduled for January 13, 1968, *Mata Hari* would be previewed at the National Theatre in Washington, D.C., and presented as a benefit for the Women's National Democratic Club. The audience of VIPs would include Lynda Bird Johnson, the president's daughter. After observing some of the rehearsals, *Washington Post* drama editor Richard L. Coe was hedging his bets about *Mata Hari*: "It could come out as the latest triumph of the American musical stage and it could resound with a shattering thud." On November 17, 1967 (a date that will live in theatrical infamy), *Mata Hari* proved to be the thud heard round the world. *Variety* declared the preview (which dragged on past midnight) a "shambles" and noted that "the advance show was a mishap almost too exaggerated to believe. . . . The audience roared with laughter in all the wrong places as far as the script was concerned. The night was so bad, there was no curtain call. . . . The direction by Vincente Minnelli is, at best, confused." Martin Charnin managed to sit through it: "All I could think of was, 'How quickly can I get the Amtrak out of Washington? Or was it legitimate to stand up on the stage at the end of the show and say to an aggregate audience, 'I apologize. This is not at all what we meant.' . . . It was purely and simply the agony of seeing something that we had created being totally destroyed with no conscious recognition of what was being done."[10] As writer Ethan Mordden recalls, "It really was a bad staging of a very good show."

In his "Window on Washington" column, Bill Henry had a field day surveying the ruins:

> The Thanksgiving holiday was made a bit merrier for people in Washington—at least for those who enjoy disasters. . . . The audience was in a gay mood when the curtain rose and was positively giddy by the time it went down when scenery fell apart, costumes came undone, dancers tripped and the whole thing began to look like something planned by Mack Sennett. Although producer David Merrick, before the curtain went up, warned the audience that "this is just a rehearsal," he hardly expected such things to happen as leading man Pernell Roberts being left stranded in his half of a cottage while the other half disappeared suddenly into the loft. And leading lady Marisa Mell, having "died" before a firing squad, raised her hand to her head just after the doctor pronounced her lifeless. Neither producer Merrick nor director Vincente Minnelli nor either of the stars showed up at the big after-the-premiere party.[11]

According to Antony DeVecchi, by that point Minnelli was long gone. "He never finished that show. He quit. He left it all in the hands of Jack

Cole. . . . Vincente's hands were tied with the stupidity of what was going on with that show. Jesus, what a nightmare it was." As Charnin recalls, at one point a desperate Merrick hit upon an idea to rescue the production: "After Washington, Merrick said, 'I got it! I know how to save it!' We all leapt to attention and he said, 'We'll do it as a spoof with Bert Lahr and Nancy Walker.'"[12] Ultimately, wiser heads prevailed. Taking a loss of approximately $700,000, Merrick canceled *Mata Hari*'s Philadelphia engagement and Broadway opening.

In 1968, the Theatre de Lys presented a pared-down version of the musical entitled *Ballad of a Firing Squad*, which Charnin directed himself. Despite encouraging reviews, the production closed after a discouraging seven performances. Although the musical's original creators made a valiant attempt to show audiences what they had intended, it seemed that nothing could obliterate the outrageous spectacle that had come before.

As set designer Jo Mielziner memorably said, *Mata Hari* was "one third Minnelli, one third Mielziner, and one third shit."

36

On a Clear Day

IF VINCENTE'S RETURN TO THE STAGE had been noteworthy for all the wrong reasons, Hollywood wanted him back—and in a big way. In June 1967, Minnelli signed on the dotted line. He was now under contract to Paramount Pictures to direct a screen version of the musical *On a Clear Day You Can See Forever*, which had been a modest success on Broadway in 1965. A year and a half would pass before principal photography began in January 1969. By that time, the Hollywood that Vincente had known intimately for three decades was beginning to disintegrate.

Despite the critical acclaim and commercial success greeting such daring, cutting-edge releases as *Bonnie and Clyde*, *The Graduate*, *Easy Rider*, and *The Boys in the Band*, the film industry still seemed largely oblivious to the civil rights movement, the sexual revolution, and the Stonewall riots. Instead, Tinseltown was almost single-mindedly obsessed with replicating the unprecedented success of a certain cinematic phenomenon.

The Sound of Music had ushered in a slew of would-be imitators— overblown, extravagantly budgeted musicals (*Doctor Dolittle*, *Finian's Rainbow*, *Sweet Charity*, *Star!*) that succeeded only in proving that *The Sound of Music* was, in the lingo of studio accountants, "a nonrecurring exception." Nevertheless, every producer in town had eyes trained on Broadway's marquees, searching for the next surefire winner in the blockbuster musical sweepstakes. Originally entitled *I Picked a Daisy*, *On a Clear Day* had plenty to recommend it. Its theatrical pedigree was impressive: book and lyrics by Alan Jay Lerner, music by Burton Lane (who had partnered with Lerner after

Richard Rodgers had left the project in its early stages), and musical numbers staged by future director Herbert Ross.

With plot elements involving reincarnation, ESP, and telekinesis, *On a Clear Day* couldn't have been more in tune with the psychedelic '60s. Lerner's story was both highly original and ahead of its time: While under hypnosis, kooky co-ed Daisy Gamble reveals that she's lived before—as Melinda Wells, eighteenth-century England's most delectable coquette. Daisy's psychiatrist, Dr. Mark Bruckner, falls for her former incarnation—the superswan Melinda—while ugly duckling Daisy is entranced by the hypnotic charms of her doctor.*

While never as celebrated as the music Lerner and Loewe had created for *My Fair Lady* or *Gigi*, the score for *Clear Day* nevertheless contained some of Lerner and Lane's finest work, including the self-affirmative title tune and one of the great, underappreciated ballads of all time, "She Wasn't You" (redressed as "He Isn't You" for the film).

Barbara Harris had won unanimous praise for her performance in the original Broadway production, though when it came time to cast Minnelli's movie, producer Howard W. Koch insisted on a major star with plenty of box-office pull. The role of the supernaturally gifted protagonist was offered to Audrey Hepburn, who turned it down, perhaps sensing that *Clear Day*'s doctor-patient relationship was in some ways too reminiscent of the professor-pupil scenario of *My Fair Lady*.

Although it didn't seem so at the time, Hepburn's turndown was a blessing in disguise, as the challenging dual role of Daisy/Melinda required a powerhouse musical-comedy star who could pull off playing Brooklyn's answer to Bridey Murphy in the contemporary scenes and then switch gears to become the elegant landed lady of the regression sequences. On the short list of performers who could handle the leap from Flatbush to Fair Lady and belt out the score besides, there seemed only one worthy contender . . . and her name was Barbra.

As Streisand herself explained, she was perfect casting: "I am a bit coarse, a bit low, a bit vulgar, and a bit ignorant. I am also part princess, sophisticate, elegant and controlled." Besides, Our Lady of Brooklyn had seen the Broadway production and pronounced it "just heaven": "The two parts are close to my schizophrenic personality. They appeal to the frightened girl and the strong woman in me."[1]

---

* Critics reviewing the Broadway version of *On a Clear Day* noted its vague resemblance to John L. Balderston's *Berkeley Square*, a three-acter from 1929 that concerned a male protagonist time traveling from 1928 to 1784 to find his one true love.

Frank Sinatra, Dean Martin, and Richard Harris were all considered for the role of Daisy's singing psychiatrist, but the part was ultimately awarded to Yves Montand, who finally landed in a Minnelli production after being passed over for the Henri Baurel role in *An American in Paris* and wisely rejecting the male lead in the ill-fated *Mata Hari*.

To surround Streisand, Paramount assembled a supporting cast composed of every available male in the Screen Actor's Guild: Larry Blyden signed on as Daisy's too tightly wound fiancé Warren Pratt; John Richardson would play Melinda's weak-willed husband; and for the small role of Daisy's "ex-stepbrother," Minnelli chose a refugee from Roger Corman B-movies, an offbeat newcomer named Jack Nicholson. "I wanted to see what it would be like to be in a big Vincente Minnelli musical," Nicholson would tell Rex Reed. "It's a radical departure for me, 'cause he makes a certain *kind* of movie, you know? . . . I think I got it because Minnelli was looking at a film I did called *Psych-Out* for some lighting effects and they saw me in it. . . . Boy, I'd like to make a movie of Vincente Minnelli watching *Psych-Out*, man."[2]

In the transition from stage to screen, countless changes were made. It was Vincente's idea to shift the regression scenes from the eighteenth century to the more photogenic Regency period. Some songs from the Broadway show, such as "On the S.S. *Bernard Cohn*" (which the critics had singled out for praise), were dropped, and others, such as the exquisite, Streisand-tailored "Love with All the Trimmings," were added. Melinda Wells morphed into the more exotic Melinda Tentrees, and with France's Yves Montand on board, the character of Dr. Mark Bruckner was gallicized into Dr. Marc Chabot.

Budgeted at $10 million, *On a Clear Day* would be the most expensive production of Minnelli's career. After principal photography was completed on the Paramount lot, the sumptuous flashback sequences would be shot on location in England at the jaw-dropping Royal Pavilion at Brighton.

Even before cameras rolled, industry insiders wondered if Vincente, now sixty-six, was up to such a monumental undertaking. And even if he was, would he be any match for the indomitable Streisand, who had reportedly overpowered director William Wyler while shooting *Funny Girl* and clashed with Gene Kelly during the making of *Hello, Dolly!* Imagine the company's collective surprise when Streisand's anticipated skirmishes with Minnelli never materialized.

"There was never a crisis that I remember between Barbra and Vince," says John Poer, who, at age twenty-eight, was hired as the film's second assistant director. "I was assigned to be almost completely responsible for Barbra Streisand's maintenance," Poer notes:

She was then and is now a prickly person to deal with but not a foolish one. She's a very intelligent person, and everybody quickly learned that even though she often had opinions about the way things should be done that conflicted with what was going on with the show, she was very often right—when it related to her. You can look at it from a selfish point of view or from just an intelligent one, but she didn't worry about what went on with other people. But when it concerned her, she was *very* particular. . . . I respect her and I think she's a professional. At least with *On a Clear Day*, I don't consider much of what she requested to be nonsense. I mean, I worked with Joan Collins for a long time and trust me, Barbra Streisand is a puppy dog compared to Joan Collins.[3]

Daisy Gamble was certainly no pushover either. "If I remember correctly, Barbra insisted that her trailer–dressing room be much bigger than Yves Montand's," recalls assistant art director Lawrence Paull. Streisand's meticulously designed dressing room (complete with hand-painted ceilings and an ornate bed with swan-shaped headboards) was the handiwork of legendary production designer John De Cuir. Barbra's over-the-top trailer was as stunning as the period sets De Cuir created for *Clear Day*. As the ultimate star perk, it left no doubt in anybody's mind who wielded the most power on the set. As Paull recalled, "She was paranoid because Yves Montand had a reputation of being a real ladies' man who bedded down a great many of his leading ladies over the years. . . . I think there was a concern there for awhile. She didn't want to be taken in by his guiles, so to speak. From what I remember, he kept a very, very low profile on the whole film."[4]

With a story that seesawed between 1814 and 1969, Minnelli had an opportunity to create what Molly Haskell would describe as "a contemporary world which is set in quotation marks, and a historical one in double quotations." Not since *Gigi* had Minnelli's camera been this inspired. "Visually, when it's exciting, that is all about Vince," says John Poer. "In fact, it's possible that he was better at the look of the film than he was with directing the cast. . . . I think he knew what the action was supposed to look like and he'd just hope that the actors got it right. It's that old gag of hire really good talent and then stay out of the way. And I think to a great extent, he was doing that." Or, as Lawrence Paull puts it, "My impression was that at that point, he was basically walking through it."[5]

Liza Minnelli recalled that there was at least one element of *On a Clear Day* that completely captivated Vincente. Before shooting began, father and daughter were sitting in a pancake house on Sunset Boulevard when Vincente suddenly had a revelation. "He said, 'I know what it's gotta be . . . I just know what it's gotta be,'" Liza recalled. "He said, 'You've got to be so interested in those flashbacks that you can't wait to get back to them.'"[6] Vincente's fixation with the regression sequences would infuse those scenes with an unusual beauty and power. Reviewing the film in the *New York Times*, Vincent Canby noted that "the movie, Minnelli and Miss Streisand burst into life in the regression sequences. . . . Minnelli's love of décor transforms the movie into very real fantasy."[7]

In fact, *On a Clear Day* contains one of the most sublime and wholly satisfying sequences of Minnelli's entire career. In the Royal Pavilion's sumptuous Banqueting Room, Melinda seduces her future husband with a strategically placed wine goblet (buried in her bosom) as her thoughts are telepathically transmitted to the tune of "Love with All the Trimmings." The sequence succeeds not only because it's exquisitely crafted but also because Minnelli and Streisand are painting from the same palette. Like Melinda, director and star are experts in the art of seduction; in many ways, *On a Clear Day* is something of a shared autobiography. Streisand had transformed herself from a fatherless *mieskeit* into a multimedia goddess in much the same way Melinda ascends from the Angel of Mercy Orphanage to the House of Lords, whereas for Minnelli, the story of a gifted yet unfulfilled individual with an alternate identity buried within must have seemed somewhat familiar.

With a spellbinding star at the peak of her powers and a collection of consummate talents contributing to every facet of the production, Minnelli seemed to have the makings of a four-star musical, but a funny thing happened on the way to the release print.

With the dawning of the "Age of Aquarius," lavish road-show musicals suddenly resembled woolly mammoths. When Paramount's two other tune-packed extravaganzas, *Paint Your Wagon* and *Darling Lili*, both tanked upon release, the studio cast a cynical eye at *Clear Day*. It wasn't long before the executive order came down: The road-show concept was out. *Clear Day* would be dumped into general release. An overture and intermission were scrapped. Paramount then began hacking away at Minnelli's version, excising several musical numbers. Among the casualties were Nicholson's "Who Is There Among Us Who Knows?"; Streisand and Larry Blyden's rooftop duet, "Wait Til We're Sixty-Five"; and Montand's "People Like Me,"* plus his half of "He Isn't You/She Isn't You," which had been intended as a duet.

---

* Even among die-hard *Clear Day* fans, this missing number is something of a mystery. It's often referred to as "E.S.P.," which may have been the song's title at one point. Stills of Streisand in a wild, futuristic outfit at the Central Park Zoo have surfaced, offering what appears to be a tantalizing glimpse of this deleted sequence. In Lerner's script dated April 18, 1969, Montand's character croons "People Like Me," which features the lyrics, "To a sober-minded man of reason, E.S.P. is worse than treason." It's been suggested that throughout the song, there would have been cutaways to Streisand in her various incarnations—past, present, and future.

Barbra Streisand wearing one of
Cecil Beaton's eye-popping
ensembles in *On a Clear Day You
Can See Forever*. Minnelli said of
his star: "We got along beautifully.
She's very creative. . . . She realizes
there are twenty ways of playing a
scene and I'm inclined to think that
way myself, so the great fun was
finding it together."
PHOTO COURTESY
OF PHOTOFEST

Perhaps the most damaging cuts involved Minnelli's favorite part of the
film—Daisy's sumptuous past-life regressions. Pamela Brown, who had appeared in *Lust for Life*, saw her substantial role as Mrs. Fitzherbert whittled
into a walk-on. Scenes depicting Melinda's marriage and her metaphysical
machinations in her husband's business were eliminated. The absence of
these episodes pointed up the film's most obvious flaw: Melinda's story is
never resolved, it just goes away. "Those flashbacks—although they were the
essence of the whole story—they were also a problem that Alan never quite
resolved," says Alan Jay Lerner's assistant, Stone Widney. "Second acts in
a musical are a bitch. Sometimes you just get lucky and it falls out right.
Other times, you're pushing the story around to make something happen
that is positive."[8]

The cuts to *Clear Day* were so extensive that the titles of two songs that
survived, "What Did I Have That I Don't Have?" and "Come Back to Me,"
seemed to be commenting on the film's dismemberment. In June 1970, the
musical was unceremoniously dumped into theaters. "What the public saw
was not the picture we envisioned," Streisand informed the press. "I learned
a very important lesson about final control." Costar Yves Montand announced
that he had learned some lessons of his own: "Streisand had the right to cut
this film herself, so she cut me out so there could be more of her," the actor
grumbled to a reporter, overlooking the fact that virtually all of the excised
scenes featured Streisand.[9]

The reviews for Minnelli's final screen musical ran the gamut. Joseph Morgenstern gave it a thumbs-down in *Newsweek*: "The movie . . . keeps regressing, back through the Technicolored mists of time, to some of the dreariest, fustiest, mustiest habits of Hollywood's great musical-comedy era." Stuart Byron, on the other hand, offered a glowing tribute: "Vincente Minnelli has always been the most misunderstood of great American directors, and never more so than with *On a Clear Day You Can See Forever*. Here the man created an authentic masterpiece, a unique personal statement—perhaps his most personal statement—and once again he found himself treated as a mere 'stylist.'"[10]

"I suppose it's the Barbra Streisand curse but I've always wondered why people don't get it," says Jeanine Basinger:

> Was it that the picture came out a time when people really needed to be cynical? Is that what happened? And people just don't look at it anymore. I wonder what the problem with that really is? Is it because there's something so beautiful and rapturous about that movie and so heartbreaking and touching that people don't want to accept it? The message is self-affirmation and it's sumptuously presented. And Minnelli really does right by her. He really concentrates on presenting her in quite a marvelous way. I think in some ways, he must have identified Barbra Streisand with Judy Garland. The fact that Streisand really sort of popped out to the public on *The Judy Garland Show*. The fact that she could sing so powerfully as Garland did. Although they're very different, he must have made that association.[11]

Only weeks after production closed on *Clear Day*, Vincente received a call from Liza informing him that Judy had died of an accidental overdose in London. She was forty-seven years old. Though deeply saddened, Vincente chose not to attend the funeral service at Frank Campbell's in New York. He preferred to grieve privately, while vowing not to "wallow in useless tears." "Judy would have been so contemptuous of them," he wrote. "She didn't carry herself as a tragic person, and we took the cue from her."[12]

There were other endings as well. Denise informed Vincente that their marriage was over. Two years later, the gossip columns filled everybody in: "If her California divorce from film director Vincente Minnelli goes through on schedule, Yugoslavian-born Denise Minnelli, whose parties and pigtails were the talk of Beverly Hills during her Hollywood period, will marry Prentis Cobb Hale, the multimillionaire department store tycoon in San Francisco." The *New York Times* reported that "the dissolution hearing took ten seconds." Like almost everything concerning Denise, her divorce from Minnelli and marriage to Prentis Cobb Hale had everybody talking. And talking.

***

IN THE EARLY 1970S, a writer named Joel E. Siegel (who had authored a book on *Cat People* producer Val Lewton) began working on an ambitious biography of Minnelli. Siegel's friend Howard Mandelbaum remembers that the would-be biographer went to extraordinary lengths preparing what he hoped would be the definitive exploration of Minnelli's life and career:

> Joel worked on it for a long time and he went and interviewed lots of [Minnelli's] collaborators and friends. He spent a lot of time with Minnelli and he told me how difficult it was for Minnelli to communicate and to remember, which of course makes the ultimate title of Minnelli's own book [*I Remember It Well*] a little ironic. . . . Imagine Joel's surprise—as his book was nearing completion, it was announced that Minnelli had signed a contract to publish his autobiography, which Hector Arce collaborated on. So, Joel's stories were no longer going to be fresh, because all of this material that he had pulled out of Minnelli was going to be reused in Minnelli's own book. . . . Joel saw this as a real betrayal.[13]

It has been suggested that Minnelli went forward with the publication of his autobiography in part because of his dwindling finances. After the divorce from Denise, some of Minnelli's friends noticed that the house on Crescent Drive looked rather "threadbare." Vincente had not directed a film since *On a Clear Day* in 1969, and the offers weren't exactly pouring in. Another motivating factor may have been the fact that, although the entire world was now on a first-name basis with superstar Liza, her father seemed to be slipping below the radar. Was it possible that despite his Academy Award–winning credentials and remarkable cinematic legacy, Minnelli might be forgotten? It often seemed that Vincente's industry had a memory as short as his own. As Bob Fosse, William Friedkin, and Peter Bogdanovich were riding high in the swinging '70s, golden-age directors such as Minnelli, Mankiewicz, and Cukor were written off as old-fashioned and out of touch. The publication of Minnelli's memoir might remind readers that a certain Oscar-winning auteur was still around and available to direct members of the "me" generation.

Published in 1974, *I Remember It Well* was generally well received. Gene Siskel called it "a splendid and surprisingly personal recollection." Other readers noted that the memoir seemed to suffer from significant memory lapses, as key figures and controversial episodes from Minnelli's life were conspicuously missing. Older brother Paul Minnelli, Uncle Frank's suicide, and Lester Gaba—all of this was banished from the autobiography. And throughout the text, Minnelli presented himself as exclusively heterosexual. "Read with pleasure but read with caution," advised John Coleman in his *Washington Post* review.

The year *I Remember It Well* was published was also the year that MGM celebrated its fiftieth anniversary with the release of the spectacular documentary *That's Entertainment!* Written, produced, and directed by Liza's second husband-to-be, Jack Haley Jr., the movie presented clips culled from nearly a hundred of MGM's glittering extravaganzas. Garland was glimpsed singing "Over the Rainbow." Astaire danced on the ceiling in *Royal Wedding*. But it came as no surprise to movie buffs that many of the most memorable sequences were highlights from Minnelli productions. The ballet from *An American in Paris* was singled out as "MGM's masterpiece" (though purists griped that an abbreviated version was included, and not the full seventeen-minute ballet). Haley's film proved to be a sleeper smash, which spawned two sequels.

While furthering the nostalgia craze that swept through the '70s, *That's Entertainment!* also revived interest in Minnelli's movies, which were suddenly in demand in art houses and on college campuses. It was around this time that cults formed around some of Vincente's more esoteric efforts, especially *The Pirate* and *Yolanda and the Thief*. In the psychedelic '70s, Minnelli's Technicolor fantasylands and surrealistic dream sequences suddenly found a very receptive—if heavy-lidded—audience.

In 1975, writer and documentarian Richard Schickel interviewed Minnelli on camera for his acclaimed eight-part television series *The Men Who Made the Movies*, which profiled master directors such as Alfred Hitchcock and Howard Hawks. "I stayed in touch with Vincente a little bit after *The Men Who Made the Movies*," says Schickel. "He was a very kindly gentleman. He was kind of inarticulate—stammering and so forth. And sort of hidden in certain ways. You know, he wrote that autobiography *I Remember It Well* and I always laugh when I look at that title on the shelf because he didn't remember anything. But he was a fabulous filmmaker. You know, as the years go on and you look at Vincente's contributions, he seems to loom larger in film history than maybe he seemed to at the time."[14]

37

A Matter
of Time

FOR YEARS, VINCENTE AND LIZA had searched for the perfect project on which to collaborate. At one point, the Minnellis thought they had found an ideal vehicle in Nancy Milford's acclaimed 1970 biography of Jazz Age icon Zelda Fitzgerald. Milford's recounting of the life of F. Scott Fitzgerald's free-spirited though deeply troubled wife seemed like natural biopic material. Although Paramount initially expressed interest, this *Zelda with a "Z"* was not to be. Undaunted, Vincente turned his attention to a story that had long fascinated him. "When I first read the English translation of Maurice Druon's *Film of Memory*, I felt it would make a marvelous picture," Vincente recalled. "The book had been optioned by several film producers over the years. Whenever I got my offer in, it was either too little or too late. I had given up hope that I'd ever be involved with that lovely story."[1]

Published in 1955, Maurice Druon's novel *The Film of Memory* seemed ready-made for Minnelli.* The story concerned Carmela, a timid, impressionable chambermaid living vicariously through the memories of the half-mad Contessa Sanziani, a resident in the dilapidated hotel where Carmela works. The old Renaissance queen's recollections of her glamorous past as a coveted European courtesan inspire Carmela to fantasize about an exotic existence beyond her mindless routine of changing bed sheets.

Teetering on the edge of insanity, the contessa tutors the unworldly fifth-floor maid in the fine art of living. As La Sanziani retreats further into her

---

* The novel was originally published as *La Volupté d'Etrê* in 1954.

hallucinatory film of memory, she is more than a few frames out of synch with the world around her, and her decline seemed to eerily mirror Vincente's fading status in the film industry. In an era dominated by the likes of Francis Ford Coppola, Steven Spielberg, and Martin Scorsese, the seventy-two-year-old Minnelli was seen as an out-of-touch, fusty relic and one totally dependent on his daughter's star power to secure financing for any new endeavors. Friends recalled that after *On a Clear Day*, Vincente seemed perfectly content ensconced in his Crescent Drive sanctuary, lounging in an elegant silk robe and painting. Why should he have to trouble himself with mounting another elaborate film production when most of his colleagues were enjoying a quiet retirement?

"I think he did it because of Liza," says screenwriter John Gay, who was tasked with transferring Druon's psychologically layered prose to film. "[Vincente] looked at it as a project to star his daughter and they always wanted to work together. They really were devoted to each other." Naturally, Liza would be playing Carmela*—though an eternally sequined, Studio 54 habitué seemed more suitably cast as the hedonistic Sally Bowles in *Cabaret* than a mousy maid from the provinces. "I have to tell you I was a little bit surprised," Gay says of casting Liza, the glittering showstopper, as a shrinking violet. "I mean, I know why he wanted his daughter for it but Liza is like you see her on the screen. I mean, she's just *all over*. I thought the personality of Liza would be a little bit over the top, shall we say, and she'd have to hold it down to play the maid."[2]

Even with a red hot, post-*Cabaret* Liza on board, a character-driven drama about a dreamy chambermaid and a senile countess didn't seem destined for box-office glory. As *Carmela* would be competing against the likes of *Mother, Jugs and Speed*, and *Corvette Summer*, the story the Minnellis were pitching seemed almost hopelessly quaint—about as up-to-the-minute as the Victrola. From a marketing standpoint, there was no sizzling romance to exploit, at least not one of the traditional Streisand-Redford variety.

"Actually, the thing was a love story between the chambermaid and the countess, if you want took at it that way. That's really what it was all about," says Gay.[3] But who would finance such a commercially risky venture? The major studios, including MGM (which for a time had optioned the property) took turns turning down the Minnellis. "I found myself, in a way, auditioning the project before the money men," Vincente recalled. It was a humiliating experience. Despite his legendary Oscar-winning track record, the elder

---

* The character was eventually renamed *Nina*, which served as the film's title before it was changed to *A Matter of Time*.

Minnelli wasn't received with open arms by junior executives in search of the next big roller-boogie cash cow.

Then came a glimmer of hope from a most unlikely source. Samuel Z. Arkoff's American International Pictures was famous for such four-star schlock as *The Ghost in the Invisible Bikini* and *Attack of the Puppet People*. AIP, which had launched the careers of Jack Nicholson and "King of the B's" director Roger Corman, expressed interest in cofinancing Vincente Minnelli's long-awaited return. In taking on *Carmela* (as the project was then titled), Arkoff would be acquiring two Oscar-winning Minnellis at bargain-basement prices, plus a prestige project that might single-handedly obliterate the memory of such dubious Arkoff enterprises as *I Was a Teenage Werewolf* and *Girls In Prison*. A Vincente Minnelli movie was AIP's opportunity to finally go legit.

John Gay attempted to warn the film's leading lady about the type of fly-by-night producers they now found themselves in bed with. "I said to Liza, 'These guys are very tough. I mean, Vincente better watch out.' She said, 'Are you kidding? Daddy may look flighty but he's hard as nails. He can handle any of these guys.' But Vincente was weaker at that time. He was getting older. I don't think that Vincente had the old stamina that Liza said he always had."[4]

Arkoff was being cautioned as well. As the producer recalled, "A couple of my friends in Hollywood warned me, '[Minnelli] hasn't done a picture in a number of years. Be careful what you're getting yourself into. When he was making the big musicals, MGM surrounded him with the best cameramen and best set designers. All of them knew what the pictures needed without even asking him.'"[5]

With both factions forewarned, the producers turned their attention to the crucial casting of the secondary lead. Two-time Oscar-winner Luise Rainer and Italian leading lady Valentina Cortesa were both considered for the pivotal role of the grandest dowager of them all, the Contessa Sanziani. AIP and its Italian cofinancier, however, insisted on an actress with more potent box-office allure, and they got exactly that in the form of the incandescent Ingrid Bergman, who had recently won her third Oscar for her supporting role in *Murder on the Orient Express*. Although Bergman readily accepted the challenging role, she was quick to point out that she was nothing like her character: "She is just the opposite of myself, because she is destroying herself by dreams of her youth. I don't dream about my past. I accept my age [sixty] and make the best of it."[6]

Cast as Lucrezia Sanziani's former husband was Minnelli favorite Charles Boyer, who had appeared opposite Bergman in *Gaslight* and *Arch of Triumph*. With such a high-profile cast assembled, it seemed as though everything had finally fallen into place for Minnelli. Nevertheless, once shooting began—on location in Rome—it wasn't long before word leaked out that the production was floundering; the director known for his attention to the most microscopic details was said to be having inordinate difficulty focusing. Present on the set to interview Liza, writer Clive Hirschhorn observed that Vincente was no longer in full command. "He was really doddery and old and he was shouting '*Action!*' when he meant to say, '*Cut!*' and vice-versa," Hirschhorn says. "It was a very sad occasion. No one seemed to know what they were doing."[7]

Tongue-tied and unintelligible even under the best of circumstances, Vincente found himself at a loss for words on the set. To make matters worse, he was attempting to address a largely non–English speaking crew. Pacing—never Vincente's strong suit—was another challenge. "Almost immediately, . . . the production fell behind schedule," Arkoff remembered. "When I was on the set, Vincente would talk endlessly about the sets and costumes, but he just couldn't seem to pull the picture together. . . . I tried to talk to him a few times—'Vincente, I think you need to take stronger control of the picture. These actors need more guidance from you.'"[8]

But the rigors of shooting a major production in a foreign location were proving to be too much for Minnelli, who was grappling with challenges far greater than the movie. "We didn't realize it yet, but Vincente was already in the early stages of Alzheimer's disease," Liza's half sister, Lorna Luft, would recall in her memoir:

> There wasn't much knowledge of Alzheimer's at the time, and we didn't understand why Vincente was acting so strangely. We kept trying to laugh it off when he made odd mistakes. One day he came into the dressing room and called Liza "*Yolanda.*" . . . We comforted ourselves with the notion that he was getting older, and that he hadn't directed a movie in many years. It was tragic to watch the brilliant man who'd directed *An American in Paris* struggling just to function.[9]

By all accounts, Liza offered Vincente unwavering support throughout the production, though even she felt the need to turn to others for guidance, including screenwriter John Gay. "There was one scene where the contessa is by the window," Gay recalls:

> [Liza and Ingrid] had this scene together and the Contessa talks about the birds. And just before that scene, Liza said to me, "Oh, I'm so worried about this scene. Would you please watch it to see how I do?" So, I did. I watched

The Minnellis and Ingrid Bergman on the set of *A Matter of Time*. Vincente's final film was mutilated by American International Pictures, motivating director Martin Scorsese to publish a protest in Hollywood trade papers signed by over thirty directors.
PHOTO COURTESY OF PHOTOFEST

the scene and I was so elevated by Bergman. She was so absolutely wonderful in that scene. When it was over, I rushed over to Bergman and I said, "That was wonderful . . ." and I turned to Liza and I realized I should have gone to her first. She asked me to watch the scene. She was nervous about the scene. Oh, that was a real faux pas.[10]

While production wrapped on March 13, 1976, Vincente's real battles were only beginning. The rough cut of the picture, now retitled *A Matter of Time*, seemed unusually long even by Minnelli standards. The psychological subtleties and emotional nuances of the story were apparently lost on Arkoff, who found Vincente's initial assembly incoherent and interminable. When asked to outline his intentions, Minnelli had difficulty verbalizing his overall vision of the film. Frustrated and impatient, the producer announced that he would supervise a drastic re-edit. After Vincente and Liza pleaded with Arkoff for an opportunity to rework the footage, the producer relented, but he would only allow Vincente to use the footage from his initial assembly—nothing more. Arkoff deemed Minnelli's second attempt unsatisfactory as well and sharpened his scissors.

Vincente had endured studio tampering with his work before. *The Pirate*, *The Cobweb*, *Two Weeks in Another Town*, and *On a Clear Day You Can See Forever* had all fallen prey to the editor's sheers, but nothing could have prepared Minnelli for the ensuing massacre. Arkoff gutted the picture. Scenes in which "Sanziani dragged the little maid across Europe on a tour of hallucination" (as Maurice Druon had put it) were mercilessly pruned.[11] Virtually all of Edmund Purdom's scenes were axed. Anna Proclemer's role as the contessa's faithful confidante, Jeanne Blasto, was hacked out entirely, though references to her character remain in the release print.

But Arkoff didn't stop there. Believing that his middle initial gave him license to dabble in a little David O. Selznick–style showmanship, the man who gifted the world with *Reform School Girls* decided that *A Matter of Time* was sorely lacking in *La Dolce Vita*. Arkoff insisted on bookending the film with scenes of Nina as a fur-draped, limo-riding superstar. Although Minnelli had shot this footage to placate the meddlesome producer, he never intended to actually incorporate any of it into the picture. A muddled and disjointed film now had to contend with a flashback device straight out of *Funny Girl*.

AIP's mutilation of *A Matter of Time* was so reckless and arbitrary that the release print unreels like one of the countess's hallucinations. The picture is an insane jumble, though at the same time oddly moving. Every so often it's even fascinating, especially in those stretches that are pure and unadulterated Minnelli. In the film's most beautiful and fully realized scene, Bergman's Sanziani, seated by a window, observes thousands of birds flying over Rome. "At the sunset hour, these starlings fly over Rome—thousands of them. It's one of the mysteries of nature. And did you know the noise of the rain so often heard in the music of Berlioz—it's the chirping of these little birds?" After this wistful observation, the contessa hands the chambermaid an ornate Florentine mirror and invites her to take a different look at herself, "You're only what you wish to be. . . . Take it all. Take everything you can from life. It never gives anything back."

Amid the shattered remains of the movie are the fragments of what many hoped would be Ingrid Bergman's "Norma Desmond" performance. Deprived of a complete characterization, the viewer must be satisfied with tantalizing bits: During a solitary dinner, Sanziani absentmindedly reaches for a treasured watch she was forced to pawn; in another sequence, the contessa whips herself into a hysterical frenzy as she realizes that she is seventy-two, the age at which a fortune teller prophesied that she would meet her doom. In these moments, there are glimmers of what might have been. But surrounding this

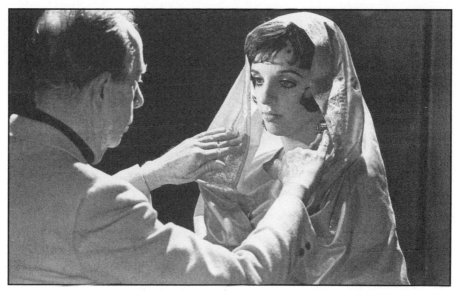

Minnelli on Minnelli: Vincente prepares Liza for a scene in *A Matter of Time*.
PHOTO COURTESY OF PHOTOFEST

are Arkoff's amateurish and arbitrarily inserted travelogue shots of Rome, a pair of inspired but out-of-place John Kander and Fred Ebb songs, and such incompetent post-production dubbing that the synchronization on *Godzilla vs. the Smog Monster* seems Oscar-worthy by comparison.

According to Arkoff, it was Liza who suggested that her then husband, director Jack Haley Jr., be brought in to attempt to salvage *A Matter of Time*. As Arkoff recalled, "By the end of our meeting, I told him, 'Why don't you see what you can do with the picture? Maybe you can save it.' Haley went to work on the picture, although we never publicly announced his involvement in the movie. . . . Despite Haley's best efforts, even he couldn't rescue it."[12]

"God, did they rearrange that movie," says John Gay. "It was so painful when that thing got butchered every which way. It was hard to look at it, you know? I just wiped it out." So did the director. When *A Matter of Time* opened at Radio City Music Hall (of all places) in October 1976, Vincente refused to see it. In later years, it remained a sensitive subject and one Minnelli was reluctant to discuss, as film scholar Joe McElhaney found out. "When I met Vincente, the first question I asked him was, 'Is there any chance that we'll ever get to see the original cut of *A Matter of Time*?,' which was the wrong question to ask him," McElhaney said. "He went completely white and his face fell. He talked in this very tiny voice about the production circumstances of the film and how unhappy it all was and he said, 'No. There's no chance of it ever being restored.'" This was not some overproduced spectacle like *The Four Horsemen of the Apocalypse*, but a poignant character study that Minnelli had genuinely cared about—to see his final film destroyed would stand as one of the great tragedies of his career.[13]

"Vincente Minnelli's *A Matter of Time* has been grossly tampered with," Pauline Kael announced in *The New Yorker*. "From what is being shown to the public, it is almost impossible to judge what the tone of his film was, or whether it would have worked at any level." Though Kael panned what remained of the movie, she saluted Ingrid Bergman's contessa. "She has a glamour in this role beyond anything she's had before onscreen. . . . Bergman's role has been reduced to shreds, so one cannot judge whether her performance had any rhythm; scene after scene has been cut. Still, there's something going on when she's on the screen, and with her gowns hanging straight down from her shoulders, she's as tall as a legend."[14]

While most critics scratched their heads, Minnelli devotees saw *A Matter of Time*—even its gutted form*—as a moving culmination of the director's career. As the greatest love goddess in all of Europe offers life lessons to an awkward chambermaid, there are echoes of Aunt Alicia taking her niece under her wing in *Gigi*. The time-traveling episodes are reminiscent of *On a Clear Day*, while the film-studio scenes recall *Two Weeks in Another Town* (though never quite *The Bad and the Beautiful*). Beyond the self-reflexive nods to his own work, *A Matter of Time* poignantly mirrored the director's own situation. One Minnelli at the end of a remarkable career was passing the mirror on to another who was just beginning.

---

* When Vestron Video released *A Matter of Time* to the home video market in the early 1980s, Liza's rendition of the Gershwin's "Do It Again" was deleted, apparently because of music clearance issues. With one of the film's few unanimously praised sequences excised, the video incarnation of the film achieved the dubious distinction of mutilating an already mutilated work.

38

Lonely Feet

THOUGH TYPICALLY DESCRIBED AS an "elegant Scotswoman," Vincente Minnelli's fourth wife, Margaretta Lee Anderson, was born (somewhere around 1909) in Croydon, England. In the summer of 1940, Anderson and ninety-six other passengers fled war-torn England by boarding the *Eastern Prince* and sailing to America. Although most of the ocean liner's passengers would make ends meet by living with friends and relatives for the duration of the war, Lee Anderson (who had already dropped the "Margaretta") had come to America to marry a millionaire.

Two years earlier, actress Anderson had met Eugene Francois Suter, the developer of a permanent-wave hair-styling process. The same year that Suter met Lee, he divorced his first wife, who was the mother of his only child. Anderson married Suter in 1940 but the union proved to be short lived. Nine months after exchanging vows, the couple divorced. Although she always exuded an air of "to the manor born," Anderson apparently did not profit from her marriage to Suter. She would have to work her way into society's upper echelon, which is where she met her second husband.

Anderson's next millionaire spouse, Arizona cattle rancher/rodeo star Marion Getzwiller, landed Lee a Beverly Hills address, though this marriage would also end in divorce in 1946. Single once again, the aspiring actress soon scored some legitimate stage work, including an appearance opposite future *Gigi* star Eva Gabor in the comedy *Candle-Light*. Anderson's full-time occupation, however, seemed to involve getting her name in the society columns. Throughout the '40s and '50s, Lee's every move was chronicled by

L.A.'s reigning gossipmongers. There she was . . . lunching with Lana Turner, sunning with heiress Kay Spreckles, or reporting that her $35,000 ruby earrings (a gift from an Indian maharajah to her late father) had been stolen.[1] In 1948, Anderson became the social director of the Palm Springs Tennis Club, and it was here that she began to hobnob with the well heeled and highly influential, particularly her fellow British expatriates.

For someone as adept at self-promotion as Lee Anderson, it surprised no one when she ascended to the position of vice president of a Westwood-based public relations firm. "Lee was a real promoter," says Hollywood insider Scotty Bowers. "If you had someone who had a few bucks and they had a lovely house but they didn't know anybody, and they wanted to work their way into a certain social set, they would pay Lee as a party promoter. Lee would do her thing and all of a sudden, there would be a hundred people at the party. And that was Lee . . . always promoting something."[2]

Somewhere between keeping company with billionaire bachelor John Gillin and vying for the title of one of L.A.'s best twisters, Anderson managed to attend her first high-powered Hollywood party (upstairs at Romanoff's) and chat up legendary gossip columnist Louella Parsons. "Every star in the world you can imagine was there," Lee remembered. "Parsons took a liking to me and she said, 'You sit by me.'" An elegant-looking gentleman with "big black eyes" caught Anderson's attention and she asked Parsons about him. Louella gave Lee the inside scoop on the very married Vincente Minnelli. "I thought he was so wonderful," Anderson said. "And I thought, 'Oh my God, I am never going to see that handsome Italian again.' This was awful. Dreadful."[3]

Several years later, while attending yet another glitzy Hollywood gathering, Lee Anderson met Denise Giganti, who announced that she was about to marry Minnelli. Anderson was devastated. "My heart sank to my boots," she recalled.[4] There was still a glimmer of hope, however. Denise befriended Lee, and throughout the '60s Anderson was often the "extra woman" at the Minnelli's star-studded dinner parties.

Anderson would later admit that she carried a torch for her mild-mannered host for years. "I would look across the room and say to myself, 'Oh, that's the only man I've ever really been in love with.'" Lee's prayers seemed to be answered the day Denise called to inform her that she was leaving Vincente for San Francisco millionaire Prentis Cobb Hale (whose wife, Marialice King Hale, died under mysterious circumstances in 1969). It was Denise who encouraged Lee to take over. "Lee is a very nice lady," Denise told a society columnist. "Vincente really needed somebody to take care of him and Lee was marvelous at looking after him."[5]

It wasn't long before Lee was ensconced in Minnelli's Beverly Hills home. The two were inseparable—though, to some, it was the classic coupling of convenience. When the *New York Post* asked if there was any truth to the marriage rumors floating around, the couple laughed and Minnelli responded, "Why ruin a friendship?" But Lee remained hopeful that Vincente would change his mind and ask her to become his fourth wife. And she wasn't the only one. "Everybody was rooting for Lee to marry Vincente," remembered columnist Doris Lilly.[6] All of the cheerleading finally paid off on April 2, 1980, as seventy-seven-year-old Vincente married seventy-one-year-old Lee (the press reported the bride's age as "fiftyish" and she made no attempts to correct them). The couple was married by Judge Edward Brand in the living room of socialite Virginia Milner.

When asked if he was directing the proceedings, Vincente told reporter Jody Jacobs, "I'm just one of the . . . well, company." To which Liza responded, "Daddy . . . you're the star."[7] And befitting an MGM production, the star was backed by a glittering supporting cast. MCA founder Jules Stein was best man. The reception was attended by the likes of Al and Betsy Bloomingdale, Charlton and Lydia Heston, and Henry and Ginny Mancini. The orange blossoms came courtesy of Tony Duquette. The red velvet cushion that housed the wedding bands was a gift from designer Luis Estevez. Every detail had been attended to—except one. Hollywood's greatest director of musicals would have to get married without musical accompaniment. But nobody seemed to mind, especially not the groom.

"I think I'm the happiest man in the world," Vincente told his guests.[8]

***

"MY FATHER IS FURIOUS," Liza Minnelli announced to the star-studded crowd attending Vincente's eightieth birthday party at the Museum of Modern Art in March 1983. The guest of honor was unable to attend his own celebration because he was in a Los Angeles hospital undergoing tests for the respiratory problems that had been plaguing him. "He's the sweetest, gentlest man in the world, but he has a temper and I'm sure he's driving the nurses mad," Liza told the more than two hundred well-wishers who had gathered to pay tribute to the absent director. Several of Vincente's stars were in attendance, including Joan Bennett, Hermione Gingold, and Farley Granger. Lillian Gish, who had appeared in *The Cobweb*, hailed Liza as "Vincente's greatest production."[9]

A month earlier, Minnelli had attended an even glitzier event in his honor at the Palm Springs Desert Museum, which was presenting a retrospective of Vincente's films along with an exhibition of his artwork. At $1,000 per

Vincente escorts fourth wife Lee Anderson to an industry event. Before they tied the knot in 1980, Minnelli wasn't exactly eager to marry again: "Why ruin a beautiful friendship?"
PHOTO COURTESY OF PHOTOFEST

person, the swanky affair seemed to have taken MGM's philosophy to heart: "Do it big, do it right, and give it class." Artist Frances Balcomb was tasked with transforming the museum's Annenberg Wing into the Maxim's of *Gigi*. Frank Sinatra, Kirk Douglas, Gregory Peck, and Lucille Ball looked on as Liza serenaded her father with a medley of her mother's songs from *Meet Me in St. Louis*. "Tonight was the first time I could get through it," she admitted, having choked up during rehearsals.[10]

The evening's most poignant moment came when Liza brought her father on stage and persuaded him to perform "Embraceable You," the winsome Gershwin tune that Vincente had been known to sing during intimate gatherings with friends. As Vincente performed the song in his own inimitable style (and in his unmistakable voice), Liza sat before him cross-legged and completely enraptured. There wasn't a dry eye in the house. As honorary chair Leonore Annenberg observed, "You'll never see anything like that again, it was such a show of love."[11]

***

BY THE SUMMER OF 1986, Vincente's health was rapidly deteriorating. For nearly a year, he had been in and out of the hospital, battling emphysema, pneumonia, and what would now be recognized as Alzheimer's disease. In June, Liza postponed a series of concerts in Indianapolis to be at her father's bedside at Cedars-Sinai Medical Center. The press began providing daily updates on his condition, and there was an outpouring of support and get-well wishes from the Hollywood community.

In late July, Vincente and Liza shared another two days together before she flew to France for a concert engagement. After Liza's departure on Friday, July 25, Lee prepared Vincente's favorite dinner (baby scallops with tomato and fresh basil sauce). Minnelli, now gravely ill, barely touched a bite. "He didn't eat much and that surprised me," Lee told reporters, adding that she phoned for an ambulance after Vincente fell asleep as she "didn't like the color of his face."[12] Minnelli went to sleep and never woke up. At 6:30 P.M., the director was rushed from his Crescent Drive home to Cedars-Sinai, where he was pronounced dead on arrival. Within hours, the news of Vincente's passing hit the wires. When Frank Sinatra heard the reports, he contacted the airport in Nice so that Liza could receive the news of her father's death from a family friend instead of the paparazzi. After speaking with Sinatra, Liza reboarded and headed back to Los Angeles.

The same consideration and sensitivity that Sinatra had shown Liza was not extended to Minnelli's other daughter, Tina Nina. Tina, who resided in Mexico with Vincente's grandchildren, Vincente and Xeminia, would receive the news of her father's death from her stepfather, who happened to catch an announcement on the radio.

In his will, Minnelli had requested that there be no funeral service, but there certainly was one, and it was the kind of high-profile, star-studded event that Louis B. Mayer would have been proud of. "The King of Pop," Michael Jackson, escorted Liza and Lee Anderson into the Wee Kirk o' the Heather chapel. After Father George O'Brien performed a brief Catholic service, Minnelli was eulogized by Kirk Douglas and Gregory Peck.

"Goodbyes don't always have to be sad," Kirk Douglas said. "Because Vincente left us with much to be happy about . . . adventures in love, laughter and wonderment." The actor also talked about the man he knew—or at least attempted to know. "I loved Vincente but I found that he was a difficult man to know. . . . He was a man of mystery; the mystery unfolds in his work, in the vivid memories he has given the world for generations to come." Peck honored Minnelli as "a man who literally gave his life to reach for the distant star, to create works that 100 years later will glow with life and power."[13]

The Douglas and Peck tributes were piped over loud speakers outside the chapel for the benefit of the news media. This drew large crowds that lingered. Many admitted that they didn't really know who Minnelli was. They were there to ogle such celebrities as Jimmy Stewart, Kenny Rogers, and

Bob Hope. As mourners filed out of the chapel, the organist played "Embraceable You."

Although Minnelli had stipulated that his remains be cremated, he was instead buried in Glendale's Forest Lawn Memorial Park. Vincente had often joked that he wanted his tombstone to read, "Here Lies Vincente Minnelli. He Died of Hard Work." But instead the epitaph would read:

IN LOVING MEMORY OF
VINCENTE MINNELLI
1903–1986
beloved father and husband, weaver of dreams,
you filled our hearts with love,
you touched our souls,
you made this world more beautiful.
our lives were enriched by knowing you.
you are missed. our best beloved.[14]

* * *

A WEEK AFTER VINCENTE'S DEATH, the details of his will (dated March 25, 1982) were made public. The bulk of Minnelli's $1.1 million estate (including artwork, jewelry, house furnishings, and memorabilia) was left to Liza. Wife Lee Anderson would receive $100,000. Under the conditions of the will, Lee would be allowed to reside in the Crescent Drive mansion for as long as she wanted. Tina Nina was bequeathed the comparatively modest sum of $5,000. A note from Minnelli explained that he knew that his youngest daughter was "already well provided for" (presumably by Georgette's immediate family—her Aunt Christiane, the former Miss Universe, was now married to an affluent businessman).[15]

Eventually Tina Nina would contest the will on the grounds that Liza had "exercised undue influence" over the ailing Vincente and that her father was of unsound mind when he prepared the document. While some rushed to Liza's defense—she had made mortgage payments on her father's Crescent Drive house and always footed the bill for Vincente and Lee's travel expenses—others believed Tina Nina had a legitimate complaint. After all, wasn't it Georgette—Tina's mother—who had arranged Vincente's MGM pension for him? And, according to Tina Nina, Vincente had always stressed that he wanted her to receive her fair share. Tina told writer Wendy Leigh: "I didn't question the will for the money. I questioned it because I wanted to do what daddy wanted. And he always wanted Liza and me to share the house. Many times, my father told me, 'I want you to know that in my will, the house will be half for you and half for Liza.' . . . He knew I was in financial need and that Liza didn't need money and that my children were his only grandchildren." Eventually, Tina Nina's lawsuit was resolved through an out-of-court settlement and her two children were named beneficiaries. Although the legal wrangling was over, the sibling rivalry remained. "There was always a power struggle between us," Tina Nina would say of her relationship with her older sister. "Liza was always jealous of me because all her life she has wanted to be Vincente Minnelli's only daughter."[16]

* * *

MAY 1987. CARNEGIE HALL. In a series of sold-out performances, Liza Minnelli captivated her audiences with powerhouse renditions of some of her trademark tunes—"New York, New York," "Cabaret," and "Ring Them Bells." At one point, in between the high-voltage hits, she turned the volume down and performed a lovely though obscure song called "Lonely Feet." It had been written by Jerome Kern and Oscar Hammerstein II for a forgotten 1934 musical entitled *Three Sisters*. Only the most erudite musical theater buffs might recognize the tune, and yet Liza had included it as a tribute to her father.

"He taught me this song when I was six," she explained. "It was not a very well-known song but he just loved it. So, I would like to sing it . . . for him."[17] The wistful ballad, which concerned a wallflower's romantic longings, seemed like a mini Minnelli movie set to music:

> *Lonely feet*
> *While others go gliding by*
> *Here am I, waiting to dance . . .*
> *Lonely waist, intended for arms to hold*
> *Lonely waist, un-embraced, waits for a dance*
> *If any boy would be*
> *Willing to dance with me*
> *Wouldn't we dance*
> *And wouldn't I find him simply divine?*

Was it any wonder that the song was one of Vincente's favorites? It was told from the point of view of a character envisioning those lonely feet out on the dance floor . . . fantasizing about being partnered . . . imagining one's deepest dreams taking flight. The sentiment behind the song was something Vincente understood all too well.

"Liza told me about this time she took him to see a show," Tina Nina remembered. "When they came out, he suddenly stopped, clutched Liza's arm, looked at her and said, 'You know, I live inside myself.'"[18] Even in an advanced

state of Alzheimer's, it was as though Vincente had experienced a moment of genuine revelation. He had suddenly figured out what everyone else had long suspected—that Vincente Minnelli had always been living two lives. There was the life that everyone could see, in which he directed Oscar-winning movies, married glamorous women, and attended all the right parties. Then there was the other life—the more important one—that he lived "inside himself." It was by far the more important existence, and though most people (who didn't know any better) would dismiss this as a fantasy life, it was actually the more authentic one.

Occasionally, he would venture out of this private world—but he wouldn't head out as Vincente Minnelli (too conspicuous) and certainly not as Lester Minnelli (too dangerous). Instead, he would appear as an ecstatic doctor's wife waltzing out of control . . . a terrified trick-or-treater taking on Halloween . . . a tormented artist desperately attempting to communicate on canvas . . . a clairvoyant coquette turning heads at the Royal Pavilion . . . a half-mad contessa randomly wandering through her memories . . . a senorita pining for the pirate of her dreams . . . a lonely schoolboy in need of tea and sympathy . . . and a courtesan that never was.

Yes, he had been living inside himself all these years, but even so, that life was there for everyone to see.

INTERVIEWS

Perry Sheehan Adair, India Adams, Cris Alexander, Jayne Meadows Allen, Eva Anderson, Evangela Anderson, John Angelo, Brian Avery, Lauren Bacall, Don Bachardy, David Balaban, Virginia Barber, Richard Barrios, Jeanine Basinger, Pam Beery, Patricia Beeson, Rudy Behlmer, William Berkson, Nita Bieber, Mary Bills, Judi Blacque, Betsy Blair (2003 interview), Scotty Bowers, Irving Brecher, Nadine Buchner, Don Burnett, Barbara Butler, Carleton Carpenter, Brent Carson, Dr. Drew Casper, Willy Cassell, Marge Champion, Esme Chandlee, Martin Charnin, David Chierichetti, Gerald Clarke (2000 interview), Bob Claunch, David Patrick Columbia, Betty Comden, Norman Corwin, Robert Crutchfield, Tony Curtis, Mary DeLiagre, Antony DeVecchi, Anne Dinovo, Mike Dinovo, Sam Dinovo, Kirk Douglas, R. Bobby Ducharme, David Ehrenstein, John Epperson, Luis Estevez, Nanette Fabray, David Fantle, Michael Feinstein (2003 interview), George Feltenstein, John Fitzpatrick, Polly Flahive, Tucker Fleming, Dorothy Florance, Nina Foch, Hugh Fordin, Harriet Frank Jr., John Fricke, David Galligan, Betty Garrett, John Gay, Ben Geary, Beth Genne, Dr. David Gerstner, William Gibson, Michael Grace, Farley Granger, Jess Gregg, Roberta Hagood, George Hamilton, Bill Hanrahan, Monika Henreid, Darryl Hickman, Clive Hirschhorn, Marian Horosko, Marsha Hunt, Jack Hurd, Kay Duke Ingalls, Sir Gerald Kaufman, Peter Keyes, Peggy King, Hilary Knight, Miles Krueger, Gavin Lambert (2000 interview), Angela Lansbury, Tony LaRocco, Jack Larson, John LeBold, John Leggett, June Lockhart, Carolyn Lopez, A. C. Lyles, Frank Lysinger, Jim Mahoney, Randal Malone, Howard Mandelbaum, Jon Marans, Gloria Marlen, Caren Marsh-Doll, Hugh Martin (1998 interview), Michael Maule, Bert May, Urie McCleary Jr., Joe McElhaney, John Meyer, Denny Miller, James Mitchell, Peggy Moffit, Hank Moonjean, Ethan Mordden (2001 interview), Robert K. Moyer, Morton Myles, Margaret O'Brien, Lawrence Paull, Gigi Perreau, John Poer, Meredith Ponedel, Rev. Lynn Ramey, Ann Rapp, Irving Ravetch, Jack Reavley, Charlene Regester, Gene Reynolds, Barbara Freed Saltzman, Richard Schickel, Mort Sheinman, Leonard Stanley, Skipper Steely, Stella Stevens, Thomas Sydes, Russ Tamblyn, Steve Terrell, Bob Thomas, Matthew Tinkcom, Audrey Totter, Judy Trott, Monique Van Vooren, Margaret Whiting, Stone "Budd" Widney, Jill Wiest, Judi B. Witty, Peter Woodburn.

⟨ ASSISTANCE & CORRESPONDENCE ⟩

Charlene Abel (Madison-Jefferson Public Library),Woolsey Ackerman, Robert Anderson, Greg Astor, Lygia Bagdanovich, Joanne Bartlett, Craig Bentley, Bill Blackwell, Windy Bolduc, Bruce Broughton, Lea Carlson, Paula J. Carter, Maryann Chach, Steve Chou, Gerald Clarke, Tess Cleary, Ned Comstock, Julia Coopersmith, Vickie Copeland, Len J. Cortigiano, Robert Diamond, Adelaide Docx, Richard Dyer, Alan Eichler, Angela Encarnacion, Scott Eyman, Edward Field, Jean Flahive, Dena Flekman (Corymore Corporation), Arlene Flower, Tom Frederiksen, Chris Freeman, Peter Garza-Zavaleta, James Gavin, Susan Ginsburg, Rolande Griffin, May Haduong, Barbara Hall, Ernie Harburg, Susan M. Hart (University of Missouri), Peter Hay, Max D. Hipp (Oxford–Lafayette County Chamber of Commerce), Steve Hodel, Stuart Hodes, Bob Hofler, Mark Horowitz (Library of Congress), Julie Houston (Delaware Historical Society), J. C. Johnson, Jim Johnson, Gai Jones, Marion Herwood Keyes, Ty King, Howard Kissel, Bob Kurtz, Richard Lamparski, Janet Landry, Nan Lansinger, Jaime Larkin (Motion Picture and Television Fund), Thomas Lee (Office for the Arts at Harvard), Dell Lemmon (a guardian angel in so many ways), Peter Levy, Jaelithe Lindblom (Louisville Free Public Library), Ron Mandelbaum, William J. Mann, Nick Markovich, Michael Mascioli, Laurence Maslon, Patrick McGilligan, Amy Meadows, Linda Harris Mehr, Lily Meltzer, Dee Michel, Joan Miller (Wesleyan Cinema Archives), David Moyer, Brian Mulcahy, Eric Myers, Ronald Neame, Keary Nichols (chef, chauffeur, graphic designer extraordinaire), Peggy Northcraft (Hannibal Free Public Library), Sandy Nyberg, Bob Oliver, Marvin Paige, Brent W. Phillips, Laura and Tony Ratcliff, Karen Richards, Jaydon Riendeau, Emily Saladino, Scott Schechter, Rebecca Sherman, Ed Sikov, (the very legendary) Charles Silver, Stephen M. Silverman, Larry Simms, Caroline Sisneros (AFI Library), Victoria Skurnick, Carol Ann Small, James Spada, Francine Stock (BBC), Kevin Stoehr, Henry Sweets (Mark Twain Boyhood Home and Museum), Lou Valentino, Judy Vardamis, Walter Vatter, Melissa Veilleux, Phet Walker, Marc Wannamaker, Ann Wikoff, Fredric Woodbridge Wilson, Charles Winecoff, Melissa Wolf, Lauren Wolk, Mike Wood, Sheryl Woodruff, Dan Works, Jack Wrangler, Larry Yudelson.

Academy of Motion Picture Arts and Sciences, American Film Institute, Boston University (Howard Gotlieb Archival Research Center), Chicago History Museum, Delaware Historical Society (Delaware, Ohio), Greenwich Village Society for Historic Preservation, Harburg Foundation, Harvard Theatre Collection (Office for the Arts at Harvard), Library of Congress (Music Division), Lewiston Public Library, Maine Public Broadcasting Network, Margaret Herrick Library, Museum of Modern Art (Film Study Center), New York Public Library for the Performing Arts (Billy Rose Theatre Collection; Rodgers and Hammerstein Archives of Recorded Sound), Shubert Archive, St. Petersburg Museum, Turner Entertainment, University of California at Los Angeles (Film and Television Archive), University of Southern California.

NOTES

INTRODUCTION

1. Vincente Minnelli, with Hector Arce, *I Remember It Well* (Garden City, NY: Doubleday, 1974).

2. Jeanine Basinger, interview with author, April 2008.

3. Vincente Minnelli, interview with Richard Schickel for *The Men Who Made the Movies*, produced by WNET/13, aired November 4, 1973, on the Public Broadcasting Service.

4. Vincente Minnelli, interview with Henry Sheehan, available at "Henry Sheehan, Film Criticism and Commentator: Vincente Minnelli," http://www.henrysheehan.com/interviews/mno/minnelli.html. Sheehan does not recall if the interview was in 1977 or 1978.

5. Jon Marans, interview with author, 2009.

6. Tucker Fleming, interview with author.

7. Nina Foch, interview with author, 2007.

8. George Feltenstein, interview with author, August 2007.

1. DELAWARE DAYS

1. S. J. Perelman, "That Felli Minnelli," *Stage*, April 1937; Jesse J. Currier, "A Delaware Saga Moves from a Torchlit Tent Show to Broadway: Minnelli Gains Acclaim as Theatrical Designer," *Columbus Dispatch*, November 10, 1935.

2. Minnelli Brothers Mighty Dramatic Company Under Canvas advertisement from the period, when the operation was headquartered at 39 West Fountain Avenue in Delaware, Ohio.

3. "Minnelli Bros. Are Here," undated article in the *Delaware Daily Journal Herald*.

4. Undated newspaper announcement alerting readers to the fact that the Minnelli Brothers were expected to perform in Marion, Indiana. Mina Gennell was set to star in "The Girl of My Dreams." Ladies would be admitted for 15 cents.

5. Ibid.

6. References to Mina Gennell as "The Dresden China Doll" appear in *The Billboard*, April 15, 1911.

7. The publicity photo of Mina Gennell appeared in the *Delaware Daily Journal Herald*, January 11, 1908, 5.

8. Minnelli, *I Remember It Well*. Records from the Department of Health, City of Chicago, provided details on the deaths of William Francis Minnelli and Mina's other children. The date of death listed for William Francis Minnelli is January 28, 1898.

9. Lynn Ramey, interview with author, 2007.

10. Alice Hughes, "B'way Hails Minnelli as New Master," *New York American*, January 4, 1937.

11. Minnelli, *I Remember It Well*. A slightly different version of the *East Lynne* anecdote appears on p. 246 of Richard Schickel, *The Men Who Made the Movies* (New York: Atheneum, 1975).

12. Currier, "A Delaware Saga."

13. Ruth Arell, "From a Tent Show to the Showplace of the Nation," *Cleveland Plain Dealer*, December 30, 1934.

14. Anne Dinovo, interview with author, 2008.

15. *Delaware Daily Journal Herald*, January 11, 1908.

16. Schickel, *The Men Who Made the Movies*.

17. Minnelli, *I Remember It Well*, 37.

18. Dorothy Florance, interview with author.

19. Minnelli, *I Remember It Well*.

20. Ibid.

21. Ibid.

22. Ibid.

23. Margaret Brawley's quotes are taken from a video interview that Delaware historian Brent Carson conducted with her. The video interview was later included in Carson's self-produced documentary *A Night with Vincente Minnelli*. (There are no dates for the Brawley footage or for when the documentary was first screened.)

24. Bill Hanrahan, interview with author, 2008.

25. Brent Carson, interview with author, 2007.

26. Virginia Barber, interview with author.

27. The line is a quote from William Shakespeare's *Much Ado About Nothing*, Act III, scene 2. The editors of the *Junior Bulletin* also mentioned Minnelli's nicknames, "Les" and "Taxi" (the latter an apparent reference to the fact that Lester Minnelli was always looking for a ride somewhere).

28. Minnelli, *I Remember It Well*.

29. The quotation is from the unpublished notes for Vincente Minnelli's autobiography, archived in the Minnelli collection at the Margaret Herrick Library, Academy of Motion Picture Arts and Sciences, Beverly Hills, California.

30. "F. P. Minnelli Ends His Life by Shooting," *Delaware Daily Journal Herald*, August 30, 1921.

31. Dorothy Eveland, "Saga of the Minnelli Family," *Pickaway Quarterly* (Winter 1989), 14–15.

32. Barbara Butler, interview with author.

2. WINDOW DRESSING THE WORLD

1. Vincente Minnelli, with Hector Arce, *I Remember It Well* (Garden City, NY: Doubleday, 1974), 43. The Chicago newspaper headlines are from the following: "$22,000 to Fight Booze" was the headline of the *Chicago Daily Tribune* on December 10, 1925. "Bandits Bind Miss Bingham, Steal $1,500" is from the same edition. "To Uphold Law in Scopes Trial, Prayers Go On" is from the July 15, 1925, *Chicago Daily Tribune*.

2. Minnelli, *I Remember It Well*, 46.

3. Unpublished notes for Vincente Minnelli's autobiography, archived in the Minnelli collection at the Margaret Herrick Library, Academy of Motion Picture Arts and Sciences, Beverly Hills, California; Minnelli, *I Remember It Well*.

4. Morton Myles, interview with author.

5. Lester Gaba, *The Art of Window Display* (New York: The Studio Publications, 1952).

6. Hugh Troy, "Never Had a Lesson," *Esquire*, June 1937.

7. Richard Schickel, *The Men Who Made the Movies* (New York: Atheneum, 1975), 246.

8. The quote is from the unpublished notes for Minnelli's autobiography, Margaret Herrick Library, Academy of Motion Picture Arts and Sciences; Stone is also described in Minnelli, *I Remember It Well*, 49.

9. Unpublished notes for Minnelli's autobiography, Margaret Herrick Library, Academy of Motion Picture Arts and Sciences.

10. E. R. Pennell and J. Pennell, *The Life of James McNeil Whistler* (Philadelphia: J. B. Lippincott, 1908); Stanley Weintraub, *Whistler: A Biography* (New York: Weybright and Talley, 1974).

11. Morton Myles, interview with author.

12. Minnelli, *I Remember It Well*, 51.

13. David Balaban, interview with author.

14. Ibid.

15. Minnelli, *I Remember It Well*, 54.

3. A GLORIOUS GARDEN OF WONDERS

1. This is a line from "Babes on Broadway," performed by Judy Garland and Mickey Rooney in the MGM production of the movie of the same name, which was directed by Busby Berkeley and released in 1941. The lyricist was Ralph Freed and the composer was Burton Lane.

2. Vincente Minnelli, with Hector Arce, *I Remember It Well* (Garden City, NY: Doubleday, 1974).

3. U.S. Census Bureau, Fifteenth Census of the United States, 1930, enumerated April 14, 1930.

4. Hugh Troy, "Never Had a Lesson," *Esquire*, June 1937.

5. Minnelli, *I Remember It Well*, 57.

6. William Berkson, interview with author.

7. Minnelli, *I Remember It Well*, 59.

8. The quote is from a Brooks Atkinson review that ran in the *New York Times* on December 28, 1932; quoted in *The Radio City Music Hall: An Affectionate History of the World's Greatest Theater* (New York: E. P. Dutton, 1979).

9. Miles Krueger, interview with author, 2008.

10. Minnelli, *I Remember It Well*, 61.

11. Ibid., 62.

12. Ibid.

13. Kevin Thomas, "Minnelli Back on the Scene," *Los Angeles Times*, February 14, 1969.

14. Steven Bach, *Dazzler: The Life and Times of Moss Hart* (New York: Alfred A. Knopf, 2001).

15. "Artist and Model," *House Beautiful*, December 1938, 52–53; "'A Girl Needs a Background: Lester Gaba Designed a Perfect One for Me' Says Cynthia," *House and Garden*, December 1941, 46–47, 75, 84.

16. Morton Myles, interview with author.

17. *Discovering America's Past: Customs, Legends, History and Lore of Our Great Nation* (Pleasantville, NY: Reader's Digest Association, 1993).

18. Lester Gaba, *The Art of Window Display* (New York: The Studio Publications, 1952).

19. Morton Myles, interview with author.

20. Troy, "Never Had a Lesson."

21. Minnelli, *I Remember It Well*, 65.

22. Peter Keyes, interview with author, 2008.

4. "A NEW GENIUS RISES IN THE THEATER"

1. Lyrics from Billy Strayhorn and Duke Ellington, "Something to Live For," 1939.

2. Jack Hurd, interview with author, 2007.

3. David Gerstner, interview with author.

4. The line comes directly from the show itself. A rare audio recording exists—the one I heard was a presentation of the Council for Musical Theatre and Global Distribution Records Ltd. (London/Los Angeles).

5. Letter from J. J. Shubert to William Klein, August 2, 1935; Kevin Thomas, "Minnelli Back on the Scene," *Los Angeles Times*, February 14, 1969.

6. Beatrice Lillie, with John Philip and James Brough, *Every Other Inch a Lady* (Garden City, NY: Doubleday, 1972).

7. "Prodigy," *The New Yorker*, October 12, 1935.

8. Elliot Norton, "'At Home Abroad' Real Hit," *Boston Post*, September 4, 1935.

9. "The Play: Beatrice Lillie and Ethel Waters in a Musical Travelogue Entitled 'At Home Abroad,'" *New York Times*, September 20, 1935; "Name Your Poison," *The New Yorker*, n.d.

10. Vincente Minnelli, with Hector Arce, *I Remember It Well* (Garden City, NY: Doubleday, 1974), 31, 40.

11. Vernon Duke, *Passport to Paris* (Boston: Little, Brown, 1955).

12. Quoted in the liner notes of the Decca Broadway Original Cast Album of *Ziegfeld Follies of 1936*, released by Universal in 2002.

13. Norton, "'At Home Abroad' Real Hit."

14. Elliot Norton, Profile of Minnelli, n.d.; Minnelli, *I Remember It Well*, 81.

15. Minnelli, *I Remember It Well*.

16. Minnelli, *I Remember It Well*.

17. Shubert Theatre press release for "The Show Is On," by C. P. Greneker.

18. "His Old Dream of 'Cock-Eyed' Show Is True," *New York Tribune*, December 20, 1936; Beatrice Lillie, "aided and abetted by John Philip, written with James Brough," *Every Other Inch a Lady: An Autobiography* (New York: W. H. Allen, 1973).

19. John Lahr, *Notes on a Cowardly Lion: The Biography of Bert Lahr* (New York: Alfred A. Knopf, 1969).

20. R. Bobby, interview with author.

21. William A. H. Birnie, "A Chorine Thought and Was Wrong," *World Telegram*, November 14, 1936.

22. Minnelli, *I Remember It Well*.

23. Letter from Vincente Minnelli to E. Y. Harburg, April 11, 1936 (courtesy of the Yip Harburg Foundation).

24. Helen Eager, "A New Genius Rises in the Theater," *Boston Traveler*, 1936.

5. A SMALL BUT EXQUISITE TALENT

1. Vincente Minnelli, with Hector Arce, *I Remember It Well* (Garden City, NY: Doubleday, 1974).

2. James Aswell, "My New York," *Hammond Times*, November 10, 1937, 26.

3. Minnelli, *I Remember It Well*.

4. Elinor Hughes, "The Theater: Ed Wynn's New Vehicle Good-Natured Satire on League of Nations," *Boston Herald*, October 31, 1937, 6.

5. Hugh Martin, interview with author.

6. "News of the Stage," *New York Times*, September 20, 1938.

7. Eve Arden, *Three Phases of Eve* (New York: St. Martin's Press, 1985).

8. John Leggett, interview with author.

9. Minnelli, *I Remember It Well*.

6. "A PIECE OF GOOD LUCK"

1. Marsha Hunt, interview with author.

2. Hugh Fordin, interview with author.

3. Betty Comden, interview with author.

4. Richard Schickel, interview with author; Betty Garrett, interview with author.

5. Barbara Freed Saltzman, interview with author.

6. Ibid.

7. Hugh Fordin, *The World of Entertainment: Hollywood's Greatest Musicals* (New York: Doubleday, 1975).

8. *Musicals Great Musicals: The Arthur Freed Unit at MGM*, 1996, Alternate Current, NHK, Thirteen/WNET, and Turner Entertainment in association with BBC Television and La Sept Arte, produced by Margaret Smilow, directed by David Thompson, released through Warner Home Video.

9. Frank Lysinger, interview with author.

10. Jess Gregg, interview with author.

11. Michael Feinstein, interview with author, 2003.

12. *Musicals Great Musicals*.

13. Matthew Tinkcom, interview with author.

14. Jess Gregg, interview with author.

15. The Horne quote is from the documentary *That's Entertainment! III*, directed by Bud Friedgen and Michael J. Sheridan, MGM/Turner Entertainment, 1994; Hilary Knight, interview with author.

16. Fordin, *The World of Entertainment*.

17. Vincente Minnelli, with Hector Arce, *I Remember It Well* (Garden City, NY: Doubleday, 1974).

18. Ibid.

19. Ibid.

20. Ibid.

21. Ibid.

22. *Judy: Beyond the Rainbow*, documentary initially broadcast on the A&E Network in 1997, produced by John Fricke.

23. Jess Gregg, interview with author.

24. Judi Blacque, interview with author.

7. "HONEY IN THE HONEYCOMB"

1. Vincente Minnelli, with Hector Arce, *I Remember It Well* (Garden City, NY: Doubleday, 1974).

2. Gail Lumet Buckley, *The Hornes: An American Family* (New York: Alfred A. Knopf, 1986).

3. Horne's quotes are taken from her audio commentary on the Warner Home Video DVD version of *Cabin in the Sky*.

4. Minnelli, *I Remember It Well*; Ethel Waters, *Her Eye Is on the Sparrow* (New York: Doubleday, 1950).

5. Buckley, *The Hornes*.

6. Waters, *Her Eye Is on the Sparrow*.

7. Buckley, *The Hornes*.

8. *Hollywood Reporter*, February 10, 1943; *New York Times*, May 28, 1943. Both are quoted in Hugh Fordin, *The World of Entertainment: Hollywood's Greatest Musicals* (New York: Doubleday, 1975).

9. Charlene Regester, interview with author.

10. Eva Anderson, interview with author.

11. David Gerstner, interview with author.

12. *Time*, November 24, 1943.

8. 5135 KENSINGTON AVENUE

1. Irving Brecher, interview with author.

2. Irving Brecher, interview with author.

3. Ibid.

4. Ibid.

5. Vincente Minnelli, with Hector Arce, *I Remember It Well* (Garden City, NY: Doubleday, 1974).

6. Margaret O'Brien, interview with author.

7. Gerald Kaufman, *BFI Film Classics:* Meet Me in St. Louis (BFI, 1994).

8. Minnelli, *I Remember It Well.*

9. Mary Astor, *A Life on Film* (New York: Delacorte Press, 1967).

10. June Lockhart, interview with author.

11. Hugh Martin, interview with author, 1998.

12. Ibid.

13. Meredith Ponedel, interview with author.

14. John Meyer, interview with author.

15. Author interviews with June Lockhart, Meredith Ponedel, and Hank Moonjean.

16. Darryl Hickman, interview with author.

17. John Fricke, interview with author.

18. MGM memo from Margaret Booth to Vincente Minnelli, March 2, 1944, Margaret Herrick Library, Academy of Motion Picture Arts and Sciences, Beverly Hills, California.

19. Irving Brecher, interview with author.

20. Howard Barnes, review of *Meet Me in St. Louis, New York Herald Tribune*, November 29, 1944; Bosley Crowther, review of *Meet Me in St. Louis, New York Times*, November 29, 1944.

9. "A JOY FOREVER, A SWEET ENDEAVOR . . ."

1. Leonard Stanley, interview with author.

2. Howard Thompson, *Fred Astaire: A Pictorial Treasury of His Films* (New York: Crescent Books, 1970); Vincente Minnelli, with Hector Arce, *I Remember It Well* (Garden City, NY: Doubleday, 1974).

3. Matthew Tinkcom interview with author.

4. William Fadiman, "Minnelli Remembers When: Memoirs of Make Believe," *Los Angeles Times,* September 6, 1974.

5. Peter Lehman, Marilyn Campbell, and Grant Munro, "Two Weeks in Another Town: An Interview with Vincente Minnelli," *Wide Angle* 3, no. 1 (1979).

6. Joe Morella and Edward Z. Epstein, *Judy: The Films and Career of Judy Garland* (Secaucus, NJ: Citadel Press, 1969); Christopher Finch, *Rainbow: The Stormy Life of Judy Garland* (New York: Ballantine Books, 1975).

7. David Ehrenstein, interview with author.

8. Hugh Fordin, *The World of Entertainment: Hollywood's Greatest Musicals* (New York: Doubleday, 1975), 140.

9. Minnelli, *I Remember It Well*; Gerald Clarke, *Get Happy: The Life of Judy Garland* (New York: Random House, 2000).

10. "IF I HAD YOU"

1. Hugh Fordin, *The World of Entertainment: Hollywood's Greatest Musicals* (New York: Doubleday, 1975).

2. John Meyer, interview with author.

3. John Fricke, *Judy Garland: A Portrait in Art and Anecdote* (New York: Bulfinch, 2003).

4. Vincente Minnelli, with Hector Arce, *I Remember It Well* (Garden City, NY: Doubleday, 1974).

5. Ibid.; Fordin, *The World of Entertainment.*

6. Minnelli, *I Remember It Well.*

7. *Learning from Performers,* audio recording of Vincente Minnelli at Harvard University, recorded on November 10–15, 1980, at Carpenter Center.

8. Gloria Marlen, interview with author.

9. *Time*, May 14, 1945.

10. Manny Farber, "Dream Furlough," *New Republic*, May 21, 1945.

11. Joyce Haber, "Vincente Minnelli Remembers It Well . . . Some of It, Anyway," *Los Angeles Times*, September 29, 1974.

11. DADA, DALI, AND TECHNICOLOR

1. Judi Blacque, interview with author.

2. Lee Server, *Screenwriter: Words Become Pictures* (Pittstown, NJ: Main Street Press, 1987).

3. Aljean Harmetz, *The Making of* The Wizard of Oz (New York: Alfred A. Knopf, 1977).

4. Clive Hirschhorn, interview with author.

5. Gerald Clarke, *Get Happy: The Life of Judy Garland* (New York: Random House, 2000).

6. Hilary Knight, interview with author.

7. Margaret Whiting, interview with author.

8. Vincente Minnelli, interview with Richard Schickel for *The Men Who Made the Movies*, produced by WNET/13, aired November 4, 1973, on the Public Broadcasting Service.

9. Bob Claunch, interview with author.

12. UNDERCURRENT

1. Vincente Minnelli, with Hector Arce, *I Remember It Well* (Garden City, NY: Doubleday, 1974).

2. Ibid.

3. Jayne Meadows Allen, interview with author.

4. Jeanine Basinger, interview with author.

5. *Time* magazine review, November 1946.

6. Jayne Meadows Allen, interview with author.

7. Ibid.

13. VOODOO

1. Hilary Knight, interview with author.

2. Hugh Fordin, *The World of Entertainment: Hollywood's Greatest Musicals* (New York: Doubleday, 1975).

3. Hugh Martin, interview with author, 1998.

4. Vincente Minnelli, with Hector Arce, *I Remember It Well* (Garden City, NY: Doubleday, 1974).

5. Ibid.

6. John Fricke, interview with author.

7. Minnelli, *I Remember It Well*.

8. Ibid.; Christopher Finch, *Rainbow: The Stormy Life of Judy Garland* (New York: Ballantine Books, 1975).

9. Minnelli, *I Remember It Well*.

10. John Fricke, interview with author.

11. George Stevens Jr., *Conversations with the Great Moviemakers of Hollywood's Golden Age at the American Film Institute* (New York: Alfred A. Knopf, 2006).

12. John Fricke, interview with author.

13. Fordin, *The World of Entertainment*.

14. Richard Barrios, interview with author.

15. Vincente Minnelli, interview with *Cahiers du Cinéma*, quoted in Fordin, *The World of Entertainment*.

16. Alvin Yudkoff, *Gene Kelly: A Life of Dance and Dreams* (New York: Back Stage Books, 1999), 182.

17. Minnelli, *I Remember It Well*.

14. "I AM MADAME BOVARY"

1. Vincente Minnelli, with Hector Arce, *I Remember It Well* (Garden City, NY: Doubleday, 1974).

2. Ibid.

3. Ibid.

4. Drew Casper, interview with author.

5. Gustave Flaubert, *Madame Bovary*, Part I, Chapter 9.

6. Drew Casper, interview with author.

7. Richard Schickel, *The Men Who Made the Movies* (New York: Atheneum, 1975); Flaubert, *Madame Bovary*, Part I, Chapter 8.

8. Miklos Rozsa, *Double Life: The Autobiography of Miklos Rozsa* (New York: Hippocrene Books, 1982).

9. *Time*, August 15, 1949.

10. John Fitzpatrick, interview with author.

11. Bosley Crowther, "Movie Review: Madame Bovary (1949)," *New York Times*, August 26, 1949.

12. "There'll Always Be an Encore," *McCall's*, January 1964; Gerald Clarke, *Get Happy: The Life of Judy Garland* (New York: Random House, 2000).

15. "A FEW WORDS ABOUT WEDDINGS . . ."

1. Vincente Minnelli, with Hector Arce, *I Remember It Well* (Garden City, NY: Doubleday, 1974).

2. Richard Schickel, *The Men Who Made the Movies* (New York: Atheneum, 1975).

3. Carleton Carpenter, interview with author.

4. Russ Tamblyn, interview with author.

5. Ellis Amburn, *The Most Beautiful Woman in the World: The Obsessions, Passions and Courage of Elizabeth Taylor* (New York: Cliff Street Books, 2000).

6. *Box Office*, May 13, 1950; Otis L. Guernsey Jr., "On the Screen," May 19, 1950.

7. Beth Genne, interview with author.

8. Esme Chandlee, interview with author.

9. Minnelli, *I Remember It Well*.

10. Ibid.; Tom Donnelly, "Vincente Minnelli: 'I Remember It Well,'" *Washington Post*, August 11, 1974.

16. THE TIME IN HIS MIND

1. Hugh Fordin, *The World of Entertainment: Hollywood's Greatest Musicals* (New York: Doubleday, 1975).

2. Deena Rosenberg, *Fascinating Rhythm: The Collaboration of George and Ira Gershwin* (New York: Dutton, 1991).

3. Donald Knox, *The Magic Factory: How MGM Made An American in Paris* (Westport, CT: Praeger, 1973).

4. Ibid.

5. Ibid.

6. Nina Foch, interview with author.

7. "Who Could Ask for Anything More? Michael Feinstein in Conversation with Saul Chaplin," liner notes interview included with *The Original Motion Picture Soundtrack of* An American in Paris, Turner Classic Movies Music/Rhino Movie Music, 1996.

8. Knox, *The Magic Factory*.

9. Album jacket for the CBS Records release of *Gershwin: An American in Paris*, 1981.

10. Knox, *The Magic Factory*.

11. Ibid.

12. Marian Horosko, interview with author, 2008.

13. Ibid.

14. Nina Foch, interview with author.

15. Vincente Minnelli, with Hector Arce, *I Remember It Well* (Garden City, NY: Doubleday, 1974); Rose Pelswick, "One of the Best Ever Made," *New York Journal American*, October 5, 1951.

16. Mason Wiley and Damien Bona, *Inside Oscar: The Unofficial History of the Academy Awards* (New York: Ballantine Books, 1986).

17. Saul Chaplin, *The Golden Age of Movie Musicals and Me* (Norman: University of Oklahoma Press, 1994).

18. Minnelli, *I Remember It Well*.

19. Liza Minnelli, on-camera interview on *Biography: Liza Minelli;* A&E series, originally aired June 11, 2004.

20. Candice Bergen, *Knock Wood* (New York: Linden Press/Simon and Schuster, 1984).

21. Nina Foch, interview with author.

22. Associated Press, December 21, 1950.

23. Minnelli, *I Remember It Well*.

24. *Judy: Beyond the Rainbow*, documentary initially broadcast on the A&E Network, 1997, produced by John Fricke.

25. Stone Widney, interview with author.

26. Richard Bernstein, "Hollywood-on-the-Wire," *Independent Film Journal*, October 6, 1951.

27. Minnelli, *I Remember It Well*.

28. "Party Protests Blackface Scenes," Associated Press, September 29, 1951.

29. Minnelli, *I Remember It Well*.

30. Marge Champion, interview with author.

31. Minnelli, *I Remember It Well*.

32. Marge Champion, interview with author.

33. Minnelli, *I Remember It Well*.

34. Farley Granger, interview with author.

35. John Angelo, interview with author.

36. Farley Granger, interview with author.

17. TRIBUTE TO A BAD MAN

1. John Houseman, *Front and Center* (New York: Simon and Schuster, 1983).

2. Sam Staggs, *Close-Up on* Sunset Boulevard (New York: St. Martin's Press, 2002), 164.

3. Vincente Minnelli, with Hector Arce, *I Remember It Well* (Garden City, NY: Doubleday, 1974).

4. Kirk Douglas, interview with author.

5. Houseman, *Front and Center*.

6. Lana Turner, *Lana: The Lady, the Legend, the Truth* (New York: Dutton, 1982).

7. Houseman, *Front and Center*.

8. Peggy King, interview with author.

9. Tom Shales, "The Magic of Minnelli," *Washington Post*, July 28, 1986.

10. Sir Gerald Kaufman, interview with author.

11. David Raksin's comments are from his liner notes for the recording *David Raksin Conducts His Great Film Scores:* Laura, The Bad and the Beautiful *and* Forever Amber, RCA Records, 1976.

12. Josh Rosenfield, review of *The Bad and the Beautiful*, *Dallas Morning News*, n.d.

18. NEW SUN IN THE SKY

1. Betty Comden, interview with author.

2. Vincente Minnelli, with Hector Arce, *I Remember It Well* (Garden City, NY: Doubleday, 1974); Betty Comden, interview with author.

3. Nanette Fabray, interview with author.

4. James Mitchell, interview with author.

5. Minnelli, *I Remember It Well*.

6. Hugh Fordin, *The World of Entertainment: Hollywood's Greatest Musicals* (New York: Doubleday, 1975).

7. Pauline Kael, *5001 Nights at the Movies* (New York: Henry Holt, 1991).

8. Michael Feinstein, audio commentary for Warner Home Entertainment DVD edition of *The Band Wagon*, 2005 (film originally released in 1953).

9. Jim Brochu, *Lucy in the Afternoon: An Intimate Memoir of Lucille Ball* (New York: William Morrow, 1990).

10. Perry Sheehan Adair, interview with author.

11. Richard Barrios, interview with author.

12. *Time*, February 22, 1954.

19. ALMOST LIKE BEING IN LOVE

1. Harrison Carroll, "Behind the Scenes in Hollywood," *Los Angeles Herald Express*, December 24, 1953.

2. Brooks Atkinson, *New York Times*, March 14, 1947 (reviewing the Broadway stage version of *Brigadoon*).

3. Tony Martin and Cyd Charisse, as told to Dick Kleiner, *The Two of Us* (New York: Mason/Charter, 1976).

4. Vincente Minnelli, with Hector Arce, *I Remember It Well* (Garden City, NY: Doubleday, 1974).

5. Michael Maule, interview with author.

6. Van Johnson, in the documentary *MGM: When the Lion Roars* (1992). A DVD version was released by Warner Home Video in 2009.

7. Stone Widney, interview with author.
8. Beth Genne, interview with author.
9. Farley Granger, interview with author.

20. COBWEBS

1. Philip K. Scheuer, "Drama: MGM in New Whack at 'Green Mansions,'" *Los Angeles Times*, October 29, 1953.
2. Letter from Alan Jay Lerner to Arthur Freed, February 9, 1954, from the Arthur Freed Collection, University of Southern California Cinema Television Library.
3. Hugh Fordin, *The World of Entertainment: Hollywood's Greatest Musicals* (New York: Doubleday, 1975).
4. *Time* magazine office memorandum, from Jim Lebenthal to George Nichols, May 10, 1954, contained in the Arthur Freed Collection, University of Southern California Cinema Television Library.
5. Vincente Minnelli, with Hector Arce, *I Remember It Well* (Garden City, NY: Doubleday, 1974).
6. Richard Schickel, *The Men Who Made the Movies* (New York: Atheneum, 1975).
7. William Gibson, interview with author.
8. John Houseman, *Front and Center* (New York: Simon and Schuster, 1983).
9. William Gibson, interview with author.
10. Houseman, *Front and Center*.
11. Minnelli, *I Remember It Well*; Houseman, *Front and Center*.
12. Schickel, *The Men Who Made the Movies*.
13. William Gibson, interview with author.
14. Lauren Bacall, interview with author.
15. William Gibson, interview with author.
16. Houseman, *Front and Center*.
17. William Gibson, interview with author.

21. STRANGER IN PARADISE

1. Vincente Minnelli, with Hector Arce, *I Remember It Well* (Garden City, NY: Doubleday, 1974).
2. Howard Keel, with Joyce Spizer, *Only Make Believe: My Life in Show Business* (Fort Lee, NJ: Barricade Books, 2005).
3. Ibid.
4. Don Bachardy, interview with author.
5. Hugh Fordin, *The World of Entertainment: Hollywood's Greatest Musicals* (New York: Doubleday, 1975).
6. Hank Moonjean, interview with author.
7. Nita Bieber, interview with author.
8. Keel, *Only Make Believe*.
9. Minnelli, *I Remember It Well*.
10. Wendy Leigh, *Liza: Born a Star* (New York: Dutton, 1993).
11. Ibid.

22. MAELSTROMS AND MADMEN

1. Jan Hulsker, *Vincent and Theo van Gogh: A Dual Biography* (Ann Arbor, MI: Fuller Technical Publications, 1990).
2. Letter from Vincent van Gogh to Theo van Gogh, August 17, 1883, available online at http://www.webexhibits.org/vangogh/letter/12/312.htm?qp=fear.shyness.
3. Norman Corwin, interview with author.
4. John Houseman, *Front and Center* (New York: Simon and Schuster, 1983).
5. Vincente Minnelli, with Hector Arce, *I Remember It Well* (Garden City, NY: Doubleday, 1974).
6. Ibid.; Adrian Turner, "An American in London," *The Guardian*, July 19, 1980.
7. Norman Corwin, interview with author.
8. Ibid.; Houseman, *Front and Center*.
9. Anthony Quinn, *The Original Sin: A Self-Portrait* (Boston: Little, Brown, 1972).
10. Kirk Douglas, interview with author.
11. Alice Hughes, "B'way Hails Minnelli as New Master," *New York American*, January 4, 1937.

12. *The Celluloid Closet*, documentary, directed by Rob Epstein and Jeffrey Friedman, produced by Bernie Brillstein, Sony Pictures, 1995.

13. Minnelli, *I Remember It Well*.

14. Quoted in Mason Wiley and Damien Bona, *Inside Oscar: The Unofficial History of the Academy Awards* (New York: Ballantine Books, 1986).

15. Unpublished notes for Vincente Minnelli's autobiography, archived in the Minnelli collection at the Margaret Herrick Library, Academy of Motion Picture Arts and Sciences, Beverly Hills, California.

23. SISTER BOY

1. Robert Anderson, interview with Mike Wood, February 22, 1994, William Inge Center for the Arts, available at http://www.ingecenter.org/interviews/robertandersontext.htm; Richard Dyer, on-camera remarks in *The Celluloid Closet*, documentary, directed by Rob Epstein and Jeffrey Friedman, produced by Bernie Brillstein, Sony Pictures, 1995.

2. Vincente Minnelli, with Hector Arce, *I Remember It Well* (Garden City, NY: Doubleday, 1974).

3. Eric Braun, *Deborah Kerr* (New York: St. Martin's Press, 1977).

4. Thomas M. Pryor, "Hollywood Clicks: MGM Solves Its 'Tea and Sympathy' Script Problem," *New York Times*, September 25, 1955.

5. Letter from Deborah Kerr to Vincente Minnelli, January 24, archived in the Minnelli collection at the Margaret Herrick Library, Academy of Motion Picture Arts and Sciences, Beverly Hills, California. (No year is given, but it was more than likely 1956.)

6. Minnelli, *I Remember It Well*.

7. Ibid.

8. Jack Larson, interview with author.

9. Darryl Hickman, interview with author.

10. Don Burnett, interview with author.

11. Darryl Hickman, interview with author.

12. Telegram from Pandro S. Berman to Arthur Loew (of Loew's Inc.), September 5, 1956.

13. Interoffice MGM memo from Vincente Minnelli to Pandro Berman, September 6, 1956.

14. William K. Zinsser, "Screen: 'Tea and Sympathy,'" *New York Herald Tribune*, September 28, 1956.

15. Justin Gilbert, "Justin Gilbert's Movies: 'Tea and Sympathy' Is Fine on Film," *Daily Mirror*, September 28, 1956; Leo Mishkin, "Screen Reviews: Weakened 'Tea,' but Still Moving," *Morning Telegram*, September 28, 1956.

16. Braun, *Deborah Kerr*.

17. David Gerstner, interview with author.

18. David Gerstner, "The Production and Display of the Closet: Making Minnelli's *Tea and Sympathy*," in *Vincente Minnelli: The Art of Entertainment*, edited by Joe McElhaney (Detroit: Wayne State University Press, 2009), 275–294.

19. Peter Lehman, Marilyn Campbell, and Grant Munro, "Two Weeks in Another Town: An Interview with Vincente Minnelli," *Wide Angle* 3, no. 1 (1979).

24. "THERE'LL BE SOME CHANGES MADE"

1. David Chierichetti, interview with author.

2. Lauren Bacall, *By Myself* (New York: Alfred A. Knopf, 1979).

3. Vincente Minnelli, with Hector Arce, *I Remember It Well* (Garden City, NY: Doubleday, 1974).

4. Gary Fishgall, *Gregory Peck: A Biography* (New York: Scribner, 2002).

5. Lauren Bacall, interview with author.

6. Stephen Harvey, *Directed by Vincente Minnelli* (New York: Harper and Row, 1989).

7. William Gibson, interview with author.

8. "Cinema: The New Pictures," *Time*, April 1, 1957.

9. Minnelli, *I Remember It Well*.

10. Review of *The Seventh Sin*, *Cue* magazine, n.d.

25. UNACCEPTABLE, OBJECTIONABLE, AND UNCLEAN

1. Vincente Minnelli, with Hector Arce, *I Remember It Well* (Garden City, NY: Doubleday, 1974).

2. Hugh Fordin, *The World of Entertainment: Hollywood's Greatest Musicals* (New York: Doubleday, 1975).

3. Fordin, *The World of Entertainment*.

4. Alan Jay Lerner, *The Street Where I Live* (New York: W. W. Norton, 1978).

5. Leslie Caron, on-camera interview for the Warner Video/Turner Entertainment documentary *Thank Heaven! The Making of* Gigi, 2008.

6. Lerner, *The Street Where I Live*.

7. Hank Moonjean, interview with author.

8. Ibid.

9. Monique Van Vooren, interview with author.

10. Hank Moonjean, interview with author.

11. Wendy Leigh, *Liza: Born a Star* (New York: Dutton, 1993).

12. Fordin, *The World of Entertainment*.

13. Ibid.

14. *MGM: When the Lion Roars* (1992). A DVD version was released by Warner Home Video in 2009.

15. Lerner, *The Street Where I Live*.

16. Ibid.

17. Stone Widney, interview with author.

18. Minnelli, *I Remember It Well*.

26. A GLITTERING TIARA

1. Alexander Walker, *Fatal Charm: The Life of Rex Harrison* (London: Weidenfeld and Nicolson, 1992).

2. Angela Lansbury, interview with author.

3. Ibid.

4. *Stars and Stripes*, May 5, 1958.

5. *News Brief* (Lima, Ohio), January 3, 1958.

27. SOME CAME RUNNING

1. Shirley MacLaine, *My Lucky Stars: A Hollywood Memoir* (New York: Bantam Books, 1995).

2. Peter Woodburn, interview with author.

3. MacLaine, *My Lucky Stars*.

4. Ibid.

5. Martha Hyer Wallis, *Finding My Way: A Hollywood Memoir* (New York: HarperCollins, 1990).

6. Denny Miller, interview with author.

7. Ibid.

8. Richard Schickel, *The Men Who Made the Movies* (New York: Atheneum, 1975).

9. Joe McElhaney, interview with author.

28. "MINNELLI'S TEXAS"

1. Unpublished notes for Vincente Minnelli's autobiography, archived in the Minnelli collection at the Margaret Herrick Library, Academy of Motion Picture Arts and Sciences.

2. Vincente Minnelli, with Hector Arce, *I Remember It Well* (Garden City, NY: Doubleday, 1974); Harriet Frank Jr., interview with author.

3. Harriet Frank Jr., interview with author.

4. George Hamilton, interview with author, 2008.

5. Ibid.

6. Ibid.

7. George Hamilton and William Stadiem, *Don't Mind if I Do* (New York: Simon and Schuster, 2008); Minnelli, *I Remember It Well*.

8. George Hamilton, interview with author, 2008.

9. Mark Shivas, "Minnelli's Method," *Movie* (London), June 1962.

10. David Siegel and Scott McGehee, "Hysteria," *Sight and Sound* 33.

11. Philip T. Hartung, "The Screen," *Commonweal* 71, no. 25 (March 1960).

29. BETTER THAN A DREAM

1. Betty Comden, interview with author.

2. Gavin Lambert, *On Cukor* (New York: Rizzoli International, 2000).

3. Brooks Atkinson, "Theatre: 'Bells Are Ringing' for Judy Holliday," *New York Times*, November 30, 1956, 18.

4. Letter to Betty Comden from Arthur Freed, quoted in Hugh Fordin, *The World of Entertainment: Hollywood's Greatest Musicals* (New York: Doubleday, 1975).

5. Jon Whitcomb, "Judy and the 'Bells,'" *Cosmopolitan*, February 1960.

6. Ibid.

7. Gary Carey, *Judy Holliday: An Intimate Life Story* (New York: Seaview Books, 1982); Vincente Minnelli, with Hector Arce, *I Remember It Well* (Garden City, NY: Doubleday, 1974).

8. Bosley Crowther, "Screen: It's All Holliday," *New York Times*, June 24, 1960.

9. MGM press release, "'Bells' Tops Million Mark at Radio City Music Hall," August 3, 1960.

30. APOCALYPSE

1. Eleanor Lambert, "She," *Waterloo Sunday Courier* (Waterloo, Iowa), July 19, 1964.

2. Elisabeth Laurence, "Lives of Style: Denise Hale," *The Examiner*, June 2, 2007.

3. C. Robert Jennings, "The Hollywood Establishment," *Los Angeles Times*, November 26, 1967.

4. Barbara Wilkins, "Who's on Top in Hollywood? Only Joyce Haber's Exercise Man Knows for Sure," *People*, April 25, 1977.

5. Luis Estevez, interview with author.

6. Ibid.; Vincente Minnelli, with Hector Arce, *I Remember It Well* (Garden City, NY: Doubleday, 1974).

7. "MGM to Remake 'Four Horsemen,'" *New York Times*, March 3, 1960.

8. John Gay, interview with author.

9. Minnelli, *I Remember It Well*, 341; George Feltenstein, interview with author.

10. Brian Avery, interview with author.

11. Ibid.

12. Ibid.

13. Letter from Harry Schein to Paul Kohner, December 31, 1960, archived at the Margaret Herrick Library, Academy of Motion Pictures Arts and Sciences, Beverly Hills, California.

14. Hank Moonjean, interview with author.

15. George Feltenstein, interview with author; Brian Avery, interview with author.

16. John Gay, interview with author.

17. Monika Henreid, interview with author.

18. Telegram from Bob Mochrie to Vincente Minnelli, December 22, 1961.

19. Paul V. Beckley, review of *The Four Horsemen*, *New York Herald Tribune*, March 10, 1962.

20. George Feltenstein, interview with author.

31. DON'T BLAME ME

1. Stephen Harvey, *Directed by Vincente Minnelli* (New York: Harper and Row, 1989).

2. George Hamilton, interview with author.

3. Peggy Moffit, interview with author.

4. Tony Martin and Cyd Charisse, as told to Dick Kleiner, *The Two of Us* (New York: Mason/Charter, 1976).

5. Kirk Douglas, *The Ragman's Son* (New York: Simon and Schuster, 1988).

6. Bosley Crowther, "Screen of Degradation: 'Two Weeks in Another Town' at Paramount," *New York Times*, August 18, 1962.

7. Peter Bogdanovich, review of *Two Weeks in Another Town*, *Film Culture*, no. 26 (Fall 1962).

32. HAPPY PROBLEMS

1. John Hallowell, "Every Shift Swings at the Factory," *Los Angeles Times*, September 15, 1968.

2. C. Robert Jennings, "The Hollywood Establishment," *Los Angeles Times*, November 26, 1967; Joyce Haber, "Familiar Line in Another Go Around," *Los Angeles Times*, December 16, 1968.

3. Interview with author. Interview subject prefers to remain anonymous.

4. Luis Estevez, interview with author.

5. Interview with author. Interview subject prefers to remain anonymous.

6. John Gay, interview with author.

7. Liza Minnelli on the recording *Liza Minnelli at Carnegie Hall*, Telarc International, 1987.

8. Ron Howard, interview with Brian Linehan for the series "City Lights," part 3, 1982, Canada National Screen Institute website, www.nsi-canada.ca.

9. Stella Stevens, interview with author.

10. Carlos Losilla, translated by Amity Joy Phillips, "The Immobile Journey of Helen Corbett: On *The Courtship of Eddie's Father*," in *Vincente Minnelli: The Art of Entertainment*, edited by Joe McElhaney (Detroit: Wayne State University Press, 2009).

11. Stella Stevens, interview with author.

12. Audio commentary on DVD edition of *The Courtship of Eddie's Father*, Warner Video/Turner Entertainment, 2003.

13. Ibid.

14. Stella Stevens, interview with author.

33. IDENTITY THEFT

1. Syd Cassyd, "MGM Pairs Art Freed, Irving Berlin Again," *Box Office*, May 6, 1963.

2. Barbara Freed Saltzman, interview with author.

3. Quoted in *Ms.* magazine, August 1972. (The quote appeared a decade after Monroe's death.)

4. Vincente Minnelli, with Hector Arce, *I Remember It Well* (Garden City, NY: Doubleday, 1974).

5. "Theatre: Expanded Vaudeville Sketch," *New York Times*, December 17, 1959; Minnelli, *I Remember It Well*.

6. Tony Curtis, interview with author.

7. Ellen Burstyn, *Lessons in Becoming Myself* (New York: Riverhead Books/Penguin Group, 2006), 127.

8. Tony Curtis, interview with author.

9. John Epperson, interview with author.

10. Tony Curtis, interview with author.

34. THE SHADOW OF YOUR SMILE

1. "Who Pays the Sandpiper Calls the Tune," *Life*, July 16, 1965.

2. Unpublished notes for Vincente Minnelli's autobiography, archived in the Minnelli collection at the Margaret Herrick Library, Academy of Motion Picture Arts and Sciences, Beverly Hills, California.

3. Liz Smith, *Natural Blonde: A Memoir* (New York: Hyperion, 2000).

4. Robert Crutchfield, interview with author.

5. Ibid.

6. Richard Barrios, interview with author.

35. "AT BEST, CONFUSED"

1. Martin Charnin, interview with author.

2. Ibid.

3. Eugenia Sheppard, "Minnelli Spied on Mata Hari," *Washington Post and Times Herald*, August 24, 1967.

4. Hugh Fordin, interview with author.

5. Ibid.

6. Antony DeVecchi, interview with author.

7. Martin Charnin, interview with author.

8. William Goldman, *The Season: A Candid Look at Broadway* (New York: Harcourt, Brace and World, 1969).

9. Antony DeVecchi, interview with author.

10. *Variety*, November 22, 1967; *Variety*, November 17, 1967; Martin Charnin, interview with author.

11. Bill Henry, "Window on Washington," *Los Angeles Times*, November 29, 1967.

12. Antony DeVecchi, interview with author; Martin Charnin, interview with author.

36. ON A CLEAR DAY

1. Shaun Considine, *Barbra Streisand: The Woman, the Myth, the Music* (New York: Delacorte Press, 1985).

2. Rex Reed, *People Are Crazy Here* (New York: Delacorte Press, 1974).

3. John Poer, interview with author.

4. Lawrence Paull, interview with author.

5. Molly Haskell, "Film: *On a Clear Day*," *Village Voice*, June 25, 1970; John Poer, interview with author; Lawrence Paull, interview with author.

6. Vincente Minnelli, with Hector Arce, *I Remember It Well* (Garden City, NY: Doubleday, 1974).

7. Vincent Canby, "Screen: 'On a Clear Day You Can See Forever' Begins Its Run," *New York Times*, June 18, 1970.

8. Stone Widney, interview with author.

9. Considine, *Barbra Streisand*; Jonathan Black, *Streisand* (New York: Nordon Publications, 1975).

10. Stuart Byron, "On a Clear Day You Can See Minnelli," *December* 14, nos. 1–2 (1972).

11. Jeanine Basinger, interview with author.

12. Minnelli, *I Remember It Well*.

13. Howard Mandelbaum, interview with author.

14. Richard Schickel, interview with author.

37. A MATTER OF TIME

1. Vincente Minnelli, with Hector Arce, *I Remember It Well* (Garden City, NY: Doubleday, 1974).

2. John Gay, interview with author.

3. Ibid.

4. Ibid.

5. Sam Arkoff, with Richard Trubo, *Flying Through Hollywood by the Seat of My Pants* (New York: Birch Lane Press, 1992).

6. Donald Spoto, *Notorious: The Life of Ingrid Bergman* (New York: HarperCollins, 1997).

7. Clive Hirschhorn, interview with author.

8. Arkoff, *Flying Through Hollywood*.

9. Lorna Luft, *Me and My Shadows: A Family Memoir* (New York: Pocket Books, 1998).

10. John Gay, interview with author.

11. Maurice Druon, *The Film of Memory* (New York: Scribner, 1955).

12. Arkoff, *Flying Through Hollywood*.

13. John Gay, interview with author; Joe McElhaney, interview with author.

14. Pauline Kael, *When the Lights Go Down* (New York: Holt, Rinehart and Winston, 1980).

38. LONELY FEET

1. "Earrings Worth $35,000 Stolen," *Los Angeles Times*, January 15, 1962.

2. Scotty Bowers, interview with author.

3. Robin Abcarian, "The Divine Mrs. M," *Los Angeles Times Magazine*, August 22, 1999.

4. Ibid.

5. Wendy Leigh, *Liza: Born a Star* (New York: Dutton, 1993).

6. Ibid.

7. Jody Jacobs, "Caught the Bridal Bouquet: Minnelli-Anderson Vows Said," *Los Angeles Times*, April 4, 1980.

8. Ibid.

9. "The Evening Hours," *New York Times*, March 4, 1983.

10. Jody Jacobs, "Minnelli Tribute 'A Show of Love,'" *Los Angeles Times*, February 21, 1983.

11. Ibid.

12. "Obituaries: Vincente Minnelli, Versatile Director of Acclaimed Musicals," *Chicago Tribune*, July 27, 1986.

13. Jerry Belcher, "Minnelli's Works Praised at Services," *Los Angeles Times*, July 31, 1986.

14. A picture of the tombstone appears on the "Find a Grave" website at http://www.findagrave.com/cgi-bin/fg.cgi?page=pv&GRid=2106&PIpi=133663.

15. United Press International, "Minnelli Leaves Bulk of Estate to Liza: His Wish for Cremation Ignored," August 1, 1986.

16. Leigh, *Liza: Born a Star*.

17. *Liza Minnelli at Carnegie Hall*, Telarc International, 1987.

18. Leigh, *Liza: Born a Star*.

SOURCES

Amburn, Ellis. *The Most Beautiful Woman in the World: The Obsessions, Passions and Courage of Elizabeth Taylor*. New York: HarperCollins, 2000.

Amory, Cleveland. *Celebrity Register: An Irreverent Compendium of American Quotable Notables*. New York: Harper and Row, 1963.

Andersen, Christopher. *Barbra: The Way She Is*. New York: William Morrow, 2006.

Arden, Eve. *Three Phases of Eve*. New York: St. Martin's Press, 1985.

Arkoff, Sam, with Richard Trubo. *Flying Through Hollywood by the Seat of My Pants*. New York: Birch Lane Press, 1992.

Astaire, Fred. *Steps in Time: An Autobiography*. New York: Harper and Row, 1959.

Astor, Mary. *A Life on Film*. New York: Delacorte Press, 1967.

Bacall, Lauren. *By Myself*. New York: Alfred A. Knopf, 1979.

Bach, Steven. *Dazzler: The Life and Times of Moss Hart*. New York: Alfred A. Knopf, 2001.

Barrios, Richard. *Screened Out: Playing Gay in Hollywood from Edison to Stonewall*. New York: Routledge, 2003.

Benson, Sally. *Meet Me in St. Louis*. New York: World Publishing Company/Random House, 1944.

Bergen, Candice. *Knock Wood*. New York: Simon and Schuster/Linden Press, 1984.

Black, Jonathan. *Streisand*. New York: Nordon Publications, 1975.

Black, Shirley Temple. *Child Star: An Autobiography*. New York: McGraw-Hill, 1979.

Braun, Eric. *Deborah Kerr*. New York: St. Martin's Press, 1977.

Brochu, Jim. *Lucy in the Afternoon: An Intimate Memoir of Lucille Ball*. New York: William Morrow, 1990.

Buckley, Gail Lumet. *The Hornes: An American Family*. New York: Alfred A. Knopf, 1986.

Bucklin, Linda Hale. *Beyond His Control: Memories of a Disobedient Daughter*. Pasadena, CA: Hope Publishing, 2007.

Burstyn, Ellen. *Lessons in Becoming Myself*. New York: Riverhead Books/Penguin Group, 2006.

Carey, Gary. *Judy Holliday: An Intimate Life Story*. New York: Seaview Books, 1982.

Casper, Joseph Andrew. *Vincente Minnelli and the Film Musical*. Cranbury, NJ: A. S. Barnes, 1977.

Castelluccio, Frank, and Alvin Walker. *The Other Side of Ethel Mertz: The Life Story of Vivian Vance*. Manchester: Knowledge, Ideas and Trends, 1998.

Chaplin, Saul. *The Golden Age of Movie Musicals and Me*. Norman: University of Oklahoma Press, 1994.

Clarke, Gerald. *Get Happy: The Life of Judy Garland*. New York: Random House, 2000.

Considine, Shaun. *Barbra Streisand: The Woman, the Myth, the Music*. New York: Delacorte Press, 1985.

Crowther, Bosley. *Hollywood Rajah: The Life and Times of Louis B. Mayer*. New York: Holt, Rinehart and Winston, 1960.

Dietz, Howard. *Dancing in the Dark*. Chicago: Quadrangle, 1974.

Duke, Vernon. *Passport to Paris*. Boston: Little, Brown, 1955.

Finch, Christopher. *Rainbow: The Stormy Life of Judy Garland*. New York: Ballantine Books, 1975.

Fishgall, Gary. *Gregory Peck: A Biography*. New York: Scribner, 2002.

Flaubert, Gustave. *Madame Bovary*. London: Penguin Books, 1992.

Fordin, Hugh. *The World of Entertainment: Hollywood's Greatest Musicals*. New York: Doubleday, 1975.

Francisco, Charles. *The Radio City Music Hall: An Affectionate History of the World's Greatest Theater*. New York: E. P. Dutton, 1979.

Frank, Gerold. *Judy*. New York: Harper and Row, 1975.

Freedland, Michael. *Maurice Chevalier*. New York: William Morrow, 1981.

Fricke, John. *Judy Garland: A Portrait in Art and Anecdote*. New York: Bulfinch Press, 2003.

———. *Judy Garland: World's Greatest Entertainer*. New York: Henry Holt, 1992.

Gaba, Lester. *The Art of Window Display*. New York: The Studio Publications, 1952.

Gallick, Sarah, and Nicholas Maier. *Divinely Decadent: Liza Minnelli*. Boca Raton, FL: AMI Books, 2003.

Gibson, William. *The Cobweb*. New York: Alfred A. Knopf, 1954.

Golden, Eve, with Kim Kendall. *The Brief, Madcap Life of Kay Kendall*. Kalamazoo: University Press of Kentucky, 2002.

Goldman, Herbert G. *Fanny Brice: The Original Funny Girl*. Oxford: Oxford University Press, 1992.

Goldman, William. *The Season: A Candid Look at Broadway*. New York: Harcourt, Brace and World, 1969.

Gottlieb, Robert. *George Balanchine: The Ballet Maker*. New York: HarperCollins, 2004.

Guilaroff, Sydney, as told to Cathy Griffin. *Crowning Glory: Reflections of Hollywood's Favorite Confidante*. Santa Monica, CA: General Publishing, 1996.

Haber, Joyce. *The Users*. New York: Dell, 1976.

Halliwell, Leslie. *The Filmgoer's Companion*. New York: Avon Books, 1978.

Hamilton, George, with William Stadiem. *Don't Mind if I Do*. New York: Simon and Schuster, 2008.

Haney, Lynn. *Naked at the Feast: A Biography of Josephine Baker*. New York: Dodd, Mead, 1981.

Harmetz, Aljean. *The Making of* The Wizard of Oz. New York: Alfred A. Knopf, 1977.

Harvey, Stephen. *Directed by Vincente Minnelli*. New York: Harper and Row, 1989.

———. *Fred Astaire*. New York: Pyramid Books, 1975.

Haskins, James, with Kathleen Benson. *Lena: A Personal and Professional Biography of Lena Horne*. New York: Stein and Day, 1984.

Hay, Peter. *MGM: When the Lion Roars*. Atlanta: Turner Publishing, 1991.

Henreid, Paul, with Julius Fast. *Ladies' Man: An Autobiography*. New York: St. Martin's Press, 1984.

Higham, Charles, and Joel Greenberg. *The Celluloid Muse: Hollywood Directors Speak*. Chicago: Henry Regnery Company, 1969.

Hirschhorn, Clive. *Gene Kelly: A Biography*. Chicago: Regnery Publishing, 1975.

Horne, Lena, and Richard Schickel. *Lena*. New York: Doubleday, 1965.

Houseman, John. *Front and Center*. New York: Simon and Schuster, 1983.

Hudson, W. H. *Green Mansions: A Romance of the Tropical Forest*. New York: Random House/Modern Library, 1944.

Hulsker, Jan. *Vincent and Theo van Gogh: A Dual Biography*. Ann Arbor: Fuller Technical Publications, 1990.

Jablonski, Edward. *Alan Jay Lerner: A Biography*. New York: Henry Holt, 1996.

———. *Harold Arlen: Happy with the Blues*. Garden City, NY: Doubleday, 1961.

Jablonski, Edward, and Lawrence D. Stewart. *The Gershwin Years*. New York: Doubleday, 1958.

Kael, Pauline. *500 Nights at the Movies*. New York: Henry Holt and Company, 1985.

———. *For Keeps: 30 Years at the Movies*. New York: Dutton, 1994.

———. *When the Lights Go Down*. New York: Holt, Rinehard and Winston, 1980.

Kaufman, Gerald. *BFI Film Classics: Meet Me in St. Louis*. New York: BFI, 1994.

Keel, Howard, with Joyce Spizer. *Only Make Believe: My Life in Show Business*. Fort Lee, NJ: Barricade Books, 2005.

Kissel, Howard. *David Merrick: The Abominable Showman*. New York: Applause Books, 1993.

Knox, Donald. *The Magic Factory: How MGM Made An American in Paris*. New York: Praeger, 1973.

Lahr, John. *Notes on a Cowardly Lion*. New York: Alfred A. Knopf, 1969.

Lambert, Gavin. *On Cukor*. New York: Rizzoli International, 2000.

Leigh, Wendy. *Liza: Born a Star*. New York: Dutton, 1993.

Lerner, Alan Jay. *The Street Where I Live*. New York: W. W. Norton, 1978.

Levant, Oscar. *The Memoirs of an Amnesiac*. New York: G. P. Putnam's Sons, 1965.

Lillie, Beatrice, with John Philip and James Brough. *Every Other Inch a Lady*. New York: Doubleday, 1972.

Luft, Lorna. *Me and My Shadows: A Family Memoir*. New York: Pocket Books, 1998.

MacLaine, Shirley. *My Lucky Stars: A Hollywood Memoir*. New York: Bantam Books, 1995.

Madsen, Axel. *The Sewing Circle*. New York: Birch Lane Press, 1995.

Mandelbaum, Ken. *Not Since Carrie: Forty Years of Broadway Musical Flops*. New York: St. Martin's Press, 1991.

Mann, William J. *Behind the Screen: How Gays and Lesbians Shaped Hollywood*. New York: Viking, 2001.

Marill, Alvin H. *Katharine Hepburn: The Pictorial History of Film Stars*. New York: Galahad Books, 1973.

Martin, Tony, and Cyd Charisse, as told to Dick Kleiner. *The Two of Us*. New York: Mason/Charter, 1976.

McElhaney, Joe. *Vincente Minnelli: The Art of Entertainment*. Detroit: Wayne State University Press, 2009.

Meyerson, Harold, and Ernie Harburg. *Who Put the Rainbow in* The Wizard of Oz? *Yip Harburg, Lyricist*. Ann Arbor: University of Michigan Press, 1993.

Miller, Denny. *Didn't You Used to Be What's His Name?* Las Vegas: To Health With You Publishers, 2004.

Minnelli, Vincente, with Hector Arce. *I Remember It Well*. Garden City, NY: Doubleday, 1974.

Mitchell, Yvonne. *Colette: A Taste for Life*. New York: Harcourt Brace Jovanovich, 1975.

Moonjean, Hank. *Bring in the Peacocks . . . or Memoirs of a Hollywood Producer*. Bloomington, IN: Author House, 2004.

Mordden, Ethan. *The Hollywood Musical*. New York: St. Martin's Press, 1981.

Morella, Joe, and Edward Z. Epstein. *Judy: The Films and Career of Judy Garland*. Secaucus, NJ: Citadel Press, 1969.

Parish, James Robert, and Ronald L. Bowers. *The Golden Era: The MGM Stock Company*. New York: Bonanza Books, 1977.

Pennell, E. R., and J. Pennell. *The Life of James McNeil Whistler*. Philadelphia: J. B. Lippincott Company, 1908.

Phelps, Robert. *Earthly Paradise: Colette's Autobiography, Drawn from the Writings of her Lifetime*. New York: Farrar, Straus and Giroux, 1966.

Prideaux, Tom, and the editors of Time-Life Books. *The World of Whistler: 1834–1903*. New York: Time-Life Books, 1970.

Reed, Rex. *People Are Crazy Here*. New York: Delacorte Press, 1974.

Reynolds, Debbie, and David Patrick Columbia. *Debbie: My Life*. New York: William Morrow, 1988.

Rose, Helen. *Just Make Them Beautiful*. Santa Monica, CA: Dennis-Landman, 1976.

Rosenberg, Deena. *Fascinating Rhythm: The Collaboration of George and Ira Gershwin*. New York: Dutton, 1991.

Rozsa, Miklos. *Double Life: The Autobiography of Miklos Rozsa*. New York: Hippocrene Books, 1982.

Russo, Vito. *The Celluloid Closet*. New York: HarperCollins, 1981.

Sanders, Coyne Steven. *Rainbow's End: The Judy Garland Show*. New York: William Morrow, 1990.

Sarde, Michele. *Colette: Free and Fettered*. New York: William Morrow, 1978.

Schickel, Richard. *The Men Who Made the Movies*. New York: Atheneum, 1975.

Sharaff, Irene. *Broadway and Hollywood Costumes Designed by Irene Sharaff*. New York: Von Nostrand Reinhold, 1976.

Server, Lee. *Robert Mitchum: "Baby, I Don't Care."* New York: St. Martin's Press, 2001.

———. *Screenwriter: Words Become Pictures*. Pittstown, NJ: Main Street Press, 1987.

Silverman, Stephen M. *Dancing on the Ceiling: Stanley Donen and His Movies*. New York: Alfred A. Knopf, 1996.

———. *The Fox That Got Away*. Secaucus, NJ: Lyle Stuart, 1988.

Smith, Liz. *Natural Blonde: A Memoir*. New York: Hyperion, 2000.

Spoto, Donald. *Notorious: The Life of Ingrid Bergman*. New York: HarperCollins, 1997.

Stevens, George, Jr. *Conversations with the Great Moviemakers of Hollywood's Golden Age at the American Film Institute*. New York: Alfred A. Knopf, 2006.

Streeter, Edward. *Father of the Bride*. New York: Simon and Schuster, 1948.

Thomas, Bob. *Astaire: The Man, the Dancer*. New York: St. Martin's Press, 1984.

Thurman, Judith. *Secrets of the Flesh: A Life of Colette*. New York: Alfred A. Knopf, 1999.

Tinkcom, Matthew. *Working Like a Homosexual: Camp, Capital, Cinema*. Durham: Duke University Press, 2002.

Toby, Mark. *The Courtship of Eddie's Father*. New York: B. Geis Associates/Random House, 1961.

Turner, Lana. *Lana: The Lady, the Legend, the Truth*. New York: Dutton, 1982.

Twiss, Clinton. *The Long, Long Trailer*. New York: Thomas Y. Crowell, 1951.

Valentino, Lou. *The Films of Lana Turner*. Secaucus, NJ: Citadel Press, 1976.

Walker, Alexander. *Fatal Charm: The Life of Rex Harrison*. London: Weidenfeld and Nicolson, 1992.

Wallis, Martha Hyer. *Finding My Way: A Hollywood Memoir*. New York: HarperCollins, 1990.

Waters, Ethel. *His Eye Is on the Sparrow*. New York: Doubleday, 1950.

———. *To Me It's Wonderful*. New York: Harper and Row, 1972.

Weintraub, Stanley. *Whistler: A Biography*. New York: Weybright and Talley, 1974.

Wiley, Mason, and Damien Bona. *Inside Oscar: The Unofficial History of the Academy Awards*. New York: Ballantine Books, 1986.

Yudkoff, Alvin. *Gene Kelly: A Life of Dance and Dreams*. New York: Back Stage Books, 1999.

ACKNOWLEDGMENTS

I would like to give special thanks to many people who supplied invaluable assistance during the research and preparation of this book: the incomparable Don Weise, who launched this project and offered support, kind words, and encouragement from start to finish; the unflappable Jonathan Crowe, who very patiently and thoughtfully answered my countless questions; Bruce Shenitz, who kept asking me about that Vincente Minnelli biography I planned to write someday, and who proved to be a terrific little matchmaker; Ms. Karen Richards, research assistant extraordinaire (whether it was *The Fundamental Principles of Balaban & Katz Theatre Management*, Peter Bogdanovich's birthdate, or a listing in the 1926 Illinois Bell white pages, you somehow found anything and everything that I asked for; as I said innumerable times, I couldn't have done this without you); Dell Lemmon, for divine intervention whenever I needed it; Paula J. Carter, for her captivating caricature of Mr. Minnelli and his trio of screen goddesses; Bingo wizard Greg Astor, for getting me an agent; Dan Works, the information technology oracle, (who made sure hundreds of hours of interviews were kept safe and sound); and Keary Nichols, who gave his all and then some more.

INDEX

MARK GRIFFIN has been a writer and reviewer for many publications, including the *Boston Globe*, *MovieMaker*, *Film Score Monthly*, *Genre*, and the *Portland Phoenix*. He lives in Maine and is now at work on a screenplay.